BIOMOLECULAR NETWORKS

BIOMOLECULAR NETWORKS

Methods and Applications in Systems Biology

LUONAN CHEN
Osaka Sangyo University, Japan

RUI-SHENG WANG
Renmin University of China, China

XIANG-SUN ZHANG
Chinese Academy of Science, China

A JOHN WILEY & SONS, INC., PUBLICATION

Published by John Wiley & Sons, Inc., Hoboken, New Jersey
Published simultaneously in Canada

For general information on our other products and services or for technical support, please contact our
Customer Care Department within the United States at (800) 762-2974, outside the United States at
(317) 572-3993 or fax (317) 572-4002.

Wiley also publishes its books in variety of electronic formats. Some content that appears in print may
not be available in electronic formats. For more information about Wiley products, visit our web site at
www.wiley.com.

Library of Congress Cataloging-in-Publication Data:

Chen, Luonan, 1962-
   Biomolecular networks : methods and applications in systems biology / Luonan Chen, Rui-Sheng Wang,
Xiang-Sun Zhang.
       p. cm.
   Includes bibliographical references and index.
   ISBN 978-0-470-24373-2 (cloth)
1.   Molecular biology–Data processing.   2.   Computational
biology.   3.   Bioinformatics.   4.   Biological systems–Research–Data processing
I.   Wang, Rui-Sheng.   II.   Zhang, Xiang-Sun, 1943-   III.   Title.
QH506.C48 2009
572.80285—dc22

                                                                    2009005776

Printed in the United States of America

10   9   8   7   6   5   4   3   2   1

We Dedicate This Book to Our Colleagues and Our Families

CONTENTS

PREFACE

Network-based systems biology (or Network Systems Biology), an emerging area focusing on various biomolecular networks, is a multidisciplinary intersection of mathematics, computer science, and biology. Burgeoning high-throughput data are driving the integrative study from describing complex phenomena to understanding essential design principles, from studying individual components to understanding functional networks for biomolecular systems, cells, organs, and even entire organisms. To elucidate the fundamental mechanisms of cellular systems, study of biomolecular networks is increasingly attracting much attention from many academic fields such as mathematics, information science, and the life sciences. A major challenge in network systems biology is to investigate how cellular systems facilitate biological functions by various interactions (pathways and networks) between genes, proteins, and metabolites. Based on analytical and computational methodologies, network systems biology studies how an organism, viewed as a dynamical or interacting network of biomolecules (e.g., genes, proteins, and complexes) and biochemical reactions, eventually gives rise to a complex life. In contrast to individual molecules, biomolecular networks governed by universal laws offer a new conceptual framework that could potentially revolutionize our view of biology and pathology. Therefore, it is mandatory that mathematicians and computer scientists provide theoretical and computational methodologies to reveal the essential biological mechanisms of living organisms from a system or network perspective.

Keeping this in mind, this book comprehensively covers the contents and the topics on modeling, inferring, and analyzing biomolecular networks in cellular systems on the basis of available experimental data, in particular stressing the aspects of network, system, integration, and engineering. Each topic is treated in depth with specific biological problems and novel computational methods. From a biological viewpoint, this book, based on the authors' research work and experience in studying biomolecular networks, describes a variety of research topics related to biomolecular networks with deep analysis of many real examples and detailed descriptions of the latest trends, such as gene regulatory networks, transcription regulatory networks, protein interaction networks, metabolic networks, signal transduction networks, and integration of heterogenous networks. On the other hand, from a computational perspective, this book covers many theoretical or computational methods from several areas, such as optimization, differential equations, probability theory, statistics, graph theory, complex systems, network analysis, statistical thermodynamics, graphical modeling, and machine learning, which are all applied in the analysis of biomolecular networks.

The goal of this book is to help readers understand the state-of-the-art techniques in bioinformatics and systems biology, particularly the theory and application of biomolecular networks.

The potential readers are (1) specialists and advanced students in systems biology and computational biology and practitioners in industry, (2) researchers and graduate students in computer science and mathematics who are interested in systems biology, and (3) molecular biologists who are interested in using computational tools to analyze biological networks. Hence, any university or research institute with a bioinformatics or systems biology program in this field will find this book useful.

The contents of this book are based mainly on collaborative studies and discussions with many researchers, including Drs. Yong Wang (Chapters 3, 8), Dong Xu (Chapter 3), Ling-Yun Wu (Chapter 5), Zhenping Li (Chapters 6, 7, 9), Shihua Zhang (Chapters 6, 7), Guangxu Jin (Chapter 7), Xing-Ming Zhao (Chapters 8, 10), and Zhi-Ping Liu (Chapter 11). Collectively and individually, we express our gratitude to these people for their collaboration.

LUONAN CHEN
RUI-SHENG WANG
XIANG-SUN ZHANG

October 2008

ACKNOWLEDGMENTS

To those colleagues who contributed the materials for this book and shared their expertise and vision, the authors express their sincerest gratitude and appreciation. In particular, the authors thank Prof. Dong Xu in University of Missouri, Columbia, Drs. Yong Wang, Ling-Yun Wu, Shihua Zhang, Guangxu Jin in Academy of Mathematics and Systems Science, CAS, Prof. Zhenping Li in Beijing Wuzi University, and Drs. Xing-Ming Zhao, Ruiqi Wang, Achyut Sapkota, Prof. Zengrong Liu in Shanghai University, Dr. Zhi-Ping Liu in Osaka Sangyo University for their cooperation in bringing this book to completion.

LUONAN CHEN
RUI-SHENG WANG
XIANG-SUN ZHANG

LIST OF ILLUSTRATIONS

Figures

Tables

ACRONYMS

2DE	Two-dimensional gel electrophoresis
AGPS	Annotating genes with positive samples
AMC	Average motif correlation
ANOVA	Analysis of variance
APM	Association probabilistic method
APMM	Association probabilistic method with multidomain pairs
ASNM	Association numerical method
BIND	Biomolecular Interaction Network Database
BOLS	Bayesian orthogonal least squares
BTR	Binary transitive reduction
CAGE	Cap analysis of gene expression
CATH	Class, Architecture, Topology, and Homologous superfamily database
CBB	Coomassie Brilliant Blue
CBM	Conserved Binding Mode database
CD	Czekanowski-Dice (distance)
CDD	Conserved Domain Database
ChIP	Chromatin immunoprotein
COG	Cluster(s) of orthologous groups
CPM	Clique percolation method
DBN	Dynamical Bayesian network
DDI	Domain–domain interaction
DDIB	Database of domain interactions and bindings
DIP	Database of Interacting Proteins
DP	Dynamic programming
DPEA	Domain pair exclusion analysis
EBI	European Bioinformatics Institute
EC	Enzyme Commission
EGF	Epidermal growth factor
EM	Expectation maximization
ERF	Ethylene response factor
ERK	Extracellular signal-regulated kinase
FA	Factor analysis
FBA	Flux balance analysis
GAP	GTPase-activating protein
GEF	Guanine exchange factor

GEO	Gene expression omnibus
GGM	Graphical Gaussian model
GO	Gene ontology
GRN	Gene regulatory network
HCS	Highly connected subgraph
ICA	Independent component analysis
ILP	Integer linear programming
IQP	Integer quadratic programming
IST	Interaction sequence tag
KEGG	Kyoto Encyclopedia of Genes and Genomes
LP	Linear programming
LPBN	LP-based method for binary interaction data
LPNM	LP-based method for numerical interaction data
M3D	Many Microbe Microarray Database
MAMC	Mean of average motif correlations
MAPK	Mitogen-activated protein kinase
MCL	Markov clustering algorithm
MCMC	Markov chain Monte Carlo
MCSA	Monte Carlo simulated annealing
mDH	Motif date hub
MESC	Minimum exact set cover
MFGO	Modified and faster global optimization
MILP	Mixed-integer linear programming
MIPS	Munich Information Center for Protein Sequences
MLE	Maximum-likelihood estimation
MNI	Modification by network identification
MODY	Mature-onset diabetes of the young
mPH	Motif party hub
MRF	Markov random field
MS	Mass spectrometry
MSC	Minimum set cover
MSSC	Maximum-specificity set cover
NCA	Network component analysis
NIR	Network identification by (multiple) regression
NMR	Nuclear magnetic resonance
ODE	Ordinary differential equation
ORF	Open reading frame
PCA	Principal-component analysis
PCC	Pearson correlation coefficient
PCR	Polymerase chain reaction
PDB	Protein Data Bank
PDE	Partial differential equation
PDGF	Platelet-derived growth factor
PE	Parsimony explanation
PLDE	Piecewise-linear differential equation

PLS	Partial least squares
PPI	Protein–protein interaction
PVC	Pseudovertex collapse
PWM	Position weight matrix
QP	Quadratic programming
RBF	Radial basis function
RKIP	Raf kinase inhibitor protein
RMSE	Root-mean-square error
RNAP	RNA polymerase
RNSC	Restricted neighborhood search clustering
ROC	Receiver operating characteristic
SAGE	Serial analysis of gene expression
SAMC	Standard deviation of average motif correlation(s)
SCOP	Structural classification of proteins
SDE	Stochastic differential equation
SGD	Stanford Gene expression Database
SIM	Signal-input motif
SPA	Selective permissibility algorithm
SPC	Superparametric clustering
STN	Signal transduction network
SVD	Singular value decomposition
SVM	Support vector machine
TAIR	The Arabidopsis Information Resources
TAP	Tandem affinity purification
TC	Transcription complex
TF	Transcription factor
TFA	Transcription factor activity
TFBS	Transcription factor binding site
TRN	Transcriptional regulatory network
TSNI	Time-series network identification
TSS	Transcription start site
Y1H	Yeast one-hybrid
Y2H	Yeast two-hybrid

CHAPTER 1

INTRODUCTION

1.1 BASIC CONCEPTS IN MOLECULAR BIOLOGY

We introduce some basic and central concepts in modern molecular biology in this section to help readers understand the related problems discussed in the later chapters. Note that this is a very general and brief introduction, and arranged mainly for computer scientists and mathematicians who are trying to acquire a reading knowledge about molecular biology. Biology-oriented researchers can skip the details in this section. For more detailed and systematic biological knowledge, readers can refer to professional books (e.g., [Sta02], [Kar02], [Bro02], [Sad07]).

All living things, whether simple or complex organisms, are composed of cells, which are the basic units of structure and function in an organism [Sta02]. Each cell is a complex system consisting of many different building blocks. According to their sizes and types of internal structures, cells are classified as prokaryotic cells and eukaryotic cells, which, in turn, distinguish organisms into prokaryotic organisms (or prokaryotes) and eukaryotic organisms (or eukaryotes). Prokaryotic organisms, represented by bacteria and blue algae, are made up of prokaryotic cells that are smaller and have simpler internal structures, whereas eukaryotic organisms such as fungi, plants, and animals are composed of structurally complex eukaryotic cells [Kar02]. The distinction between eukaryotes and prokaryotes leads to the vast differences between many cellular building blocks and life processes in these two organism types.

Both eukaryotic and prokaryotic cells contain a nuclear region with the genetic materials of living organisms. However, the genetic materials of a prokaryotic cell

Biomolecular Networks. By Luonan Chen, Rui-Sheng Wang, and Xiang-Sun Zhang
Copyright © 2009 John Wiley & Sons, Inc.

are contained in a nucleoid without a boundary membrane, whereas a eukaryotic cell has a nucleus that is separated from the rest of the cell by a complex membranous structure or nuclear envelope. Note that besides nuclear membrane, both prokaryotes and eukaryotes have cell membranes or plasma membranes, which regulate the flow of nutrients, energy, and information in and out of the cell and play important roles in signal transduction. Despite this difference, eukaryotic cells have a molecular chemistry composition similar to that of prokaryotic cells. For example, both eukaryotic and prokaryotic organisms possess a genome in their cell that contains the biological genetic information needed to maintain life in that organism. Another essential feature of most living cells is their ability to reproduce and grow in an appropriate environment through cell division. New cells are generated from the reproduction of existing cells to maintain the life in living beings.

Cells consist of four basic types of molecules: (1) small molecules, (2) DNA, (3) RNA, and (4) protein. Small molecules in cells include water, sugars, fatty acids, amino acids, and nucleotides. They are either the basic building blocks of the macromolecules (DNA, RNA, proteins) or independent units with important roles, such as signal transduction and energy sources. Most eukaryotic and prokaryotic genomes consist of deoxyribonucleic acid (DNA), but a few viruses have ribonucleic acid (RNA) genomes [Bro02]. DNA and RNA are polymeric large molecules made up of chains of monomeric subunits.

DNA is the hereditary material in almost all organisms. Most DNA is located in the cell nucleus, but a small amount of DNA can also be found in the mitochondria. DNA is a linear polymer of four chemically distinct nucleotides consisting of three components: $2'$-deoxyribose (a type of sugar composed of five carbon atoms labeled from $1'$ to $5'$), a phosphate group attached to the $5'$-carbon of the sugar, and a nitrogenous base. Four kinds of nucleotides differ in their nitrogenous bases: adenine (A), cytosine (C), guanine (G), and thymine (T), which are usually referred to as *bases*, denoted by their initial letters, A, C, G, and T (Fig. 1.1). Hence, a DNA sequence can always be denoted by a string of A, C, G, T. Individual nucleotides are linked by phosphodiester bonds between their $5'$-carbon and $3'$-carbon in any order to form a DNA chain called a polynucleotide. A DNA molecule is actually double-stranded, and its nucleotide bases on two strands form complementary pairs: A pairing with T, and C pairing with G. The orientations of DNA strands are determined by the carbons at their ends which conventionally start from the $5'$ ends to the $3'$ ends (Fig. 1.1). The two strands are tied together and form a stable structure known as the *DNA double helix*, which was identified in 1953 in Cambridge by Watson and Crick. (Fig. 1.2).

RNA is also a polynucleotide, and its structure is similar to that of DNA except for two main differences [Bro02]: (1) the sugar in a RNA nucleotide is ribose rather than deoxyribose, and (2) RNA contains uracil (U) instead of thymine (T). In addition, the structure of RNA generally does not form a double helix as does the structure of DNA. The functions of DNA and RNA for living cells are also different. Generally, DNA is responsible for encoding genetic information and performs one essential function, while several types of RNA perform different functions, such as ribosomal RNAs and transfer RNAs. RNA also contains $3'-5'$ phosphodiester bonds, but these

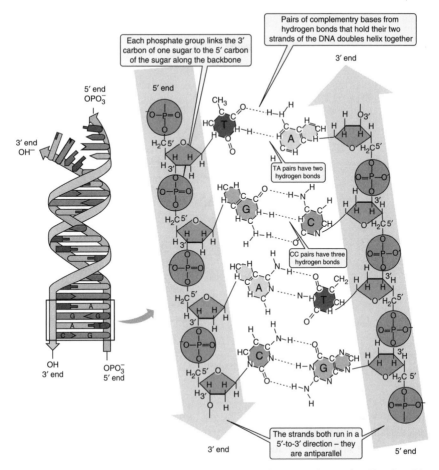

Figure 1.1. The double-helix DNA backbone with complementary base pairs. [Reprinted from [Sad06] © (2006) with permission of Sinauer Associates, Inc.]

bonds are not as stable as those in a DNA polynucleotide [Bro02]. In RNA polynu-cleotide, A complements or "pairs" with U, and C pairs with G. Such complementary base-pairing leads to folded structures of RNA that help RNA molecules carry out their functions in the expression of genes.

DNA encodes RNA and protein molecules through a law dominating the whole biology, which is called as the central "dogma" of molecular biology (Fig. 1.3). It pro-vides a framework for understanding the flow of information from DNA via RNA and then to protein. Three important biological processes in the central "dogma" of mol-ecular biology are replication, transcription, and translation. First, certain contiguous DNA segments containing biological information must be duplicated through a replication process to transmit the genetic information from parents to progeny. Then, the information contained in a section of DNA is transferred to a newly assembled piece of messenger RNA (mRNA) through a transcription process,

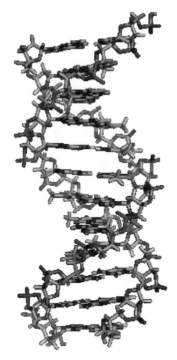

Figure 1.2. The double-helix structure of a DNA.

in which RNA polymerase and transcription factors play an important role. This transcription process is completed in the cell nucleus with the synthesis of RNA molecules. Finally, mRNAs are transported into a protein-synthesizing "factory" (i.e., ribosome) and read by the ribosome as triplet codons through a translation

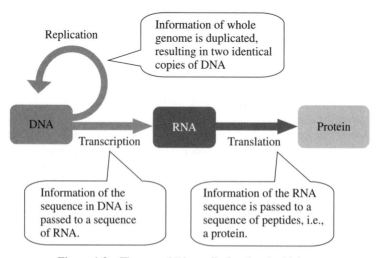

Figure 1.3. The central "dogma" of molecular biology.

process, which further synthesizes proteins. In Sections 1.1.1–1.1.3 we will describe these biological processes in detail.

1.1.1 Genomes, Genes, and DNA Replication Process

According to the number of cells that they contain, organisms may be unicellular or multicellular. Bacteria and baker's yeast are representative examples of unicellular organisms that consist of only one cell. Most organisms consist of two or more cells. Each cell contains one or more DNA molecules. A chromosome is formed from a single DNA molecule. In prokaryotes, DNA is organized in the form of a circular chromosome. In eukaryotes, chromosomes have a complex structure where DNA is wound around structural proteins called histones. Most of the DNA in eukaryotes is located in the cell nucleus and is called chromosomal DNA. But a small amount of DNA can also be found in the mitochondria, which is called mitochondrial DNA. Both chromosomal and mitochondrial DNA in a cell constitute a genome. Owing to DNA replication in the process of cell division, all cells in an organism contain identical genomes with few rather special exceptions. The total number of chromosomes and genome size differ quite considerably in different organisms. For example, each cell in Homo sapiens has 23 pairs of chromosomes, whereas a fruit fly has 4 pairs and a yeast has 12 pairs of chromosomes. The human genome has about 3 billion base pairs. Determining the four-letter order for a given DNA molecule is known as *DNA sequencing*. Since the first full genome for a bacterium was sequenced in 1995, genomes of many organisms have been sequenced. The well-known Human Genome Project was completed in 2001, and a draft human genome was obtained.

As mentioned earlier, information encoded in static DNA is passed to functional protein molecules through transcription and translation processes. However, not all portions of DNA are used for encoding proteins. A continuous stretch of DNA molecule that contains the information necessary to encode a protein is called a gene. Other portions are termed "junk DNA," which is actually not real "junk"; such noncoding portions have been found to perform important functions [Soo06, Lev07]. In cells, genes consist of a long strand of DNA that contains an important region for controlling gene transcription called a promoter. In addition to promoter regions, genes in eukaryotic organisms contain regions called introns and exons (Fig. 1.4). The introns will be removed from mRNAs in a process called *splicing*. The regions encoding gene products are called exons, which are interspersed with noncoding introns. The number and size of introns and exons differ considerably between different genes and different species. In eukaryotes, a single gene can encode multiple proteins through different alternative splice variants, that is, the same pre-mRNA produces different mRNAs by different arrangements of exons known as alternative splicing. In prokaryotes, genes seldom have introns and thereby there is no splicing.

DNA replication is the process of copying a double-stranded DNA molecule or a whole genome, a process essential in all known life forms. The general mechanisms of DNA replication are also different in prokaryotic and eukaryotic organisms. As each DNA strand holds the same genetic information, both strands can serve as templates for the reproduction of the opposite strand. The template strand is preserved in its

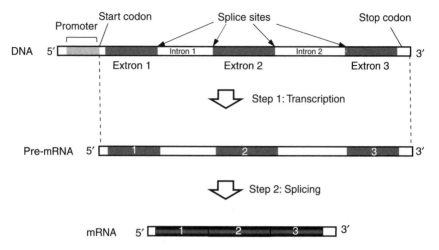

Figure 1.4. The structure of eukaryotic genes and splicing process.

entirety and the new strand is assembled from nucleotides. This process is called semiconservative replication. The resulting double-stranded DNA molecules are identical; proofreading and error-checking mechanisms exist to ensure extremely high fidelity. In a cell, DNA replication must occur before cell division. Prokaryotes replicate their DNA throughout the interval between cell divisions. On the other hand, the replication of eukaryotic cells progresses through a regular cycle of growth and division termed as cell cycle, consisting of four phases: S phase, during which DNA is synthesized; M phase, during which the actual cell division or mitosis occurs; and two gap phases, G1 and G2, which fall between M and S phases and between S and M phases, respectively. In other words, the replication timings of DNA in eukaryotes are highly regulated, and this occurs during the S phase of the cell cycle, preceding mitosis.

1.1.2   Transcription Process for RNA Synthesis

In all organisms, there are two major steps necessary for DNA producing proteins: (1) information of the DNA on which the gene resides is transcribed to messenger RNA (mRNA), and (2) information on the mRNA is translated to the protein. Transcription is the process of producing mRNA using genes as templates. In the transcription process, one strand of DNA molecule is copied into a complementary pre-mRNA by an enzyme called RNA polymerase II. To initiate transcription, the two-stranded double-helix structure of DNA molecule is "unzipped." The DNA strand whose sequence matches that of the RNA is known as the coding strand and the strand to which the RNA is complementary is the template strand. Then, RNA polymerase II first recognizes and binds a promoter region of the gene. It begins to read the template strand in the $3'-5'$ direction, splice the introns, and synthesize the primary transcript mRNA from $5'$ to $3'$. It is worth noting that the splicing of introns present within the transcribed region is unique to eukaryotes. In prokaryotes, transcription occurs in the cytoplasm. In contrast, transcription in eukaryotes necessarily occurs in the nucleus. After such a transcription process, mRNA is synthesized and will be transported to ribosomes to form proteins. However, the mature mRNA may be further modified by other biochemicals, such as noncoding RNA, before the translation.

The process of producing functional molecules such as RNA or protein is called *gene expression*. In addition to transcription and translation, the steps in the gene expression process may be further modulated, including the posttranscriptional regulation of an mRNA and the posttranslational modification of a protein. Messenger RNA can be quantitatively measured by many techniques such as DNA microarray technology, which is now widely adopted to study many problems in biology.

1.1.3 Translation Process for Protein Synthesis

Translation is a process of forming proteins by using a mature mRNA molecule as a template. It is the second stage of protein biosynthesis and an important part of gene expression. Translation takes place in the cytoplasm where ribosomes are located. In the translation process, mRNA is decoded to produce a specific polypeptide according to the rules known as triplet or genetic code, which specifies the mapping from mRNA nucleotide bases (codons) to 20 specific amino acids (Fig. 1.5). There are start and stop codons to indicate the beginning and ending of a gene. Since there are 64 codons and only 20 amino acids, the code is redundant; that is, an amino acid may be represented

Second letter

First letter		U		C		A		G		Third letter
		UUU	Phenyl	UCU		UAU	Tyrosine	UGU	Cysteine	U
	U	UUC	alanine	UCC	Serine	UAC		UGC		C
		UUA	Leucine	UCA		UAA	Stop codon	UGA	Stop codon	A
		UUG		UCG		UAG		UGG	Tryptophan	G
		CUU		CCU		CAU	Histidine	CGU		U
	C	CUC	Leucine	CCC	Proline	CAC		CGC	Arginine	C
		CUA		CCA		CAA	Glutamine	CGA		A
		CUG		CCG		CAG		CGG		G
		CUU		ACU		AAU	Asparagine	AGU	Serine	U
	A	CUC	Isoleucine	ACC	Threonine	AAC		AGC		C
		CUA		ACA		AAA	Lysine	AGA	Arginine	A
		CUG	Methionine; Start codon	ACG		AAG		AGG		G
		GUU		GCU		GAU	Aspartic	GGU		U
	G	GUC	Valine	GCC	Alanine	GAC	acid	GGC	Glycine	C
		GUA		GCA		GAA	Glutamic	GGA		A
		GUG		GCG		GAG	acid	GGG		G

Figure 1.5. The mapping rules (genetic codes) from codons to amino acids.

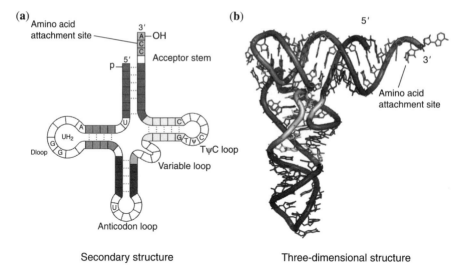

Figure 1.6. The structure of tRNA.

by more than one codon. For example, histidine is encoded by CAT and CAC, but a single codon can represent only one amino acid.

After the transcription process, mRNA carries genetic information encoded as a ribonucleotide sequence from chromosomes to ribosomes. In cytoplasm, mRNA forms a complex with ribosomes. Transfer RNA (tRNA) is a small noncoding RNA chain that transports amino acids to the ribosome and makes the connection between a codon and the corresponding amino acid (Fig. 1.6). Ribosome and tRNA molecules read the ribonucleotides by translational machinery and guide the synthesis of a chain of amino acids to form a protein. After the translation process, gene expression is completed. The final product of gene expression is a protein. The protein is still subject to multiple posttranslational biochemical modifications before becoming a mature, active, and functional molecule, such as degradation, dimerization, and phosphorylation. It is worth noting that, as a result of alternative splicing and posttranslational modifications, one gene can produce multiple proteins. After its synthesis, the new protein folds to its active three-dimensional structure before carrying out cellular functions.

1.2 BIOMOLECULAR NETWORKS IN CELLS

Through the transcription and translation processes, gene products such as mRNA and protein are produced. Gene, mRNA, and protein are known as biological molecules or basic components. The complicated relations and interactions between these components are responsible for diverse cellular functions. At the genome or DNA level, transcription factors (TFs) function as DNA-binding proteins and can activate or inhibit the transcription of genes to synthesize mRNAs by regulating the activities of genes. Since these TFs themselves are products of genes, the ultimate effect is that genes regulate each other's expression as part of a transcription (or transcriptional) regulatory network (TRN) or gene regulatory network (GRN). Similarly, at the proteome or protein level, proteins can participate in diverse posttranslational modifications of other proteins or form protein complexes and pathways together with other proteins that assume new roles. Such local associations between protein molecules are called protein–protein interactions (PPIs), which form a protein inter-action network. The biochemical reactions in cellular metabolism can likewise be inte-grated into a metabolic network whose fluxes are regulated by enzymes that catalyze the reactions. In many cases, these interactions at different levels are integrated into a signaling network. For example, external signals from the exterior of a cell are first mediated to the inside of that cell by a cascade of protein–protein interactions of the signaling molecules. Then, both biochemical reactions and transcription regu-lations including protein–DNA interactions trigger the expression of some genes to respond the signals [Alb05]. In short, although cells consist of various biological molecules, their cellular processes and functions are actually achieved by bio-molecular networks with the collaborative effects of those individual components. Figure 1.7(b) illustrates several typical molecular networks at different levels in cellu-lar systems, which are the backbone of network systems biology. From the viewpoint of network architecture, main ingredients in this book are molecules, interactions, pathways, and networks. Their hierarchical relations are conceptually shown in Figure 1.7(a), where a cellular system can also be viewed to be formed conceptually from individual molecules, to pairwise interactions, to local structures (including network motifs, modules, pathways, and subnetworks), and eventually to global net-works. In other words, basic components in a cellular system are individual molecules, which affect each other by their pairwise interactions. A cascade of those pairwise interactions forms a local structure (i.e., linear pathway or a subnetwork) which trans-forms local perturbations into a functional response. And all of linear pathways or sub-networks are assembled into a global biomolecular network which eventually generates global behaviors and holds responsibility for complicated life in a living organism. In terms of interactions, each type of molecular network is assembled by the following different pairwise interactions: transcription regulatory network: TF–DNA interactions; gene regulatory network: gene–gene interactions (or genetic interactions); protein interaction network: protein–protein interactions; metabolic network: enzyme–substrate interactions; signaling network: molecule–molecule interactions.

The completion of the Haemophilus influenzae genome sequence in 1995 marked the beginning of the genomic era [Fle95]. The advent of whole-genome sequencing technologies leads to hundreds of complete genome sequences. Especially after the release of the draft version of the human genome sequence [Ven01], we are now enter-ing into a postgenomic era and begin to analyze the transcriptome and the proteome of many model organisms. In this era, various high-throughput experimental techniques in molecular biology can provide genome-scale measurements from biological mol-ecules that exist within the cell such as genes (DNA), proteins, RNA, metabolites,

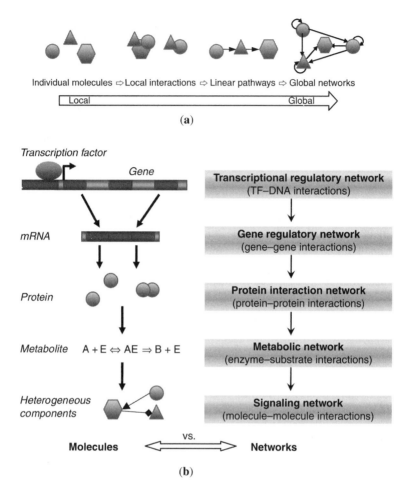

Figure 1.7. Ingredients in cellular systems in terms of network architecture. (a) Hierarchical relations of molecules, interactions, pathway, and networks. (b) Hierarchical relations of various biomolecular networks. In (a), "Local interactions" are mainly pairwise interactions, and "Linear pathways" are local network structures, including pathways, modules, communities, network motifs and subnetworks.

and other molecules, and have resulted in an enormous amount of component data. In addition, the functional genomic and proteomic approaches have generated a variety of protein–protein, protein–DNA, and other component–component interaction mappings, which make it possible to study biomolecular networks mentioned above. The resulting datasets by these experimental techniques run through the information flow of the central dogma of molecular biology, and include genome, transcriptome, proteome, metabolome, localizome, and interactome components, which are collectively referred to as "omic" data and provide comprehensive descriptions of all

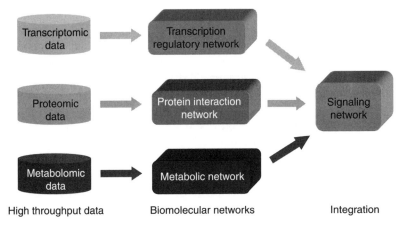

Figure 1.8. Omic data and biomolecular networks.

components and interactions within the cell [Joy06]. Figure 1.8 illustrates the relations between omic data and biomolecular networks.

- *Transcriptomic Data–Transctiption Regulatory Network.* Transcriptome profiling is one of the first omic approaches developed. DNA chips, microarrays and serial analysis of gene expression (SAGE) are the most widely used approaches for examining the expression of thousands of genes simultaneously under various experimental conditions and have generated large amounts of mRNA transcripts [Har05]. Such data have been applied to many fields, such as identifying differentially expressed genes in stem cells, classifying the molecular subtypes of human cancers, and monitoring the host cell transcriptional response to pathogens. Gene expression is the result of transcription factors regulating target genes; hence it is possible to retrieve the interaction relationships between different genes from a large amount of gene expression data. Such pairwise interaction relationships are combined into gene regulatory networks. In addition, the ChIP-chip technique helps determine protein–DNA interactions [LeT02], which constitute transcription regulatory networks describing special functional modules of interest. In addition, transcription factors regulate genes by binding to upstream and downstream regulatory regions of transcription start sites. With the availability of whole-genome sequences, identification of regulatory regions and transcription factor binding sites has become feasible from a computational viewpoint.
- *Proteomic Data–Protein Interaction Network.* Although the analysis of proteomics has lagged behind that of transcriptomics, the functions of all proteins and how they form complexes during various conditions are now beginning to be systematically explored. Two-dimensional gel electrophoresis (2DE) and mass spectroscopy (MS) have been used to identify and quantify the activity, binding, and other cellular levels of proteins [Par03]. For protein spot detection,

conventional staining techniques such as colloidal Coomassie Brilliant Blue (CBB) and silver staining are being popular. Yeast two-hybrid (Y2H) is one of the first methods for high-throughput protein–protein interaction mapping and has been used to determine the interactomes of many organisms. Besides Y2H, tandem affinity purification (TAP) and phage library display are also used. Such protein–protein interactions can be represented as a protein interaction network, from which much useful knowledge can be extracted. For example, protein interactions provide rich information for protein function and signaling pathway information.

- *Metabolomic Data–Metabolic Network.* As one of the new types of omic data, the methods used to generate the complete set of metabolites of many organisms are still being refined. MS, nuclear magnetic resonance (NMR) spectroscopy, and vibrational spectroscopy have been used to analyze the metabolite contents that are extracted from isolated cells or tissues [Joy06]. The resulting data make it possible to study the dynamic metabolic response of living systems to environmental stimuli or genetic perturbations through analyzing metabolic networks, in which the nodes denote metabolites and the edges represent reactions or enzymes. A metabolic network provides not only a list of metabolite components but also a functional readout of the cellular state. Given the highly diverse set of biomolecules and the large dynamic range of metabolite concentrations, sophisticated computational techniques are needed to reconstruct and analyze various biochemical reaction pathways and networks.

- *Integrated Data–Signaling Network.* Integrating the above mentioned interaction data at different levels leads to a signaling network or a hierarchical molecular network. A signaling network involves the transduction of a variety of signals such as energy and stimuli from the outside to the inside of the cell. It is one of the main parts of cellular communication and relies on an underlying series of biochemical reactions, transcription regulations, and protein interactions. Except in a very few cases, experimentally determining a complete signaling network is a time-consuming and also costly task. However, with the increasing deposition of various types of data, reconstructing a signaling network from multiple information sources is becoming a promising topic and feasible task that attracts much attention from the researchers in systems biology and computational biology. Depending on the types of data, the integrated system may be not only a hierarchical but also a heterogeneous molecular network with diverse substructures.

In contrast to component data such as genomic and proteomic data providing a specific molecular content of a cellular system, pairwise interaction data include protein–DNA interactions, protein–protein interactions, and protein–ligand (enzyme–substrate) interactions, which determine the local connectivity that exists among the molecular species, and provide a network scaffold within the cell system [Joy06]. The subsequent function data are closely related to the interaction data since many biological processes in cells are not performed by individual components but through gene regulations, signal transduction, and interactions between biomolecules. It is the local interactions of those components that are assembled into a global network and are ultimately responsible for an organism's form and functions [Bar04, Har99]. Generally, a living organism can be viewed as a huge nonlinear biochemical reaction system characterized by the interactions of biomolecules, including genes, RNAs, proteins, and metabolites. Such local and pairwise interactions are often represented by a global biomolecular network in which each node is a biological molecule or complex, and each edge represents an interaction or association of two molecules. Generally, biomolecular networks include gene regulatory networks (gene–gene interactions), transcription regulatory networks (TF–gene interactions), signaling networks (integrated interactions among molecules), protein interaction networks (protein–protein interactions), metabolic networks (enzyme–substrate interactions), and hybrid networks. These biomolecular networks indispensably exist in cell systems and play fundamental and essential roles in giving rise of life.

In short, with various interaction data available, the focus of biological research is being transformed from analyzing individual components to studying global networks from a systematic perspective. Without depreciating the importance of individual molecules, the more recent research results indicate that a cellular function is actually the contribution of various kinds of interactions between a myriad of cellular constituents. In particular, a cellular system can be viewed as a networked biological system. Therefore, an important challenge for biology is to understand the cell's function organization by investigating the structure, function, and dynamics of complex biomolecular networks in living cellular systems.

1.3 NETWORK SYSTEMS BIOLOGY

To elucidate the essential principles of cellular systems, study of biomolecular networks is increasingly attracting much attention from various science and engineering communities. High-throughput experimental methods in molecular biology have resulted in an enormous amount of data, including interactions, networks and pathways [Bar04]. Hence, it is crucial that mathematicians and computer scientists provide computational tools to reveal the essential biological mechanisms from a system perspective. To meet such a challenge, rather than analyzing individual components or partial aspects of the organism, network systems biology, is to study an organism viewed as a dynamical interaction network of genes, proteins, and biochemical reactions by developing sophisticated theoretical methodologies and computational tools.

The goal of network systems biology is to mine knowledge on the basis of the networked data generated from high-throughput techniques by exploiting special features of the biological system, and gain biological insight by further interpreting them in a systematic manner. For example, understanding the process of specific gene regulations and signal transduction provides deep insight into the mechanisms of cellular systems. From a computational viewpoint, modeling the gene regulation process and signal transduction by appropriate mathematical models will enhance such knowledge. Given a large amount of gene expression data from microarray techniques, identifying gene–gene interactions and signaling pathways is by no means a trivial thing. A large number of genes with few timepoints are a main characteristic of microarray data that hinders us from achieving this task. With the ChIP-chip data, estimating the activity profiles of transcription factors (TFs) is also a very important task, since measuring the activity of a TF is still experimentally difficult owing to chemical modifications after the translational process. At the same time, inferring the relationships between TFs and their targets from experimental data is of utmost importance for understanding direct interactions as well as the complex regulatory mechanisms in cellular systems.

A living organism or a cell is a highly organized system of interacting macromolecules and metabolites, which can be viewed as a huge molecular network formed by those local interactions of molecules, as shown in Figure 1.7. Therefore, as a discipline related closely to systems biology, network biology emphasizes local interactions and global networks of molecules **that characterize various biological systems**, and attempts to understand biology from the viewpoint of the global and local systems properties of molecular networks by **offering a quantifiable description of the interactions and networks**. The research subject of network systems biology or network biology is rich and diverse. For example, the huge deposit of gene expression profiles and protein–DNA interactions makes it possible to quantitatively study the regulatory relationships between genes. Reverse engineering of regulatory networks is one of main computational problems in this field. Protein interaction data from high-throughput techniques are highly "noisy" and incomplete with unknown portion of false positives. We are required to systematically integrate these data and further estimate their confidence by statistical techniques. This problem is known as protein interaction prediction. Interacting proteins are believed to have similar functions. The annotation of proteins is currently far from complete. We can enhance it by employing protein interaction data and other biological sources. This is the challenge of protein function prediction. With the current technologies, experimental determination of protein complexes and functional modules is not cost-effective. Actually, it is not only expensive but also time-consuming, and the result is not reliable. Can this be done by mining the data from protein interaction networks to provide a rough estimation for biologists? This is the problem defined as functional module detection. Given protein interaction networks or metabolic networks from multiple species, how can we compare these networks and extract important knowledge related to evolution? Given a concerned pathway, how can we find a similar one in a protein interaction network? These are problems of network alignment and query. In addition, in order to understand the structure and function of a living cell, we also should investigate the structure and dynamics of these biological networks. This is the challenge of dynamical modeling or qualitative analysis of biomolecular networks. In contrast to qualitative studies, quantitative simulation can directly predict the dynamic behaviors of living cells, and is an important topic related to the development of highly efficient computation algorithms on both stochastic and deterministic dynamic models. Do biomolecular networks have topological properties similar to those of other complex networks? Are the topological patterns (e.g., network motifs, modules, or hubs) of biomolecular networks related to specific biological functions? How can we reconstruct metabolic pathways and identify active subnetworks from a large set of biochemical reactions?

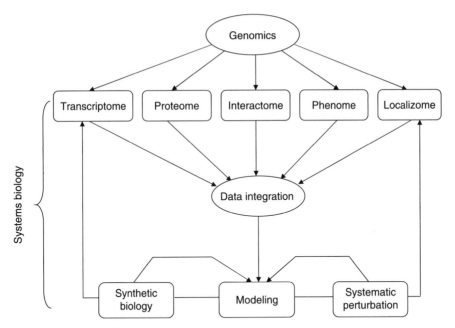

Figure 1.9. Systems biology focusing on integrating omic data. [Reprinted from [GeH03] © 2003 with permission from Elsevier.]

How can we detect signal transduction pathways or drug targets from data of perturbed biological experiments? Can we design or construct a synthetic biological network representing a whole or partial cellular system (i.e., forward engineering of biomolecular networks)? All of these problems are expected to be solved by computational means, which are the main research focuses of network systems biology.

With increasingly accumulated data from high-throughput technologies, biomolecular networks and their functional roles have been studied extensively from various aspects of living organisms. This research not only helps scientists understand complicated biochemical phenomena but also reveals the fundamental mechanisms of living organisms from a system perspective. Hence, systems biology with emphasis on networks is anticipated to enhance our understanding of cellular systems by integrating comprehensive data of molecular components in different layers and studying how the multitudes of interactions facilitate the complicated biological functions within a cell. Figure 1.9 illustrates the main research focus of systems biology. In this book, we particularly emphasize four aspects for network systems biology, represented by four keywords—network, dynamics, system, and integration:

- *Network.* A cellular system can be viewed as a huge biochemical reaction network that orchestrates the sophisticated and complex functions of the cells and thus gives rise to life. Living organisms differ from each other not only because of the differences of their constituting proteins but also because of the architectures of their molecular networks. The availability of genome sequences for hundreds of organisms including humans leads to a transition from molecular biology to modular biology [Har99]. Since most gene products function in unison, cellular processes are considered to be the results of complex networks of individual components. Therefore, to elucidate fundamental cellular behaviors, it is essential to focus on the interactions between individual components and the functional states of these networks resulting from the assembly of all such local and pairwise interactions. It has been recognized that a complicated living organism cannot be fully understood by merely analyzing individual components, and that the global network of those components is ultimately responsible for an organism's form and governs the organism's behavior.

- *Dynamics.* Life is dynamic, and dynamics exists in living organisms at each level. Cellular systems are commonly modeled by nonlinear dynamical systems such as ordinary differential equations [ChL02, ChL04, WaR08], or stochastic processes such as the chemical master equation [ChL05, WaR08], based on mass action law and enzyme reaction kinetics. The ultimate goal of network systems biology is to understand a complex biological process in sufficient detail to enable us to build a computational network model for the process and gain deep insight into the principles of living organisms. Clearly, dynamic simulations of a cellular system can provide a more thorough quantitative understanding of its principles, mechanism and function [Zho05, LiC07a]. From both theoretical and experimental perspectives, it is a very challenging problem in biological science to model, analyze, and further predict the dynamic behaviors of biosystems [Zho08]. One of the most widely best studied dynamic or rhythmic phenomena so far is circadian oscillation [WaR08], which is assumed to be produced by limit cycle oscillators at the molecular level from the gene regulatory feedback loops or protein interaction loops. With the rapid advances in mathematics and experiments concerning the underlying regulatory mechanisms, developing more sophisticated theoretical models and general quantitative simulation techniques is increasingly necessary for elucidating dynamical behaviors in a cell at the system level.

- *System.* In cells, an individual component always receives signals and outputs information. There is a regular communication between different cells [ChL05, Zho05], which mediates their collective behaviors. All the components are wound together to form into a complex cellular system that collectively performs biological function and system behavior [WaR08, LiC06a]. The system behaviors are essentially coordinated responses resulting from the local interactions of individual components in both prokaryotes and eukaryotes. Such a mechanism is an absolute requisite to ensure appropriate and robust coordination of cell activities at all levels of organisms under an uncertain environment. Each cellular process can be studied in a systematic way, which means not only that the interactions of homogeneous components are important but also that the functional relationships between heterogeneous components are essential. In addition, perturbation is an approach often adopted in systems biology. When genes or proteins in a cellular system are systematically perturbed, responses from other parts of the system can be recorded and the information obtained can be incorporated into the basic model [GeH03].

- *Integration.* Integration has multiple implications, including integrating different data sources, integrating different levels of systems, integrating different technologies, integrating different disciplinary areas, and even integrating different human resources. To make full use of high-throughout data, clearly we need to integrate not only heterogeneous data sources but also different methodologies and different levels of systems. Most cellular processes involve some components of gene regulation as well as protein interactions. For example, a membrane protein receiving an external signal may trigger a cascade of protein interactions that results in one or more genes being expressed in the genome. Understanding this interplay between proteins and DNA clearly requires data integration. When proteins interact to accomplish a specific process, some of the genes encoding them may be expressed in a coordinated manner. Therefore, integrating microarray gene expression data and protein interaction network can provide new insights. In another view, the knowledge on most biological processes studied for many years in individual labs is fragmentary and stored in countless scientific papers. Hence, integrating various sources of knowledge on interactions and regulations from scientific literature is also necessary and imperative. Finally, different computational methods and tools have their own advantages and limitations, and integrating methodologies could also enhance our ability to analyze the large amount of data in an accurate and robust manner.

Except for the main characteristics of systems biology, sophisticated computational and analytical methods are definitely indispensable as tools of network systems biology. For instance, reverse-engineering gene regulatory networks requires optimization models to fit time-series experimental data. Mining useful knowledge from the topological properties of biomolecular networks cannot be done without machine learning and data-mining methods. Dealing with noise and uncertainty underlying experimental data demands appropriate probabilistic or statistical methods. In particular, integrating all kinds of omic data necessitates efficient data integration techniques such as kernel methods and Bayesian methods. Finally, a network itself is a kind of graph, and thus graph-theoretic methods are an effective tool for systems biology. Combining these computational methods with the systematic framework of studying cell mechanism, systems biology stressing on networks, or network systems biology is an increasingly promising discipline for studying complex life phenomena (Fig. 1.10).

One of the great challenges in this area is to build a complete and high-resolution description of molecular topography and connect biomolecular interactions with physiological responses. By investigating the relationships and interactions between various parts of a biological system such as gene regulatory systems, protein interaction networks, metabolic pathways, organelles, cells, physiological systems, and organisms, we expect to eventually develop an understandable model of the whole

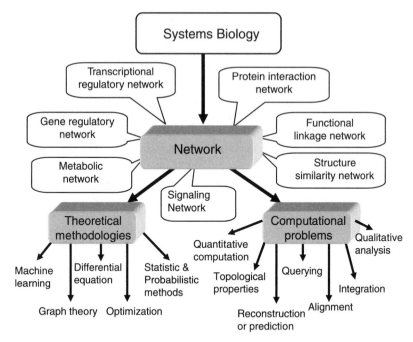

Figure 1.10. The research focus of network systems biology.

cellular system, which is critical for a thorough understanding of the essential mechanisms of living organisms.

1.4 ABOUT THIS BOOK

This book focuses primarily on various kinds of biomolecular networks, with particular emphasis on computational problems, methods, and applications in bioinformatics and systems biology. It provides a general theoretical and methodological framework for analyzing biomolecular networks. In the book, many mathematical concepts and methods, such as graph theory, optimization theory, probability theory, statistics, thermodynamical theory and differential equations, are adopted to solve the computational problems in bioinformatics and systems biology (Fig. 1.11), and these methods play important roles in many interesting and sophisticated applications. In contrast to conventional bioinformatics, which studies mainly the individual components or local interactions of biological systems, this book presents a new research area, where machine learning and computation techniques, such as text mining, classification, clustering, and visual techniques, find their alternative applications on global networks. Computer scientists or mathematicians will find that it is in high demand to develop new techniques suited for this increasingly important area, to enable them to deal with large-scale networks, heterogeneous data, and intense computation. This book also gives a comprehensive survey for biomolecular networks and the biological

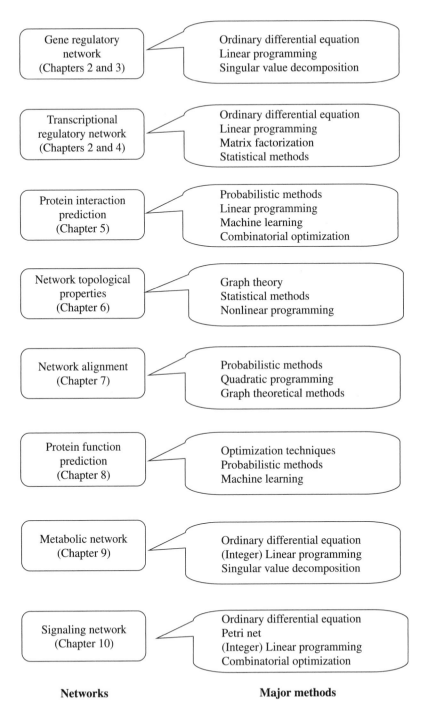

Networks   **Major methods**

Figure 1.11. Biomolecular networks with major computational tools applied in this book.

relations between them, which can significantly enhance the understanding and knowledge of the essential mechanisms of living organisms from a system viewpoint. On the other hand, biologists will find in this book many useful tools, and algorithms that can be utilized to analyze biological networks and further design biological experiments, such as network inference tools, network alignment tools, functional module detection tools, and drug target detection tools. The book assumes basic knowledge of molecular biology with each chapter covering the necessary materials. The objective of this book is to help biology-oriented researchers and other researchers understand the state-of-art techniques in bioinformatics and systems biology. It covers extensive topics related to biomolecular networks and the latest trends such as

- Reverse engineering of gene regulatory networks
- Inferring transcriptional interaction and regulator activity*
- Protein–protein interaction prediction
- Topological analysis of biomolecular networks
- Alignment of biomolecular networks
- Network-based function prediction and annotation
- Uncovering signal transduction networks
- Metabolic network modeling and reconstruction
- Drug target detection in metabolic networks
- Integration of heterogenous data and heterogeneous networks

The remainder of this book is organized as follows:

- Chapter 2 introduces basic concepts related to gene regulation and gene expression, as well as microarray technologies. In this chapter, gene regulatory networks and transcription regulatory networks are described with basic kinetic models.
- Chapter 3 first presents several mathematical models for modeling gene regulatory networks, and then reviews several representative methods for reconstructing gene regulatory networks, particularly emphasizing the approaches integrating multiple datasets.
- Chapter 4 describes the basic principle of ChIP-chip technology and reports the most recent advances of quantitative studies on transcription regulation, including how to infer transcriptional interactions, reveal combinatorial regulation mechanisms, and reconstruct TF activity profiles.
- Chapter 5 is one of the main parts of this book. In this chapter, we first introduce some experimental techniques for determining protein–protein interactions and then focus on computational prediction methods based on domain information. Among various approaches, we introduce probabilistic approaches, optimization

*Identifying the regulatory roles of microRNAs in the process of post transcription regulation.

methods, and other topics. Finally, several methods, particularly designed for domain interaction prediction, are discussed.

- Chapter 6 discusses the statistical properties of protein interaction networks from the topological viewpoint. In particular, hubs, motifs, and modularity are described and utilized with their explorative biological roles. In addition, a new criterion, modularity density D for characterizing the modularity structure of complex networks is also described.

- Chapter 7 introduces a variety of network alignment methods including pairwise network alignment and multiple network alignment. In particular, a quadratic programming approach for pairwise network alignment is discussed in detail. Subnetwork and pathway query methods are also covered.

- Chapter 8 focuses on protein function prediction and is also an important part of this book. First, methods for detecting functional modules and for creating protein function linkages are extensively explored, and then several protein function prediction methods based on high-throughput data are discussed, including optimization methods and machine learning methods. Finally, we report the most recent advances of annotation approaches for domain function.

- Chapter 9 describes the biological principle of metabolism and introduces some analysis methods for metabolic pathways and networks in living organisms. Computational approaches for reconstructing and simulating metabolic networks are included. In addition, on the basis of available metabolic networks, we introduce an effective drug target detection method.

- Chapter 10 first introduces the biological principles of signal transduction and discusses mathematical modeling of signaling pathways. Then we describe several computational methods for uncovering signaling networks from high-throughput data sources or experimental evidences.

- Chapter 11 discusses some new and promising topics on both artificial and real networks to conclude this book, such as protein structure networks, integrated heterogeneous networks, and the posttranscriptional regulation networks for noncoding RNAs (e.g., microRNAs).

PART I

GENE NETWORKS

CHAPTER 2

TRANSCRIPTION REGULATION: NETWORKS AND MODELS

2.1 TRANSCRIPTION REGULATION AND GENE EXPRESSION

Although genome stores biological information, it is unable to release the information by itself to the cell. Only through the coordinated activity of enzymes and other proteins participating in a series of biochemical reactions can the biological information be passed and utilized to functional molecules [Bro02]. Regulation of gene expression or activity is one of the most important processes in a cellular system. It transmits static information encoded in the DNA sequence into mRNA in transcription process and further into functional proteins in translation processes, which in turn control most of the cellular processes [Gib04]. Through gene expression, the inheritable information that comprises a gene (DNA segment) is made manifest as a physically and biologically functional gene product, such as RNA or protein. In this section, we first introduce the biological processes and principles in gene regulation, then review more recent technologies for measuring the products of transcriptional regulation: transcripts or mRNA abundance. The ChIP-chip technique, which screens binding proteins for a promoter, is also described.

2.1.1 Transcription and Gene Regulation

As introduced in Chapter 1, a gene consists of a coding region (transcribed region) and a regulatory region (promoter region). The coding region is the part that will be transcribed into mRNA and then further translated into a protein. The regulatory region is the part of the DNA sequence that contributes the transcription of the

Biomolecular Networks. By Luonan Chen, Rui-Sheng Wang, and Xiang-Sun Zhang
Copyright © 2009 John Wiley & Sons, Inc.

gene. It contains the binding sites of a type of protein called the *transcription factor* (TF). A transcription factor or called a sequence-specific DNA binding factor is a protein that binds to specific DNA sequences to control the transfer of genetic information from DNA to RNA. Transcription factors act as an activator to promote, or act as a repressor to block the recruitment of RNA polymerase to specific genes, by performing this function alone or with other proteins (e.g., cofactors) in a complex. Each transcription factor has a key feature, that is, it contains one or more DNA binding domains which attach to specific sequences or regulatory region of DNA adjacent to the gene. In prokaryotes, the regulatory region is typically short and contains binding sites for a small number of TFs. In contrast, the regulatory region in eukaryotes can be very long and contains binding sites for multiple TFs [Gib04]. The transcriptional regulation of a gene is achieved by TFs that attach to a specific DNA promoter region and exert their effects positively or negatively on binding of RNA polymerase (RNAP) to the promoter region of the gene. RNAP is an enzyme which performs the transcription of genetic information from DNA to RNA. TFs rarely bind solely; in other words, these TFs recruit other proteins or cofactors to form chromatin-modifying complexes and transcription apparatus to initiate RNA synthesis together with RNAP (see Fig. 2.1).

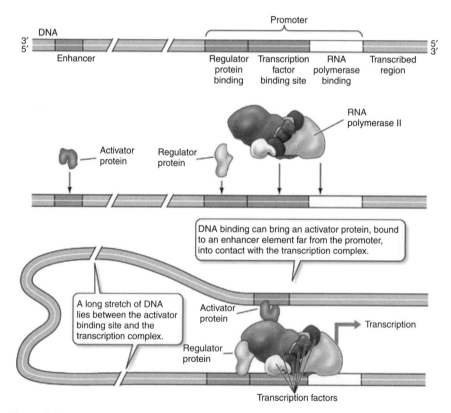

Figure 2.1. Gene structure and transcription process. [Reprinted from [Sad06] © (2006) with permission of Sinauer Associates, Inc.]

Specifically, transcription process consists of three stages: initiation, elongation, and termination. Although transcription is chemically and enzymatically similar to DNA replication, it does not need a primer to start. In prokaryotes, transcription occurs in the cytoplasm alongside translation, and transcription initiation is rather simple. Transcription begins with the direct binding of RNAP to the promoter region in DNA and then unwinds the DNA to create a chromatin-modifying complex so that RNAP has access to the single-stranded DNA template. In eukaryotes, transcription occurs primarily in the nucleus, and the produced transcript is then transported into the cytoplasm for translation. Transcription initiation in eukaryotes is far more complex. RNAP itself seldom binds directly to the core promoter sequences owing to the low affinity. It is first assembled with transcription factors to form a transcription initiation complex that is able to bind to the promoter with a much higher affinity and initiate the transcription. After RNAP binds to the promoter, the second stage of transcription begins. RNAP traverses the template strand of the DNA and uses base-pairing complementarity with the DNA template to create an RNA copy. Unlike DNA replication, transcription can involve multiple RNA polymerases on a single DNA template and make multiple rounds of replication, so many mRNA

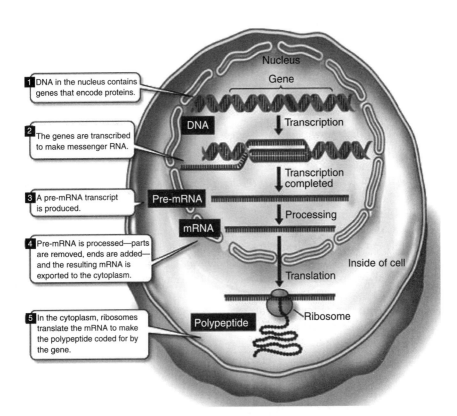

Figure 2.2. The whole process of gene expression. [Reprinted from [Sad06] © (2006) with permission of Sinauer Associates, Inc.]

molecules can be produced from a single copy of a gene. After the RNA copy is made, transcription enters into the final stage to process a pre-mRNA into a mature mRNA.

The process of gene expression involves a series of complex biochemical events such as transcription, cooperativity and competition of multiple TFs, intron splicing, posttranscriptional modification, translation, posttranslational modification, degradation, and other mechanisms. Figure 2.2 illustrates the whole gene expression process, in which a series of important events are involved. First, the DNA double helix should be unzipped to ensure that the genes on the genome are accessible. Then, a set of proteins with a RNA polymerase is assembled into a transcription initiation complex to initiate the transcription control. After this, several events such as RNA synthesis (i.e., the gene is copied into RNA), RNA processing (i.e., RNA splicing and posttranscriptional modification), and RNA degradation are involved. Subsequently, translation initiation complex is assembled near the 5′ termini of coding RNA molecules, which is a prerequisite for translating these RNA molecules into proteins. Finally, a series of events follow, such as synthesis of protein, protein folding and processing, and protein degradation.

2.1.2 Microarray Experiments and Databases

Generally, the amount of mRNA synthesized during transcription measures how active or functional a gene is. Thousands of genes and their products (RNAs and proteins) in living organisms function in a complicated and coordinated way and create the mystery of life. However, traditional methods in molecular biology that examine gene expression levels were limited to a small scale per experiment. With the development of high-density DNA chip technology, a new technology called *DNA microarray* has enabled researchers to monitor the whole genome at the transcriptional level on a single chip and detect mRNA expression levels of thousands of genes simultaneously. It can be used to detect the abundance of RNAs that may or may not be translated into active proteins. This kind of analysis is referred to as *expression analysis* or *expression profiling*. The first use of microarrays for gene expression profiling was Schena et al. [Sch95].

The DNA microarray, also known as *gene* or *genome chip*, *DNA chip*, or *gene array*, is typically a glass or plastic slide. It is a collection of microscopic DNA spots that utilize the preferential binding of complementary single-stranded nucleic acid sequences by using short lengths of nucleotides called *probes*. Such probes represent single genes, arrayed on a solid surface by covalent attachment to a chemical matrix. Thousands of probes can be placed in known locations on a single DNA microarray. Hence, each microarray experiment can potentially accomplish the equivalent number of genetic tests in parallel. The resulting gene expression data can be used to study the effects of drug treatment, diseases, developmental genetics, and so on. For example, microarray-based gene expression profiling has been widely used to identify disease genes by comparing their expression profiles in diseased and normal tissues.

Complementary DNA (cDNA) microarrays and oligonucleotide microarrays are two technologies of DNA microarray. Note that cDNA in genetics is DNA synthesized from a mature mRNA template in a reaction catalyzed by the enzyme reverse

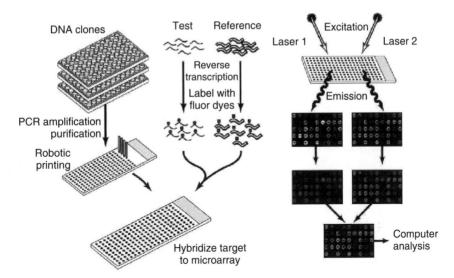

Figure 2.3. Scheme of the cDNA microarray technique. [Reprinted by permission from Macmillan Publishers Ltd: Nature Genetics [Dug99] © 1999.]

transcriptase. Figure 2.3 illustrates the scheme and principle of cDNA microarray. First, templates for genes of interested (oligonucleotides, cDNA) are obtained and amplified by polymerase chain reaction (PCR). Following purification and quality control, aliquots (~5 nL) are printed on the coated glass microscope slides using a computer-controlled high-speed robot. Total RNAs from both the test and reference samples are labeled with two different fluorophores (Cye5, Cye3). The two samples are mixed and hybridized to a single microarray that is then scanned in a microarray scanner to visualize fluorescence of the two fluorophores. Laser excitation of the incorporated targets yields an emission with a characteristic spectra, which is measured using a scanning confocal laser microscope. Monochrome images from the scanner are imported into software in which the images are pseudocolored and merged. Information about the clones, including gene name, clone identifier, intensity values, intensity ratios, normalization constant, and confidence intervals, is attached to each target. Data from a single hybridization experiment are viewed as a normalized ratio (Cye3/Cye5) in which significant deviation from 1 (no change) is indicative of increased (>1) or decreased (<1) levels of gene expression relative to the reference sample. Finally, data from multiple experiments can be examined using data-mining tools [Dug99].

Microarray techniques have been used to produce massive amounts of data. There are many useful links in which a variety of microarray data sets are deposited, including those for different organisms, conditions, biological processes, or tissues. Table 2.1 lists some microarray databases and their Websites, where the data can be analyzed by different computational methods and help elucidate the underlying biological processes.

TABLE 2.1. Some Microarray Databases and Their Websites

Databases	Websites
Stanford Microarray Database	http://genome-www5.stanford.edu/
SIEGE	http://pulm.bumc.bu.edu/siegeDB/
Gene Expression Omnibus	http://www.ncbi.nlm.nih.gov/geo/
UNC Microarray database	https://genome.unc.edu/
ArrayExpress at EBI	http://www.ebi.ac.uk/arrayexpress/
ExpressDB	http://twod.med.harvard.edu/ExpressDB/
Yale Microarray Database	http://info.med.yale.edu/microarray/
Human Gene Expression Index	http://www.biotechnologycenter.org/hio/
ChipDB	http://staffa.wi.mit.edu/chipdb/public/
M3D	http://m3d.bu.edu/
GXD	http://www.informatics.jax.org/mgihome
Escherichia coli Gene Expression Database	http://chase.ou.edu/oubcf/
Plant Expression Database	http://www.plexdb.org/
Rice Expression Database	http://red.dna.affrc.go.jp/RED/
Tomato Expression Database	http://ted.bti.cornell.edu/
Pancreatic Expression Database	http://www.pancreasexpression.org/
RNA Abundance Database	http://www.cbil.upenn.edu/RAD/
Riken Expression Array Database	http://read.gsc.riken.go.jp/
Genevestigator	https://www.genevestigator.ethz.ch/
Yeast Microarray Global Viewer	http://www.transcriptome.ens.fr/ymgv/
Bodymap	http://bodymap.ims.u-tokyo.ac.jp/

2.1.3 ChIP-Chip Technology and Transcription Factor Databases

More recently, many experimental and computational techniques have been applied to identify TFs and their target genes in several organisms such as *S. cerevisiae*, *E. coli*, and *D. Melanogaster* [LeT02, Har04]. One such important technique is ChIP-chip technology, also known as genomewide location analysis. This technique combines a modified chromatin immunoprecipitation (ChIP) assay with microarray technology and can identify the DNA sequences (target genes) occupied by specific DNA-binding proteins (TFs) in cells. These binding sites may indicate functions of various transcription regulators and help to identify their target genes during animal development or disease progression. The purpose of ChIP assay is to determine which proteins bind to a particular region on the endogenous chromatin of living cells or tissues. The principle underpinning this assay is that DNA-bound proteins, including transcription factors in living cells, can be crosslinked to the chromatin on which they are situated. Figure 2.4 illustrates the process and principle of ChIP-chip experiment.

The ChIP-chip experiment process is achieved in five steps [Zhe07]:

1. Let proteins bind to DNA. In other words, bound transcription factors and other DNA-associated proteins are crosslinked to DNA with formaldehyde.
2. Chop the DNA sequences into small fragments, using sonication to break genomic DNA sequences into small DNA fragments while the transcription factors are still bound to DNA.

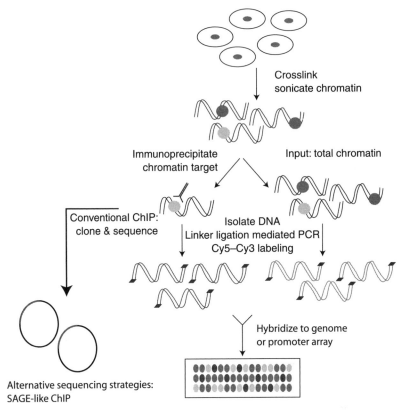

Figure 2.4. Scheme of the ChIP-chip experiment process. [Reprinted from [Haw06] © 2006 by permission of Oxford University Press.]

3. Isolate the DNA fragments bound by proteins by chromatin immunoprecipitation (ChIP).
4. Crosslinking between DNA and protein is reversed and DNA is released, amplified by ligation-mediated polymerase chain reaction (LM-PCR) and labeled with a fluorescent dye (Cy5). A sample of DNA, which is not enriched by the abovementioned immunoprecipitation process, is also amplified by LM-PCR and labeled with another fluorescent dye (Cy3).
5. Both IP-enriched and -unenriched DNA pools of labeled DNA are hybridized to the same high-density oligonucleotide arrays (chip). The microarray is then scanned and two images corresponding to Cy5 and Cy3, respectively, are extracted.

Through such ChIP-chip technique, target genes regulated by given TFs can be identified. Experimental TF–gene interactions associated with ChIP-chip techniques are deposited in several databases such as YEASTRACT [Tei06], RegulonDB [Sal06], and TRANSFAC. YEASTRACT (Yeast Search for Transcriptional Regulators And Consensus Tracking) is a curated repository of regulatory associations

TABLE 2.2. Experimental and Predicted Transcription Factor Databases

Databases	Websites
YEASTRACT	http://www.yeastract.com
RegulonDB	http://regulondb.ccg.unam.mx
AtTFDB	http://arabidopsis.med.ohio-state.edu
RIKEN AtTF	http://rarge.gsc.riken.jp/rartf
DBTBS	http://dbtbs.hgc.jp
TRANSFAC	http://www.biobase-international.com
TFdb	http://genome.gsc.riken.jp/TFdb
RiceTFDB	http://ricetfdb.bio.uni-potsdam.de
PlntTFDB	http://plntfdb.bio.uni-potsdam.de
PlantTFDB	http://planttfdb.cbi.pku.edu.cn
nTFdB	http://worms.mcmaster.ca/ntfdb
PopTF DB	http://poptf.db.umu.se
FTFD	http://ftfd.snu.ac.kr
DMTR	http://bioinfo3.noble.org/dmtr
LymphTF DB	http://www.iupui.edu/tfinterx

between TFs and target genes in *S. cerevisiae* based on bibliographic references. It also includes the information of some DNA-binding sites. RegulonDB is a reference database of *E. coli* K-12 that provides rich curated knowledge of the regulatory interactions and operon organization. Its current version also includes the information of noncoding RNAs. Except for ChIP-chip techniques, other experimental methods such as yeast one-hybrid (Y1H) assay [Dep06, VeV07] have also been used to map protein–DNA interactions.

To play a fundamental role in transcription regulation, TFs are generally composed of at least two types of domains: a DNA-binding domain, which serves to interact with its cognate DNA target sequence; and a transcription regulation domain, which serves to activate or repress transcription. Different strategies have been employed to identify TFs according to this feature, including computational and experimental methods. Currently there are many databases depositing known and predicted transcription factors, which are listed in Table 2.2.

2.2 NETWORKS IN TRANSCRIPTION REGULATION

One of the most important issues in biology is how gene expression is switched on and off, that is, how gene expression is regulated. As described earlier, it has been revealed that transcription factors (TFs) play quite an important role in gene regulation. TFs regulate gene expression by binding to the gene's promoter region to either activate or repress the gene's transcription. Transcription factors are gene products themselves, and therefore in turn can be regulated by other TFs. One TF can have many target genes, depending on the target promoters, and one gene can be controlled simultaneously by the combination of multiple transcription factors. Such relationships form a directed graph called transcription regulatory network (TRN), in which nodes are genes or gene products (mRNAs and proteins including TFs), and the edges denote the physical regulatory interactions between TFs and target genes. In other words, a TRN contains the components in two spaces: the protein space and the gene space with feedback loops between them (Fig. 2.5). Note that although we use "transcription regulatory network" to represent molecular network at transcriptional level in this book, "transcriptional regulatory network" is also widely used in literature.

Instead of studying TRNs, in earlier decades, because of the difficulty in identifying direct interactions between genes and proteins, especially in identifying transcription factors, a popular method for representing gene regulation is to draw network diagrams where genes connect to other genes as if they implicitly affect each other [Bra02]. Such a network diagram is called a gene regulatory network (GRN), or genetic network, in some literature, which represents indirect interactions or genetic interactions between genes. The edges in gene networks may not be direct physical interactions from regulators to target genes since they do not represent explicitly those interactions that are mediated by the proteins and metabolites. In other words, they represent genetic or indirect interactions between different genes. Therefore, a gene regulatory network is a phenomenological model and is a projection of the whole biochemical network onto a space where the only observable components are gene transcripts (mRNAs), but the influence of the remaining biochemical system is felt implicitly [Bra02]. Figure 2.5 illustrates this point. For example, the regulatory interaction between gene 1 and gene 2 is actually implicit or indirect and mediated by protein 1. Gene regulatory networks can help us understand the cellular functions efficiently and globally by analyzing their dynamics and design principles. Constructing and modeling such gene networks are among the most challenging

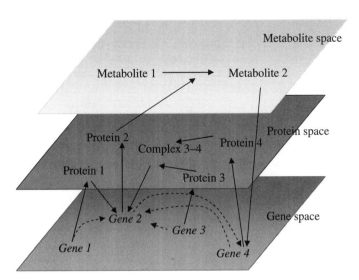

Figure 2.5. Genetic interactions in gene regulatory networks. [Reprinted from [Bra02] © 2002 with permission from Elsevier.]

problems in functional genomics. Since the expression profiling of a gene is the result of the (direct or indirect) regulatory role of other genes or gene products, such gene regulatory networks can be retrieved from gene expression profiles; this is known as the reverse-engineering problem of gene regulatory networks, which will be discussed in detail in the next chapter.

Gene regulatory network is a logical way of attempting to describe the relationships between different genes observed with transcription profiling. It is a directed network with genes as nodes and their relationships as edges and can be viewed as an input–output device. In this kind of network, each node has multiple inputs, specifically, regulatory proteins synthetically represented as mRNA levels of other genes, with one output characterized by the translated protein abundance. Figure 2.6 provides a simple illustration, where $m_i(t)$ represents the concentration of mRNA at t instant for node i, and $p_i(t)$ denotes the concentration of protein at t instant for node i. Each node (e.g., node i) has two variables or dynamical components (e.g., two variables $m_i(t)$ and $p_i(t)$) with multiple inputs $p_1(t), \ldots, p_n(t)$ and one output $p_i(t)$ [ChL02], where inputs $p_1(t), \ldots, p_n(t)$ may include $p_i(t)$ if node i is a self-regulated node or an autocatalytic node. It is such a gene regulatory network in a living cell that dynamically orchestrates the expression level of each gene in the genome by controlling whether and how the gene will be transcribed into RNA in response to various environmental and developmental signals.

Ordinary differential equations are one of the most common models for describing gene regulatory networks. Mathematically the network model of Figure 2.6 can be expressed [ChL02] as $dm_i/dt = f_i(p_1, \ldots, p_n) - d_{mi}m_i \quad dp_i/dt = s_i m_i - d_{pi}p_i$ where f_i and $s_i m_i$ are synthesis rates of mRNA$_i$ and protein$_i$ respectively, and d_{mi} and d_{pi} are degradation rates of mRNA$_i$ and protein$_i$ respectively. Generally, f_i is a nonlinear function of all related proteins, and translation rate of mRNA$_i$ is assumed to be proportional to the mRNA$_i$ (or linear function of mRNA$_i$). Figure 2.6 shows how to model a gene regulatory network with both mRNAs and proteins as variables. However, when inferring a gene regulatory network from microarray dataset, the concentrations of only mRNAs are usually taken as variables mainly because mRNAs are

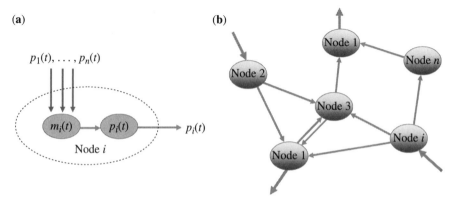

Figure 2.6. Illustrations of a gene regulatory network. (a) A single-node. (b) A gene regulatory network by connecting each node.

numerically observable values. Hence, in the framework of differential equations, a GRN is usually expressed by a set of nonlinear dynamical equations with gene expression levels (i.e., mRNA concentrations) $x(t)$ as variables [WaY06, Yeu02] because observable data reflect the abundance of mRNA from microarray experiments

$$\frac{dx(t)}{dt} = F[x(t)] - Kx(t) \tag{2.1}$$

where $x(t) = [x_1(t), \ldots, x_m(t)]^T$ denotes the expression levels of genes at time instant t, where m is the number of genes. In equation (2.1), the first term, $F(\cdot) = [F_1(\cdot), \ldots, F_m(\cdot)]^T$, is generally a nonlinear vector function denoting the synthesis rate of mRNAs, with the transcription, translation, and biochemical modification processes included. The second term, $Kx(t)$, denotes the degradation rate, where $K = \text{diag}(k_1, \ldots, k_m)$. Although gene regulations are often nonlinear, most of the existing approaches for reconstructing GRN adopt linear or additive models owing to unclearly delineated structures of biological systems and scarcity of data. A detailed review on models and algorithms for GRN is given in Jong [Jon02].

A gene regulatory network represents the interactions among genes at the level of mRNA, which characterize indirect regulatory relationships or genetic interactions between different genes [Jon02, WaY06, Hus03a]. Although GRN provides valuable information and insight on gene regulation, understanding of the direct interactions between TFs and genes is very necessary in order to elucidate regulatory mechanisms in a more accurate and detailed manner. In this sense, transcription regulatory networks (TRNs), which describe the transcription interactions between TFs and the target genes at the level of mRNA and protein, characterize the direct relationships (i.e., physical interactions) between regulators and target genes. It is defined by the integrated effects of TFs on the expression of genes with all binding relationships between TFs and promoters [Pta02]. Transcription regulatory networks are composed of protein–DNA interactions between transcription factors and their target genes, with implicit protein–protein interactions. The chemistry underlying these interactions is not fully understood yet. A long-term goal in genome biology is to map protein–DNA interaction networks of all regulatory regions in a genome of interest. Both TF and gene-centered methods can be used to systematically identify such interactions. We will discuss them in detail in Chapter 4.

Transcription regulatory networks are remarkably diverse in their structures, but they usually consist of structural building blocks such as autoregulation loops, feed-forward loops (FFL), feedback loops, single input motifs (SIM), multiple input motifs (MIM), regulator chains, and other components [Bab04, LiC07a]. Figure 2.7 illustrates the typical structural organization of TRNs. The functional building block of TRNs is the promoter region of a gene or operon, which contains the *cis*-regulatory binding sites for the relevant TFs regulating the expression of the gene. The regulatory interactions in TRNs can be classified as either negative (inhibitory) or positive (activating). If the presence of a protein P triggers the expression of a target gene Q, we say that this protein activates (positively regulates) its target gene, and that P is an activator of Q. Conversely, if the presence of a protein P represses the expression of a target gene Q, we say that this protein represses (negatively regulates) its target gene, and that P is a repressor of Q.

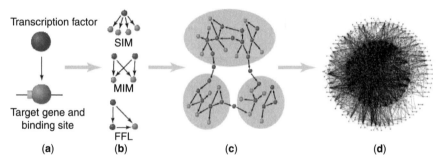

Transcription factor

SIM

MIM

Target gene and
binding site

FFL

(a)   (b)   (c)   (d)

Figure 2.7. Structural organization of transcription regulatory networks: (a) basic unit; (b) motifs; (c) modules; (d) transcriptional regulatory network (see color insert). (Reprinted from [Bab04], © 2004, with permission from Elsevier.)

Similar to the GRN represented by equation (2.1), TRN can also be described by a set of ordinary differential equations with gene expression level $x(t)$ and transcription factor activity (TFA) $a(t)$ as variables

$$\frac{dx(t)}{dt} = F[a(t)] - Kx(t) \tag{2.2}$$

where $x(t) = [x_1(t), \ldots, x_m(t)]^T$ denotes the expression level of genes where m denotes the number of genes, and $a(t) = [a_1(t), \ldots, a_n(t)]$ denotes TFA profile with n indicating the number of TFs. $F(\cdot) = [F_1(\cdot), \ldots, F_m(\cdot)]^T$ denotes the transcription rates of mRNAs, which include only transcription process.

Notice that an interaction in GRN [model (2.1)] is an indirect or genetic interaction from mRNA [described by $x(t)$] to mRNA [described by $x(t)$], which integrates the effects of whole biochemical reactions including transcription, translation, and gene regulation processes, while an interaction in TRN [model (2.2)] represents a direct or physical interaction from TF [described by $a(t)$] to mRNA [described by $x(t)$] including only the transcription process. It is worth noting that differential assumptions or kinetics lead to different forms of F in both (2.1) and (2.2). The main tasks for reverse engineering of GRN and TRN can be generally stated as

- Inferring GRN: derive F for given gene expression data $x(t)$.
- Inferring TRN: derive $a(t)$ and F for given gene expression data $x(t)$ and partial knowledge of F (e.g., ChIP-chip data).

2.3 NONLINEAR MODELS BASED ON BIOCHEMICAL REACTIONS

Diverse biochemical and biophysical processes are involved in the transduction of the information flow from DNA to a protein. A predictive mathematical model can be created from biochemical details. We now illustrate how to formulate a

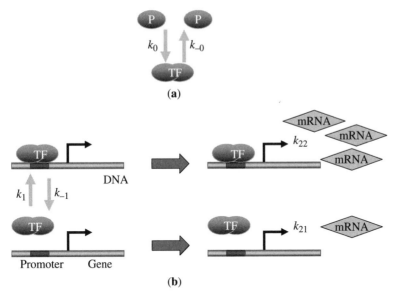

Figure 2.8. Illustrations of a TF binding to DNA and starting transcription: (a) protein–protein interaction to form a transcription complex (dimerization); (b) the transcription complex binds to DNA and starts transcription (this TF is an activator of the gene).

mathematical model in a deterministic form from a series of biochemical reactions. Although additional assumptions and constraints for the model can make the problems computationally tractable or efficient, such a nonlinear model can provide rich information for the regulatory relationships between TFs and target genes and predict the future dynamics of regulation. Note that the stochastic form of gene regulation with the consideration of random and discrete changes in the number of molecules is not the main focus of this book. Interested readers are referred to the review paper [WaR08].

Figure 2.8 illustrates a simple example of a TF that binds to DNA and then recruits RNA polymerase (RNAP), thereby initiating a transcriptional process for transcription of DNA into mRNA. The TF can be a dimer of a protein P, or a simple transcription complex. We use the notation TF $\cdot$ DNA to represent a complex with "TF bound to DNA," and so on. For simplicity, we omit the RNA polymerase binding to DNA, namely, RNAP $\cdot$ DNA. The biochemical reactions for protein–protein interaction (i.e., the dimerization process of protein) involve the following reactions:

$$1P + 1P \xrightarrow{k_0} 1TF \qquad (2.3)$$

$$1TF \xrightarrow{k_{-0}} 1P + 1P \qquad (2.4)$$

Reaction (2.3) represents the synthesis of active TF or a simple transcription complex (dimer) from monomer protein P, and reaction (2.4) is the disassociation of active TF, where k_0 and k_{-0} are reaction rates. Note that reactions (2.3) and (2.4) can be expressed by a bidirectional chemical reaction. The active TF is able to bind to the promoter of a gene to regulate the gene activity. Note that rather than individual proteins, a gene is generally regulated by one transcriptional complex or multiple transcriptional complexes formed by multiple proteins.

On the other hand, the biochemical equations in the transcription process are

$$1TF + 1DNA \xrightarrow{k_1} 1TF \cdot DNA \tag{2.5}$$

$$1TF \cdot DNA \xrightarrow{k_{-1}} 1TF + 1DNA \tag{2.6}$$

$$1DNA \xrightarrow{k_{21}} mRNA \tag{2.7}$$

$$1TF \cdot DNA \xrightarrow{k_{22}} mRNA \tag{2.8}$$

$$mRNA \xrightarrow{k_3} \varnothing \tag{2.9}$$

Biochemical reactions (2.5) and (2.6) represent the binding activity of the TF, which follows simple and complementary chemical kinetics, where k_1 and k_{-1} are the synthesis and disassociation rates respectively. Biochemical reactions (2.7) and (2.8) represent the transcription process of DNA in which mRNA is synthesized by RNA polymerase (RNAP), where k_{21} and k_{22} are transcription rates without and with the TF respectively. We omit RNAP here to simplify the expression. Biochemical reaction (2.9) denotes the degradation of mRNA, where k_3 is the degradation rate. Note that if we explicitly consider the RNAP binding, DNA should be replaced as RNAP $\cdot$ DNA in (2.7) and (2.8). If the TF is an activator, $k_{22} > k_{21}$. Otherwise, if the TF is a repressor, $k_{22} < k_{21}$.

The law of mass action in chemistry indicates that the rate of an elementary reaction defined by reduction of reactant or formation of product is proportional to the concentration of each individual species involved in this reaction. The change rate of the concentration of any given reactant is then a sum of the change rates giving rise to all elementary reactions in which it is involved. The differential equation for protein–protein interaction reactions (2.3) and (2.4) is

$$\frac{d[TF]}{dt} = k_0[P]^2 - k_{-0}[TF] \tag{2.10}$$

where [TF] and [P] denote the concentrations of TF and P, respectively. To simplify the expression of variables, we explicitly omit t in each variable, for example, $[TF] = [TF](t)$ and $[P] = [P](t)$. Similarly, the governing equations of reactions (2.5) and (2.6) in the transcription process are given by

$$\frac{d[TF \cdot DNA]}{dt} = k_1[TF][DNA] - k_{-1}[TF \cdot DNA] \tag{2.11}$$

where [TF · DNA], [TF], and [DNA] denote the concentrations of TF · DNA, TF, and DNA, respectively. The governing equation of reactions (2.7) and (2.8) is given by

$$\frac{d[\text{mRNA}]}{dt} = k_{21}[\text{TF} \cdot \text{DNA}] + k_{22}[\text{DNA}] - k_3[\text{mRNA}] \qquad (2.12)$$

where [mRNA] denotes the concentration of mRNA.

Generally, protein–protein interactions and binding reactions are much faster than those of transcription and translation processes, which are actually chain reactions with multiple steps depending on the lengths of gene and mRNA sequences. In other words, equations (2.10)–(2.11) can be viewed as fast dynamics corresponding fast reactions (e.g., lasting less than seconds), whereas (2.12) is slow dynamics corresponding to a slow reaction (e.g., lasting more than a minute). Hence, we assume that (2.10)–(2.11) quickly reach a quasiequilibrium state:

$$\frac{d[\text{TF}]}{dt} = 0, \qquad \frac{d[\text{TF} \cdot \text{DNA}]}{dt} = 0$$

Then we have

$$[\text{TF}] = \frac{k_0}{k_{-0}}[\text{P}]^2 = K_{eq0}[\text{P}]^2 \qquad (2.13)$$

and

$$[\text{TF} \cdot \text{DNA}] = \frac{k_1}{k_{-1}}[\text{TF}][\text{DNA}] = K_{eq}[\text{TF}][\text{DNA}] \qquad (2.14)$$

where $K_{eq0} = k_0/k_{-0}$ and $K_{eq} = k_1/k_{-1}$ are called the equilibrium constants of those two fast reactions. Since there is generally one DNA or one specific gene in one eukaryotic cell, there is a conservation condition for the number of DNA. For example, assume [TF · DNA] + [DNA] = 1 or a specific constant. Hence, [DNA] = 1 − [TF · DNA] = 1 − K_{eq}[TF][DNA], which means

$$[\text{DNA}] = \frac{1}{1 + K_{eq}[\text{TF}]}$$

Therefore, we can obtain an ordinary differential equation describing the dynamics of the gene regulation process

$$\begin{aligned}
\frac{d[\text{mRNA}]}{dt} &= k_{21}\frac{1}{1 + K_{eq}[\text{TF}]} + k_{22}[\text{TF}]\frac{1}{1 + K_{eq}[\text{TF}]} - k_3[\text{mRNA}] \\
&= \frac{k_{21} + k_{22}[\text{TF}]}{1 + K_{eq}[\text{TF}]} - k_3[\text{mRNA}] \qquad (2.15)
\end{aligned}$$

which is the well-known Michaelis–Menten equation. Such a model has been widely used to formulate transcription regulatory networks, which will be discussed in detail in the later chapters. Replacing [TF] in equation (2.15) with [P] in equation (2.13), that is, $[TF] = K_{eq0}[P]^2$, we can also express (2.15) with the variable [P]. Clearly, if $k_{22} > k_{21}$, the TF is an activator of the gene, which is the case in Figure 2.8. Otherwise, if $k_{22} < k_{21}$, the TF is a repressor of the gene.

When two or more TFs bind to the promoter of a gene, similar biochemical reactions can be derived but with higher-order Michaelis–Menten terms. For instance, assume that there are two regulators, TF1 and TF2, for regulating one gene with one binding site. Then, there are four states for binding of DNA and TFs: (1) no TF bound to DNA, (2) TF1 bound to DNA, (3) TF2 bound to DNA, and (4) both TF1 and TF2 bound to DNA. Hence, we have the following biochemical reactions:

$$1TF1 + 1DNA \xrightarrow{k_1} 1TF1 \cdot DNA \tag{2.16}$$

$$1TF1 \cdot DNA \xrightarrow{k_{-1}} 1TF1 + 1DNA \tag{2.17}$$

$$1TF2 + 1DNA \xrightarrow{k_2} 1TF2 \cdot DNA \tag{2.18}$$

$$1TF2 \cdot DNA \xrightarrow{k_{-2}} 1TF1 + 1DNA \tag{2.19}$$

$$1TF1 + 1TF2 + 1DNA \xrightarrow{k_3} 1TF1 \cdot TF2 \cdot DNA \tag{2.20}$$

$$1TF1 \cdot 1TF2 \cdot DNA \xrightarrow{k_{-3}} 1TF1 + 1TF2 + 1DNA \tag{2.21}$$

$$1DNA \xrightarrow{k_4} mRNA \tag{2.22}$$

$$1TF1 \cdot DNA \xrightarrow{k_5} mRNA \tag{2.23}$$

$$1TF2 \cdot DNA \xrightarrow{k_6} mRNA \tag{2.24}$$

$$1TF2 \cdot 1TF2 \cdot DNA \xrightarrow{k_7} mRNA \tag{2.25}$$

$$mRNA \xrightarrow{k_8} \emptyset \tag{2.26}$$

where (2.16)–(2.17), (2.18)–(2.19), and (2.20)–(2.21) are all bidirectional reactions respectively, and $k_1, k_{-1}, k_2, k_{-2}, k_3, k_{-3}, k_4$–$k_8$ are all reaction rates. Note that RNAP binding to DNA in reactions (2.23)–(2.25) is again omitted. A similar analytic process will lead to the following differential equation by assuming the conservation condition of DNA number: $[DNA] + [TF1 \cdot DNA] + [TF2 \cdot DNA] + [TF2 \cdot TF2 \cdot DNA] = 1$ or a constant

$$\frac{d[mRNA]}{dt} = \frac{k_4 + k_5[TF1] + k_6[TF2] + k_7[TF1][TF2]}{1 + K_{eq1}[TF1] + K_{eq2}[TF2] + K_{eq3}[TF1][TF2]} - k_8[mRNA] \tag{2.27}$$

where the equilibrium constants $K_{eq1} = k_1/k_{-1}, K_{eq2} = k_2/k_{-2}, K_{eq3} = k_3/k_{-3}$. This equation can characterize the binding cases of two TFs in detail by observing the values of the coefficients and has been applied in formulating the dynamics of transcription regulatory networks with multioutput motifs. Clearly, k_7 and k_{eq3} represent the cooperativity between the two TFs. In other words, if all TFs interact with the binding site independently, that is, if there is no cooperativity between them, k_7 and k_{eq3} are zero. For the example described by reactions (2.16)–(2.26), the activation and inhibition roles of TF1 and TF2 depend on the relative values between k_4, k_5, k_6, k_7. Note that the form of equation (2.27) depends on the combination of TFs and binding sites, which can be explored to derive a general model for transcription regulatory networks. In addition, to approximate the diffusion and transportation processes, time delays are usually introduced in the right-hand first term of equation (2.27), replacing [TF1](t) and [TF2](t) by [TF1]$(t - \tau_1)$ and [TF2]$(t - \tau_2)$ respectively, where τ_1 and τ_2 approximately represent the effects of diffusion and transportation processes.

In contrast to the transcriptional process to produce mRNA, protein is synthesized by the corresponding mRNA at the ribosome during the translational process. The translation rate is generally assumed to be linearly proportional to the concentration of the mRNA, specifically

$$\frac{d[\text{protein}]}{dt} = k_9[\text{mRNA}] - k_{10}[\text{protein}] \qquad (2.28)$$

where [protein] is the concentration of the protein. Equation (2.28) represents two biochemical reactions, translation and degradation, respectively:

$$\text{mRNA} \xrightarrow{k_9} \text{protein} \qquad (2.29)$$

$$\text{protein} \xrightarrow{k_{10}} \varnothing \qquad (2.30)$$

where k_9 and k_{10} are the synthesis rate and degradation rate of the protein, respectively. Depending on the problem under study, equations (2.27) and/or (2.28) are required to be derived. As similar to the transcription, the translational process is a chain reaction, which is much slower than other biochemical reactions and thereby is viewed as slow in terms of the dynamics.

Generally, assume that there are multiple TFs, where each TF has multiple binding sites for the ith gene. Then, in the same way that we derived equation (2.27), we can obtain the cis-regulation function of this case. For such a case, possible states for the transcription are all combinations of TFs and binding sites for the ith gene. Therefore, the number of terms for the synthesis function in the TRN exponentially increases with numbers of TFs and binding sites. Specifically, assume that there are m_i TFs, and that the jth TF has s_{ij} binding sites for the ith gene. Then, both the denominator and numerator of the synthetic rate for the ith gene of the TRN, namely, the first term on the right side of equation (2.27), have all of the following combination terms: [TF]$_{i1}^{q_{i1}}$ [TF]$_{i2}^{q_{i2}} \cdots$ [TF]$_{im_i}^{q_{im_i}}$, where $q_{ik} = 0, 1, \ldots, s_{ik}$ for $k = 1, \ldots, m_i$.

Based on statistical thermodynamics, a general TRN can be also derived. Specifically, in terms of thermodynamics, a general nonlinear model of TRN with n genes can be expressed as

$$\frac{d[\text{mRNA}]_i}{dt} = k_{Ri}\text{Pr}(\text{RNAP}_i) - d_{Ri}[\text{mRNA}]_i \tag{2.31}$$

$$\frac{d[\text{protein}]_i}{dt} = k_{Pi}[\text{mRNA}]_i - d_{Pi}[\text{protein}]_i \tag{2.32}$$

where $i = 1, \ldots, n$, k_{Ri}, k_{Pi} denote the synthesis rates of mRNA and protein, respectively, and d_{Ri}, d_{Pi} represent the degradation rates of mRNA and protein, respectively. $\text{Pr}(\text{RNAP}_i)$ can be viewed as the probability that the RNA polymerase is bound to DNA or the ith gene. It has the following form

$$\text{Pr}(\text{RNAP}_i) = \sum_{c_i \in C} \text{Pr}(c_i) \text{Pr}(\text{RNAP}_i|c_i) \tag{2.33}$$

where C is the set of all possible configurations of TFs on the DNA, $\text{Pr}(c_i)$ is the distribution over TF configurations on the DNA, and $\text{Pr}(\text{RNAP}_i|c_i)$ is the probability that the RNA polymerase is bound given the constellation of TFs bound to the ith gene in configuration c_i. Here, we assume that the expression level of the gene i, that is, the concentration of mRNA, is proportional to the probability that RNA polymerase occupies its regulatory sequence.

We further assume that the transcription and translation rates are much slower than other biochemical reactions, such as binding and dimerization. Therefore, the system is in a state of thermodynamic equilibrium such that each configuration is achieved with a probability proportional to its probability under the Boltzmann distribution. If there are m_i TFs, and the jth TF has s_{ij} binding sites for the ith gene, then

$$\text{Pr}(\text{RNAP}_i) = \frac{\sum_{q_{i1}=0,\ldots,q_{im_i}=0}^{s_{i1},\ldots,s_{im_i}} w(1, q_{i1}, \ldots, q_{im_i})[\text{RNAP}][\text{TF}]_{i1}^{q_{i1}} \cdots [\text{TF}]_{im_i}^{q_{im_i}}}{1 + \sum_{q_0=0}^{1} \sum_{q_{i1}=0,\ldots,q_{im_i}=0}^{s_{i1},\ldots,s_{im_i}} w(q_0, q_{i1}, \ldots, q_{im_i})[\text{RNAP}]^{q_0}[\text{TF}]_{i1}^{q_{i1}} \cdots [\text{TF}]_{im_i}^{q_{im_i}}} \tag{2.34}$$

where $w(q_0, q_{i1}, \ldots, q_{im_i})$ are the parameters related to the thermodynamic coefficients on the system. Hence, substituting (2.34) into (2.31), we have the nonlinear dynamical equation of the TRN (2.31)–(2.32).

As a special example, assume that all TFs independently bind at available distinct sites of a gene's promoter region without interacting with each other, that is, there is no cooperativity between TFs. Then the TRN with n genes can be mathematically expressed as

$$\frac{d[\text{mRNA}]_i}{dt} = d_{i0} + d_i \left(1 - \prod_{j \in R_i^+} \rho\left([\text{TF}]_j, s_{ij}, \theta_{ij}\right) \right)$$

$$\times \prod_{j \in R_i^-} \rho\left([\text{TF}]_j, s_{ij}, \theta_{ij}\right) - d_i[\text{mRNA}]_i \tag{2.35}$$

where $i = 1, \ldots, n$ and $\rho([\text{TF}], s, \theta) = 1/(1 + \theta[\text{TF}])^s$. Let R_i be the regulator set of the ith gene. Then, R_i^+ is the set of activators in R_i, and R_i^- is the set of inhibitors in R_i. Hence, $R_i = R_i^+ \cup R_i^-$. s_{ij} represents the number of binding sites for the jth TF, and θ_{ij} stands for the affinity constant for the jth TF to the binding site. d_{io} is the initiation transcription rate of the ith gene, and d_i is the degradation rate of the ith gene. According to the assumption of independence between TFs, there is a much smaller set of parameters in equation (2.35).

2.4 INTEGRATED MODELS FOR REGULATORY NETWORKS

As described earlier, a major process for gene regulation is the transcription control by TFs, which exert their effects positively or negatively on the binding of RNA polymerase to the promoter region of the gene to synthesize the gene product. In other words, it is the accumulated effects of all TFs that recruit RNA polymerase so as to initiate the transcription of the gene, with each TF playing a different role.

To describe such effects, generally a gene or transcriptional regulatory network can be expressed by the following nonlinear differential equations with each gene expression level as variables

$$\frac{dx(t)}{dt} = sg[u(t)] - dx(t). \tag{2.36}$$

where $x(t) = [x_1(t), \ldots, x_n(t)]^T$, and $g[u(t)] = \{g[u_1(t)], \ldots, g[u_n(t)]\}^T$ with $u_i(t) = \sum_{j=1}^{n} J_{ij}x_j(t) + I_i$ for $i = 1, \ldots, n$. $x_i(t)$ is the expression level (mRNA concentration or protein concentration) of gene i at timepoint t, and n is the number of genes. The diagonal matrices $s = \text{diag}(s_1, \ldots, s_n)$ and $d = \text{diag}(d_1, \ldots, d_n)$ represent the production rates and degradation rates of mRNA x, respectively, which are positive matrices. This model combines the processes of transcription and translation into a single production process. $g(u_i)$ specifies the production efficiency of gene i, as a function of the weighted summation over all x_j modified by the gene's activation threshold or external stimulus I_i. In the model, if $J_{ij} > 0$, then we interpret gene j as an activator of gene i. On the other hand, if $J_{ij} < 0$, then gene j is a repressor of gene i. I_i is set to be zero when there is no external input. Figure 2.9 illustrates such a formalism for a single gene [ChL02].

In model (2.36), $g(u)$ is generally expressed as a sigmoidal transfer function:

$$g[u(t)] = \frac{1}{1 + e^{-u(t)}} \tag{2.37}$$

There are $n^2 + 3n$ parameters corresponding J_{ij}, I_i, s_i, and d_i in this nonlinear model, in contrast to the conventional $n^2 + n$ parameters corresponding to J_{ij} and I_i in linear model. In other words, unknown parameters of (2.36) are in the same order as that of linear equations, although it is in a nonlinear form. This formalism has been widely adopted to model or reconstruct gene regulatory networks. $sg(u)$ in (2.36) represents mainly the accumulated effects of regulators on recruiting RNA polymerase to initiate the transcription of gene i.

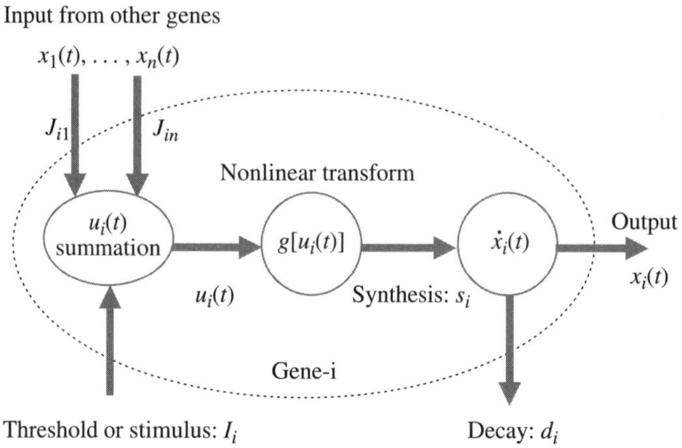

Input from other genes

$x_1(t), \ldots, x_n(t)$

Figure 2.9. Scheme of a node in a nonlinear gene regulatory network.

Assume that there are m timepoints totally for a given experimental condition, namely, $t_1, \ldots, t_m$. For the nonlinear model (2.36), when x_i is sufficiently small, we have $\dot{x}_i(t) \approx s_i \sum_{j=1}^{n} J_{ij}x_j(t) - d_i x_j(t) + s_i I_i + \frac{1}{2}$ by linearizing $g[u]$, which is equivalent to the conventional linear formalism. Here, $\dot{x}_i(t) = dx_i(t)/dt$ for the simplicity. On the other hand, according to (2.36), we have

$$g^{-1}\left(\frac{\dot{x}_i(t) + d_i x_i(t)}{s_i}\right) = u_i(t) = \sum_{j=1}^{n} J_{ij}x_j(t) + I_i \qquad (2.38)$$

for $i = 1, \ldots, n$, which is a typical linear form provided that the parameters d and s are given. Such a fact suggests that we can exploit the existing algorithms for linear gene regulatory networks [WaY06] to efficiently infer nonlinear regulatory networks by adopting a two-phase strategy, specifically, deriving parameters s and d for the given J and I in the first phase, then inferring J and I for given s and d in the second phase. The optimal solution is eventually obtained by the iteration of these two phases.

For the model (2.36) or (2.38), generally $2n$ parameters s_i and d_i are nonzero because of their biological meanings, while the matrix J with n^2 elements is assumed to be sparse; that is, most of its elements are zero. Notice that it is a major task to derive n^2 elements of J in computational biology because J is the regulatory strength matrix between genes. In the next chapter, we give a detailed algorithm for inferring all parameters J_{ij}, I_i, s_i, and d_i by exploiting a linear programming algorithm [WaY06].

2.5 SUMMARY

In this chapter, we briefly introduced the basic principle of transcriptional regulation and microarray technologies, and described some main gene expression databases and transcription factor databases. The concepts of gene regulatory networks and transcription regulatory networks were also introduced. Finally, we discussed transcriptional regulation process from the viewpoint of biochemical reactions, and introduced several mathematical models of gene networks including gene regulatory networks and transcription regulatory networks in the framework of differential equations. These concepts as well as databases and models are presented for the next two chapters, where we will describe how to computationally reconstruct regulatory networks from a huge deposition of microarray data.

CHAPTER 3

RECONSTRUCTION OF GENE REGULATORY NETWORKS

3.1 MATHEMATICAL MODELS OF GENE REGULATORY NETWORK

As described in the preceding chapter, a gene regulatory network (GRN, or genetic network) is a collection of genes in a cell that interact with each other (indirectly through their products, i.e., RNAs and proteins) and the regulatory relationships between gene activities are mediated by proteins and metabolites. In other words, gene regulatory networks are high-level descriptions of cellular biochemistry, in which only the transcriptome is considered and all biochemical processes underlying gene–gene interactions are implicitly present. Most gene regulatory networks are large and complicated, and thereby the dynamics of detailed genetic regulatory processes is difficult to be understood by intuitive approaches alone. Generally, gene regulatory networks can be modeled and simulated by mathematical and computational approaches such as graphs, Boolean networks, Bayesian networks, and differential equations [ChT99, ChL02, Jon02, Hus03a]. Although such models are created with a set of assumptions, they can provide a qualitative or rough description of system dynamics and further behavioral predictions. Once a model is chosen, the parameters in the model need to be inferred to fit the data. Such a computational process is known as gene regulatory network inference or reverse engineering of gene regulatory networks. In the last few years (as of 2009), a number of methods have been developed for inferring gene regulatory networks from microarray gene expression data. We will first introduce some mathematical models and then focus on reverse engineering of gene regulatory networks modeled by differential equations.

Biomolecular Networks. By Luonan Chen, Rui-Sheng Wang, and Xiang-Sun Zhang
Copyright © 2009 John Wiley & Sons, Inc.

3.1.1 Boolean Networks

The Boolean network, $\mathcal{G}(\mathcal{V}, \mathcal{F})$, firstly introduced by Kauffman [Kau69], is defined by a directed graph with a set of nodes $\mathcal{V} = \{v_1, v_2, \ldots, v_n\}$ and a list of Boolean functions $\mathcal{F} = (f_1, f_2, \ldots, f_n) \in \{0, 1\}^n$, where Boolean functions implicitly define the graph edge set. Each node v_i stands for a gene or a stimulus with an associated steady-state expression level x_i, representing the amount of a gene or the amount of stimulus present in the cell. This level is approximated as binary states (ON or OFF), where $x_i = 1$ represents the fact that gene v_i is expressed and $x_i = 0$ means that it is not expressed. Boolean function $\mathcal{F}$ represents the rules of regulatory interactions between genes, which are combinations of logic operations AND, OR, and NOT. Figure 3.1 illustrates a small Boolean network with its truth table. It is a gene regulatory network with three genes: $x\_\{gene3\} = x\_\{gene1\}$ OR NOT $x\_\{gene2\}$, indicating that gene1 activates gene3 and gene2 inhibits gene2. As each gene has only two states, the state space of the network consists of 2^n states. The state of a gene at time t is completely determined by those of other genes through underlying logical Boolean functions. In other words, at each timestep, the new state of a node is a Boolean function of the prior states of the nodes with arrows pointing toward it

$$x_i(t+1) = f_i(x_{i_1}, x_{i_2}, \ldots, x_{i_l})$$

where $l \leq n$, $v_{i_j} \in V$. In a synchronous Boolean model, all the states of nodes are updated simultaneously in one step according to the last state of the system. In a asynchronous Boolean model, the nodes are updated in a random order, which means that the state of genes at time t is determined by the current or prior states of other genes, depending on the updating order of the nodes. The state space of a Boolean network is finite, and the network will eventually reach a steady state, which is also called a *dynamic attractor*.

The objective of reverse engineering of gene regulatory networks by Boolean networks is to infer both the underlying topology (the edges in the graph) and the Boolean functions for each gene from observed gene expression data. Boolean network modeling has been widely used for reconstructing gene regulatory networks. An early study was contributed by Liang et al. who have developed an algorithm called REVEAL to infer Boolean networks from state transition tables formulated from

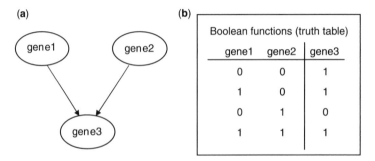

Figure 3.1. A Boolean network for three genes.

time-series data [Lia98]. Akutsu et al. gave a theoretical result on reconstructing gene networks by Boolean network [Aku99], in which they proved that $O(\log n)$ expression patterns are necessary and sufficient to identify the underlying Boolean network of n genes correctly with high probability if the maximum number of incoming edges is bounded. In another study, Akutsu et al. pointed out that many real regulatory relationships are nonlinear and using linear equations in network reconstruction methods will make the methods difficult to be applied to real data [Aku00]. In their work, on the basis of generalized mass action, they proposed a qualitative Boolean network model with noise and a power-law model called an *S system*, which has been widely used to model biological networks. Gene regulation exhibits considerable uncertainty on the biological level. Shmulevich et al. provided a comprehensive survey of Boolean networks as models of gene regulatory networks and proposed a probabilistic Boolean network that can deal with the uncertainty in gene expression data [Shm02]. More recently, Kim et al. proposed a variable selection method that can reduce Boolean network computation time significantly and at the same time obtain optimal network constructions by using chi-square (χ^2) statistics for testing the independence in contingency tables [Kim07].

Boolean models simplify the dynamics of gene networks, which enable the efficient analysis of large networks. However, Boolean networks ignore the intermediate states of gene expression and it can update genes in a asynchronous way, which may miss many important dynamic behaviors. In addition, the learning of Boolean Network both topology and Boolean functions is also a key machine learning problem. There are several ways to learn Boolean network from observed data. If the truth table is completely known, exhaustive enumeration can suffice but is not feasible for large biological systems. Many refined techniques have been developed in the machine learning community [Lah03].

3.1.2 Bayesian Networks

A Bayesian network is a graphical structure with a family of conditional probability distributions that describes a set of random variables and their probabilistic dependences. The graphical structure consists of a set of nodes V representing random variables and a set of directed edges $\mathcal{E}$ indicating the conditional dependence relations among different random variables. Figure 3.2 illustrates a small example of a Bayesian network. If a directed edge in the graph is from node A to node B, then A is called a "parent" of B and B is called a "child" of A. A Bayesian network is a directed acyclic graph and offers a simple way for expanding the joint probability in terms of conditional probabilities. Given $X_1, X_2, \ldots, X_n$ as a set of random variables represented by the nodes in the graph, if the set of parent nodes of a node X_i is denoted by $\mathrm{Pa}[X_i]$, then the joint distribution of the node values can be written as a product of the local conditional distributions of each node and its parents, which is just the characteristic of Bayesian networks:

$$P(X_1, X_2, \ldots, X_n) = \prod_{i=1}^{n} P(X_i | \mathrm{Pa}[X_i])$$

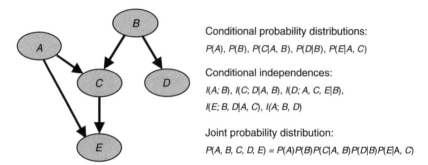

Conditional probability distributions:
$P(A)$, $P(B)$, $P(C|A, B)$, $P(D|B)$, $P(E|A, C)$

Conditional independences:
$I(A; B)$, $I(C; D|A, B)$, $I(D; A, C, E|B)$,
$I(E; B, D|A, C)$, $I(A; B, D)$

Joint probability distribution:
$P(A, B, C, D, E) = P(A)P(B)P(C|A, B)P(D|B)P(E|A, C)$

Figure 3.2. An example of a simple Bayesian network $I(x, y)$ means that for a given z, x is independent of y.

Bayesian networks are interpretable and flexible models for representing conditional dependence relations between multiple interacting quantities [Hus03a]. In order to fully specify a Bayesian network and thus fully represent the joint probability distribution, its structure should be learned to specify the probability distribution for each node X conditional on X's parents, which is a very important part of machine learning. The posterior probability of the network structure given by the training data is often treated as the objective function, which corresponds to the degree to which the inferred network structure is supported by the data. However, the number of possible structures increases exponentially with respect to the number of variables (nodes). A local search strategy can make incremental changes and improve the score of the structure. Therefore, numerical approximate algorithms are often adopted such as Markov chain Monte Carlo (MCMC).

Bayesian network can deal with the stochastic aspects of gene expression and noisy data in a natural way. In particular, it can be used when only partial knowledge of the system is available, which popularized its use as a tool for reconstructing gene regulatory networks [Fri04]. Bayesian networks were first applied to analyze gene expression data by Friedman et al. [Fri00]. When the Bayesian network is used in the inference of gene networks, the nodes in its graph structure are associated with genes and their expression levels, and the edges represent the interactions between different genes. Pe'er et al. introduced a procedure that calculates how many discrete levels of expression are needed for each gene [Pee01]. They used a Bayesian network framework to infer a finer interaction structure between different genes, such as mediation, activation, and inhibition. Husmeier discussed how to evaluate the inferred genetic networks by Bayesian methods [Hus03a]. He suggested using synthetic data generated from a known Bayesian network to test whether the inferred network is consistent with the true network in terms of true positives and false positives (ROC curves). In another study, Husmeier presented a realistic simulation study to test the viability of the dynamic Bayesian network paradigm for gene regulatory networks [Hus03b], where artificial gene expression data are generated by simulating a known biological network involving DNAs, mRNAs, inactive protein monomers, and active protein dimers. This work provides important insights on how to evaluate

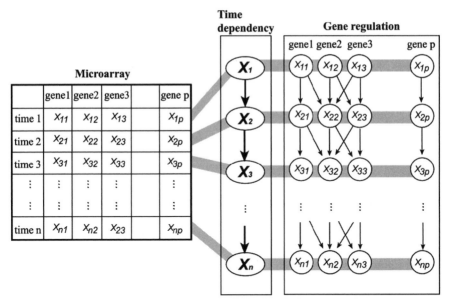

Figure 3.3. Graphical view of a dynamic Bayesian network model. (Reprinted from [Kim03] © 2003 by permission of Oxford University Press.)

the inferred gene networks. Although Bayesian networks are widely adopted to reconstruct gene regulatory networks, a serious limitation is their acyclicity constraint, which rules out recurrent structures such as feedback loops. Since feedback is an essential feature of biological systems, the usefulness of Bayesian networks for modeling gene regulatory interactions seems questionable [Hus03b]. Hence, to proceed with modeling gene networks by Bayesian network more practically, many researchers turn their attention to dynamic Bayesian networks.

Compared with Bayesian networks, dynamical Bayesian networks can describe cyclic regulations using time-delay information. Dynamic Bayesian network is a representation of stochastic evolution of a set of random variables $X = \{X_1, \ldots, X_n\}$ over discretized time. It consists of a directed graph representing conditional independences and a family of conditional distributions $P(X_i(t)|\text{Pa}[X_i(t-1)])$. Figure 3.3 gives a graphical view of a dynamical Bayesian network for modeling gene regulatory networks. The temporal process of a dynamic Bayesian network is assumed to be a time-homogenous Markov process:

$$P[X(t)|X(0), X(1), \ldots, X(t-1)] = P[X(t)|X(t-1)]$$

The joint distribution over all the possible trajectories of the process is decomposed into the following product form:

$$P[X(0), X(1), \ldots, X(T)] = P(0) \prod_{t=1}^{T} P[X(t)|X(t-1)]$$

Therefore, given an initial state of random variables, their evolution is given by

$$P[X(1), \ldots, X(T)|X(0)] = \prod_{t=1}^{T} P[X(t)|X(t-1)]$$

$$= \prod_{i=1}^{n} \prod_{t=1}^{T} P(X_i(t)|\mathrm{Pa}[X_i(t-1)])$$

Kim et al. gave a comprehensive review of the applications of DBNs in inferring gene networks from time-series microarray data and presented a general framework for DBN modeling [Kim03]. To improve prediction accuracy and reduce computational time, Zou and Conzen presented a new DBN-based approach that can limit the number of potential regulators and consequently reduce the search space [Zou05]. The time-lag estimation between regulator genes and target genes increases the accuracy of predicting gene regulatory networks. Dojer et al. extended the framework of dynamic Bayesian networks to incorporate perturbations [Doj06]. They proposed an exact algorithm for inferring an optimal network and a discretization method specialized for time-series data from perturbation experiments.

3.1.3 Markov Networks

Generally, graphical models can be classified mainly into directed graphical models and undirected graphical models. In contrast to Bayesian networks, which represent directed acyclic structures and belong to directed graphical model, Markov networks (or Markov random fields) are undirected graphical models but can describe cyclic or feedback regulations. For Markov networks, if nodes X_i and X_j represent conditional independence on other node X_s, then the joint probability distribution is expressed by $P(X_i, X_j, X_s) = P(X_i, X_s)P(X_j, X_s)$, where $s \neq i$ or j. Figure 3.4 illustrates a simple example of a Markov network.

A graphical Gaussian model (GGM) is a simplest form of Markov networks. Specifically, a GGM is an undirected probabilistic graphical model with the assumption that the nodes (random variables) $X = \{X_1, X_2, \ldots, X_n\}$ follow a multivariate

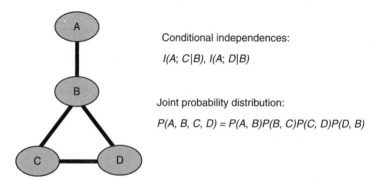

Figure 3.4. A simple example of a Markov network.

Gaussian distribution, and the edges denote the conditional dependence relations among the nodes. It has been widely used to model the relationships among a set of variables. The key idea behind GGMs is to use partial correlations as a measure of independence of any two nodes, which makes it straightforward to distinguish direct from indirect relationships. Inferring a GGM entails estimation of the partial correlation coefficients based on the covariance matrix C of the Gaussian distributions, whose element C_{ik} is related to the correlation coefficient between nodes X_i and X_k. In GGMs, missing edges (low correlation coefficients) indicate conditional independence. In contrast, a high correlation coefficient between two nodes may indicate a direct or indirect interaction between them [Wer06]. Partial correlation coefficients provide a strong measure of dependence and offer only a weak criterion of independence. The interaction measured by the partial correlation coefficient ρ_{ik} describes the correlation between nodes X_i and X_k conditional on all other nodes in the network and tends to be direct interaction. Partial correlation coefficients ρ_{ik} are related to the inverse C^{-1} of the covariance matrix C in the following way

$$\rho_{ik} = -\frac{C_{ik}^{-1}}{\sqrt{C_{ii}^{-1} C_{kk}^{-1}}}$$

which straightforwardly represent a gene regulatory network after truncating small values to zero. When a G.GM is used to reconstruct a gene regulatory network, an important step is to estimate the covariance matrix and its inverse from the expression profiles of genes. Reliable and stable estimation of the covariance matrix requires a large number of observations, which makes it a major challenge for use in reverse engineering since microarray datasets generally have much more genes than samples.

Toh and Horimoto developed a method combining cluster analysis with a classical GGM to infer genetic networks from gene expression data [Toh02]. Wille et al. presented a modified graphical Gaussian modeling approach for reverse engineering of genetic regulatory networks with many genes and few experimental observations by considering GGMs for all triples of genes [Wil04]. They applied their methods in modeling of the isoprenoid gene network in *Arabidopsis thaliana*. Aburatani et al. designed a procedure for graphical chain modeling to analyze the expression profiles of genes that can be classified into several blocks in a natural order [Abu06]. Werhli et al. numerically compared the performance of three related models—relevance networks, GGMs, and Bayesian networks—in reconstructing gene regulatory networks [Wer06]. As another application example, a more recent work on adopting a regularized GGM to infer an *Arabidopsis* gene network was contributed by Ma et al. [Ma07].

3.1.4 Differential Equations

Gene regulation processes involve several biochemical events such as transcription factor binding, mRNA synthesis, mRNA degradation, protein synthesis, and protein degradation. In this process, the concentrations of mRNAs, proteins, and other elements affect each other and form a dynamic system. In other words, gene regulation can be modeled by reaction-rate equations expressing the rate of production of a gene product (protein or mRNA) as a function of the concentration of other elements of the system. Differential equation models provide a general framework for modeling gene regulation processes. By making certain assumptions, any system of chemical reactions and physical constraints can be essentially transformed into a system of ordinary differential equation (ODE), whose variables are concentrations of proteins, mRNAs, and other material [Gib04]. ODE is the most widespread formalism used to model dynamical systems in science and engineering, and has been widely used to model and analyze gene regulatory systems. Equation (2.27) is one example of such formalism.

Generally, a gene regulatory network with n genes can be expressed by a set of non-linear ODEs with the expression level of each gene as a variable

$$\frac{dx_i(t)}{dt} = f_i[x(t)], \qquad x_i(t) \geq 0; \quad 1 \leq i \leq n \tag{3.1}$$

where $x(t) = [x_1(t), \ldots, x_n(t)]^T \in R^n$ is the vector of concentrations of proteins, mRNAs, or small metabolites, and f_i is usually a continuous nonlinear function. $dx_i(t)/dt$ denotes the rate of synthesis of species i that is dependent on the concentration $x(t)$. If external stimuli such as externally supplied nutrients are taken into account as input elements, equation (3.1) can be extended as follows

$$\frac{dx_i(t)}{dt} = f_i[x(t), u(t)], \qquad x_i(t) \geq 0; \quad 1 \leq i \leq n \tag{3.2}$$

where $u(t) \geq 0$ is the concentration vector of input elements.

The regulatory relationships between two genes usually involve many hidden reactions; for example, a gene is first transcribed into a mRNA and translated into a protein, which then exerts a certain effect on the transcription of the second gene. This implies that the interaction between two genes is not instantaneous. The effect of the regulatory interaction happens with a time delay after its cause. Therefore, equation (3.1) can be adapted to account for discrete time delays arising from the time required to complete transcription, translation, and so on [Jon02, ChT99]

$$\frac{dx_i(t)}{dt} = f_i[x_1(t - \tau_{i1}), x_2(t - \tau_{i2}), \ldots, x_n(t - \tau_{in})], \qquad x_i(t) \geq 0; \quad 1 \leq i \leq n \tag{3.3}$$

where $\tau_{ij} \geq 0, j = 1, 2, \ldots, n$ denotes time delays.

Although gene regulations are often nonlinear, most of the existing approaches for gene regulatory network inference use piecewise-linear or linear models because of the unclear structures of biological systems and lack of detailed knowledge of reaction mechanisms [Gla98, Jon02]. Piecewise-linear differential equations (PLDEs) for the reaction-rate equations of a gene regulatory network has the following form

$$\frac{dx_i(t)}{dt} = b_i[x(t)] - r_i x_i(t), \qquad x_i(t) \geq 0; \quad 1 \leq i \leq n \tag{3.4}$$

where b_i is a piecewise-constant function. The second term $-r_i x_i(t)$ corresponds to the degradation of species i and r_i is the degradation rate constant. With respect to dynamical systems, linear equations can at least capture the main features of network structure and function, in particular around a steady state of the system. The linear form of equation (3.1) with appropriate normalization is

$$\frac{dx_i(t)}{dt} = Jx(t) + u_i(t), \qquad x_i(t) \geq 0; \quad 1 \leq i \leq n \tag{3.5}$$

where $J = (J_{ij})_{n \times n} = \partial f(x)/\partial x$ is an $n \times n$ Jacobian matrix, $f = (f_1, f_2, \ldots, f_n)$, and $u = (u_1, \ldots, u_n)^T \in R^n$ is a vector representing the external stimuli or environmental conditions, which is set to zero when there is no external input.

Except for the deterministic ODEs, stochastic differential equations (SDE) have also been used to model gene regulatory networks with the consideration of the uncertainty in gene regulation [Gil77, McA97]. Also, Li et al. adopted a SUM model [LiC06b, LiC07b] that factored in stochastic noise to represent gene regulations. We will not give detailed introduction here.

Although linear models are less realistic for some nonlinear systems, they are mathematically simple and can employ a large amount of tools available from linear algebra such as least-squares methods. D'haeseleer et al. showed that a simple linear model could identify biologically relevant regulatory relationships from real data [Dha99, Dha00]. Chen et al. presented a linear model including both mRNA and protein concentrations with two methods to reconstruct the model from gene expression data [ChT99]. Unlike that by linear models, reconstruction of gene regulatory networks using nonlinear models requires more general and sophisticated techniques because of the complexity of the problems. One such technique is the S system, which has been widely used to model nonlinear gene regulatory networks [Aku00], and another one is monotone dynamical system which has been adopted to design and analyze nonlinear gene regulatory networks. In addition, we will show in next section that sigmoid functions can also been used to represent nonlinear gene regulatory networks.

3.2 RECONSTRUCTING GENE REGULATORY NETWORKS

With the recent advances in biotechnology technologies, it has become possible to measure mRNA expression level of genes on a genomewide scale. Mining these data can provide insights into biological processes at a systemwide level. The first stage in analyzing microarray data is to cluster gene expression profiles for functional analysis [Zha06]. Although clustering genes provides a computationally cost-effective way to extract useful information from gene coexpression for large-scale data, it cannot give a fine resolution of the interaction processes between the genes [Hus03a]. Another hot topic on gene expression data analysis is the reconstruction of gene regulatory networks, also known as *reverse engineering of gene regulatory networks*, the objective of which is to reveal the underlying network of gene–gene interactions from the measured dataset of gene expression. Constructing gene regulatory networks is helpful for a thorough understanding of the regulatory mechanisms of coordinated genes in cellular systems. More recently, various reverse engineering methods of gene regulatory networks have been developed, including those based on the mathematical models described in the last section. In this section, we introduce two classes of approaches based on ODE in detail: singular value decomposition (SVD) methods and model-based optimization methods.

3.2.1 Singular Value Decomposition

Singular value decomposition (SVD) as a dimension reduction method has been widely used for analyzing large-scale expression data for a long time [Alt00, Hol01, Alt03, Hol00]. For example, Alter et al. used SVD to transform genomewide expression data from *genes* × *arrays* space to diagonalized *eigengenes* × *eigenarrays* space [Alt00], where the eigengenes (or eigenarrays) are unique orthonormal superpositions of the genes (or arrays). They enable meaningful comparison of the expression of different genes across different arrays by filtering out the eigengenes (and eigenarrays) that represent noise or experimental artifacts. Holter et al. explored the fundamental patterns underlying the noisy gene expression data by SVD [Hol00]. In contrast to these applications in exploring patterns in microarray data, Holter et al. in another study, modeled the time evolution of gene expression levels by using a time translational matrix to predict future expression levels of genes on the basis of their expression levels at some initial time [Hol01], which is similar to modeling a gene regulatory network from gene expression data. Alter et al. adopted generalized singular value decomposition to develop a mathematical framework for comparative analysis of genome-scale expression datasets from two different organisms [Alt03].

Although SVD has been already used in analyzing gene expression data, Yeung et al. enhanced its application in reverse engineering of gene regulatory networks in a different way [Yeu02]. Their method is based on the empirical observation that gene regulatory networks are typically large and sparse. First, SVD is used to construct a family of candidate solutions that are consistent with the measured data, and then a robust regression is adopted to identify the solution with the smallest number of connections (the sparsest one) as the most likely solution. This method can overcome the limitations caused by scarce data to some extent [Yeu02]. To reduce the complexity, only systems that operate near a steady state are considered. Therefore, the dynamics can be approximated by a linear system of ordinary differential equations:

$$\frac{dx_i(t)}{dt} = -\lambda_i x_i(t) + \sum_{j=1}^{n} W_{ij} x_j(t) + b(t) + \xi_i(t) \quad \text{for } i = 1, 2, \ldots, n \qquad (3.6)$$

Here, $x_i(t)$, $i = 1, 2, \ldots, n$ is the concentration of the mRNA that reflects the expression level of gene i, λ_i is the self-degradation rate constant of gene i, $b(t)$ is the external stimuli, and $\xi_i(t)$ represents noise. W_{ij} is the element of regulation matrix that describes the type and strength of the influence of the jth gene on the ith gene, with a positive sign indicating activation, a negative sign indicating repression, and zero indicating no regulatory relation.

Yeung et al. used the perturbed microarray data by applying a prescribed stimulus $(b_1, b_2, \ldots, b_n)^T$ and simultaneously measuring the concentrations of all n different mRNAs: $(x_1, x_2, \ldots, x_n)^T$. After such a procedure is repeated m times, a microarray dataset with m measurements can be obtained and denoted as

$$X_{n \times m} = \begin{pmatrix} x_1(1) & x_1(2) & \cdots & x_1(m) \\ x_2(1) & x_2(2) & \cdots & x_2(m) \\ \vdots & \vdots & \ddots & \vdots \\ x_n(1) & x_n(2) & \cdots & x_n(m) \end{pmatrix}$$

where $x_i(j)$ is the concentration of the ith mRNA for the jth sample. Equation (3.6) can be rewritten in the following matrix form

$$\dot{X} = JX + B \tag{3.7}$$

where noises are neglected and the self-degradation rates are absorbed into the coupling constants W_{ij} to simplify the notation. $\dot{X} = dX(t)/dt$, $J_{ij} = W_{ij} - \delta_{ij}\lambda_i$, where δ_{ij} is the delta function, that is, $\delta_{ij} = 1$ when $i = j$; otherwise $\delta_{ij} = 0$, and $B = [b_i(j)]$, $i = 1, 2, \ldots, n, j = 1, 2, \ldots, m$. By adopting SVD, we can decompose X^T into $(X^T)_{m \times n} = U_{m \times n} E_{n \times n} V^T_{n \times n}$, where U is a unitary $m \times n$ matrix of left eigenvectors, $E = \text{diag}(e_1, \ldots, e_n)$ is a diagonal $n \times n$ matrix containing the n eigenvalues, and V^T is the transpose of a unitary $n \times n$ matrix of right eigenvectors. Without loss of generality, let all nonzero elements of e_k be listed at the end: $e_1 = \cdots = e_l = 0$ and $e_{l+1}, \ldots, e_n \neq 0$. Then, a particular solution with the smallest L_2 norm for the connection matrix $\hat{J} = (\hat{J}_{ij})_{n \times n}$ is given as

$$\hat{J} = (\dot{X} - B)UE^{-1}V^T \tag{3.8}$$

where $E^{-1} = \text{diag}(1/e_i)$ and $1/e_i$ is set to be zero if $e_i = 0$. Thus, the general solution of the connection matrix $J = (J_{ij})_{n \times n}$ is

$$J = (\dot{X} - B)UE^{-1}V^T + YV^T = \hat{J} + YV^T \tag{3.9}$$

where $Y = (y_{ij})$ is an $n \times n$ matrix. y_{ij} is zero if $e_j \neq 0$ and otherwise an arbitrary scalar coefficient. Solutions of (3.9) represent a network family, that is, all possible networks that are consistent with the microarray dataset, depending on arbitrary Y.

Because SVD leads to nonunique solutions, additional constraints are needed to isolate the true solution from the entire family. Yeung et al. suggested that sparseness is a biologically reasonable constraint, since real gene regulatory networks are often sparse and generally each gene interacts with only a small percentage of all the genes in the entire genome [Yeu02]. Hence, they have chosen L_1 regression, that is, minimizing the sum of the absolute values of the errors: $\min_Y |\hat{J} + YV^T|$.

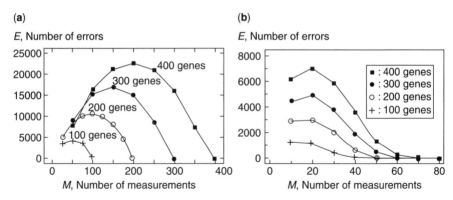

Figure 3.5. Number of errors E as function of number of measurements for four linear networks of the form (3.6) with different sizes made by SVD (a) without and (b) with sparseness constraint. (Reprinted from [Yeu02] © 2002 National Academy of Sciences, U.S.A.)

To measure the discrepancies between the true network and the inferred network with n genes, a simple criterion E_0 is adopted to assess the basic recovering ability

$$E_0 = \sum_{i=1}^{n} \sum_{j=1}^{n} I \|J_{ij}^T - J_{ij}^R\| > \delta \tag{3.10}$$

where I takes 1 if $\|J_{ij}^T - J_{ij}^R\| > \delta$, otherwise 0. δ is a prescribed small value for error tolerance related to noise level of the system. J_{ij}^T and J_{ij}^R are interaction strengths from gene j to gene i in the true and inferred networks, respectively. E_0 evaluates gene regulatory networks directly by emphasizing the importance of the topology structure.

Yeung et al. illustrated by several experiments that the SVD scheme with sparseness constraint can reconstruct gene regulatory networks more accurately, and at the same time uses fewer data than does SVD alone (see Fig. 3.5) [Yeu02]. In addition, for a timecourse dataset, they showed that the smallest number of timepoints needed is $O(\log n)$ to reconstruct the $n \times n$ connection matrix for an n-gene network (see Fig. 3.6). Such results provide rough information about whether we can infer the gene networks correctly under a certain number of samples. It should be noted that this result is numerically obtained and may be suitable only for the linear model of gene regulatory networks.

3.2.2 Model-Based Optimization

Reverse engineering of gene regulatory networks is essentially to fit the observed expression data to a proper model with as small error as possible. Hence, with such a requirement, optimization approaches provide a natural way for reconstructing genetic networks. Dasika et al. proposed a mixed-integer linear programming framework for inferring gene networks with time delay [DaM04]. Thomas et al. developed a mixed-integer nonlinear programming method for regulatory network inference based

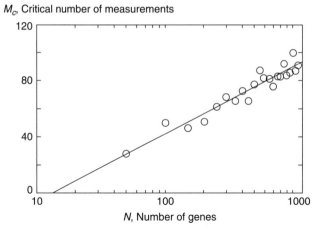

Figure 3.6. Critical number of measurements required to recover the entire connectivity matrix correctly versus network size for linear systems of the form (3.6). (Reprinted from [Yeu02] © 2002 National Academy of Sciences, U.S.A.)

on the *S*-system model for both transcription and translation processes [Tho04, Tho07]. In addition, the least-squares scheme, as a special optimization model, has also been used to infer a variety of biochemical networks including genetic networks [KiJ07, KiC07]. Although it is difficult to find a global optimum for a general nonlinear programming problem, such a model usually can be transformed as a convex programming problem, which can be exactly solved because of its convexity. Han et al. proposed a convex optimization scheme to infer biomolecular interaction networks including gene networks from perturbed concentrations of components [Han07]. Next, we introduce some of them in detail.

Gene regulation processes actually include time delay, which has been widely reported in the literature. Time delay in gene regulation stems from the delays characterizing various underlying processes such as transcription, translation, and transport processes. Das et al. used linear differential equations with time delay to describe the regulatory inputs for each gene [Das04]

$$\dot{x}_i(t) = \sum_{\tau=0}^{\tau^{\mathrm{max}}} \sum_{j=1}^{n} W_{ij\tau} x_j(t - \tau) \tag{3.11}$$

where $x_i(t)$ is the expression level of gene i at time t, $t = 1, 2, \ldots, m$; τ indicates the time delay; $W_{ij\tau}$ is the regulatory coefficient that captures the regulatory effect of gene j on gene i with a time delay τ; τ^{max} denotes the longest time delay; n is the total number of genes; and m is the total number of timepoints (samples). To reduce the solution space, they assume a single time delay τ for every regulatory interaction and limit the maximal number of regulatory inputs to each gene. Letting binary variable $y_{ij\tau}$ denote whether gene j regulates gene i with a time delay τ, the gene network inference problem with time delay is formulated as the following mixed-integer linear programming (MILP) model:

$$\min \; \frac{1}{nm} \sum_{i=1}^{n} \sum_{t=1}^{m} [e_i^+(t) + e_i^-(t)] \tag{3.12}$$

$$\text{s.t.} \quad \dot{x}_i(t) - \sum_{\tau=0}^{\tau^{\max}} \sum_{j=1}^{n} W_{ij\tau} x_j(t-\tau) = e_i^+(t) - e_i^-(t) \tag{3.13}$$

$$r^{\min} y_{ij\tau} \leq W_{ij\tau} \leq r^{\max} y_{ij\tau} \tag{3.14}$$

$$\sum_{\tau}^{\tau^{\max}} y_{ij\tau} \leq 1 \tag{3.15}$$

$$\sum_{\tau}^{\tau^{\max}} \sum_{j=1}^{n} y_{ij\tau} \leq n_i \tag{3.16}$$

$$y_{ij\tau} \in \{0, 1\}, \; e_i^+(t) \geq 0, \; e_i^-(t) \geq 0 \tag{3.17}$$

$$i, j = 1, 2, \ldots, n, \; \tau = 1, 2, \ldots, \tau^{\max}, \; t = 1, 2, \ldots, m \tag{3.18}$$

where the objective function is to minimize the total absolute error between predicted and experimental expression values, $r^{\min}$ and $r^{\max}$ are respectively the lower and upper bounds on regulatory coefficients, and n_i is the maximal number of regulatory genes to gene i. $\dot{x}_i$ is defined as $dx_i(t)/dt$, and s.t. means "subject to." This model can infer the time delays associated with each regulation relationship, and the computational results indicate that incorporation of time delay causes the inferred networks to be sparser and more accurate.

In contrast to linear differential equations, Thomas et al. adopted a special nonlinear differential equation called the *S system* to model gene networks with both transcription process and translation process [Tho04, Tho07]

$$\frac{dm_i(t)}{dt} = V_{sm,i} - V_{dm,i} = \alpha_i \prod_{j=1}^{n} p_j^{\varepsilon_{ij}}(t) - \beta_i m_i(t) \tag{3.19}$$

$$\frac{dp_i(t)}{dt} = V_{sp,i} - V_{dp,i} = \gamma_i m_i(t) - \delta_i p_i(t) \tag{3.20}$$

where $m_i(t)$ and $p_i(t)$ are the concentration of mRNA i and protein i, respectively, $V_{sm,i}$ and $V_{dm,i}$ denote the rates of synthesis and degradation of the ith mRNA, whereas $V_{sp,i}$ and $V_{dp,i}$ denote the rates of synthesis and degradation of the ith protein. α_i, γ_i are the synthesis constants of transcription and translation, and β_i, δ_i are the decay constants of the mRNA and protein, respectively. ε denotes the regulation strength of protein j on mRNA i. To infer the regulation strengths and rate constants that best fit the dynamic model from a given set of gene expression data, y_{ij} is defined as a binary variable to denote whether gene j interacts with gene i, and the following mixed-integer nonlinear programming model is developed

$$\min \tilde{E} + \sum_{i=1}^{n} \tau_i^2 \parallel \varepsilon \parallel \tag{3.21}$$

$$\text{s.t.} \quad -D y_{ij} \leq \varepsilon_{ij} \leq D y_{ij} \tag{3.22}$$

$$\sum_{j=1}^{n} y_{ij} \leq k \tag{3.23}$$

$$y_{ij} \in \{0, 1\}, \quad \alpha_i \geq 0, \quad \gamma_i \geq 0 \tag{3.24}$$

$$m_i^c \geq 0, \quad p_i(0) \geq 0 \tag{3.25}$$

$$i, j = 1, 2, \ldots, n, \quad t = 1, 2, \ldots, m \tag{3.26}$$

where m_i^c is a reference state for gene i, $P_i(0)$ is the initial concentration of protein i, $\varepsilon_i = (\varepsilon_{i1}, \ldots, \varepsilon_{in})$ and

$$\tilde{E} = \sum_{i=1}^{n} \sum_{t=1}^{m} \left[\log\left(\frac{d\tilde{m}_i(t)}{dt} + \beta_i \tilde{m}_i(t) \right) - \log(\alpha_i) - \sum_{j=1}^{n} \varepsilon_{ij} \log[\tilde{p}_j(t)] \right]^2$$

is the error term between the observed expression data and the reconstructed model, $\bar{\varepsilon}_i$ represents the vector of regulatory interactions on gene i, τ_i is a regularization parameter for each gene i, D is a positive number that limits the strength of an interaction, and k is the maximal number of regulatory genes to gene i. $\tilde{m}_i(t)$ and $\tilde{P}_j(t)$ are respectively the discrete approximation of $m_i(t)$ and $P_j(t)$ based on some techniques involving m_i^c and $P_j(0)$ [Tho07]. Because of the hardness of mixed-integer programming in terms of computational complexity, they used a heuristic iterative technique to repeatedly deal with the problem estimating γ_i, m_i^c, $p_i(0)$ and then problem fixing ε_i and $\log(\alpha_i)$ to solve the optimization model presented above. They found that the ability of a method to infer regulatory interactions correctly is related to the similarity in the expression profiles of some or all of the genes. The less similar the expression profiles are to each other, the easier it is to infer the regulatory interactions. In addition to the inferred genetic networks, this method can also be used to estimate the concentrations of proteins.

3.3 INFERRING GENE NETWORKS FROM MULTIPLE DATASETS

In this section, we describe a new methodology for inferring gene interactions by exploiting multiple datasets. As mentioned in Chapter 2, microarray gene expression data generated by different labs worldwide are increasingly accumulated for many species and deposited in public-domain databases or individual Websites. However, the regulatory interactions between thousands of genes have to be learned from datasets typically containing only a few dozen timepoints. In other words, the number of genes far exceeds the number of timepoints. Therefore, a major difficulty in gene network inference from microarray data for all methods is the scarcity of timepoints or the dimensionality problem [Dha00, Zak03, Hus03b], which makes the problem of inferring network structure an ill-posed one. Most of existing methods generally use a single timecourse dataset under a specific experimental condition, and hence it is difficult to construct gene networks accurately.

Although each microarray dataset has only a limited number of timepoints, if so many data from different experiments are combined and further exploited in an integrative manner, the scarcity of data can be overcome to a great extent and gene networks can be constructed more accurately. In other words, in order to enhance the inference accuracy of gene regulatory networks, we need to explore multiple microarray datasets simultaneously or employ other prior sources of genomic data. It is worth mentioning that simply arranging multiple timecourse datasets into a single one is inappropriate because of data normalization issues and lack of temporal relationships among these datasets. Some researchers have moved ahead on this line to integrate datasets from different sources. For example, Nariai et al. proposed a statistical method to unify Bayesian networks and Markov networks, and infer gene regulatory networks and protein interaction networks simultaneously by integrating DNA microarray data, protein interaction data, and other genomewide data [Nar05]. Redestig et al. developed a covariance-based method to extract the regulatory relationships between transcription factors and target genes in *Arabidopsis thaliana* by using multiple time-series expression datasets [Red07]. Wang et al. presented a linear programming framework to combine multiple timecourse datasets from different conditions for inferring gene regulatory networks [WaY06]. Geier et al. adopted linear Gaussian dynamic Bayesian networks and a variable selection scheme based on F statistics for reconstructing gene regulatory networks from time series data, knockout data, and prior knowledge [Gei07]. Shi et al. presented a probabilistic framework for inferring time-lagged regulatory relationships from multiple time-series expression experiments with varying timescales [Shiy07]. Except for reconstruction of gene regulatory networks, integrating multiple datasets or data sources has been also applied to other fields such as clustering and meta-analysis of gene expression data [ChH07].

In addition to the scarcity of data, another problem existing in conventional approaches is that the derived gene regulatory networks often have densely connected regulatory relationships among genes, which are not biologically plausible. A biological gene regulatory network is expected to be sparse, and should also be reflected in the procedure of network reconstruction [Yeu02]. Some inference methods attempted to achieve the sparseness of the inferred gene networks by limiting the maximum number of regulatory inputs of each gene [DaM04, Tho07]. Although such a scheme is reasonable, determining the upper bounds is a tricky problem and usually heuristically done.

Wang et al. proposed a method for combining a wide variety of microarray datasets from different experiments for inferring gene regulatory networks (GRN) with the consideration of sparseness of regulatory matrices [WaY06]. A gene network

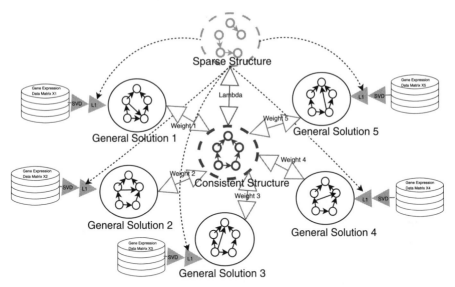

Figure 3.7. The scheme of GRNInfer for inferring gene regulatory networks. (Reprinted from [WaY06] © 2006 by permission of Oxford University Press.)

reconstruction tool called GRNInfer was developed using a decomposition procedure by exploiting the general solutions created from each microarray dataset using a linear programming model. This method is theoretically able to find a most consistent regulatory network with respect to all microarray datasets of interest. Such integration of multiple datasets can not only alleviate the problem of data scarcity but also improve the accuracy of network inference. GNRInfer is coded by FORTRAN and available from http://intelligent.eic.osaka-sandai.ac.jp/chenen/index.htm, http://www.isb.shu.edu.cn, or http://zhangroup.aporc.org/ResourceBioinformatics.

Figure 3.7 illustrates the scheme of GRNInfer. Gene regulatory networks are modeled by a set of linear differential equations. First, a general solution representing a GRN family created from each dataset based on singular value decomposition (SVD) is obtained by using the method described in Section 3.2.1. On the basis of such general solutions from each single dataset, the GRN reconstruction problem is formulated as an optimization problem, with the objective of finding a consistent gene regulatory network with respect to all microarray datasets of interest. The optimization problem is actually equivalent to a linear programming (LP). Owing to the absolutes of objective function and special structure of constraints in the optimization model, rather than solving this LP directly, an efficient decomposition algorithm is developed.

3.3.1 General Solutions and a Particular Solution of Network Structures for Multiple Datasets

In Section 3.2.1, we described how to obtain a general solution for the inference problem of a gene regulatory network by using the SVD technique when a single dataset is employed. Now assume that multiple microarray datasets from one organism are available, and that each of them is measured assuming a certain environmental condition. With application of the SVD technique, each dataset corresponds to a general solution in the form of (3.9), which represents all possible networks that are consistent with this dataset. Specifically, assume that we have N timecourse datasets. Then, N sets of putative regulatory networks can be inferred in the following way since Y^k is arbitrary

$$J^k = (\dot{X}_k - B_k)U_k E_k^{-1} V_k^T + Y^k V_k^T = \hat{J}^k + Y^k V_k^T \qquad (3.27)$$

where the subscript $k = 1, \ldots, N$ is the index of the dataset k. Each general network (3.27) corresponds to one dataset. Note that without normalization, J^k for each dataset is actually a normalized matrix even for different experimental conditions with different time intervals due to the form of (3.8). Note that we assume that the gene regulatory network for differential individuals is assumed to be identical provided that they are the same organism.

With N sets of putative regulatory networks available, as illustrated in Figure 3.7, the next step is to find a final gene regulatory network $J = (J_{ij})_{n \times n}$ that is as consistent with all of these putative networks as possible, meanwhile considering the sparseness of the network structure. In other words, we are to find a particular solution of network structures from the N general solutions. Mathematically, it can be achieved by solving the following optimization problem

$$\min_{Y,J} \sum_{k=1}^{N} \sum_{i=1}^{n} \sum_{j=1}^{n} \left[\omega^k |J_{ij} - J_{ij}^k| + \lambda |J_{ij}| \right] \qquad (3.28)$$

where J_{ij}^k is a function of Y^k according to (3.27), and $Y = (Y^1, \ldots, Y^N)$. The variables of this optimization problem are Y and J. The first term in the objective function is the error term, which forces J to be consistent with all J^k, whereas the second term is the sparseness term, which makes J sparse and biologically reasonable owing to the L_1 norm. λ is a positive parameter balancing the error term and the sparseness term. Since different datasets may have different qualities (e.g., different technologies, number of replicates in measurements, etc.), a weight coefficient is used to represent the reliability of each dataset. ω^k is a positive weight coefficient for the dataset k with $\sum_{k=1}^{N} \omega^k = 1$. Such a weight can be determined according to the number of time points in a microarray dataset [WaY06]. Assume that the number of repeated experiments for dataset k is N_k using the same type of microarray. Then ω^k can be set as

$$\omega^k = \frac{N_k}{\sum_{i=1}^{N} N_i} \qquad (3.29)$$

Of course, more sophisticated methods for estimating the weight of each dataset can be employed since this is crucial for data integration. Cross-validation is a widely used strategy for determining the values of parameters.

The optimization problem (3.28) is a mathematical programming with a positive combination of L_1 norm of variables. It can be transformed into a linear programming by removing the absolutes in the model. However, removing the absolutes entails adding many extra variables and thus increases the complexity of the problem significantly. A decomposition procedure is adopted to solve (3.28) iteratively [WaY06]. Because of the L_1 norm, generally the optimal solution of (3.28) has the property of as many zeros as possible for $|J_{ij} - J_{ij}^k|$ and $|J_{ij}|$, which exactly serves purpose of finding a consistent and sparse gene regulatory network.

3.3.2 Decomposition Algorithm

For the problem (3.28), if J is fixed or known, it becomes equivalent to N independent linear programming (LP) subproblems. Similarly, if Y is fixed or known, (3.28) is actually a single linear programming problem. Hence, the optimization problem (3.28) can be iteratively solved using the following model [WaY06]:

$$\min_{J} \min_{Y} \sum_{k=1}^{N} \sum_{i=1}^{n} \sum_{j=1}^{n} [\omega^k |J_{ij} - J_{ij}^k| + \lambda |J_{ij}|] \qquad (3.30)$$

The steps involved in the decomposition algorithm are outlined in detail as follows.

GRNInfer Algorithm

- *Step 0 (Initialization)*. Compute the particular solution $\hat{J}^k$ for each microarray dataset k by the SVD technique from (3.8), and ω^k by (3.29). Set initial values for the regulation matrix $J_{ij}(0) = 0$, $Y_{ij}^k(0) = 0$ and $J_{ij}^k(0) = \hat{J}^k$, and positive numbers λ, ε. Let the iteration index be q, and set $q = 1$.
- *Step 1*. Let $J^k(q) = J^k(q-1) + Y^k(q)V_k^T$. Fix $J(q-1)$ and obtain $Y^k(q) = [y_{ij}^k(q)]$ at iteration q by solving the following subproblem for $k = 1$, $\dots, N$ with given $J(q-1)$:

$$\min_{Y^k(q)} \sum_{i=1}^{n} \sum_{j=1}^{n} |J_{ij}(q-1) - J_{ij}^k(q)| \qquad (3.31)$$

Note that $y_{ij}^k(q) = 0$ if $j > l_k$ according to (3.9).
- *Step 2*. Given all $y_{ij}^k(q)$ obtained in step 1, obtain $J_{ij}(q)$ at iteration q by solving the following problem with all $J^k(q)$ fixed:

$$\min_{J(q)} \sum_{k=1}^{N} \sum_{i=1}^{n} \sum_{j=1}^{n} [\omega^k |J_{ij}(q) - J_{ij}^k(q)| + \lambda |J_{ij}(q)|] \qquad (3.32)$$

- *Step 3*. If J converges, that is, if $\|J(q) - J(q-1)\| < \varepsilon$, then the computation stops. Otherwise, $q = q + 1$ and go to step 1.

Now we describe the detailed procedures of solving (3.31) and (3.32). The subproblems (3.31) are actually the same as

$$\min_{Y^k(q)} \sum_{i=1}^{n} \sum_{j=1}^{n} |J_{ij}(q-1) - J_{ij}^k(q-1) - Y^k(q)V_k^T| \qquad (3.33)$$

where $J_{ij}(q-1)$, $J_{ij}^k(q-1)$ and V^T are given. Without loss of generality, the problems can be expressed as the standard form

$$\min_{X} |AX - B| \qquad (3.34)$$

where the coefficient A is an $n^2 \times nl_k$ matrix, and l_k is the number of zero elements in E_k^{-1} in (3.27). X and B are $n \times l_k$ and $n \times n$ matrices, respectively. In fact, we do not need to solve such a large linear programming problem. We observe that A has a special structure as

$$A = \begin{bmatrix} A_1 & & & \\ & A_2 & & \\ & & \cdots & \\ & & & A_n \end{bmatrix}$$

The size of A_i, $i = 1, 2, \ldots, n$ is $n \times l_k$. Similarly, X and B can be decomposed into $X = [X_1, X_2, \ldots, X_n]$ and $B = [B_1, B_2, \ldots, B_n]$, and the solution of the original problems (3.31) can be obtained by solving the following n small problems, respectively

$$\min_{X_i} |A_iX_i - B_i| \quad i = 1, 2, \ldots, n \qquad (3.35)$$

where the dimensions of A_i, X_i, and B_i are $n \times l_k$, $l_k \times 1$ and $n \times 1$, respectively. The LP problem with such a scale can be addressed directly by the simplex method even for $l_k \approx n$ in a large-scale sparse gene regulatory network. Clearly the decomposition scheme reduces the storage space from $O(n^4)$ to $O(n^2)$ and requires $O(n^4)$ computations. Furthermore, it provides a formulation for parallel computation so as to rapidly find the regulatory relationship between the key genes with a high priority.

Although (3.32) formally is a large-scale LP problem, it can be solved very efficiently by a decomposition technique. Since every element of J_{ij} is an independent variable, this problem can be decomposed into N^2 one-dimensional subproblems. Specifically, letting $\zeta = J_{ij}$, $\zeta^k = J_{ij}^k$, $k = 1, 2, \ldots, N$, the one dimensional optimization subproblem is expressed as

$$\min_{\zeta} \sum_{k=1}^{N} [\omega^k |\zeta - \zeta^k| + \lambda|\zeta|] \qquad (3.36)$$

Let $\omega^{N+1} = N\lambda$ and $\zeta^{N+1} = 0$. Then

$$\min_{\zeta} \sum_{k=1}^{N+1} \omega^k |\zeta - \zeta^k| \tag{3.37}$$

The optimal solution is easily obtained by sorting ζ^k, $k = 1, 2, \ldots, N+1$ and analyzing the $N+2$ cases, respectively. Specifically, suppose that the sorted non-decreasing array is also ζ^k with $k = 1, 2, \ldots, N+1$, and the $N+2$ intervals are $(-\infty, \zeta^1], (\zeta^1, \zeta^2], \ldots, (\zeta^{N+1}, \infty)$. Then, the function value F_i of $\sum_{k=1}^{N+1} \omega^k |\zeta - \zeta^k|$ is easily computed when ζ is in the ith interval, where we assume that the corresponding optimal solution is ζ_i^* (choose any one when multiple optimal solutions exist). Without loss of generality, assuming $F_k^* = \min\{F_1, F_2, \ldots, F_{N+2}\}$, the corresponding solution ζ_k^* is the optimal solution of problem (3.37).

In order to evaluate the network inference method and the inferred gene regulatory network, Wang et al. introduced several measures [WaY06]. Specifically, let the optimal solution of (3.28) be J^* and Y^{*k}. Then, the variance v_{ij} and deviation σ_{ij} of each element J_{ij} for J can be estimated by

$$v_{ij} = \sum_{k=1}^{N} \omega^k \frac{[J_{ij}^* - J_{ij}^k(Y^{*k})]^2}{N} \tag{3.38}$$

$$\sigma_{ij} = \sqrt{v_{ij}} \tag{3.39}$$

By computing their average, we can obtain the deviation σ_{ij} by

$$\bar{\sigma} = \sum_{i=1}^{n} \sum_{j=1}^{n} \frac{\sigma_{ij}}{n^2} \tag{3.40}$$

To measure the accuracy of the inferred gene regulatory network, the following two criteria, E_1 and E_2, have been defined in addition to the E_0 in Section 3.2.1

$$E_1 := \sum_{i=1}^{n} \sum_{j=1}^{n} |J_{ij}^T - J_{ij}^R| \tag{3.41}$$

$$E_2 := \sum_{i=1}^{n} \sum_{j=1}^{n} \left(J_{ij}^T - J_{ij}^R\right)^2 \tag{3.42}$$

which are L_1 norm and L_2 norm errors, respectively, for all interaction strengths, and J_{ij}^T, J_{ij}^R have the same meaning as those in E_0.

3.3.3 Numerical Validation

A common problem in evaluating the accuracy of a network inference method is lack of a goldstandard test set since no full experimentally determined gene regulatory networks are available. In most cases, only partial information can be used. Therefore,

Husmeier et al. suggested that realistic simulation is a good choice for validation of network inference [Hus03a, Hus03b].

3.3.3.1 *Simulated Data*

A small synthesized network is used to test the inferred gene regulatory networks by using GRNinfer to integrate multiple simulated datasets [WaY06]. This example is a simulated network with five genes whose structure and dynamics are governed by

$$\dot{x}_1(t) = -2x_2(t) + \xi_1(t)$$
$$\dot{x}_2(t) = -x_3(t) + \xi_2(t)$$
$$\dot{x}_3(t) = -3x_4(t) + \xi_3(t)$$
$$\dot{x}_4(t) = -1.5x_5(t) + \xi_4(t)$$
$$\dot{x}_5(t) = 2x_1(t) + \xi_5(t)$$

where x_i reflects the expression level of gene i and $\xi_i(t)$ represents noise for $i = 1, 2, 3, 4, 5$. Clearly, the system is a negative gene regulation loop with genes 2,3,4,5 repressing genes 1,2,3,4, respectively, and with gene 1, in turn, activating gene 5. By using the Matlab command `ode45`, a simulated timecourse dataset can be generated by setting an initial condition of the system shown above and taking several timepoints of x. Different initial conditions lead to different datasets. With three initial conditions, three timecourse datasets with four, four and three timepoints are generated, respectively, on which GNRInfer can be applied to reconstruct the connection matrix J.

The numerical results of GRNInfer on the simulated data without adding any noise are depicted in Figure 3.8, where the arrows and arcs denote activation and repression, respectively. We can see that the more datasets there are, the more accurate the inferred network. Clearly, when only one dataset is employed (Fig. 3.8b), the relation between x_5 and x_3 cannot be correctly inferred. For the case where two datasets are used, the topology of the network is correctly identified (Fig. 3.8c). If all three datasets are used, the predicted regulation matrix is very close to the true one even for the quantitative values of the strengths (Fig. 3.8d). Such results imply that integrating multiple datasets is helpful for solving the highly ill-posed problem in an accurate manner.

The function of parameter λ in GNRInfer is to control the sparseness of the inferred network. As indicated in the case of a single dataset in Section 3.2.1, sparseness can also overcome the ill-posedness to some extent. The benefit of sparseness is illustrated in the results when noises are added (Fig. 3.9). The distribution function of the noise in microarray is believed to be a Gaussian distribution. Figure 3.9 shows the results when noises obeying normal distribution $N(0, 0.005)$ are added to the dynamics, from which we can see that the network cannot be correctly inferred even using all three datasets due to the effect of noises. At this time, the additional constraint of sparsity plays an important role, as shown in Figure 3.9d.

To evaluate the accuracy of GRNInfer for network inference, Table 3.1 shows the accuracies in terms of different error criteria, specifically, E_0, E_1, and E_2 in the two cases (without noise and with noise), where E_0 reflects the accuracy of the network topology, and E_1 and E_2 reflect the accuracy of regulation strengths. From Table 3.1, we can see that the more datasets there are, the smaller are the E_0, E_1,

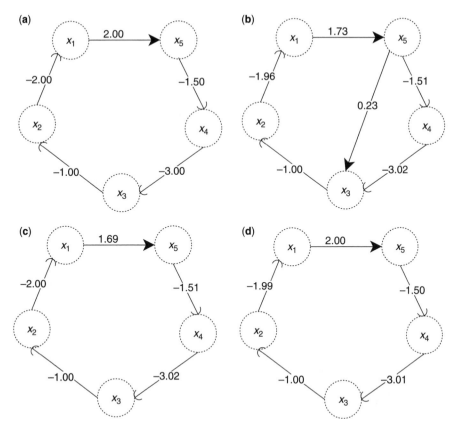

Figure 3.8. A simulated example with $\lambda = 0$ and without noise: (a) a true network; (b) using one dataset; (c) using two datasets; and (d) using three datasets. (Reprinted from [WaY06] © 2006 by permission of Oxford University Press.)

and E_2 values, which again justifies the benefit of integrating multiple datasets. The deviation $\bar{\sigma}$ in Table 3.1 is introduced to evaluate the confidence of the inferred network. The tendency of $\bar{\sigma}$ also indicates that integration of multiple datasets improves the confidence of the network inference.

3.3.3.2 Experimental Data In addition to simulated data, several real datasets based on genomewide Affymetrix chip experiments were used to test the ability of GRNInfer, such as yeast cell cycle data and *Arabidopsis* stress response data [WaY06]. These datasets are from Stanford Microarray Database (SMD) and AtGenExpress database (see Table 2.1). Yeast cell cycle data have been generated from the study by Spellman et al. [Spe98], and are actually measured under four different experimental conditions. Therefore, four datasets with 18, 17, 23, and 14 timepoints, respectively, are available for integration. Of all the yeast genes, 140 undergo twofold changes up or down in at least 20% of the expression conditions across all datasets and are selected as the components of the yeast cell cycle

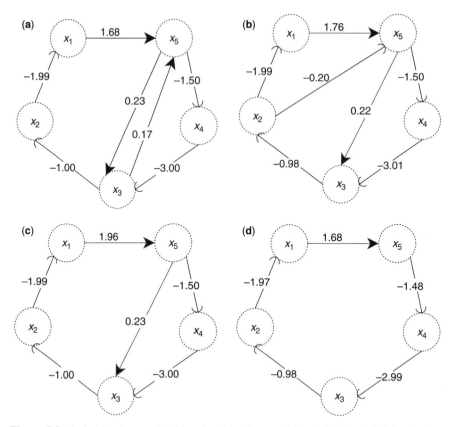

Figure 3.9. A simulated example with noise: (a) using one dataset with $\lambda = 0.0$; (b) using two datasets with $\lambda = 0.0$; (c) using three datasets with $\lambda = 0.0$; and (d) using three datasets with $\lambda = 0.3$. (Reprinted from [WaY06] © 2006 by permission of Oxford University Press.)

TABLE 3.1. Accuracies in Terms of Different Error Criteria and Confidence Evaluation

Number of Datasets	λ	E_0	E_1	E_2	$\bar{\sigma}$
		Without Noise			
One	0.0	1	1.38	0.22	0.4145
Two	0.0	0	1.16	0.21	0.0075
Three	0.0	0	0.93	0.15	0.0032
		With Noise			
One	0.0	2	1.42	0.27	0.4105
Two	0.0	2	1.36	0.21	0.0131
Three	0.0	1	0.93	0.13	0.0035
Three	0.3	0	0.93	0.19	0.0197

Source: Wang et al. [WaY06].

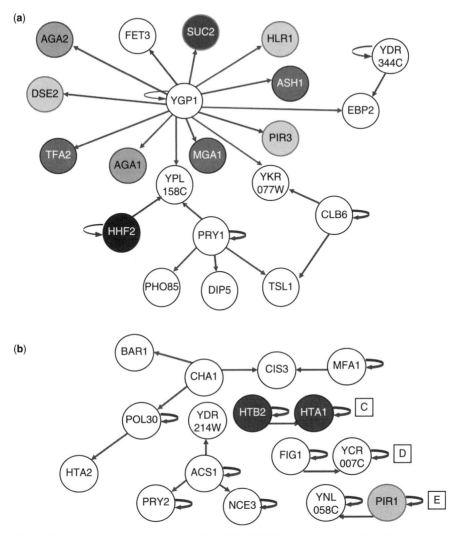

Figure 3.10. Two connected subnetworks of the 64-link inferred yeast cell cycle regulatory network. (Reprinted from [WaY06] © 2006 by permission of Oxford University Press.)

regulatory network. By applying GRNInfer with varying parameter λ, putative regulatory networks with different sizes can be obtained. Figure 3.10 shows a partial representation of the inferred 64-link yeast cell cycle regulatory network, where arrows represent the interactions between genes. Some of these regulatory interactions are confirmed by the information from literature.

Arabidopsis thaliana as a typical model organism has been widely studied in the biological field. From The Arabidopsis Information Resources (TAIR) Website, nine microarray datasets related to the stress responses are available, each with six or more timepoints. Wang et al. selected 226 genes for the root experiments and

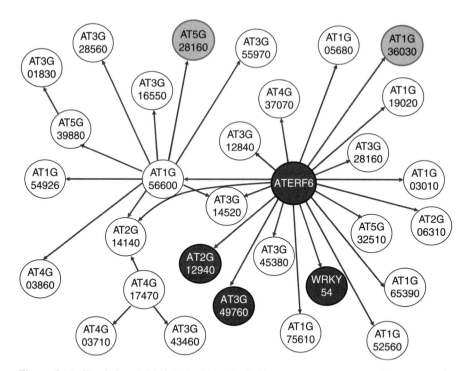

Figure 3.11. The inferred 35-link *Arabidopsis thaliana* stress response regulatory network. (Reprinted from [WaY06] © 2006 by permission of Oxford University Press.)

246 genes for the shoot experiments based on twofold change in at least 70% of the ratios of a gene [WaY06], which represents the most significant genes differentially expressed under stress in root and shoot experiments. Figure 3.11 illustrates an inferred 35-link regulatory subnetwork in shoots related to *Arabidopsis* stress response. The inferred regulatory network matches certain existing knowledge, and also contains some novel regulations. For example, ATERF6 is a member of the ERF (ethylene response factor) subfamily B3 of ERF/AP2 transcription factor family. It is predicted to activate three genes encoding known or putative transcription factors: AT2G12940, AT3G49760, and AT2G40750. AT2G12940 is similar to transcription factor VSF-1; AT3G49760 is a Bzip transcription factor. AT2G40750 is a member of the WRKY transcription factor family. Such novel predicted regulations provide insights for biologists in further biological experiments.

3.4   GENE NETWORK-BASED DRUG TARGET IDENTIFICATION

Knowledge of a drug's mode of action (molecular targets), which mediates its therapeutic effects and side effects, is important for drug development. A drug's mode of action is based primarily on its targets and the action mechanisms of the chemical compounds involved. However, for many drug candidates, the targets are unknown and difficult to be identified from the thousands of gene products in a genome [Ber05]. Fortunately, more recent developments of DNA microarray technology can be used to measure the concentration of all mRNAs within an organism, including gene expression profiles following perturbation of some gene or compound of interest. The expression profiles of genes responding to drug treatments or disease conditions can also be measured. However, gene expression profiles alone cannot distinguish the targets or mediators of a treatment response from so many genes [Xin06]. Computational tools are needed to identify the drug targets or the action mode of the compound through the inferred regulatory networks or other means. Actually, if a compound or drug is viewed as a gene, then the drug targets can be directly inferred by the methods of gene network reconstruction from microarray data, based on the inferred regulatory relations between the drug and genes. Gardner et al. proposed a method called network identification by multiple regression (NIR) for identifying the compound mode of action [Gar03]. Bansal et al. developed an algorithm called time-series network identification (TSNI) to infer the local network of gene–gene interactions surrounding a gene of interest [BaM06]. Their method is based on the gene expression profiles at multiple timepoints generated by perturbing the gene of interest. Hallén et al. designed a CutTree algorithm and applied it to whole-genome expression datasets for identifying the primary affected genes of a chemical compound [Hal06]. The advantage of this method is that it needs only a limited set of experimental perturbations without requiring any prior information about the underlying pathways. In contrast, Wang et al. presented a linear programming framework that can not only integrate multiple perturbation expression datasets but also identify compound of action by regulatory network inference [WaY09]. In addition to those methods using gene networks, other data sources such as protein–protein interactions have also been employed for drug target identification. In this section, we will introduce some of these methods that identify mode of action based on gene expression profiles.

3.4.1 Network Identification Methods

In the problem of drug target identification, system identification in engineering plays an important role. In 2003, Gardner proposed the NIR method to identify a compound model of action [Gar03]. They assumed that near a steady-state point, the nonlinear differential equations modeling a gene regulatory network can be approximated by a linear system of equations

$$\frac{dx(t)}{dt} = Ax(t) + u(t)$$

where $x(t)$ is a vector representing the concentrations of n mRNAs in the network and $u(t)$ is a vector denoting external perturbations to the rates of accumulation of the species $dx(t)/dt$. A is the regulation matrix of $n \times n$ describing the regulatory interactions between the species in x. Then, from the steady-state mRNA expression data obtained by perturbing the linear systems with the external perturbation term, a connection matrix of the network A is inferred. For large-scale networks, it is not practical to perform n perturbation experiments, which makes the network inference an underdetermined problem. To overcome this problem, it is assumed that each gene has a maximum of k regulatory inputs with $k < n$, which is reasonable since biological networks are observed to be sparse. With this assumption, the underdetermined problem is transformed into an overdetermined problem, rendering the network inference biologically tractable and robust to measurement noise and the incompleteness of datasets. The next step in NIR is to apply multiple linear regression to calculate all possible combinations of k regulatory coefficients for each gene. The one that fits the expression data with the smallest error is chosen as the best approximation of A. The final step is to use the inferred network model to predict expression changes and network behaviors such as a compound's model of action. For example, suppose that the activity of a compound is treated as a set of unknown perturbations u_p and the change of mRNA expression resulting from treatment with that compound is x_p. Then, by calculating the unknown perturbations through the equations

$$u_p(t) = -Ax_p(t)$$

one can identify the direct targets of the compound, specifically, those genes that exhibit statistically significant values in u_p. The NIR method was tested on a nine-transcript subnetwork of the SOS pathway in *E. coli* using a set of nine-perturbation expression profiles, which showed that NIR can infer the local regulatory network around a gene of special interest and meanwhile identify the targets of pharmacological compounds.

The NIR method has proved highly effective in inferring small gene networks. But, as pointed by Bansal et al. it requires prior knowledge, specifically, which genes are involved in the network of interest [BaM06]. In addition, it requires the measurement of gene expressions at steady state after the perturbation. These factors make it challenging for large networks. Most importantly, it is not applicable if there is no prior knowledge of the genes belonging to the network [BaM06]. To overcome these disadvantages, Bansal et al. presented an algorithm called time-series network identification (TSNI) [BaM06]. Instead of using all-gene perturbation, this method can infer the local gene network surrounding a gene of interest by measuring gene expression profiles at multiple timepoints following perturbation of the gene.

Bansal et al. used a set of linear differential equations to represent the rate of mRNA synthesis as a function of the concentration of other mRNAs in a cell and the external perturbations [BaM06]

$$\dot{x}(t) = Jx(t) + Pu(t), \quad t = t_1, \ldots, t_m \tag{3.43}$$

where $x(t) = [x_1(t), \ldots, x_n(t)]^T \in R^n$, $x_i(t)$ is the expression level (mRNA concentration) of gene i at timepoint t; $\dot{x}(t) = dx(t)/dt$ is the change rate of concentration of gene transcript mRNA at time t; and J is an $n \times n$ connection matrix, composed of element J_{ij}, which represents the effect of gene j on gene i with a positive, zero, or negative sign indicating activation, no interaction, and repression, respectively. P is an $n \times s$ matrix representing the effect of the s perturbations or s compounds on x, and $u(t) \in \mathcal{R}^s$ represents the external perturbations for s compounds at time t. A nonzero element P_{ij} of P implies that the ith gene is a direct target of the jth pertur-bation or compound. By identifying P, the approach can be a powerful methodology for the drug design and function discovery of molecules. Equation (3.43) can be rewritten in a compact form for all timepoints of one dataset using matrix notation, thus we have

$$\dot{X} = JX + PU \tag{3.44}$$

where $X = [x(t_1), \ldots, x(t_m)]$ and $\dot{X} = [\dot{x}(t_1), \ldots, \dot{x}(t_m)]$ are all $n \times m$ matrices. Suppose that there are s external perturbation compounds. Then $U = [u(t_1), \ldots, u(t_m)]$ is an $s \times m$ matrix representing the s perturbations. The unknown variables to be calculated are the connection matrix J and matrix P, which constitute a predictive model and can be used to identify the direct target of a perturbation or compound.

Typically, solving equation (3.44) is an underdetermined problem since we usually have fewer timepoints than genes. Bansal et al. overcame this difficulty by applying a cubic smoothing spline filter to the gene expression data and interpolated the smoothed data using piecewise cubic spline interpolation to increase the number of timepoints. Then principal component analysis (PCA) was applied to the dataset to reduce its dimensionality [BaM06]. To avoid noise-level increase resulting from the addition of derivatives, Bansal et al. converted equation (3.44) to its discrete form

$$X(t_{k+1}) = J_d X(t_k) + P_d U(t_k) \tag{3.45}$$

where J_d and P_d are respectively the discrete counterparts of J and P in the discrete space [Lju99]. The equation (3.45) can be reformed as

$$X(t_{k+1}) = [J_d \ P_d] \begin{bmatrix} X(t_k) \\ U(t_k) \end{bmatrix} \tag{3.46}$$

which can be written for all timepoints

$$X = HY \tag{3.47}$$

where $H = [J_d \ P_d]$ and

$$Y = \begin{bmatrix} X(t_k) \\ U(t_k) \end{bmatrix}$$

Dimensions of X, U, H, and Y are $n \times (m - 1)$, $s \times (m - 1)$, $n \times (n + s)$, and $(n + s) \times (m - 1)$, respectively. Then, PCA was applied to reduce the dimension of equation (3.47) by decomposing Y using SVD, so the following equation can be obtained

$$X = HVDW^T \tag{3.48}$$

where V is an $(n + s) \times (n + s)$ matrix of left singular vectors and D is a diagonal matrix containing the $n + s$ singular values arranged in descending order. The rows of W^T are right singular vectors which form an $(n + s) \times (m - 1)$ matrix. By selecting the top k singular values, we have $X = Z_d Y_R$, where Z_d is obtained by taking the first k columns of HV and Y_R is the data in the reduced dimension obtained by taking the first k rows of DW^T. By taking the pseudoinverse of Y, it follows that

$$Z_d = X Y_R^T (Y_R Y_R^T)^{-1}$$

Hence, J_d and P_d can be obtained from Z_d and V. Their continuous counterparts J and P can be computed by the following transformation [Lju99]

$$J = \frac{2(J_d - I)}{\delta_t (J_d + I)}$$
$$P = (J_d + I)^{-1} J P_d$$

where I is the square identity matrix with dimension $n \times n$ and δ_t is the sampling interval. The advantage of TSNI is that it requires a limited amount of data to infer a local regulatory network surrounding a gene of interest and thus would be a powerful methodology for drug discovery.

In contrast to the abovementioned methods using linear differential equations to model gene networks, Bernardo et al. developed a method for predicting the mode of action of compounds based on nonlinear (actually loglinear) differential equations [Ber05]

$$\dot{x}_i(t) = u_i(t) \prod_{j=1}^{n} [x_j(t)]^{J_{ij}} - d_i x_i(t) \tag{3.49}$$

where d_i is the rate constant of degradation of transcript i, and other symbols have the same meaning as in the previous equations. Their approach, called *mode-of-action by network identification* (MNI) [Ber05, Xin06], has a framework similar to those of the two methods described above. Figure 3.12 illustrates the scheme of the MNI method. First, a set of treatments such as knockouts, compounds, overexpression, or RNAi is applied to an organism. RNAi means RNA interference, and is a highly evolutionally conserved process of post-transcriptional gene silencing by which double stranded RNA causes sequence-specific degradation of homologous mRNA sequences when introduced into a cell. The expression profiles of a set of genes of interest in compound-treated cells are measured as training data. Then, the microarray data from the samples are processed by the MNI algorithm to infer a predictive model of the regulatory interactions between genes in the organism under the conditions treated by those external perturbations. Finally, by inputting the microarray data from the test treatment into the reconstructed regulatory model, the molecular targets of the test treatment can be identified by examining the values of the predicted u. The software for the MNI algorithm is coded by Matlab and can be downloaded from the authors' website, http://gardnerlab.bu.edu.

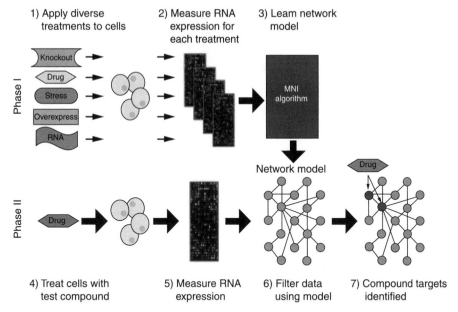

1) Apply diverse treatments to cells
2) Measure RNA expression for each treatment
3) Leam network model

Phase I

Knockout
Drug
Stress
Overexpress
RNA

MNI algorithm

Network model

Phase II

Drug

Drug

4) Treat cells with test compound
5) Measure RNA expression
6) Filter data using model
7) Compound targets identified

Figure 3.12. Schematic overview of the mode-of-action by network identification (MNI) method. (Reprinted by permission from Macmillan Publishers Ltd: Nature Protocols [Xin06] © 2006.)

3.4.2 Linear Programming Framework

To integrate multiple microarray datasets and various prior biological information from experimental results, Wang et al. developed a linear programming (LP) approach to reconstruct gene networks which can be further used to identify compound targets by considering the external perturbations or compound treatments [WaY09a]. As a network identification method, the model is used to correlate the changes in transcript concentration from one gene to another and to the external perturbations [BaM06]. An *external perturbation* means an experimental treatment (e.g., a drug) or an input that can alter the transcription rates of the genes in the cell. An example of perturbation is the treatment with a chemical compound, or a genetic perturbation involving overexpression or downregulation of particular genes. Figure 3.13 illustrates the scheme of the linear programming framework. In the LP framework, microarray timecourse datasets from different experiment conditions or perturbations are collected as matrices. A gene regulatory network is described by ordinary differential equations (ODEs). To infer the relationships between genes, the coexpression information and prior observations from the literature or databases are compiled to form documented structure and coexpression, structure, respectively, acting as supervised information. On the other hand, each timecourse dataset gives a general solution for the network inference by the SVD technique. Finally, a consistent gene network is obtained with an LP-based algorithm by comparing all network structures.

Gene regulation with external perturbations can also be modeled by using the linear differential equation (3.44). In contrast to using the discrete counterpart of the model,

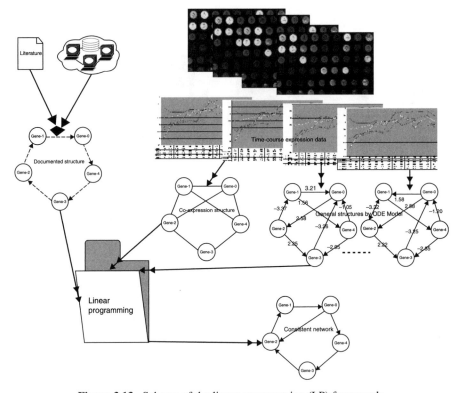

Figure 3.13. Scheme of the linear programming (LP) framework.

an approximate difference scheme based on the first-order derivatives is adopted, specifically

$$\dot{x}_i(t_j) = \frac{x_i(t_{j+1}) - x_i(t_j)}{t_{j+1} - t_j}$$

for $i = 1, \ldots, n; j = 1, \ldots, m$. Although the forward difference approximation here is utilized for numerical computation of $\dot{x}$, backward or other difference approximation methods can be applied similarly. By adopting SVD to $[X^T\ U^T]$, it follows that

$$\begin{bmatrix} X \\ U \end{bmatrix}^T_{m \times (n+s)} = W_{m \times (n+s)} D_{(n+s) \times (n+s)} V^T_{(n+s) \times (n+s)} \tag{3.50}$$

where W is an $m \times (n + s)$ matrix of left eigenvectors, D is a diagonal $(n + s) \times (n + s)$ matrix containing the $(n + s)$ eigenvalues, and V^T is the transpose of an $(n + s) \times (n + s)$ matrix of right eigenvectors. As in Sections 3.2.1 and 3.3, a particular solution for regulation matrix $[J, P]$ can be created from each dataset with the least L_2 norm in the following way

$$[\hat{J}\ \hat{P}] = \dot{X} W D^{-1} V^T \tag{3.51}$$

where $D^{-1} = \text{diag}(1/d_i)$ with $1/d_i$ taken to be zero if $d_i = 0$. Here we mean that the diagonal element of the matrix D^{-1} is obtained by the following rules: If $d_i = 0$, we set it to zero and if $d_i \neq 0$ we set it to $1/d_i$.

Assuming that N microarray datasets are available, then N special regulatory networks can be obtained by

$$[\hat{J}^k \ \hat{P}^k] = X^k W^k (D^k)^{-1} V^{kT} \tag{3.52}$$

where the subscript $k = 1, \ldots, N$ is the index of the dataset k. Thus, the general solution of the Jacobian matrix $J^k = (J_{ij}^k)_{n \times n}$ and $P^k = (P_{ij}^k)_{n \times s}$ for each dataset k is expressed by

$$[J^k \ P^k] = [\hat{J}^k \ \hat{P}^k] + Y^k V^{kT} \tag{3.53}$$

which represents all of the possible regulatory networks that are consistent with this dataset due to the arbitrary variables Y^k. $Y^k = (y_{ij}^k)_{n \times (n+s)}$ is an $n \times (n + s)$ matrix, where y_{ij}^k is zero if $d_j^k \neq 0$ and is otherwise an arbitrary bounded scalar coefficient. With N general solutions available, a linear programming framework can be used to construct the most consistent gene regulatory network $[J\ P]$ from all $[J^k\ P^k], k = 1, \ldots, N$, by determining Y^k through an optimization procedure similar to GRNInfer.

In addition to combining multiple microarray datasets, the linear programming framework can also incorporate various prior knowledge from experiments or the literature. Hence, before introducing the details of the method, next we examine what information can be employed and integrated into the network inference model.

3.4.2.1 Coexpression Information

A common observation in earlier studies is that genes that behave similarly during a timecourse are functionally related and may also be involved in the same regulatory mechanism. It has been shown that compound targets belonging to the same single- and multiple- input motifs tend to be coexpressed, and that the level of coexpression is higher when multiple transcript factors are involved. In other words, similarities and differences between expression profiles and changes in expression levels provide important insight into regulatory relationships. Hence, the coexpression information can be combined with equation (3.53) to infer a reliable gene network.

Multiple datasets $X^k, k = 1, \ldots, N$ are arranged into one expression profile dataset $X = [X^1, \ldots, X^N]$. Letting $m = m_1 + \cdots + m_N$, we then compute the correlation coefficient of gene i and gene j as cc_{ij} and construct the coexpression matrix as $CC = (cc_{ij})_{n \times n}$:

$$cc_{ij} = \sum_{k=1}^{m} \frac{(X_{ik} - \bar{X}_i)(X_{jk} - \bar{X}_j)}{\sigma_{X_i} \sigma_{X_j}} \tag{3.54}$$

Clearly, $-1 \leq cc_{ij} \leq 1$ here. Dynamic expression data are the vectors of the first-order difference. Some genes may have associated dynamic behaviors. Similarly, let $\dot{\bar{X}} = [\dot{X}^1, \ldots, \dot{X}^N]$. By computing the correlation coefficient of gene i and gene j in matrix $\bar{X}$ as dcc_{ij}, the dynamic coexpression matrix can be constructed as $DCC = (dcc_{ij})_{n \times n}$:

$$dcc_{ij} = \sum_{k=1}^{m-N} \frac{(\dot{X}_{ik} - \bar{\dot{X}}_i)(\dot{X}_{jk} - \bar{\dot{X}}_j)}{\sigma_{\dot{X}_i} \sigma_{\dot{X}_j}} \qquad (3.55)$$

where, clearly, $-1 \leq dcc_{ij} \leq 1$. The purpose of studying gene expression dynamics is that the existing static data cannot recover all the important relationships.

In addition to correlation coefficients, the mutual information between two genes can also elucidate their relationships on the basis of their expression profiles. For the expression profiles $X = [X^1, \ldots, X^N]$, we can compute the mutual information of gene i and gene j as MI_{ij} and construct the coexpression matrix as $MI = (mi_{ij})_{n \times n}$

$$mi_{ij} = \frac{1}{m} \sum_{k=1}^{m} \log \frac{g(X_{ik}, X_{jk})}{g(X_{ik})g(X_{jk})} \qquad (3.56)$$

where $g(\vec{z}) = (1/m) \sum_{k=1}^{m} h^{-2} G(h^{-1} \| \vec{z} - \vec{z}_k \|)$ and $\vec{z} = \{x, y\}$, $\vec{z}_k = \{X_{ik}, X_{jk}\}$, $k = 1, \ldots, m$. $G(\cdot)$ is the bivariate standard normal density. $g(x)$ and $g(y)$ are the margins of $g(\vec{z})$. The software ARACNE [Bas05] is used to obtain the mutual information estimation, which allows the optimal choice of the parameter h (Gaussian kernel width). Clearly, $0 \leq mi_{ij} \leq 1$.

Besides correlation, there may exist a timeshift relationship between two gene expression profiles, which can be examined by aligning the expression profiles of the genes of interests by dynamic programming approach. For dataset X^k, the aligned score of genes i and j by dynamic programming is denoted by ce_{ij}^k, which constitutes the matrix $CE^k = (ce_{ij}^k)_{n \times n}$, where $ce_{ij}^k \geq 0$. The iteration formula is

$$ce_{ij}^k(k, l) = ce_{ij}^k(k-1, l-1) + \max\{0, X_{ik} \times X_{jl}\}, \qquad k, l = 2, \ldots, m_k \quad (3.57)$$

Then the multiple coexpression matrices CE^k, $k = 1, \ldots, N$ are combined into CE with each element as $CE_{ij} = \min\{CE_{ij}^k, k = 1, \ldots, N\}$.

Incorporating the coexpression information mentioned above into the network inference model can make the results more biologically reasonable. CC and DCC are normalized by simply taking the absolute value of every element, and linear normalization is applied to CE to make elements in $[0, 1]$:

$$ce_{ij} = \frac{ce_{ij} - \min_{i,j}\{ce_{ij}\}}{\max_{i,j}\{ce_{ij}\} - \min_{i,j}\{ce_{ij}\}} \qquad (3.58)$$

CC, DCC, and CE also denote the normalized matrices. The final coexpression matrix $E = \{e_{ij}\}$, $i = 1, \ldots, n$, $j = 1, \ldots, n$ is combined from CC, DCC, MI, and CE by the following formula:

$$e_{ij} = \min\{\max\{0, cc_{ij} - \eta_1\}, \max\{0, dcc_{ij} - \eta_2\},$$
$$\max\{0, mi_{ij} - \eta_3\}, \max\{0, ce_{ij} - \eta_4\}\} \qquad (3.59)$$

where η_1, η_2, η_3, and η_4 are the thresholds for matrices CC, DCC, MI, and CE respectively, and also play a role as weights for combining the four matrices.

3.4.2.2 Documented and Prior Regulations   Although full genetic networks for many biological processes are not available, some fragmentary regulatory relationships from the literature and databases can be collected and used as supervised information for the gene network inference. For example, much work on regulatory networks has focused on *E. coli* and yeast *S. cerevisiae*. Many regulatory interactions in *E. coli* have been collected manually from the literature and deposited in the RegulonDB database [Sal06]. In yeast, manually compiled data in YEASTRACT [Tei06] have been greatly augmented by large-scale DNA-binding data from ChIP-chip experiments. Let the documented network be $K = (k_{ij})_{n \times n}$, which is an $n \times n$ matrix and represents the known gene regulation information. If the element k_{ij} is nonzero, this means that gene j has regulatory effect on gene i (activation or repression depends on the sign of k_{ij}), and this regulatory relationship is assumed to be prior knowledge from biological experiments. Since many such prior regulatory relationships are qualitative instead of quantitative, quantitative relationships described by k_{ij} is seldom available. Wang et al. incorporate such qualitative prior interactions into the linear programming framework by setting $k_{ij} \geq 0$ or $k_{ij} \leq 0$ as a hard constraint depending on the activating or inhibiting information [WaY09a]. For prior interactions without activation information, such as ChIP-chip data, they are treated as soft constraints, removing the related elements from the objective function of LP. As mentioned in Section 3.2.1, for a large system, the minimum number of timepoints needed is $O(\log n)$ to reconstruct the $n \times n$ connection matrix for an n-gene network. Hence, a proper incorporation of the documented and coexpression information in the algorithm will alleviate the requirement and dependence on accuracy of microarray data.

3.4.2.3 Decomposition Algorithm Based on LP   With the N general solutions $[J^k \ P^k]$, the coexpression matrix E and prior interactions K, the next step is to find a consistent and also biologically reasonable solution by determining variable $Y^k, k = 1, \ldots, N$. Wang et al. developed a method by exploiting L_1 norm in the formulation of the objective function to infer a sparse and consistent gene network with an ability of identifying compound targets [WaY09a]:

$$\min_{Y,L} \sum_{k=1}^{N} \sum_{i=1}^{n} \sum_{j=1}^{n+s} [\omega^k |L_{ij} - L_{ij}^k| + \lambda |L_{ij}|]$$

$$\text{s.t.} \quad L_{ij}^k \geq 0 \quad \text{if} \quad k_{ij} \geq 0$$

$$\qquad\quad L_{ij}^k \leq 0 \quad \text{if} \quad k_{ij} \leq 0 \qquad\qquad (3.60)$$

$$\qquad\quad L_{ij}^k = 0 \quad \text{if} \quad e_{ij} = 0$$

$$\qquad\quad i, j \in \{1, \ldots, n\}, k \in \{1, \ldots, N\}$$

where L_{ij}^k is a function of Y^k and $Y = (Y^1, \ldots, Y^N)$. The first term in the objective function is a matching term that forces the matching of L and L^k, whereas the second term is the sparsity term, which forces L sparse, due to L_1 norm. λ is a positive parameter, which balances the matching and sparsity terms in the objective function. The first and second constraints are used to add the documented information, and the third one is used to incorporate the coexpression information. The variables in (3.60) are L_{ij} and all of nonzero y_{ij}^k. ω^k is a positive weight coefficient for the dataset k and $\sum_{k=1}^{N} \omega^k = 1$. The optimization problem (3.60) is an LP with L_1 norm, which is a widely studied problem. It is known that L_1 gives the most robust answer comparing with L_2 and L_∞. Documented regulations are added as hard constraints according to their activation or repression role, and the strength will be decided from the algorithm. Here the coexpression data of genes are added as equality constraints only for those zero or weak linkages of coexpression. It is possible that no regulatory effect exists if genes i and j are shown to be weakly co-regulated on the basis of the four prior matrices (i.e., $e_{ij} = 0$). For documented regulations without activation or repression conditions (e.g., ChIP-chip data), they are treated as soft constraints by removing the related elements of L_{ij} (corresponding to the documented possible interactions) from the objective function so that those removed elements are not taken as sparse terms.

Equation (3.60) has a large number of variables. Removing the absolutes in the LP model will also increase the number of variables. To solve problem (3.60) efficiently, a decomposition algorithm is used based on the special structure of (3.60) based on two subproblems [WaY09a]. Specifically, we first can fix L to solve N small-size matching subproblems $LP^1, LP^2, \ldots, LP^N$, and then update L by solving (3.60) with fixed Y^1, $Y^2, \ldots, Y^N$ obtained from the N subproblems. The procedure continues until it converges. Each decomposed subproblem is formulated as follows:

- *Subproblem 1.* Set $L^k(q) = L^k(q-1) + Y^k(q)V^{k^T}$. Obtain $y_{ij}^k(q)$ at iteration q through solving subproblems $LP^1, LP^2, \ldots, LP^N$ in the following form

$$\min_{Y^k(q)} \sum_{i=1}^{n} \sum_{j=1}^{n+s} |L_{ij}(q-1) - L_{ij}^k(q)|$$

$$\begin{aligned}
\text{s.t.} \quad & L_{ij}^k(q) \geq 0 \quad \text{if} \quad k_{ij} \geq 0 \\
& L_{ij}^k(q) \leq 0 \quad \text{if} \quad k_{ij} \leq 0 \\
& L_{ij}^k(q) = e_{ij} \quad \text{if} \quad e_{ij} = 0 \\
& i, j \in \{1, \ldots, n\}
\end{aligned} \tag{3.61}$$

where $L_{ij}(q-1)$ is fixed.

- *Subproblem 2.* Calculate $L_{ij}(q)$ at iteration q by solving the following problem with all of $L^k(q)$ fixed:

$$\min_{L(q)} \sum_{k=1}^{N} \sum_{i=1}^{n} \sum_{j=1}^{n+s} [\omega^k |L_{ij}(q) - L_{ij}^k(q)| + \lambda |L_{ij}(q)|] \tag{3.62}$$

The procedures of solving (3.61) and (3.62) and the choice of parameter λ are similar to those in Section 3.3. Clearly, the procedure above can be viewed as an extension of GRNInfer.

Next, we give a brief proof of the convergence. Letting $Y^k(q)$ be the solution of subproblem (3.61) at the qth iteration with the fixed $L(q-1)$, the objective function satisfies

$$\sum_{k=1}^{N}\sum_{i=1}^{n}\sum_{j=1}^{n+s} [\omega^k |L_{ij}(q-1) - L_{ij}^k(q)| + \lambda |L_{ij}(q-1)|]$$

$$\leq \sum_{k=1}^{N}\sum_{i=1}^{n}\sum_{j=1}^{n+s} [\omega^k |L_{ij}(q-1) - L_{ij}^k(q-1)| + \lambda |L_{ij}(q-1)|]$$

Fixing $L_{ij}^k(q)$, subproblem (3.62) is solved. Letting the solution be $L(q)$, then

$$\sum_{k=1}^{N}\sum_{i=1}^{n}\sum_{j=1}^{n+s} [\omega^k |L_{ij}(q) - L_{ij}^k(q)| + \lambda |L_{ij}(q)|]$$

$$\leq \sum_{k=1}^{N}\sum_{i=1}^{n}\sum_{j=1}^{n+s} [\omega^k |L_{ij}(q-1) - L_{ij}^k(q)| + \lambda |L_{ij}(q-1)|]$$

which means that the objective function decreases with the iteration. Since the objective function and y_{ij}^k are bounded, the solution space of $(L, Y^1, \ldots, Y^N)$ is a bounded set. Monotonic decrease for the objective function implies that there is a subsequence converging to a local solution of the original problem, which proves the convergence of the algorithm. Clearly, the proof also holds fpr the algorithm of GRNInfer.

3.4.2.4 Simulated Gene Expression Data

To test whether the linear programming framework can infer gene networks accurately as well as identify the targets of perturbations, a small simulated network with six genes is used with dynamics governed by

$$\begin{bmatrix} \dot{x}_1(t) \\ \dot{x}_2(t) \\ \dot{x}_3(t) \\ \dot{x}_4(t) \\ \dot{x}_5(t) \\ \dot{x}_6(t) \end{bmatrix} = \begin{bmatrix} -1.0 & 0.0 & 0.01 & 0.0 & 0.03 & 0.03 \\ 0.2 & -1.2 & 0.0 & 0.4 & -0.05 & 0.0 \\ 0.0 & 0.0 & -1.0 & 0.0 & 0.0 & -0.05 \\ 0.0 & -0.05 & 0.0 & -1.5 & 0.0 & 0.0 \\ 0.0 & 0.0 & 0.2 & 0.0 & -1.2 & 0.0 \\ 0.0 & 0.03 & 0.0 & -0.01 & 0.0 & -1.0 \end{bmatrix} \times \begin{bmatrix} x_1(t) \\ x_2(t) \\ x_3(t) \\ x_4(t) \\ x_5(t) \\ x_6(t) \end{bmatrix} + \begin{bmatrix} 2.0 \\ 0.0 \\ 0.0 \\ 0.0 \\ 0.0 \\ 0.0 \end{bmatrix} u_0$$

where x_i reflects the expression level of the gene i for $i = 1, \ldots, 6$. One perturbation is applied ($s = 1$) to gene 1, which is indicated by $P = [2.0, 0.0, 0.0, 0.0, 0.0, 0.0]^T$. P has all its elements equal to 0 except for the gene that is the direct target of the perturbation. u_0 indicates which kind of perturbation is applied. Then four timecourse datasets are generated according to the different initial conditions. The first dataset is obtained by taking perturbation $u_0 = 1$ as a constant and the timestep as 0.1. The second dataset is also obtained by taking $u_0 = 1$ as a constant but the timestep as 0.15. The perturbation varies with time and gradually increases from $u_0 = 1$ to $u_0 = 2$ in generating the third dataset, where the timestep is 0.2. The fourth dataset is obtained without perturbation with timestep 0.2. The initial value of the system is randomly generated from [1.0, 1.1], and Gaussian noise is added to the data matrix with zero mean and $\sigma = 0.2\|X\|$ (standard deviation), where $\|X\|$ is the L_∞ norm of data matrix X. The parameter λ is set to 0.1 to make the inferred network sparse. The supervised information K is denoted by the following matrix:

$$K = \begin{pmatrix} -1.0 & 0.0 & 0.0 & 0.0 & 0.0 & 0.03 \\ 0.0 & 0.0 & 0.0 & 0.4 & -0.05 & 0.0 \\ 0.0 & 0.0 & 0.0 & 0.0 & 0.0 & 0.0 \\ 0.0 & 0.0 & 0.0 & 0.0 & 0.0 & 0.0 \\ 0.0 & 0.0 & 0.2 & 0.0 & 0.0 & 0.0 \\ 0.0 & -0.05 & 0.0 & 0.0 & 0.0 & 0.0 \end{pmatrix}$$

The LP framework integrates multiple simulated timecourse datasets and/or the prior information to infer regulatory networks. The results are depicted in Figure 3.14, where the arrrows and arcs denote activation and repression, respectively. We can see that supervised prior information can make the network inference more accurate in terms of correctly predicted interactions. The accuracies of the inferred networks are assessed by E_1 and E_2. Again, supervised information can reduce the inference error. For example, E_1 decreases by 0.7139 (minus the error reduction 1.73 introduced by K) and E_2 decreases by 1.4857 (minus the error reduction 1.20 introduced by K). In addition, the LP method is able to properly identify the target genes of perturbation and thus can be applied to the drug design and function discovery of molecules. For example, the inferred perturbation vector without supervised information is $P = [0.35, -0.08, 0.09, 0.0, 0.0, 0.0]$, whereas the prediction results with supervised information are improved to $P = [1.25, 0.0, -0.01, 0.0, 0.0, -0.03]$. These results show that the LP method can correctly identify gene 1 as the

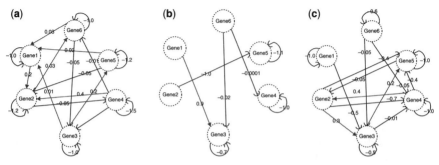

Figure 3.14. Results of the LP approach on the simulated network: (a) true network; (b) a network without supervised learning; and (c) a network with supervised learning.

target of the perturbation applied. But the result with supervised information is more accurate and statistically significant.

3.4.2.5 SOS Network of E. coli

The SOS pathway in *E. coli* regulates cell survival and repairs the cell after DNA damage. It involves the lexA, recA, and many other genes directly or indirectly regulated by lexA and recA. A nine-gene SOS subnetwork is used to test the LP method, and this subnetwork is also used by Gardner et al. [Gar03] [BaM06]. The multiple timecourse datasets were from the Many Microbe Microarray Database (M3D), which is a resource for analyzing and retrieving gene expression data for microbes (see Table 2.1). The norfloxacin time-series data from a norfloxacin perturbation (a known antibiotic that acts by damaging the DNA) are selected. The timecourse experiments were conducted by the induction with 10 μg/mL of norfloxacin and extraction of the total RNA at 0, 12, 24, 36, 48, and 60 min from the drug treatment. Data are normalized by the average of chips luc_U_N0000_r1, luc_U_N0000_r2, and luc_U_N0000_r3, and the noise level is about 13% [BaM06].

The inferred network and perturbations by the LP method on these experimental data were compared with the ones identified in previous work [Gar03, BaM06] and with those from the literature survey. For this nine-gene SOS subnetwork, there are in total 49 known regulatory relationships, including 8 self-feedbacks. Among them, 21 connections were correctly identified by the LP method and 18 nonregulatory links were confirmed. Figure 3.15 summarizes the results, where the dashed lines indicate that there are no regulatory effects confirmed by coexpression relationships. The whole network with the weight of links obtained by the parameter $\lambda = 0$ and $\eta_1 = \eta_2 = \eta_3 = \eta_4 = 0.3$ is shown in Table 3.2, where the bold weights denote the correctly predicted connections and the italic weights denote the correctly predicted zero connections. The LP results are similar to those of previous studies with some differences for the sparsity of network structure. As indicated by Gardner et al. [Gar03], the recovered actions to gene recF are statistically nonsignificant. The results in Table 3.2 also indicate that there are no correctly recognized connections for gene

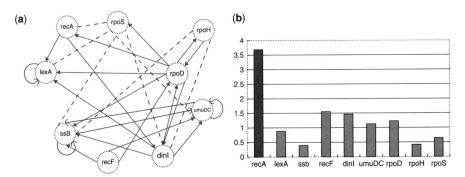

Figure 3.15. Results for SOS network: (a) predicted interactions between the nine genes of SOS network in *E. coli*; (b) the predicted perturbation.

TABLE 3.2. The SOS Network and Predicted Perturbations for *E. coli*

Gene	recA	lexA	ssb	recF	dinI	umuDC	rpoD	rpoH	rpoS	Pert.
recA	-0.0682	0.1149	0.0599	-0.0095	-0.0431	0.0000	**0.0173**	-0.0104	*0.0000*	0.1739
lexA	**0.0009**	**-0.1098**	0.0232	-0.0197	**0.0061**	0.0000	**0.0082**	0.0384	*0.0000*	0.0418
ssb	-0.0181	0.0188	**-0.0141**	**0.0279**	**0.0020**	**-0.0192**	**0.0018**	*0.0000*	*0.0000*	0.0187
recF	-0.0424	0.0015	0.0539	-0.0863	*0.0000*	-0.0090	-0.0005	0.0398	*0.0000*	0.0731
dinI	**0.0268**	0.0239	0.0538	0.0000	-0.0827	0.0769	**0.0177**	*0.0000*	*0.0000*	0.0689
umuDC	0.0000	0.0000	**-0.0527**	**0.0247**	**0.0280**	**-0.0705**	0.0000	0.0083	*0.0000*	0.0531
rpoD	-0.0525	0.0237	0.0145	**0.0009**	**0.0059**	0.0000	-0.0211	**0.0336**	*0.0000*	0.0578
rpoH	-0.0256	-0.0143	*0.0000*	-0.0111	*0.0000*	0.0335	**0.0127**	-0.0032	*0.0000*	0.0195
rpoS	*0.0000*	*0.0000*	*0.0000*	*0.0000*	*0.0000*	*0.0000*	**0.0101**	0.0091	-0.0274	0.0304

recF, which supports the theory that the inferred network is rendered more reliable by incorporating the coexpression relationships since LP uses only a single perturbation experiment and three time datasets, whereas nine different perturbation experiments are used by Gardner et al. [Gar03] and the perturbation matrix is known.

In addition, the LP method has the ability to predict the perturbation target correctly. The treatment of *E. coli* with norfloxacin is equivalent to a perturbation to gene recA. Noxfloxacin is a member of the fluoroquinolone class of antimicrobial agents that target prokaryotic type II, topoisomerase type II (DNA gyrase), and topoisomerase IV, which induce the formation of single-stranded DNA and thus activate the SOS pathway via activation of the recAp protein. Quinolones have been previously demonstrated to induce recA and other SOS-responsive genes in *E. coli*. The numerical simulation shows that recA is the strongest target (see the last column of Table 3.2 and Figure 3.15).

3.5 SUMMARY

Microarray gene expression data become an increasingly common data source that can provide insights into biological processes at a system level. Reverse engineering of gene regulatory networks is a promising means for analyzing gene expression profiles. In this chapter, we introduced some mathematical models and reconstruction approaches for gene regulatory networks. In particular, we described how to integrate multiple datasets for network inference and how to detect drug targets by inferring gene networks from perturbed gene expression data. In addition to the mathematical models introduced in this chapter, there are some other models for gene networks such as the relevance network and the finite-state machine. Several more recent related topics have appeared in this area, such as inferring scale-free genetic regulatory networks [ChG08] and identifying dynamic genetic regulatory systems [Iro07]. For further information, one can refer to some other papers (e.g., [Bas05], [Rog05]).

CHAPTER 4

INFERENCE OF TRANSCRIPTIONAL REGULATORY NETWORKS

4.1 PREDICTING TF BINDING SITES AND PROMOTERS

Understanding the fundamental mechanism that regulates the expression of genes is a major challenge in molecular biology. As described in Chapter 2, gene regulation is achieved mainly by DNA-binding proteins called transcription factors (TFs). Such TFs typically consist of at least two domains: a DNA-binding domain and a transcriptional regulation domain. The former serves to interact with a target sequence, and the latter serves to activate or repress transcription. In a transcription process, TFs usually bind to the regulatory regions of their target DNA sequences on immediate upstream and downstream of the transcription start site (TSS) known as promoters. TF-encoding genes can also be regulated by other TFs. Such regulatory interactions between TFs and target genes constitute a transcription regulatory network, which contains two types of nodes: regulatory proteins and their target genes. Identification of TF binding sites, promoters and *cis*-regulatory elements is very important for understanding the function of transcription regulatory networks. Many computational and experimental methods have been employed to identify TFs, target genes, and their interactions.

Generally, a eukaryotic gene has multiple binding sites, which means that it is usually regulated by a coordinated interaction of multiple TFs. Even some prokaryotic genes have several binding sites. Such transcription factor binding sites (TFBSs) are usually situated in the upstream of the corresponding genes and form as *cis*-regulatory modules. One method for identifying TFBSs is based on an assumption that coexpressed genes are also coregulated on the level of transcription to a certain extent.

Biomolecular Networks. By Luonan Chen, Rui-Sheng Wang, and Xiang-Sun Zhang
Copyright © 2009 John Wiley & Sons, Inc.

The advent of microarray techniques facilitates the identification of coexpressed genes by clustering gene expression data. On the other hand, by analyzing the genomic sequences of a set of coexpressed genes, statistically overrepresented motifs can be found as potential TFBSs. Accurate identification of these motifs is difficult since they are very short subsequences located in the midst of a large amount of significant false positives. A number of computational approaches have been developed for discovering unknown motifs, such as Gibbs sampling, expectation–maximization (EM), and exhaustive enumeration. Most of them search recurring or overrepresented short patterns in DNA sequences.

Another method is based on phylogenetic footprinting, which hypothesizes that functionally important regulatory sequence elements are under constraint evolutionary variance, and thus TFBSs are found on the basis of the conservation of functional *cis*-regulatory elements in closely related organisms. This method has been used to identify putative regulatory elements in yeast [Cli03], *D. melanogaster* [Gla05]. Xie and his colleagues reported the first comprehensive screen for regulatory motifs in human promoters by comparative genome analysis of several mammals, such as human, mouse, rat, and dog genomes [Xie05]. Table 4.1 lists some main TF binding site databases. TFBSs are typically stored as position weight matrices (PWM). Some databases also store the binding sites as sequence logos. A variety of computational tools make use of the position weight matrices stored in databases to predict TFBSs in DNA sequences, such as MatInspector, PhyloScan, MATCH, and YMF (Table 4.2.). A comprehensive review of computational and experimental techniques for locating TFBSs can be found in a paper by [Eln06]. There are some systematical assessment of several computational tools for discovering TFBSs [Tom05]. It is worth noting that only a small portion of all TF binding sites in genomes have been identified so far, and thus there is much room for both computational and experimental methods.

In prokaryotes, a promoter typically consists of two short sequences at -10 and -35 positions upstream from the TSS that can be recognized by RNA polymerase. However, eukaryotic promoters are much more diverse and difficult to characterize. They typically lie upstream of the gene, and the regulatory elements in them may be several kilobases away from the TSS. A number of algorithms have been developed

TABLE 4.1. Several Databases of TF Binding Sites

Databases	Websites
DBSD	http://rulai.cshl.org/dbsd
E. coli TFBSs	http://bayesweb.wadsworth.org/binding_sites
TRRD	http://www.bionet.nsc.ru/bgrs/thesis/5
TRED	http://rulai.cshl.edu
AtProbe	http://rulai.cshl.edu/cgi-bin/atprobe/atprobe.pl
AtcisDB	http://arabidopsis.med.ohio-state.edu/AtcisDB
PRODORIC	http://prodoric.tu-bs.de
JASPAR	http://jaspar.genereg.net
TRANSFAC	http://www.gene-regulation.com/pub/databases.html

TABLE 4.2. Some Software for Searching TF Binding Sites

Program	Description
MatInspector	Utilizes a large library of matrix descriptions for TFBSs to locate matches in DNA sequences
MATCH	Uses a library of mononucleotide or dinucleotide weight matrixes from TRANSFAC 3.5 for searching potential TFBSs
YMF	Does an enumerative search to find the motifs with the highest z scores
MotifSampler	Uses Gibbs sampling to find the PWM that represents the motif by modeling the background with a higher-order Markov model
PhyloScan	Uses evidence from matching sites found in cross-species to identify TFBSs
ANN-Spec	Uses an artificial neural network and a Gibbs sampling method to model the specificity of a DNA-binding protein
CONSENSUS	Searches for the PWM with the maximum information content
Weeder	Enumerates all the oligos of (or up to) a given length and determines their occurrences with possible substitutions in the input sequences
AlignACE	Uses Gibbs sampling algorithm to find a series of motifs as PWMs that are overrepresented in the input sequences
MEME	Uses EM algorithm to optimizes the E value of a statistic related to the information content of the motif
GLAM	Uses a Gibbs sampling-based algorithm that optimizes the alignment width and obtains the best possible gapless multiple alignment
STAMP	automatically builds alignments for multiple motifs and can be used to query motifs against databases of known motifs in chosen databases

to facilitate the detection of promoters and transcription start sites in genomic sequence. These methods typically utilize the sequence context or structural characteristics of promoter regions. For example, Zhao et al. developed a boosting technique with stumps called CoreBoost to select important features for locating TSSs [ZhaX07]. Bajic and Seah presented a system called "dragon gene start finder," which combines information about CpG islands, TSSs, and signals downstream of the predicted TSSs to predict gene start location [Baj03]. Other Web resources for finding promoters include PromoSer, GeneQuest, and CREME. Phylogenetic footprinting can also be used to identify promoter regions and regulatory regions, especially those farther apart from the TSS.

In addition to computational methods, several experimental approaches have been developed for transcription start site identification and promoter annotation. For example, promoter sequences are placed upstream of a fireflyluciferase reporter gene or green fluorescent protein. Gene expression assays can measure the transcript changes of a gene in response to *cis*-acting regulatory signals and thus annotate the promoters for both the murine and the human genome. Cap analysis of gene expression (CAGE) has been used to more precisely define transcription start sites in mammalian promoters [Car06]. In addition, promoters can be tested in short-term reactions known as transient transfections [Coo06]. Table 4.3 lists some predicted and experimental promoter databases for a variety of organisms.

TABLE 4.3. Databases of Promoters and TSSs

Databases	Websites
SCPD	http://rulai.cshl.edu/SCPD
CEPDB	http://rulai.cshl.edu/cgi-bin/CEPDB
LSPD	http://rulai.cshl.edu/LSPD
PlantProm DB	http://mendel.cs.rhul.ac.uk/mendel.php?topic=plantprom
EPD	http://www.epd.isb-sib.ch
CSHLmpd	http://rulai.cshl.edu/CSHLmpd2
MPromDb	http://bioinformatics.med.ohio-state.edu/MPromDb
OMGProm	http://bioinformatics.med.ohio-state.edu/OMGProm
HemoPDB	http://bioinformatics.med.ohio-state.edu/HemoPDB
OPD	http://www.opd.tau.ac.il/
HPD	http://zlab.bu.edu/mfrith/HPD.html
DCPD	http://www-biology.ucsd.edu/labs/Kadonaga/DCPD.htm
TiProD	http://tiprod.cbi.pku.edu.cn:8080/index.html
DBTSS	http://dbtss.hgc.jp/
PLACE	http://www.dna.affrc.go.jp/PLACE/

4.2 INFERENCE OF TRANSCRIPTIONAL INTERACTIONS

Gene regulation is an important biological process accounting for organismal complexity and diversity in the course of biological evolution and adaptation. More and more biological data are deposited owing to the advances of various high-throughput experiment techniques, which make it possible to quantitatively study gene regulation in a systematic way [WaR07b]. Current microarray techniques can measure the transcripts of thousands of genes simultaneously. Since the expression profiles of genes result from the network interactions between regulators and target genes, it is possible and reasonable to retrieve these interactions from gene expression data. Although gene regulation is not completely known, great progress has been made by computational approaches, such as recognizing promoter sequences, predicting binding sites and transcription factors, which have been described in the previous sections. One of the central problems in this area is to determine the direct regulatory interactions between TFs and their target genes, namely, transcriptional interactions or transcription regulatory networks (TRNs) [WaR07b]. Like gene regulatory networks (GRNs), which represents indirect interactions among genes [ChL02, ChL04, Hus03a, Jon02, WaY06, Yeu02], inferring direct regulatory interactions has utmost importance for revealing the complex regulatory mechanisms in cellular systems. More recently, a number of methods have been developed for inferring TRN from the expression data of TFs and targets, including Bayesian methods, stochastic differential equations, optimization methods, and data mining. Some of these methods also combine literature information, ChIP-chip data, or motif data. Figure 4.1 illustrates a general framework for inferring TRN from various kinds of transcription data. In this section, we describe mainly the most recent work on deriving transcriptional interactions between regulators and target genes.

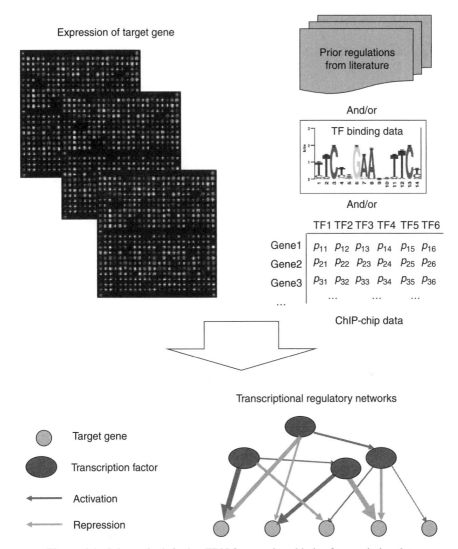

Figure 4.1. Scheme for inferring TRN from various kinds of transcription data.

4.2.1 Differential Equation Methods

As in reverse engineering of gene regulatory networks, inferring transcription regulatory networks should also be based on mathematical models describing the dependent relations between regulators and target genes. Ordinary differential equations (see Section 3.1) are widely used to model both gene regulatory networks and transcription regulatory networks. To model gene regulation, sigmoidal function is often adopted as the regulatory function of a TF

$$f[a(t):\alpha, \beta] = \frac{1}{1 + \exp\{-\alpha a(t) + \beta\}} \qquad (4.1)$$

because it has several desirable properties; For instance, it can closely represent actual systems, act as a molecular switch to control gene expression, and handle saturation and repression [Vei03]. A relatively early work on inferring TRN is contributed by Chen et al. [ChH04], where they assumed that a TRN can be represented by a set of ordinary differential equations with the following form for a specific gene i:

$$\frac{dx_i(t)}{dt} = G_i(t) - d_i x_i(t) + \xi_i(t) \qquad (4.2)$$

$G_i(t)$ and d_i are respectively the transcription rate and the self-degradation rate constant of gene i, $x_i(t)$ is the expression profile of gene i, and the last term, $\xi_i(t)$, represents noise to indicate the uncertainty of the data and the model residuals. The transcription rate $G_i(t)$ is assumed to be a linear combination of sigmoidal functions

$$G_i(t) = \sum_{j=1}^{m} \frac{a_{ij}}{1 + \exp\{-\alpha[u(t, \beta_j, \delta) - \gamma]\}}$$

where a_{ij} is an associated parameter that controls the weight of the specific switch function and $u(t, \beta_j, \delta)$ represents a triangular function whose three corners are determined by the parameters $\beta_j - \delta$, δ, $\beta_j + \delta$. On the basis of such a model, a two-step method is proposed for inferring TRN [ChH04]. In the first step, it models the dynamics of gene expression and estimates transcription rate $G_i(t)$. In the second step, it identifies potential regulators using the estimated transcription rate and computes the regulation strengths of TFs by matching the transcription rate of target gene i through a combination of a set of regulatory functions from regulators

$$G_i(t) = c_{i0} + \sum_{j \in L_i} c_{ij} f_j [x_j(t) : \alpha, \beta]$$

where f_j has the form (4.1) and c_{ij} is the regulatory capability from regulator j to target gene i. L_i is the set of regulators for gene i. Ability to quantify the regulatory ability of the TFs to a target gene is a major advantage of this method.

Vu and Vohradsky directly used sigmoidal function (4.1) as $f(\cdot)$ to model gene expression [VuT07]. The target gene expression profile is believed to result from the regulation action of the upstream TF, and each putative regulator is applied in the model to estimate the transcription pattern of a target gene i by minimizing the following deviation function

$$E = \frac{1}{Q} \sum_{t=1}^{Q} [x_i(t) - x_i^c(t)]^2$$

where $x_i(t)$ is the expression profile of gene i and $x_i^c(t)$ denotes the reconstructed profile of target gene i through differential equations. The two approaches described above adopt a nonlinear representation for gene regulation, which is more realistic than linear models. The limitation is that they examine TFs individually to correlate a target gene, which is not reasonable since the cooperative or competitive binding of multiple TFs is very common in gene regulation. In addition, these two approaches directly use the gene expression profile of a TF as its regulation activity, ignoring post-translational modification events.

In contrast to the sigmoidal model, the model proposed by [Nac04] adopted a regulatory function in nonlinear Michaelis–Menten form:

$$f[a(t) : \alpha, \beta] = \alpha \frac{a(t)}{\beta + a(t)} \tag{4.3}$$

where $a(t)$ denotes the concentration of active regulator protein, α is the rate of production, and β is the half-saturation constant. On the basis of this regulation function, their method, combining a dynamic Bayesian network to model regulons and a network structure learning algorithm, allows reconstruction of regulatory network structure and identification of quantitative kinetic parameters as well as regulator activity profiles simultaneously. The function (4.3) can also be extended to accommodate multiple regulators:

$$f[a_1(t), a_2(t) : \alpha, \vec{\beta}, \gamma_1, \gamma_2] = \alpha \frac{\beta_1 + \beta_2 a_1(t) + \beta_3 a_2(t) + \beta_4 a_1(t)a_2(t)}{1 + \gamma_1 a_1(t) + \gamma_2 a_2(t) + \gamma_1 \gamma_2 a_1(t)a_2(t)} \tag{4.4}$$

In addition, the stochastic differential equation (SDE), which is suitable for modeling irregular motion, variability, or uncertainty due to time series, has also been used to model TRN [ChK05, Cli07]. Chen et al. applied SDE to model the irregular patterns of time-continuous gene expression datasets and the transcriptional process of a target gene [ChK05]:

$$\frac{N_{t+\Delta t} - N_t}{N_t} = \frac{\Delta N_t}{N_t} = (g_t - \lambda)\Delta t + \varepsilon_{t,\Delta t} \tag{4.5}$$

where N_t denotes the exact amount of mRNA for the target gene at time t, g_t is the transcription rate, λ is the degradation rate, and $\varepsilon_{t,\Delta t}$ is the noise or random error captured by normal distribution with zero mean and variance in proportion to Δt. Generally, N_t cannot be measured directly. Let X_t denote the expression level of the gene and assume that $X_t = \log N_t$. Chen et al. adopted sigmoid regulatory functions f_i and assumed $g_t = c_0^* + \sum_{i=1}^{n} c_i f_i(X_{it})$ [ChK05]. Hence, the SDE for the dynamic gene regulation process is depicted by the generalized linear model

$$dX_t = \left[c_0 + \sum_{i=1}^{n} c_i f_i(X_{it}) \right] + \sigma dW_t \tag{4.6}$$

where W_t is the standard Brownian motion representing the source of uncertainty of random error. $c_0 = c_0^* - \lambda - \sigma^2/2$, and c_i is the contribution of regulator i to the transcription of the gene. On the basis of this linear model, a log-likelihood function is defined and the transcription rate of each target gene is associated with the regulatory functions of selected regulators resulting in the highest log-likelihood. The contributions of these selected regulators are estimated simultaneously. Climescu-Haulica and Quirk [Cli07] generalized the sigmoid regulatory functions in (4.6) into beta sigmoid functions that can keep track of the local temporal patterns of regulators and enhance the Chen group's results [ChK05]. In addition, Heron et al. used stochastic differential equations to model gene regulation and presented a Bayesian method for the inference of the Hes1 regulatory networks [Her07].

4.2.2 Bayesian Approaches

As in other fields of bioinformatics and systems biology, Bayesian methods also play an important role in reconstructing transcriptional regulatory networks. For example, Sun et al. adopted a loglinear model to describe the relationships between gene expression levels, transcription interactions and TF activities [Sun06]:

$$\frac{x_i(t)}{x_i(0)} = \prod_{j=1}^{c} \left(\frac{a_j(t)}{a_j(0)} \right)^{J_{ij}} \tag{4.7}$$

This can be seen as the steady-state or quasiequilibrium form of model (2.2). They built a Bayesian error analysis model to estimate the regulation matrix and transcription activity alternately by a Markov chain Monto Carlo (MCMC) algorithm. This loglinear model actually stems from a series of biochemical reactions occurring in the transcription regulation of a gene. They modeled mRNA regulation as a closed reacting system involving proteins, chromosomses, nucleotide bases, mRNA, and other intermediate species. The processes of TFs binding DNA sequence and recruiting RNA polymerase onto the promoter region of DNA are assumed to be accomplished by a set of reversible reactions. With an assumption that all reversible reactions reach equilibrium, an overall chemical reaction stoichiometry of transcription initiation is given in the chemical equation

$$[DNA_i] + J_{i1}[TF_1] + \cdots + J_{ic}[TF_c] + [PolII]$$
$$= [DNA_i(TF_1)_{J_{i1}} \cdots (TF_c)_{J_{ic}} PolII]$$

where there are a total of c TFs as regulators of gene i, the stoichiometric coefficient J_{ij} represents the effective abundance of bound TF_j involved in the regulation of gene i, and DNA_i is the sequence of gene i. PolII denotes the RNA polymerase II complex. The product of transcription initiation is $[DNA_i(TF_1)_{J_{i1}} \cdots (TF_c)_{J_{ic}} PolII]$, which is an immobilized compound. By assuming that there are sufficient RNA polymerase II complexes in cells and that the system attains the equilibrium state, the law of mass action in biochemistry leads to the following equation:

$$[DNA_i(TF_1)_{J_{i1}} \cdots (TF_c)_{J_{ic}} PolII] \propto \prod_j [TF_j]^{J_{ij}}$$

DNA bases are assumed to be sufficient, so that the mRNA synthesis rate reaches maximum value. With the quasi-steady-state assumption for mRNA synthesis and degradation, the following equation

$$\text{mRNA} \propto [\text{DNA}_i(\text{TF}_1)_{J_{i1}} \cdots (\text{TF}_c)_{J_{ic}} \text{PolII}]$$

leads to the loglinear model (4.7) in which $x_i(t) = [\text{mRNA}_i]_t$, $x_i(0) = [\text{mRNA}_i]_0$, $a_j(t) = [\text{TF}_j]_t$, $a_j(0) = [\text{TF}_j]_0$. Since microarray data are noisy and the biological system is intrinsically stochastic, Sun et al. developed a Bayesian hierarchical model to incorporate measurement errors in both protein–DNA-binding data and gene expression data, and used MCMC to infer model parameters [Sun06].

Sabatti and James developed a method capable of integrating literature information, DNA sequences, and expression profiles (Fig. 4.2) [Sab06]. They used literature information to determine a set of related transcription factors and employed DNA sequence data to identify potential target genes, which can result in a prior distribution on the topology of the regulatory network. Then, loglinear model (4.7) was utilized and a Bayesian hidden component model was built on gene expression data to obtain a posterior topology of regulatory network and regulation strength as well as TF activity profiles. A major advantage of this method is its ability to reconstruct regulatory

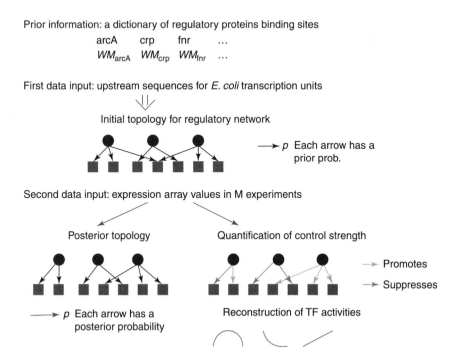

Figure 4.2. Reconstructing transcriptional regulatory networks by integrating DNA sequence and gene expression information. (Reprinted from [Sab06] © 2006 by permission of Oxford University Press.)

networks and TF activities in the studied conditions simultaneously. Hackney et al. studied transcription regulatory networks in a nonmodel organism *Entamoeba histolytica* [Hac07]. In contrast to using gene expression profiles, they primarily adopted *E. histolytica* genome sequences and used a naive Bayesian classifier to identify promoter motifs, according to which transcription regulatory relations in *E. histolytica* were constructed. Other applications of Bayesian methods in TRN can be found in papers by Beal et al. [Bea05] and Geier et al. [Gei07].

4.2.3 Data Mining and Other Methods

Generally, from a computational perspective, inferring transcription regulatory networks is much more complicated than inferring gene networks because the former involves determination of specific transcription factors and their activities. Therefore, the inference methods for TRN are diverse. In addition to differential equation approaches and Bayesian approaches, many other methods are used, including data mining and factor analysis. For example, Qian et al. used the support vector machine (SVM) to predict the targets of a transcription factor on the basis of their expression profiles [Qia03]. Dai et al. utilized gene coexpression information to convert biological sequences into reverse-complementary position-sensitive n-gram profiles [Dai07], according to which SVM is trained to build prediction models. Yu and Li adopted a factor analysis model taking the form of $X = LY + E$ to relate TF–gene interactions with transcript abundance [YuT05]. This model is actually linear or loglinear in terms of the expression of target genes and the activity of TFs. To make the model identifiable from gene expression data, a prior sparse connection matrix is used to guide the loading matrix L. They developed a matrix factorization-like method that allows one to estimate both the regulation matrix and TF activity profiles through an alternating least-squares procedure. Haverty et al. developed a TRN inference technique by combining microarray gene expression data and promoter sequences [Hav04], which can identify the transcription factors in response to a stimulus as well as their target genes. Gao et al. presented a method to determine TRNs by combining microarray mRNA expression and transcription factor binding data [Gao04]. In their method, first, the activity of each transcription factor f is estimated by multivariate regression analysis

$$E_{gt} = F_{0t} + \sum_f F_{ft} B_{fg}$$

from the mRNA expression E_{gt} of its target gene g and ChIP log–ratio B_{fg}, where the regression coefficients F_{ft} can be interpreted as inferred TF activities. Next, the regulation strength of each TF for each target gene is determined by the Pearson correlation coefficient $r(f, g)$ across different conditions between TF activity and the mRNA expression of the target gene, with an associated p-value computed by performing a t-test. Note that in this method the regression model has an implicit assumption that the roles of multiple TFs for a common target gene are independent and additive. In addition, Barrett and Palsson developed an algorithm that iteratively combines a computational procedure and an experimental procedure for constructing TRN [BaC06]. It utilizes a mathematical model to integrate a reconstructed metabolic network with a partially inferred TRN[BaC06] to identify the experiment designs with the highest potential of yielding the most new regulatory knowledge. Sayyed-Ahmad et al. presented a method for integrating gene expression microarray data and cell modeling through information theory to construct the network of cellular processes [Say07], which is also able to infer TF activities.

More approaches to identify regulators and infer TRN have been discussed [Gao04, Qia03]. Although knowledge of gene regulation has been accumulated quickly, current studies on the effects of posttranslational modifications and competitive binding of multiple TFs are in the initial stages. It is still a difficult task to quantify the effects of these biological events [Too05]. More elaborated formulations incorporating these mechanisms are needed to make the inference of TRN more realistic in the future. In addition, with an increasing number of noncoding RNA (ncRNA) shown to regulate critical pathways in prokaryotes and eukaryotes, quantitative characterization of their regulation roles in gene expression is becoming a new and important trend [Lev07, Shi07].

4.3 IDENTIFYING COMBINATORIAL REGULATIONS OF TFS

As mentioned in previous sections, even in prokaryotes, a gene may contain binding sites for multiple TFs in its promoter region. Research on transcriptional regulation indicates that combinatorial regulation mechanism is common in gene regulation, which implies that the combinations of even a small number of ubiquitous TFs are able to execute a large number of regulatory processes [Rem04]. Generally, one or more TFs recruit specific proteins together to mediate the regulation of a target gene, which implies the cooperativity between binding sites. In addition, there may be competitive binding when multiple TFs simultaneously interact with the promoter region of a target [Gib04] (see Fig. 4.3). Precisely elucidating transcriptional control is an important and challenging topic in studying gene expression and regulation. Integrating such detailed cooperative and competitive mechanisms of TFs in mathematically modeled gene regulation will make the reconstruction of TRN more realistic and practical in applications. Genomewide location technique (ChIP-chip) has been developed to measure physical interactions between TFs and their target genes [Har04, LeT02]. Although it can be used to identify possible functional TF-binding sites, it does not provide the coregulation information of multiple TFs. With the increasing availability of transcription data, such as Genomewide gene expression data, ChIP-chip binding data as well as *cis*-regulatory elements, many more recent studies have begun to explore the combinatorial control of multiple TFs in gene regulatory from a computational viewpoint, with some of them focusing on TF cooperation mechanisms and others considering general combinatorial control rules.

An early study on this topic is the expression coherence method [Pil01], in which an expression coherence (EC) score for each motif (binding site) or motif combination EC is defined as p/P, where p is the number of gene pairs whose Euclidean distance

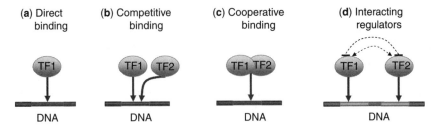

Figure 4.3. Combinatorial control in gene regulation: (a) TF1 binds directly to the motif; (b) TF1 and TF2 competitively bind to the motif; (c) TF1 and TF2 cooperatively bind to the motif; (d) two TFs respectively bind two binding sites but undergo active or repressive interactions.

is smaller than a threshold distance, and $P = K(K - 1)/2$, where K is the number of genes containing a particular motif or motif combination in their promoters. Then, the synergy of motif combinations is identified by comparing the expression coherence of genes defined by different motif combinations. In a motif combination containing two motifs, motifs A and B are considered to be "synergistic" or "cooperative" if genes containing these motifs have a significantly higher expression coherence score than do the genes containing motif A but not motif B and the genes containing motif B but not motif A. Figure 4.4 illustrates an example of expression coherence. Banerjee and Zhang integrated ChIP-chip data and gene expression data and developed a significance measure based on multivariate hypergeometric distribution for evaluating the cooperativity between two TFs according to the coexpression patterns of their target gene pairs [Ban03]

$$P = 1 - \sum_{x_{ab} < m_{ab}} \frac{\binom{n_a}{x_a} \binom{n_{ab}}{x_{ab}} \binom{n_b}{x_b}}{\binom{N}{M}} \tag{4.8}$$

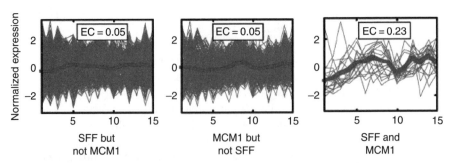

Figure 4.4. Expression profiles of genes containing the motifs Mcm1 and/or SFF. (Reprinted by permission from Macmillan Publishers Ltd: Nature Genetics [Pil01], © 2001.)

where

$$\binom{N}{M} = \frac{N!}{M!(N-M)!}$$

n_a is the number of gene pairs in the target set of TF1 (excluding the target genes of TF2), n_b is the number of gene pairs in the target set of TF2 (excluding the target genes of TF1), and n_{ab} is the number of gene pairs in the common target set of TF1 and TF2; m_a, m_b, m_{ab} are respectively the number of coexpressed gene pairs in these sets; and $N = n_a + n_b + n_{ab}$, $M = m_a + m_b + m_{ab} = x_a + x_b + x_{ab}$. This measure assumes that a combination of TFs is cooperative if the average expression correlation score of genes showing binding of both TFs is significantly greater than any set of genes with binding of either TF alone. Therefore, the rationale underlying this significance measure is consistent with that in the expression coherence method. Nagamine et al. adopted a similar idea for classifying the target genes of a TF pair into three sets [Nag05]. They claimed that genes encoding proteins that contribute to the same biological processes tend to be regulated by the same control mechanism, and proteins controlled by two cooperative TFs must be much closer to each other in protein interaction networks. Instead of using gene expression data, they used the topology of protein interaction networks to measure the extended Czekanowski–Dice distance of two proteins i and j

$$D(i, j) = \min_k D_I(i, j, k)$$

where

$$D_I(i, j, l) = \frac{\sum_{k=1}^{l} 1/k[|\text{Int}_k(i)| + |\text{Int}_k(j)|] - 2\sum_{n=1}^{l}\sum_{m=1}^{l}[2/(m+n)]|\text{Int}_m(j) \cap \text{Int}_n(j)|}{\sum_{k=1}^{l} 1/k[|\text{Int}_k(i)| + |\text{Int}_k(j)|]},$$

$\text{Int}_k(i)$ is a list (or set) of proteins whose shortest path length from the protein i is equal to k, and l denotes the range of the shortest path length to be considered. $D_I(i, j, l)$ is equal to the original Czekanowski–Dice distance. Then the p value of the Mann–Whitney U test is adopted to examine the significance of the fact that the overlap target gene set has a shorter median distance of interacting protein pairs. In addition to protein interaction data, cellular localization data and function data are also combined into the distance measure to overcome the false positives in protein interaction data. It is worth noting that this method allows prediction of cooperative TF triads and cooperative TF modules. In a similar spirit, Zhu et al. proposed a computational method for determining TF combinations by using phylogenetically conserved sequences and gene expression data [ZhZ05]. With this method, they also used the expression coherence score [Pil01] to quantify the similarity of expression profiles within a given set of genes and adopted a model based on multivariate hypergeometric distribution as in the Banerjee–Zhang paper [Ban03] to measure the overrepresentation of neighboring motifs, resulting in more coherent expression profiles. In addition, Tsai et al. directly selected TF pairs with significant associations by comparing the number of their common target genes with random expectation [Tsa05]. For these TF pairs, they further applied the analysis of variance (ANOVA) test to determine synergistic ones.

Except for the statistical significance measures for TF cooperativity, there are many other kinds of methods. For example, a multivariate adaptive regression splines model was used to correlate the occurrences of TF binding motifs in the promoter DNA and their interactions to the logarithm of the ratio of gene expression levels, which can detect both the individual motifs and synergistic pairs of motifs Das et al., 2004 [Das04]. A dynamic model has also been utilized to identify the synergy of multiple TFs [Cha06]. In that study, a stochastic discrete dynamic model of regulatory networks with a cooperativity term for TF pairs was established

$$x(t + 1) = ax(t) + \sum_{i=1}^{N} b_i f_i[x_i(t)] + \sum_{i=1}^{N-1} \sum_{j=i+1}^{N-1} c_{ij} f_{ij}[x_i(t) \cdot x_j(t)] + k + \varepsilon(t)$$

where $x(t)$ represents the mRNA expression level of the target gene at timepoint t and the parameter a indicates the effect of the present state $x(t)$ to the next state $x(t + 1)$. b_i indicates the regulatory ability of the ith TF whose regulatory function is a sigmoid function. k represents the basal level from other factors, and $\varepsilon(t)$ denotes a stochastic noise. c_{ij} denotes the regulatory ability of the cooperative TFs i and j. N denotes the number of TFs binding to the target gene. By a system identification method, the regulatory coefficients can be inferred including c_{ij}, which indicates the possible TF cooperativity. A p value is designed to measure the obtained putative cooperative TF pairs. Balaji et al. used a network transformation procedure to create a pairwise coregulatory network from yeast TRN, and analyzed combinatorial regulation among multiple TFs [Bal03]. Such a coregulatory network describes a set of all significant associations among TFs in regulating common target genes. In contrast to the methods using ChIP-chip data by simply setting a threshold on binding p values, Datta and Zhao used a loglinear model to study the cooperative binding between TFs [Dat08]. This model does not distinguish between dependent and independent variables and thus can accommodate the statistical evidence of TF binding and the cooperativity among multiple TFs by checking the mutual association between different response variables. An EM algorithm was adopted to estimate true TF bindings from the p values of ChIP-chip data.

These methods are used mainly for identifying cooperation mechanisms of two TFs in gene regulation. More recently, a method for selecting proper statistical thermodynamic models was proposed [Che08], which can determine all possible combinatorial natures of multiple TFs in transcription regulation; multiple TFs are either independent, cooperative, or competitive. Specifically, this method begins with predicting the equilibrium probability that RNA polymerase (RNAP) binds to the promoter of its targeted gene according to concentrations of associated TFs, and the interaction among TFs and RNAP. According to the number of TFs binding to the promoter, the equilibrium probability can be found in the following forms for zero TF with one binding site

$$Pr[\text{RNAP}_{\text{binding}}] = \frac{p_0}{1 + p_0}$$

or for one TF with one binding site

$$Pr[\text{RNAP}_{\text{binding}}] = \frac{p_0 + w_{11}p_0p_1}{1 + p_0 + p_1 + w_{11}p_0p_1}$$

or for two TFs with one binding site

$$Pr[\text{RNAP}_{\text{binding}}] = \frac{p_0 + w_{110}p_0p_1 + w_{101}p_0p_2 + w_{111}p_0p_1p_2}{1 + p_0 + p_1 + p_2 + w_{110}p_0p_1 + w_{101}p_0p_2}$$
$$+ w_{011}p_1p_2 + w_{111}p_0p_1p_2$$

where p_0 denotes the ratio of the probability of promoter bound by RNAP to unbound by RNAP, p_1 (p_2 respectively) denotes the ratio of the probability of promoter bound by TF1 (TF2), assuming that the weight of promoter with no TF1 (TF2) is 1 $w_{110}, w_{101},$ w_{011}, w_{111} are kinetic parameters. w_{110} and w_{101} represent the interaction between each TF and RNAP, respectively. w_{011} denotes the interaction between the two TFs. w_{111} represents the effect of the interaction among RNAP and the two TFs.

Generally, if there are m TFs, and TFj has s_j binding sites for the gene of interest, where $j = 1, \ldots, m$, and TF0 represents RNAP (i.e., p_0), then the equilibrium probability can be expressed as

$$Pr[\text{RNAP}_{\text{binding}}] = \frac{\sum_{q_1=0,\ldots,q_m=0}^{s_1,\ldots,s_m} w(1, q_1, \ldots, q_m)p_0p_1^{q_1}\cdots p_m^{q_m}}{1 + \sum_{q_0=0}^{1}\sum_{q_1=0,\ldots,q_m=0}^{s_1,\ldots,s_m} w(q_0, q_1, \ldots, q_m)p_0^{q_0}p_1^{q_1}\cdots p_m^{q_m}}$$

Clearly, the denominator represents all combination terms among TFs and RNAP, whereas the numerator contains the combination terms with only nonzero RNAP p_0 that ensure the transcription or synthesis of the RNA. $w(q_0, q_1, \ldots, q_m)$ are parameters representing the effects of interactions among molecules $p_0, p_1, \ldots, p_m$. Actually, the power of chemical species i or TFi is simply the number of molecules of TFi present in that configuration. For instance, if the molecule i is a dimer and occupies three binding sites at a specific configuration, it should be expressed in $p_i^{2\times3} = p_i^6$ in terms of monomer p_i. Figure 4.5 is an illustrative example of one TF with two binding sites, where clearly there are total eight combinations among two binding sites and RNAP binding. mRNA is synthesized with the four cases or states, namely, parts (b), (e), (f), and (g) in Figure 4.5 with RNAP binding.

A TF can serve as either an activator or a repressor, or does not interact with the RNAP, simulated by choosing appropriate parameters w. Similarly, the probability of RNAP binding under different forms of interactions among RNAP and the

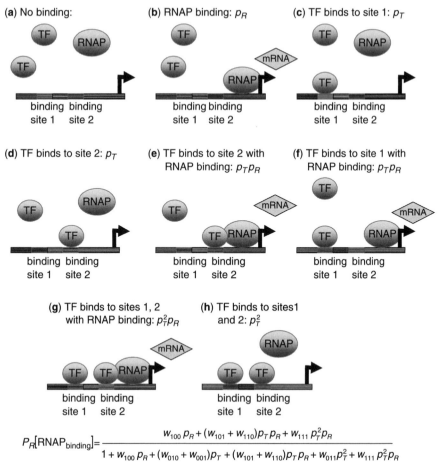

$$P_R[\text{RNAP}_{\text{binding}}] = \frac{w_{100}\, p_R + (w_{101} + w_{110})p_T p_R + w_{111}\, p_T^2 p_R}{1 + w_{100}\, p_R + (w_{010} + w_{001})p_T + (w_{101} + w_{110})p_T p_R + w_{011}p_T^2 + w_{111}\, p_T^2 p_R}$$

Figure 4.5. An illustrative example of a thermodynamic model for one TF with two binding sites.

two TFs can be obtained by adjusting the parameters w. Then, a system of ordinary differential equations is used to simulate the expression dynamics of interested genes:

$$\frac{dx(t)}{dt} = K_s\, Pr[\text{RNAP}_{\text{binding}}] - K_d\, x(t) \qquad (4.9)$$

Finally, the Pearson correlation coefficients between the observed expression pattern and the predicted expression pattern are computed to select a proper thermodynamic model, according to which combinatorial nature of TFs can be implied. In this method, the concentration of a TF is directly replaced by its mRNA level. Nevertheless, the nonlinear regulatory model here is more biologically plausible than linear ones.

The above mentioned work focuses mainly on determining the combinatorial regulation mechanisms in gene expression. With more and more tools for inferring TRN available, how to incorporate such combinatorial mechanisms into regulatory networks is clearly an interesting but challenging topic.

4.4 INFERRING COOPERATIVE REGULATORY NETWORKS

Although much research has been contributed for inferring TRNs, there are two main limits in the current methods. One is that most existing algorithms for inferring transcription regulatory networks from gene expression data implicitly require that the activities of TFs be linearly proportional to their mRNA levels. As is well known to us, this assumption is not biologically reasonable due to various posttranslational modifications and nonlinear interactions between TFs before binding to DNA sequences [Bou05]. On the other hand, as described in the last section, combinatorial regulation of multiple TFs is widespread. Except for the cooperativity among different TFs, one or more TFs usually recruit other proteins (e.g., cofactors) to form a transcription complex (TC) and regulate transcriptional reaction processes together. Therefore, the activity of a TF (TFA) can be viewed as a nonlinear function with respect to the gene expression levels of the TF and its cooperative proteins in the TC instead of the mRNA level of a single constituent gene. Incorporating the cooperation mechanisms in gene regulation into network inference methods will overcome the existing limits and make the inferred transcription regulatory networks more biologically meaningful.

Actually, inferring cooperative regulatory networks is a new trend. For example, Elati et al. proposed a data-mining system for inferring cooperative TRN from gene expression data [Ela07]. By mining candidate coregulator sets for each target gene, their method is also suitable for the detection of cooperative regulation. Regulatory relationships are modeled as a labeled two-layer regulatory network, and then a three-step heuristic approach is developed to learn TRN from expression datasets. Roy et al. developed a software system called RENCO for automatically generating transcription regulatory networks with combinatorial control of transcription by explicitly modeling protein–protein interactions among transcription factors [Roy08]. A method based on transcription complexes and the law of mass action has been developed [WaR07a] that can detect the direct regulations not only between TFs and target genes but also between coregulating proteins and target genes. Unlike other approaches, this method is based not on individual TFs but on transcription complexes, thereby reconstructing the TRN in a more accurate and reliable manner from a biological perspective. This method can adopt either a linear model or a sigmoidal model. The inference process based on both models can be formulated as a linear programming (LP) problem that scales up well to large-scale networks. Next we will introduce this method in detail.

4.4.1 Mathematical Models

Generally, transcriptional regulations are nonlinear; for instance, $f(\cdot) = [f_1(\cdot), \ldots, f_m(\cdot)]^T$ in equation (2.2) is a nonlinear vector function. However, because of the complex and unclear structures of biological systems, linear or additive models are often adopted. If the first-order approximation of f is adopted, the linear form of (2.2) is

$$\dot{x}(t) = Ja(t) + b(t) \tag{4.10}$$

where $x(t) = [x_1(t), \ldots, x_m(t)]^T$ denotes the expression levels of m genes, and $a(t) = [a_1(t), \ldots, a_c(t)]$ denotes the activity levels of TFs that are generally functions of x. $J = [J_{ij}]_{m \times c} = \partial f(a)/\partial a$ is an $m \times c$ Jacobian matrix or connection matrix. In the model, $J_{ij} > 0$ indicates that TFj is an activator of gene i, $J_{ij} < 0$ indicates that TFj is a repressor of gene i and $J_{ij} = 0$ indicates that TFj does not regulate gene i. $b(t) = [b_1(t) - k_1 x_1(t), \ldots, b_n(t) - k_n x_n(t)]$ is a vector representing the external stimuli or environment conditions with self-degradations. b_i is set to zero when there is no external input. Model (4.10) can be rewritten into the following matrix form

$$\dot{X} = JA + B \tag{4.11}$$

where $\dot{X} = [\dot{x}(t_1), \ldots, \dot{x}(t_n)]$ and $B = [b(t_1), \ldots, b(t_n)]$ are $m \times n$ matrices, and $A = [a(t_1), \ldots, a(t_n)]$ is a $c \times n$ matrix.

Although linear models are simple and easy to implement, biological systems are inherently nonlinear and show multiple stability and nonlinear oscillation that may not be appropriately expressed by a linear model of f. With this consideration, as mentioned in Section 4.2, sigmoid function (4.1) is often adopted as a regulatory function f. Therefore, a transcription regulatory network can be expressed by a set of nonlinear differential equations with gene expression levels and TFAs as variables in the following form

$$\dot{X} = \frac{1}{\alpha + \exp\{-(JA + B)\}} - KX = f(A) - KX \tag{4.12}$$

which denotes a nonlinear transcriptional regulatory network. In addition, note that both model (4.11) and model (4.12) are dynamic systems. When these systems converge to an equilibrium (i.e., $\dot{X} = 0$), it follows $X = K^{-1}f(A)$, where f is a linear or sigmoid function. Loglinear model (4.7) can be used to model the steady-state gene expression data, which can be written in the following matrix form after taking the logarithm

$$\log X = J \log A \tag{4.13}$$

where X and A are the timecourses of relative gene expression levels and TFAs, respectively.

4.4.2 Estimating TF Activity

Various biological events occur during the whole process of gene expression, where posttranslational modifications can affect the concentrations of TFs. Because of such modifications, TF activity levels may be not proportional to the mRNA levels. Hence, the TF activity cannot be measured directly by a standard microarray experiment. On the other hand, a transcription reaction is seldom mediated by a sole TF. In the transcription process, several TFs and proteins combined as a protein transcription complex (TC) cooperatively regulate the expression of a gene. However, although ChIP-chip technique can detect possible target genes occupied by TFs, coregulating

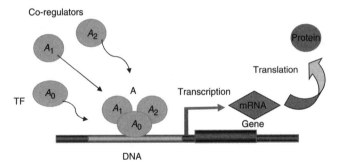

Figure 4.6. Illustration of a transcription complex participating in a transcription process. (Reprinted from [WaR07a] © 2007 by permission of Oxford University Press.)

proteins cannot be detected by ChIP-chip technique because they are non-DNA-binding proteins, despite their similar roles in regulating the target gene as TFs. Wang et al. used transcription complexes from databases to estimate the TF activities on the basis of the law of mass action [WaR07a]. A transcription complex is formed through a series of elementary biochemical reactions. This reaction mechanism obeys the law of mass action, which means that the rate of any given elementary reaction is proportional to the product of the concentrations of the reactants [Cra04, SrJ07]. The TFA profiles can be estimated from the protein composition of TCs and the expression levels of individual genes.

Figure 4.6 gives a small example, where the transcription complex A is formed from TF A_0 and proteins A_1, A_2 which take part in the transcription process of the gene. Assume that the following general chemical reaction accounts for the formation of A:

$$A_0 + A_1 + A_2 \underset{k_{-1}}{\overset{k_1}{\rightleftharpoons}} A \tag{4.14}$$

where k_1 and k_{-1} are the rate constants for the forward and backward reactions. According to the law of mass action, the velocities of the preceding reactions can be given by

$$v_1(t) = k_1 a_0(t) a_1(t) a_2(t), \quad v_{-1}(t) = k_{-1} a(t)$$

where a_0, a_1, a_2, and a are the concentrations of reactants A_0, A_1, A_2, and A, respectively. Most reactions involve a number of simultaneous elementary steps. As indicated by Crampina et al. [Cra04], the rate of change of the concentration of any given reactant is the sum of the rates of change due to the elementary reactions in which that reactant participates. Therefore, the governing equations of the reactions (4.14) are given by

$$\frac{da_i(t)}{dt} = -k_1 a_0(t) a_1(t) a_2(t) + k_{-1} a(t)$$

$$\frac{da(t)}{dt} = k_1 a_0(t) a_1(t) a_2(t) - k_{-1} a(t) \tag{4.15}$$

where $i = 0, 1, 2$. Let x_0, x_1, x_2, x represent the mRNA expression levels of the encoding genes of proteins A_0, A_1, A_2, A. As we all know, the concentrations a_0, a_1, a_2 of individual proteins A_0, A_1, A_2 before various posttranslational modifications are proportional to their mRNA expression levels, that is, $a_i \propto x_i$. Assuming that the reactions generating a are much faster than the reactions synthesizing x and can reach an equilibrium very quickly, the activity level a of A (represented by the activity of TF A_0) can be given approximately by

$$a(t) = k_0 a_0(t) a_1(t) a_2(t) \approx k x_0(t) x_1(t) x_2(t) \qquad (4.16)$$

From equation (4.16) we can see that the overall activity a of TF A_0 after recruiting proteins A_1 and A_2 is not simply proportional to its gene expression level x_0 but dependent on all the expression levels x_i of individual genes in the TC.

4.4.3 Linear Programming Models

Like the reverse engineering of gene regulatory networks, inferring TRN from experimental data based on differential equations is to find a solution J as consistent to (4.11) as possible. Wang et al. presented a linear programming framework that can accommodate multiple datasets simultaneously [WaR07a]. Assume that there are multiple datasets available for one organism and that X^k denotes the kth gene expression dataset of size $(m \times n_k)$, $k = 1, 2, \ldots, L$ and A^k denotes the kth activity dataset of TF complexes of size $(c \times n_k)$ that can be estimated by the method described in the last of Section 4.4.2. According to the differential equation (4.11) with the degradation term ignored, network inference based on LP is to find an $m \times c$ regulation matrix J so as to satisfy all the equalities $\dot{X}^k = JA^k$. Because of the noise in experimental datasets, there may not exist a solution satisfying all of the equalities presented above. A natural way is to find a connection matrix J that minimizes the total errors

$$\min_J \sum_{k=1}^{L} |\dot{X}^k - JA^k| + \lambda|J| \qquad (4.17)$$

where the first term is to minimize the error between real data and the reconstructed model, and the second term is the sparsity term, which forces J sparse by using L_1 norm. λ is a positive parameter that balances the error and sparsity terms in the objective function. Equation (4.17) is an optimization problem with positive combination of L_1 norm of variables J_{ij}, which can be transformed into a LP problem through a well-known procedure. Specifically, the model (4.17) is equivalent to

$$\min_{J_{ij}} \sum_{k=1}^{K} \sum_{i=1}^{m} \sum_{j=1}^{n_k} \left| \dot{X}_{ij}^k - \sum_{l=1}^{c} J_{il} A_{lj}^k \right| + \lambda \sum_{i=1}^{m} \sum_{l=1}^{c} |J_{il}| \qquad (4.18)$$

Letting $J_{il} = u_{il} - v_{il}$ and $\dot{X}_{ij}^k - \sum_{l=1}^{c} J_{il}A_{lj}^k = w_{ij}^k - s_{ij}^k$, then the model given above is equivalent to

$$\min_{w,s,u,v} \sum_{k=1}^{K}\sum_{i=1}^{m}\sum_{j=1}^{n_k} (w_{ij}^k + s_{ij}^k) + \lambda \sum_{i=1}^{m}\sum_{l=1}^{c} (u_{il} + v_{il})$$

$$\text{s.t.} \quad \sum_{l=1}^{c} (u_{il} - v_{il})A_{lj}^k + w_{ij}^k - s_{ij}^k = \dot{X}_{ij}^k \quad \text{for} \quad i, j, k \qquad (4.19)$$

$$w_{ij}^k, s_{ij}^k, u_{il}, v_{il} \geq 0$$

which is a linear programming model and can be solved efficiently for a global optimal solution. Because of L_1 norm, the optimal solution of (4.17) has as many zeros for the elements of the matrices $\dot{X}^k - JA^k$ and J as possible, which exactly serves the purpose of finding a consistent and sparse network.

For the sigmoidal nonlinear model of the TRN (4.12), inferring the nonlinear TRN can also be achieved by a similar LP model

$$\min_{J} \sum_{k=1}^{K} |f^{-1}(\dot{X}^k + KX^k) - JA^k| + \lambda|J| \qquad (4.20)$$

where f^{-1} is the inverse function of the sigmoid function. For the loglinear static model (4.13), an LP problem in the same framework can be obtained:

$$\min_{J} \sum_{k=1}^{L} |\log X^k - J \log A^k| + \lambda|J| \qquad (4.21)$$

Similarly, the models (4.20) and (4.21) can be transformed into linear programming in the same way as (4.19).

Network inference involves deriving the $m \times c$ elements of J, which is the strength matrix of the regulatory interactions between TFs and target genes. The software implemented by FORTRAN is called TRNinfer [WaR07a] and available from http://intelligent.eic.osaka-sandai.ac.jp/chenen/TRNinfer.html, http://www.isb.shu.edu.cn.

4.4.4 Numerical Validation

TRNinfer was tested on both simulated and experimental data [WaR07a]. The transcription activity of a TF is approximated by the corresponding transcription complex (TC) on the basis of the expression levels of individual genes through the law of mass action, and the data of TCs were collected from MIPS database [Mew06]. In the budding yeast *S. cerevisiae*, ChIP-chip experiments have been utilized to elucidate the binding interactions between 6270 genes and 113 TFs [LeT02], among which 26 TFs are contained in protein transcription complexes. Among these 26 TFs, some are related to yeast cell cycle [Spe98] and some are related to polyphosphate metabolism in *S. cerevisiae* [OgN00]. TRNinfer was tested on these two datasets.

TABLE 4.4. TFs Related to Yeast Cell Cycle and Their Transcription Complexes

TFs	TCs	Protein Members
MBP1	510.190.70	MBP1 SWI6
MCM1	510.190.120	ARG82 ARG81 ARG80 MCM1
STB1	510.190.150	STB2 STB1 RPD3 SIN3
SWI4	510.190.60	SWI4 SWI6
SWI6	510.190.60	SWI4 SWI6

4.4.4.1 Yeast Cell Cycle Data According to the ChIP-chip experiments [LeT02], 11 TFs are known to be related to cell cycle regulation, among which 5 TFs are contained in four different TCs. The details of these TFs and their TCs are given in Table 4.4. Except these five TFs, eight genes that are closely related to cell cycle according to their function information were selected. Four datasets with the number of timepoints 18, 17, 24, and 14 respectively from the gene expression data in Spellman et al. [Spe98] were utilized.

TRNinfer was applied to the above datasets and obtained a transcription regulatory connection matrix that characterizes the interactions between target genes and TFs (i.e., TCs). The corresponding transcription regulatory network is shown in Figure 4.7, where the bold edges indicate regulatory relations confirmed by documented information and the thin edges indicate potential regulations. The blunt arrows in the figure indicate repression, while the sharp arrows indicate activation. The

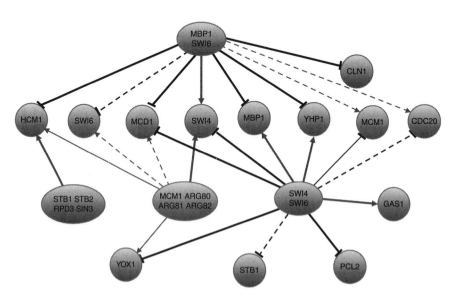

Figure 4.7. Yeast cell cycle transcriptional regulatory network. (Reprinted from [WaR07a] © 2007 by permission of Oxford University Press.)

unconfirmed inferred regulations are denoted by dashed edges. In this network, DNA-binding proteins SWI4 and SWI6 are transcription cofactors, forming a complex to regulate transcription at the G1/S transition. They are involved in several processes such as meiotic gene expression, localization regulated by phosphorylation, and potential Cdc28p substrate. SWI6 and MBP1 are believed to be involved in the same regulatory module according to many literatures. MBP1 forms a complex with SWI6 that binds to MluI cell cycle box regulatory element in promoters of DNA synthesis genes. Figure 4.7 indicates that TRNinfer can provide not only direct relations between TFs and target genes but also the interactions between coregulating proteins and target genes.

In order to justify the benefit of considering TCs, comparative experiments for three methods—LP method based on TCs, LP method based on mRNA levels of TFs, and SVD method based on mRNA levels of TFs [Yeu02]—were conducted by Wang et al. [WaR07a]. The regulations with supporting evidences in YEASTRACT are viewed as true edges (true positives), and all other regulations are viewed as true negatives. Sensitivity and specificity are used to evaluate the inference results. The results are plotted in Figure 4.8, which indicates that considering TCs can make the inference more accurate. On the other hand, it is widely believed that the activities of TFs related to the cell cycle tend to be periodic. To test the possibility of approximating TFAs by the expression levels of individual genes in TCs, of the TFs, Wichert et al. checked the periodicity of the activity levels by Fisher's g test [Wic04]. Table 4.5 lists the p values of the periodicity for the activity profiles and the gene expression profiles of some TFs, indicating that the activity profiles of these proteins show highly periodic patterns, which are consistent with common biological knowledge. In contrast, their gene expression profiles are not periodic. These results indicate that the transcription activity of a TF does not linearly correlate with the corresponding gene expression profile [Bou05, Lia03].

4.4.4.2 *Polyphosphate Metabolism Data* TRNinfer was also tested on gene expression data for polyphosphate metabolism in *S. accharomyces cerevisiae* [OgN00]. Among the TFs related to polyphosphate metabolism verified by the ChIP experiments [LeT02], there are 14 TFs in nine different transcription complexes. The details of these TFs and their TCs are given in Table 4.6. These gene expression data contain eight timepoints collectively. In total, 64 genes (including 14 TFs) form test data with a twofold change either upward or downward in at least two timepoints of the expression levels, which are believed to be closely related to polyphosphate metabolism. The inferred transcriptional regulatory network by TRNinfer has 106 links. A component with three TFs is shown in Figure 4.9, where the bold, thin, and dashed edges and arrows have the same meaning as in Figure 4.7. Genes with the same functions are denoted by the same color, and functions of the gray-colored genes are yet unknown. In this network, RTG1 and RTG3 are bHLH/Zip proteins and transcription cofactors. RTG3 forms a complex with RTG1 to activate the retrograde (RTG) and TOR pathways. Again, TRNinfer can also provide the interactions between coregulating proteins and target genes in addition to the direct relations between TFs and target genes.

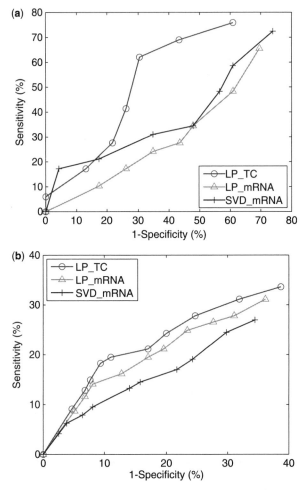

Figure 4.8. Comparison results of LP method based on TCs (LP_TC), LP method based on mRNA levels of TFs (LP_mRNA), and SVD method based on mRNA levels of TFs (SVD_mRNA): (a) on yeast cell cycle dataset; (b) on yeast polyphosphate metabolism dataset. (Reprinted from [WaR07a] © 2007 by permission of Oxford University Press.)

TABLE 4.5. p Values of Periodicity for Some TFs Related to Cell Cycle

TFs	Experimental Conditions	Expression	Activity
MBP1	alpha0min ~ alpha119min	0.525	0.003
SWI4	alpha0min ~ alpha119min	0.0064	0.00019
SWI6	alpha0min ~ alpha119min	0.367	0.00019
SWI4	cdc1510min ~ cdc15290min	0.132	0.01
SWI6	cdc1510min ~ cdc15290min	0.024	0.01

Source: Wang et al. [WaR07a].

TABLE 4.6. TFs Related to Polyphosphate Metabolism and Their Transcription Complexes

TFs	TCs	Protein Members
RTG1	510.190.130	RTG3 RTG1
RTG3	510.190.130	RTG3 RTG1
MET4	510.190.160.30	MET32 MET28 MET4
MET31	510.190.160.20	MET28 MET4 MET31
LEU3	510.190.210	LEU3
HAP5	510.160	HAP3 HAP2 HAP4 HAP5
HAP4	510.160	HAP3 HAP2 HAP4 HAP5
HAP3	510.160	HAP3 HAP2 HAP4 HAP5
GCR2	510.190.90	GCR2 GCR1
GCR1	510.190.90	GCR2 GCR1
GAL4	510.190.80	GAL3 GAL80 GAL4
CBF1	510.190.160.10	MET28 CBF1 MET4
ARG80	510.190.120	ARG81 ARG80 MCM1
ARG81	510.190.120	ARG81 ARG80 MCM1

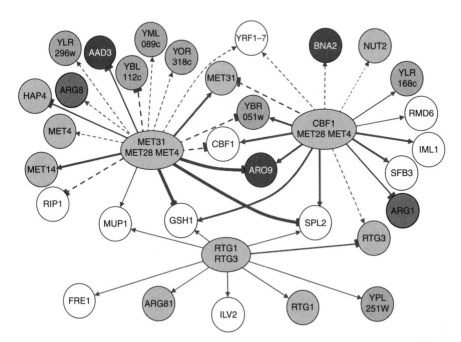

Figure 4.9. Transcription regulatory network for polyphosphate metabolism. (Reprinted from [WaR07a] © 2007 by permission of Oxford University Press.)

4.5   PREDICTION OF TRANSCRIPTION FACTOR ACTIVITY

As mentioned in Chapter 2, GRN is reconstructed based on the mRNA concentration of genes, whereas inferring TRN requires transcription factor activities (TFA), specifically, the active concentration of a TF after various posttranslational modifications such as dimerization, degradation, and phosphorylation. Most of the current methods for inferring TRN ignore posttranslational biological events in order to simplify the corresponding mathematical models; they assume that the expression level of the gene coding for a TF is an accurate proxy of the protein concentration that it produces. For some TF–gene pairs, this simplification seems reasonable. However, most posttranslational modifications definitely affect TFA [Too05], which means that mRNA abundance provides only limited information for TFA. The situation becomes even more complex in the presence of cooperativity or competition between multiple TFs that regulate a target gene [Kha07]. There is currently no reliable experiment technology for routine measurement of regulator activities. Studies on posttranslational modifications of TFs are in only the initial stages, and it is still a difficult task to quantify the effects of these biological events.

The activity of a TF determines its ability in regulating a target gene. On the other hand, the expression profiles of target genes are the regulation results of regulators and thus can provide rich information for deriving the regulator activity of their upstream TFs. Therefore, the regulator activities can be retrieved from their target gene expression profiles and the corresponding regulatory relationships. Figure 4.10 gives a general scheme for inferring TFA on the basis of the expression data of the target genes. So far, there have been many attempts to reconstruct the activity profiles of regulators from the expression data of their target genes and ChIP-chip data, including Bayesian methods [Rog07], matrix factorization [Bou05, Kao04, Lia03, LiZ06], statistical and probabilistic methods [Kha06, Kha07, San06a, San06b]. Although most of those approaches adopt a linear model of TF–gene transcription, the nonlinear model is now a new trend in this area. In this section, we briefly review computational methods for quantitatively deriving TFAs.

4.5.1   Matrix Factorization

The loglinear model (4.13) formulated from a series of biochemical reactions in the regulatory process has been widely used to define the relation between transcript abundance, TF–gene interactions, and TF activity [Sun06, Lia03, Kao04]. Such a loglinear model can be seen as the steady-state or quasiequilibrium form of model (2.2) and is suited for modeling nontimecourse datasets. This means that the expression level $x_i(t)$ of a gene is a product of an exponential function of the connection strength J_{ij} for each regulatory pair and the regulator activities $a_j(t)$. In addition, linear model (4.11) can also be used to approximately describe the dynamics of transcriptional regulatory networks. Therefore, in predicting TF activity profiles, matrix factorization methods play an important role.

Network component analysis (NCA) is the first method proposed to infer regulator activities by combining the expression data of target genes and ChIP-chip data [Lia03,

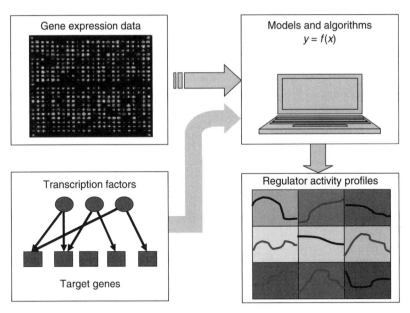

Figure 4.10. Workflow for inferring regulator activity profiles from gene expression data and ChIP-chip data [WaR07b].

Kao04]. It is actually a kind of matrix factorization scheme. Assume that the multidimensional data (here the gene expression data) are organized by an $n \times m$ matrix X with m timepoints or samples and n genes. Inferring hidden variables can be done by matrix factorization $X = JA$, where J is an $n \times c$ matrix representing the connection strength between the regulatory layer and the output signals, and A is a $c \times m$ matrix consisting of the samples of c regulatory signals (i.e., the activities of c TFs), where c is in general much smaller than n. This matrix factorization is actually not unique, which means that there may be multiple connection matrices and activity matrices that satisfy the preceding equation. Several criteria have been defined [Lia03, Kao04] by setting restrictions on the network structure J and regulator activity A to ensure the unique decomposition of the matrix X. This method uses ChIP-chip data as prior knowledge J_0 on the connection matrix and then minimizes the following objective function

$$\min_{J,A} \|X - JA\|^2 \qquad (4.22)$$

$$\text{s.t.} \quad J \in J_0 \qquad (4.23)$$

where $J \in J_0$ indicates that J must be consistent with the prior network connection pattern J_0. Then, J and A are estimated by using a two-step least-squares algorithm. Compared with independent component analysis (ICA) and principal-component analysis (PCA), which are popular methods for matrix factorization with statistical assumptions such as orthogonality or independence, NCA makes no assumption regarding the statistical properties of the regulator activity profiles and at the same time allows incorporation of prior knowledge on network structure (Fig. 4.11).

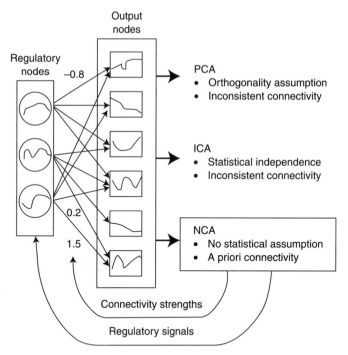

Figure 4.11. ICA, PCA, and NCA for a regulatory system in which the output data are driven by regulatory signals through a bipartite network. (Reprinted from [Lia03] © 2003 National Academy of Sciences, U.S.A.)

However, in order to ensure the existence of a unique solution, NCA establishes several criteria on the two matrices resulting from the decomposition, which limit its application for arbitrary datasets. In other words, a dataset must be reduced to satisfy the requirements of NCA. Although these criteria may ensure the existence of unique matrix decomposition, the two-step algorithm for solving matrix factorization cannot necessarily converge to this unique solution because of the notorious local minima problem.

In order to overcome the limitations of NCA mentioned just above, partial least squares (PLS) is used to extend NCA [Bou05], which offers an efficient and sound way to infer true TFAs for any given connection matrix without much restriction such as NCA. Boulesteix et al., used a linear model to relate the gene expression data to connection information [Bou05].

$$X = C + JB + E$$

where X is a data matrix for gene expression data with n genes and m samples, C is an $n \times m$ constant matrix, J is the connection matrix with n rows and c columns, and B is a $c \times m$ matrix of regression coefficients that can be interpreted as the matrix of the true TFA of the c transcription factors for each of the m samples. E is an $n \times m$ matrix containing error terms. The PLS algorithm mainly consists of several consecutive steps [Bou05]. In addition to TFA prediction, this method is also statistically sound for small samples and allows detection of functional interactions among the TFs via the notion of "meta"-transcription factors. Nguyen and D'haeseleer developed a matrix factorization method to decompose gene expression matrix, and obtained motif strength and TF activity profiles simultaneously [Ngu06]. In the algorithm, they enforced the formulated least-squares problem to ensure unique solutions by adding a sparseness term on the network structure.

Factor analysis (FA) is a statistical data reduction technique used to explain a larger number of observed variables by a smaller number of unobserved variables called the factors, by which all correlations between the observed variables are explained by common factors. It has been widely used in modeling transcription regulation, such as the state space models [San06b, LiZ06] and the probabilistic dynamical model [San06a]. Pournara and Wernisch studied factor analysis methods for predicting the protein activities of TFs [Pou07]. They explored the performance of five factor analysis algorithms on reconstructing TF activity, among which Bayesian FA methods [Wes03] allow one to infer sparse networks by enforcing sparsity through priors, and the classical FA methods [Gha97] use matrix rotation to enforce sparsity and increase the interpretability of the inferred factor loadings matrix. These factor analysis methods were further extended to incorporate existing correlation within the TF profiles and consider the sparsity present in gene regulatory networks [Pou08]. A limitation in these factor analysis methods is that they require some restrictions on the covariance matrix of data vectors. Like matrix factorization, factor analysis also assumes that the relation between target gene expression and TF activity is linear with connection matrices acting as weight parameters.

4.5.2 Nonlinear Models

In contrast to the linear models or loglinear models mentioned above, a statistical framework was developed to infer regulator activity [Kha06, Kha07], in which the Michaelis–Menten model for gene regulation was adopted

$$\dot{x}(t) = \beta \frac{a(t)}{\gamma + a(t)} + \alpha - \delta x(t)$$

where $x(t)$ is the expression profile of a regulated gene and $a(t)$ is the activity of its TF regulator, α is the basal level of gene expression production, β and δ are the rate constants of production and degradation respectively, and γ is the half-saturation constant. Then, for a single-input motif (SIM) with K target genes, a loglikelihood function is defined as

$$L_{\text{SIM}}(\Theta, \Sigma^2, a) = \prod_{k=1}^{K} L_k[x_k(t); \theta_k, \sigma_k^2, a] \qquad (4.24)$$

where Θ represents all the kinetic parameters θ_k of the Michaelis–Menten model for all genes in the SIM, and Σ^2 stands for all the scale parameters σ_k^2 of the lognormal distribution, which are also assumed to be gene-specific. $L_k[x_k(t); \theta_k, \sigma_k^2, a]$ is the gene-specific likelihood of a gene k given the observed data $x_k(t)$ and the transcription factor activity a. Finally, a conjugate gradient method in optimization theory is used to maximize the loglikelihood L_{SIM} with respect to the parameters Θ, Σ^2, and a.

Unlike the linear models, the Michaelis–Menten model is able to describe saturation effects. However, this model is appropriate only for special network motifs that consist of several target genes actively regulated by one TF (i.e., SIM). Rogers et al. extended the Khanin et al. model [Kha06, Kha07] from maximum likelihood to a Bayesian inference framework, and demonstrated the benefits of Bayesian inference, which works especially well for the limited data [Rog07]. Other related research works can be found in [BaC06]. In addition to these computational methods, it has been recognized that the knowledge and insights on posttranscriptional and posttranslational events from biological experiments, if appropriately formulated, can significantly improve the accuracy on the estimation of TFAs [ChC08].

4.6 SUMMARY

In this chapter, we introduced the most recent advances of several problems related to transcriptional regulation such as predicting TF binding sites, inferring transcriptional regulatory networks, and identifying the combinatorial regulations in gene expression as well as reconstructing regulator activities. Most of the computational methods for these problems are based on gene expression data along with ChIP-chip data. From the computational perspective, inferring transcription regulatory networks is much harder than classical gene regulatory network reverse engineering on some aspects for several reasons. For instance, for inferring a TRN, one must first determine which genes or proteins are TFs. Furthermore, it is also very difficult to measure the protein concentration levels of TFs and determine their regulatory effects on gene transcription. In particular, the effect of a TF on the transcription rate of each target is generally gene-specific. The interactions or cooperations among multiple TFs and their coregulators when they bind to the promoter region of a gene also prevent the inference of regulatory networks from being straightforward. Clearly, great progress in this field in the future requires extensive and intensive efforts from both computational and experimental aspects.

PART II

PROTEIN INTERACTION NETWORKS

CHAPTER 5

PREDICTION OF PROTEIN–PROTEIN INTERACTIONS

5.1 EXPERIMENTAL PROTEIN–PROTEIN INTERACTIONS

Many basic cellular processes such as signal transduction, transport, cellular motion, and most regulatory mechanisms are carried out not by individual proteins but by multiple proteins through molecular interactions [LiS04, Gio03]. Such interactions can be either physical or genetic interactions. Protein complexes are good examples of physical interactions in which two or more proteins form a stable functional unit. Physical interactions can be further classified as transient versus permanent interactions. Transient interactions are defined by their temporal interaction with other proteins and play a major role in signal transduction, electron cascades, and other essential physiological processes. They are the most challenging protein–protein interactions to be screened. On the other hand, many proteins are formed as permanent protein complexes by strong and stable interactions. Such permanent complexes are much easier to study, and thus many permanent interactions have been obtained from stable complexes. The case for genetic interactions is usually that one or more proteins affect the behavior of one or more other proteins without direct or physical contact. Although genetic interactions are also essential for biological mechanisms, physical interactions between proteins have been widely studied from various perspectives. In this chapter, we focus mainly on physical protein–protein interactions (PPIs).

Determining protein–protein interactions provides not only detailed functional insights into characterized proteins but also an information base for identifying biological complexes and signal transduction pathways, which is critical for

Biomolecular Networks. By Luonan Chen, Rui-Sheng Wang, and Xiang-Sun Zhang
Copyright © 2009 John Wiley & Sons, Inc.

understanding the mechanisms of biological processes at a system level. Therefore, developing both experimental and computational methods to detect and characterize protein–protein interactions is a major theme of functional genomics and proteomics. In particular, the emergence of high-throughput experimental techniques has opened up new prospects to systematically characterize physical interactions between proteins, such as yeast two-hybrid (Y2H), mass spectrometry (MS), and phage library display.

The Y2H technique is the best-known method for screening protein–protein interactions [Ito01]. It is typically carried out by screening a protein of interest against a random library of potential protein partners. Figure 5.1 gives an overview of the Y2H technique. The principle of this technique is based on the fact that many eukaryotic transcription activators have at least two distinct domains, one of which directly binds to a promoter DNA sequence known as the DNA-binding domain (BD), with the other one activating a form of transcription known as the transcription

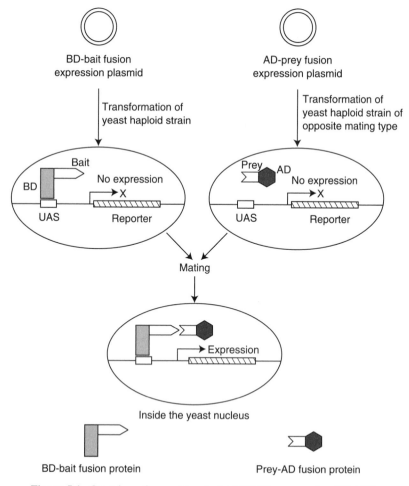

Figure 5.1. Overview of a yeast two-hybrid (Y2H) assay system [Muk01].

activation domain (AD) [Sho07a]. For instance, GAL4 is such a protein in yeast that contains two separable domains responsible for DNA binding and transcription activation and controls the expression of the LacZ gene encoding β-galactosidase. In the Y2H system, protein–protein interactions are tested by fusing one protein (bait) to the DNA-binding domain of the yeast GAL4 transcription factor. This chimeric protein is cloned in an expression plasmid, which is then transfected into a yeast cell. A similar procedure creates a chimeric sequence of another protein (prey) fused to the GAL4 activation domain. The transcription system works only if the two domains are physically close, which means that splitting BD and AD will inactivate the transcription. But the transcription can be restored if a DNA-binding domain is physically associated with an activating domain. If two proteins physically interact, the reporter gene is activated. The Y2H system is a powerful method, but it has several limitations. Firstly, it is limited mainly to detecting binary interactions and cannot screen interactions requiring three or more proteins [Ito01]. In addition, Y2H suffers from a significant number of false positives. Despite these limitations, the Y2H system is established as a standard technique in molecular biology and serves as an appropriate method for proteomic analysis [Muk01]. In particular, high-throughput Y2H techniques have been used to screen protein interactions in many organisms such as *E. coli*, *S. cerevisiae*, *C. elegans*, and *H. pylori*.

Mass spectrometry (MS) is playing an increasingly important role in determining protein interactions as it enables the rapid identification of proteins from a variety of biological samples [Vas06]. Currently, there are a diverse range of techniques coupled with MS for studying protein interactions, among which large-scale tandem affinity purification combined with MS (TAP-MS) has proved to be effective for both large-scale and targeted protein interaction mapping efforts. TAP-MS approaches typically consist of a selective purification and enrichment of a bait protein and the associated prey proteins that copurify with the bait. Figure 5.2 illustrates the main process of mapping protein–protein interactions using mass spectrometry. Firstly, appropriate TAP tags are selected. Then, tagged proteins are expressed in yeast and allowed to form physiological complexes. These complexes are affinity-purified using the appropriate tag, and the purification protein assemblies are resolved by denaturing gel electrophoresis. Resolved proteins are excised from the gel and then digested by trypsin. The resulting peptides are analyzed by MS and interacting proteins can be characterized by using bioinformatics methods [Dro05]. There are some limitations inherent in TAP-MS for mapping protein interactions. For one thing, the affinity purification process generally isolates stable complexes, but the interactions existing in the complexes seldom can usually be differentiated into direct physical interactions and indirect interactions. Thus, TAP-MS data contain both direct physical interactions and indirect interactions within a complex. In addition, although the TAP-MS strategy has been widely used for mapping yeast protein–protein interactions, its applicability to higher eukaryotes has been limited [Vas06]. Therefore, several novel affinity purification strategies for mapping protein interactions have been developed.

These high-throughput techniques have resulted in large-scale protein interaction data that are stored in several main databases. For example, the Database of

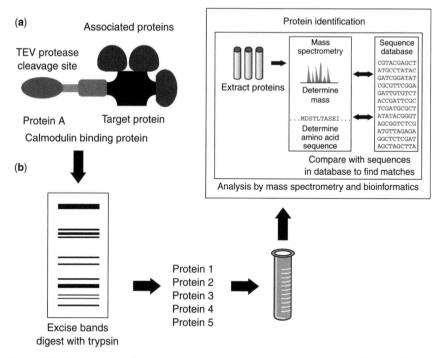

Figure 5.2. Mapping protein–protein interactions using mass spectrometry. (Reprinted by permission from [Dro05] © (2005) Society for Endocrinology.)

Interacting Proteins (DIP) contains experimentally determined protein interactions and includes a core subset of interactions with high quality. Interaction data in DIP are obtained from a variety of sources such as the literature, Protein Data Bank (PDB), and high-throughput methods, such as Y2H, DNA and protein microarrays, and TAP-MS analysis of protein complexes. MPact is a resource for accessing MIPS, which contains a manually compiled yeast protein interaction dataset collected from the literature. The resource also includes high-throughput protein interactions for yeast as a separate resource result. MIPS is often used as a standard-of-truth database for evaluating the quality of data and the accuracy of interaction prediction methods due to the high quality of protein–protein interactions that it contains. The Biomolecular Interaction Network Database (BIND) stores full descriptions of interactions, molecular complexes, and pathways, and includes high-throughput experimental datasets and protein complexes from PDB as well as a variety of manually compiled experimental data. BIND distinguishes different functional types of interactions. In addition to these databases, there are many other databases that store large-scale protein–protein interaction data, such as BioGrid, InterAct, and MINT. Table 5.1 lists some of major protein interaction databases and their Websites.

In contrast to experimental protein interactions, most of confirmed domain interactions are extracted from data of protein structures and protein interactions. For example, PIBASE is a database of all known protein structural domain interfaces

TABLE 5.1. Some Databases of Protein–Protein Interactions

Databases	Websites
MIPS	http://mips.gsf.de/proj/ppi/
MPact	http://mips.gsf.de/genre/proj/mpact/
DIP	http://dip.doe-mbi.ucla.edu/
IntAct	http://www.ebi.ac.uk/intact/index.jsp
BIND	http://www.bind.ca/
MINT	http://mint.bio.uniroma2.it/mint/
BioGRID	http://www.thebiogrid.org/
HPID	http://wilab.inha.ac.kr/hpid/
YIP	http://itolab.cb.k.u-tokyo.ac.jp/Y2H/
PID	http://www.proteinlounge.com/inter_home.asp
hp-DPI	http://dpi.nhri.org.tw/protein/hp/ORF/index.php
DroID	http://www.droidb.org/
Campy	http://proteome.wayne.edu/CampyDescription.html
MPPI	http://genome.gsc.riken.go.jp/ppi/
HPRD	http://www.hprd.org/
BRITE	http://www.genome.jp/brite/

extracted from PDB and PQS structure databases using SCOP and CATH domain definitions. The 3DID database is based on Pfam domains. It is a collection of domain–domain interactions in proteins for which high-resolution three-dimensional structures are known. iPfam contains domain–domain interactions confirmed by PDB crystal structures. It has been used as a gold standard set for evaluating predicted domain–domain interactions [Ril05, Gui06]. In addition, InterDom is also used for this purpose. It is a database of putative interacting domains derived from multiple data sources, ranging from domain fusions, protein–protein interactions, protein complexes, to scientific literature. InterDom 2.0 contains 148,938 putative pairs of domain–domain interactions with different confidence scores. The Conserved Binding Mode (CBM) database is a collection of domain interactions from the structure data where domains are defined by the Conserved Domain Database (CDD). DOMINE is a database of known and predicted protein domain interactions compiled from a variety of sources. The database contains domain–domain interactions that were observed in PDB entries, and those that were predicted by eight different computational approaches. DOMINE contains a total of 20,513 unique domain–domain interactions among 4036 Pfam domains, 4349 of which were inferred from PDB entries and 17,781 were predicted by at least one computational approach. The Domain Interaction Map (DIMA) database is a domain interaction map derived from phylogenetic profiling Pfam domains. DDIB is a database of domain–domain interactions, domain–molecule interactions, and bindings. Most of the interaction data in DDIB were extracted automatically from publication literature. It also includes many putative domain–domain interactions inferred from documented protein–protein interactions. Table 5.2 lists some of major domain interaction databases and their Websites.

TABLE 5.2. Major Databases of Domain–Domain Interactions

Databases	Websites	Domain Type
PIBASE	http://alto.compbio.ucsf.edu/pibase	SCOP/CATH
3DID	http://gatealoy.pcb.ub.es/3did/	Pfam
IPfam	http://www.sanger.ac.uk/Software/Pfam/iPfam	Pfam
InterDom	http://interdom.i2r.a-star.edu.sg	Pfam
DOMINE	http://domine.utdallas.edu/cgi-bin/Domine	Pfam
DIMA	http://mips.gsf.de/genre/proj/dima	Pfam
CBM	ftp://ftp.ncbi.nlm.nih.gov/pub/cbm	CDD
DDIB	http://www.biosino.org/DIDWeb	Pfam

5.2 PREDICTION OF PROTEIN–PROTEIN INTERACTIONS

Owing to the more recent rapid advances in high-throughput technologies, protein–protein interaction data of various species are increasingly accumulated from different experiments and stored in many databases as introduced in last section. This collection of protein–protein interaction data results in a rich but quite noisy and still incomplete source of information. In addition, experimental techniques often report protein interactions toward certain protein types and cellular localizations with a low interaction coverage and high experimental biases. Therefore, computational methods are imperatively required to analyze the noisy protein interaction data and predict unrevealed protein interactions [Sho07b]. Such methods are very helpful in increasing the confidence of protein interactions and determine potential interaction partners of interest for further experimental screening or validation.

Many efforts have contributed to an attempt to computationally predict protein–protein interactions. For instance, as classified by the type of training data, there have been gene fusion (rosetta stone) methods [Enr99, Mar99], phylogenetic profile methods [Pel99, Bow04], sequence-based methods [She07, Bur08, Naj08], structure-based methods, coevolution-based methods [Goh02, Jot06, Sat05], and domain-based methods. In terms of methodology, there are association methods [Spr01, Hay03, Che06], maximum-likelihood estimation [Den02, Liu05], optimization [Hay04], machine learning, Bayesian and probabilistic methods, and so on. Gene fusion methods employ protein sequences in different genomes [Enr99, Mar99]. It is based on the fact that two proteins in some interacting protein pairs have homologs in other genomes and are fused into one protein. Phylogenetic profile methods assume that interacting nonhomologous proteins tend to coevolve and their orthologs tend to appear in the same subset of organisms [Pel99, Bow04]. By defining a phylogenetic profile as a binary vector indicating the appearance of a protein's orthologs in different organisms, the similarity of two proteins' phylogenetic profiles provides evidence for protein interactions. In contrast to comparing phylogenetic profiles, coevolution-based methods quantify the similarity of two protein families' phylogenetic trees (defined as distance matrices) by calculating their correlation coefficients [Goh02, Jot06, Sat05]. The sequence-based approach is one of the earliest methods for protein interaction prediction and often employs sequence features such as residue frequencies, residue pairing preferences, sequence profiles, and residue neighbor lists. Some recent work reports new breakthroughs on prediction accuracy based only on sequence information [She07, Bur08, Naj08]. On the other hand, structure-based methods for protein–protein interaction prediction include extracting protein interactions from complexes with known structures and protein–protein docking. In addition, integrating multiple types of data sources for predicting protein interactions is becoming promising. For example, machine learning methods use a variety of data sources to train a classifier with proper features to learn the differences between protein interacting pairs and noninteracting pairs [Bad04, Yam04, ChX05, Ben05]. Bayesian networks have been used to combine multiple genomic features such as collocalization, coessentiality, and coexpression for predicting protein interactions [Jan03].

Domains are the basic functional units of proteins. Information of domain–domain interaction is favorable for more detailed understanding of protein–protein interactions. It is generally believed that a protein pair interacts if a domain in one protein interacts with a domain in the other protein [Hay04]. Since domains have a clear biological implication and act as basic function units, they have been widely used as intermediaries in deriving protein–protein interactions, such as in association methods [Spr01, ChL06], maximum-likelihood methods [Den02], and LP-based methods [Hay03, ZhaX06, Gui06]. Domain-based protein interaction prediction methods typically consist of two steps: (1) the interaction of each domain pair is inferred from experimental protein interaction data; (2) then, new protein interactions are predicted on the basis of the inferred domain interactions using a certain model. Some of methods involved in step (1) belong to domain interaction prediction from protein interactions. Figure 5.3 shows a scheme of protein–protein interaction prediction on the basis of domain information. We will introduce methods of this type in detail and review their applications in this field.

5.2.1 Association Methods

Association methods constitute one class of the earliest methods developed for protein interaction prediction based on domain information. Originally designed for inferring binary protein interactions, they have now been extended to the association probabilistic method (APM) for accommodating numerical interactions (interactions with confidence score or interaction strength). Owing to the simple forms and efficient implementations, they have good performance in terms of both computation time and prediction accuracy.

5.2.1.1 *Association Method*   Sequence signatures currently known as InterPro domains have been used to account for the interactions of protein pairs [Spr01]. The sequence signatures that appear in multiple interacting pairs are known as correlated sequence signatures. Overrepresented correlated sequence signatures in interacting proteins by statistical analysis are identified and used for predicting putative pairs of interacting partners. This method is known as the association method, abbreviated ASSOC.

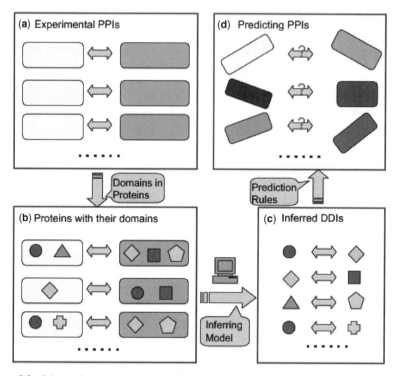

Figure 5.3. Schematic representations for inferring protein–protein interactions from domain information: (a) experimental PPIs; (b) proteins with their domains; (c) inferred DDIs; (d) predicting PPIs [Zha07].

Assume that there are N proteins indicated by $P_1, \ldots, P_N$, and M domains in the proteins represented by $D_1, \ldots, D_M$. Let P_i also denote a set of domains in the protein P_i. A protein P_i may include multiple domains D_j. Define P_{ij} and D_{mn} to represent the protein pair (P_i, P_j) and the domain pair (D_m, D_n), respectively. P_{ij} is also used to represent a set of domain pairs in P_i and P_j, that is, $P_{ij} = \{D_{mn} | D_m \in P_i, D_n \in P_j\} \subset P$, where P is the set of all protein pairs P_{ij}. Let an interaction between P_i and P_j or between D_m and D_n be represented by a random variable p_{ij} or d_{mn}. Then, $p_{ij} = 1$ if P_i and P_j interact with each other, otherwise $p_{ij} = 0$. In the same manner, $d_{mn} = 1$ if D_m and D_n interact with each other; otherwise $d_{mn} = 0$. On the basis of the observed experimental protein interaction data, the ASSOC method assigns a simple score or probability of interaction for domain pair D_m and D_n, which is defined as the fraction of interacting protein pairs among all the protein pairs containing the domain pair (D_m, D_n) [Spr01]:

$$\lambda_{mn} \equiv \Pr(d_{mn} = 1) = \frac{I_{mn}}{N_{mn}} \tag{5.1}$$

where N_{mn} is the total number of protein pairs containing domain pair (D_m, D_n) in the training dataset and I_{mn} is the number of interacting protein pairs containing domain pair (D_m, D_n) in the training dataset: $N_{mn} = \sum_{\{P_{ij}|D_{mn}\in P_{ij}\}} 1$ and $I_{mn} = \sum_{\{P_{ij}|D_{mn}\in P_{ij}\}} p_{ij}$.

5.2.1.2 Association Numerical Methods
The ASSOC method is based on binary interaction data in which the interaction information determines whether two proteins interact. In other words, there is no confidence score for each protein interaction. On the other hand, there are numerical interaction data from the repeated biological experiments. Unlike binary interaction data, such numerical interaction data imply that each protein interaction has a score to denote the interaction strength. The data include experiment ratio data based on interaction sequence tags (ISTs) [Ito01] and confidence data by integrating various data sources [Kro06]. IST is used for decoding interacting proteins in examining two-hybrid interactions. Experimental ratio data based on IST indicate that each protein interaction is provided with a ratio of the number of IST hitting in a certain number of experiments. The ratios are more informative than binary data and can be understood as the strength or probability of protein–protein interactions [Hay04]. Specifically, a ratio of interaction between P_i and P_j is defined as

$$\rho_{ij} = \frac{O_{ij}}{Z} \tag{5.2}$$

where O_{ij} is the number of times that proteins P_i and P_j are observed to interact in the experiments and Z is the total number of the experiments. In other words, ρ_{ij} is a confidence ratio of the interaction between proteins P_i and P_j, and can be considered as a natural extension of the binary variable p_{ij} from $\{0, 1\}$ to $[0, 1]$. Then, on the basis of such ratio data as well as binary interaction data, Hayashida et al. extended the association method to the association numerical method (ASNM) to accommodate numerical interactions [Hay04]. ASNM uses the summation of the strength ρ_{ij} of interaction between P_i and P_j instead of I_{mn} to define the probability of interaction between D_m and D_n as

$$\lambda_{mn} \equiv \Pr(d_{mn} = 1) = \frac{\sum_{\{P_{ij}|D_{mn}\in P_{ij}\}} \rho_{ij}}{N_{mn}} \tag{5.3}$$

where N_{mn} denotes the number of protein pairs containing domain pairs (D_m, D_n). If the ratio ρ_{ij} for each protein pair (P_i, P_j) always takes either 0 or 1, ASNM becomes equivalent to ASSOC since $I_{mn} = \sum_{\{P_{ij}|D_{mn}\in P_{ij}\}} \rho_{ij}$.

A probabilistic model describing the relations between protein–protein interactions and domain–domain interactions was proposed by Deng et al. [Den02]. This probabilistic model assumes that domain–domain interactions are independent, and that two proteins interact if at least one domain pair from the two proteins interacts. Therefore, the probability of interaction between P_i and P_j is given by

$$\Pr(p_{ij} = 1) = 1 - \prod_{D_{mn}\in P_{ij}} (1 - \lambda_{mn}) \tag{5.4}$$

After estimating a set of interacting domain pairs from experimental protein interactions by using (5.1) or (5.3), one can predict the interaction probability between a new protein pair by the probabilistic model (5.4).

5.2.1.3 Association Probabilistic Method

Methods (5.1) and (5.3) are efficient from the computational viewpoint because of their simplicity, but the prediction accuracy is not satisfactorily high [Hay04]. Each domain is a basic function unit in a protein. The probabilistic model assumes that a protein pair interacts provided that at least one domain pair interacts between the two proteins. However, the domain interaction rates in ASSOC (5.1) and ASNM (5.3) ignore the fact that some proteins contain many domains, while others may contain only one domain. Therefore, ASSOC and ASNM are actually not consistent with the probabilistic model (5.4), in particular for the ratio data. The key problem to infer protein interaction is to estimate λ_{mn} accurately from the given experimental data ρ_{ij} or p_{ij}. Chen et al. proposed a new algorithm, the association probabilistic method (APM) for solving this problem [ChL06]. APM infers protein–protein interactions through a simple computation procedure

$$\lambda_{mn} \equiv \Pr(d_{mn} = 1) = \frac{\sum_{\{P_{ij}|D_{mn}\in P_{ij}\}}[1 - (1 - \rho_{ij})^{1/|P_{ij}|}]}{N_{mn}} \qquad (5.5)$$

where $|P_{ij}|$ represents the number of domain pairs in P_{ij}. If the ratio ρ_{ij} for each protein pair (P_i, P_j) takes either 0 or 1, (5.5) is identical to (5.1) or (5.3) because of $\sum_{\{P_{ij}|D_{mn}\in P_{ij}\}}[1 - (1 - \rho_{ij})^{1/|P_{ij}|}] = \sum_{\{P_{ij}|D_{mn}\in P_{ij}\}}\rho_{ij} = I_{mn}$. λ_{mn} in (5.5) can be viewed as a reverse function of $\Pr(p_{ij} = 1)$ in (5.4) when all of λ_{mn} in P_{ij} take identical values. Thus, the protein interaction of APM is obtained by substituting λ_{mn} in (5.5) into (5.4). Both λ_{mn} and $\Pr(p_{ij} = 1)$ are straightforwardly equal to ρ_{ij} for $|P_{ij}| = 1$ (i.e., there is only one domain pair between proteins P_i and P_j). On the other hand, all the domain pairs have equal opportunity to contribute the interactions between P_i and P_j for $|P_{ij}| > 1$ under the assumption of independence for domain–domain interactions, provided that there is no prior information.

According to the statistics in experimental protein interactions, many domain pairs exist in only a single protein pair or a few of protein pairs. On the other hand, a large number of protein pairs contain multiple domain pairs. Such conditions make the prediction of domain interactions by (5.1) and (5.3) far from consistent with the probabilistic model (5.4), and also are the main reason why the accuracy of (5.1) or (5.3) is poor for the probabilistic model. For instance, Figure 5.4 illustrates an example for two proteins with totally four domains, where $P_i = \{D_1, D_2\}$, $P_j = \{D_3, D_4\}$ are proteins. D_1, D_2, D_3, D_4 are domains. There are four domain pairs: $D_{13}, D_{14}, D_{23}, D_{24}$. $P_{ij} = \{D_{13}, D_{14}, D_{23}, D_{24}\}$ denotes a set of domain pairs. If domain pairs D_{13}, D_{14}, D_{23}, D_{24} exist only in protein pair P_{ij}, and the ratio of interactions between proteins P_i and P_j by experiments is $\rho = 0.1$, then the score of interaction between each domain pair is $\lambda_{13} = \lambda_{14} = \lambda_{23} = \lambda_{24} = 0.1$ according to (5.3). Hence, the probability of interactions between P_i and P_j is $\Pr(p_{ij} = 1) = 1 - (1 - 0.1)^4 = 0.3439$ by

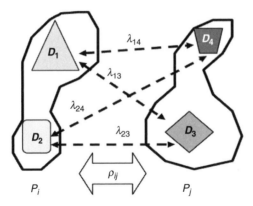

Figure 5.4. An illustrative example of two proteins with four domains total [ChL06].

the probabilistic model (5.4), which is clearly different from the experimental ratio $\rho = 0.1$. However, the score of interaction between each domain pair is $\lambda_{13} = \lambda_{14} = \lambda_{23} = \lambda_{24} = \lambda = 1 - (1 - 0.1)^{1/4}$ according to APM (5.5) due to $|P_{ij}| = 4$, which in turn gives $\Pr(p_{ij} = 1) = 1 - (1 - \lambda)^4 = 0.1$, which is consistent with the experimental ratio $\rho = 0.1$. Similarly, when a domain pair exist in multiple protein pairs, (5.5) for the inference of domain interactions will be approximately consistent with that of the corresponding protein interactions.

The APM method was compared with other four methods, that is, association methods (ASNM [Hay04], ASSOC [Spr01]), LPNM [Hay03], and the EM method [Den02] (LPNM and EM methods will be introduced in later sections) on the same training data and test data. Among those existing methods, ASSOC and EM are developed for binary data, whereas LPNM and ASNM can be applied directly on experiment ratio data. Ito's yeast interacting proteins (YIP) data [Ito01] and Uetz's two-hybrid yeast screen data (THY) [Uet00] were adopted. The binary interaction dataset can be extracted from numerical interactions by setting a threshold according to the confidence degree of experiment. Each method is evaluated by fivefold cross-validation, and the prediction accuracy is assessed by three measures: root mean-square error (RMSE), sensitivity and specificity, and correlation coefficient.

Firstly, the quality of prediction is evaluated by RMSE between the predicted probability $\Pr(p_{ij} = 1)$ by model (5.4) and the observed probability ρ_{ij}

$$\text{RMSE} = \sqrt{\sum_{P_{ij} \in P} \frac{[\Pr(p_{ij} = 1) - \rho_{ij}]^2}{|P|}} \tag{5.6}$$

where $|P|$ denotes the total number of protein pairs in training interaction data P. The performance levels of each method in terms of RMSE and elapsed training time are summarized in Table 5.3. According to Table 5.3, APM has the highest accuracy or least errors for both training (Train) and prediction (Test) of protein interactions. In addition, it is very efficient, with the same CPU consumption level as ASSOC

TABLE 5.3. Comparison of Various Methods for RMSE and Training Time on YIP Data

Train or Test (RMSE)	LPNM	EM	ASSOC	ASNM	APM
			Train		
1st	0.0139	0.4872	0.4625	0.0411	0.0125
2nd	0.0132	0.4856	0.4624	0.0375	0.0116
3rd	0.0141	0.4718	0.4425	0.0395	0.0116
4th	0.0127	0.4751	0.4471	0.0382	0.0104
5th	0.0139	0.4932	0.4672	0.0430	0.0122
Average	0.0136	0.4826	0.4564	0.0399	0.0117
Time (s)	1.5516	1.6586	0.0104	0.0096	0.0118
			Test		
1st	0.0368	0.6862	0.6592	0.0633	0.0376
2nd	0.0465	0.6171	0.5792	0.0612	0.0445
3rd	0.0502	0.6404	0.5914	0.0767	0.0491
4th	0.0505	0.6289	0.5846	0.0708	0.0487
5th	0.0362	0.5882	0.5563	0.0524	0.0365
Average	0.0441	0.6322	0.5942	0.0649	0.0434
t Test	LPNM/APM	EM/APM	ASSOC/APM	ASNM/APM	
t score	0.0838	8.7708	7.4353	2.9942	
Probability	0.4665	<0.0001	<0.0001	0.0015	

Source: Chen et al. [ChL06].

and ASNM. In terms of accuracy, t test of one-tail probability for the five tests (total 347 samples) is also performed between APM and other methods for RMSE criteria listed in Table 5.3 which indicates that APM is significantly better than others except LPNM from the statistical viewpoint. The cross-validation results on THY data are summarized in Table 5.4, which shows the results similar to those on the YIP data.

The RMSE measure is defined for nonbinary variables. Its main drawback is that the value of the quadratic distance poorly reflects the proportion of positive prediction. To compare sensitivity and specificity for both binary and ratio data, a threshold is set to process the input data and the result. Specifically, EM and ASSOC need to set a threshold for binary treatment of the numerical data before the estimation of domain–domain interactions, while LPNM, ASNM, and APM apply the threshold after the computation only for assessment. Since the ratio of the number of IST hits to the number of experiments is given for each protein pair in the numerical form, it is natural to set the IST number as the threshold. With the binary representation of the observed and predicted protein interactions, sensitivity and specificity can be used to evaluate the performance of each method. Specifically, given a set of interacting protein pairs as positive set and a set of non-interacting protein pairs as

TABLE 5.4. Comparisons of Various Methods for Average RMSE and Training Time on THY Data

	LPNM	EM	ASSOC	ASNM	APM
Train (RMSE)	0.0135	0.8130	0.7952	0.0840	0.0099
Time (s)	1.3494	0.3022	0.0026	0.0024	0.0046
Test (RMSE)	0.0453	0.8138	0.7616	0.0716	0.0414

Source: Chen et al. [ChL06].

negative set, sensitivity and specificity (denoted by SN and SP) are respectively defined as

$$SN = \frac{TP}{TP + FN}$$

and

$$SP = \frac{TN}{TN + FP}$$

where the number of true positives (TP), true negatives (TN), false positives (FP), and false negatives (FN) are estimated with respect to the given test set. Specificity and sensitivity on training data and test data are compared in Figure 5.5. The IST hit number is fixed to 3 for the observed interaction. The results indicate that APM has a very good balance between sensitivity and specificity with a high accuracy on both training and test datasets.

The reliability of YIP dataset depends on the IST hit number [Den03a]. Therefore, Chen et al. analyzed sensitivity and specificity of test data based on the reliability of the dataset by varying the IST hit threshold [ChL06]. The results are plotted in Figure 5.6, where, plots (a) and (b) correspond to IST hit numbers 1 and 8, respectively. Both plots indicate that APM has the best predictive accuracy. In particular, when the reliability of the dataset changes, the performances of LPNM, ASSOC, and EM vary greatly in contrast to APM and ASNM, which maintain stable predictive accuracy. In other words, APM is fairly robust to withstand the inconsistency of data. This feature is also very important for protein–protein interaction data because the IST hit number is generally lower than the number of experiments, for example, in the YIP dataset. According to Figures 5.5 and 5.6, some algorithms outperform APM for training data, but APM is generally better than others for test data, which implies that the other algorithms may overfit the data.

The pearson correlation coefficient is widely used by statisticians for evaluating the correlation between two vectors. Here it can measure whether there is correlation between observed and predicted interactions. The correlation coefficient is defined as

$$C(D, M) = \sum_i \frac{(d_i - \bar{d})(m_i - \bar{m})}{\sigma_D \sigma_M} \tag{5.7}$$

where D and M denote the observed and predicted sequences, respectively; $(\bar{d}, \bar{m})$ are the averages; and (σ_D, σ_M) are the corresponding standard deviations of D and M. The

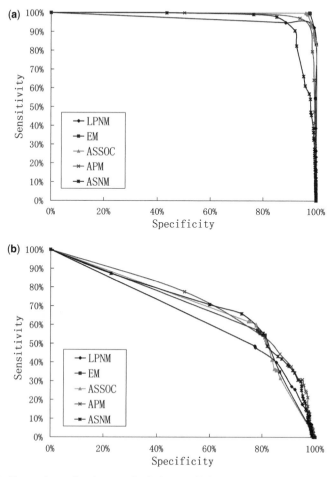

Figure 5.5. Comparison of various methods for specificity and sensitivity on yeast interacting proteins (YIP) training data and testing data [ChL06].

correlation coefficient ranges from −1 and +1. The correlation coefficient is in a global form rather than a sum of local terms, as it often provides a much more balanced evaluation of prediction. Table 5.5 lists performance levels in terms of the correlation coefficient. Again, the APM outperforms other methods in both training and test datasets.

5.2.2 Maximum-Likelihood Estimation

As in other fields, maximum-likelihood estimation (MLE) has also been applied to infer domain interactions and protein interactions [Den02]. MLE estimates the probabilities of interactions between every domain pair such that the inferred interacting domains are as consistent with the observed protein interactions as possible. The basic assumptions of the MLE method are that domain–domain interactions are

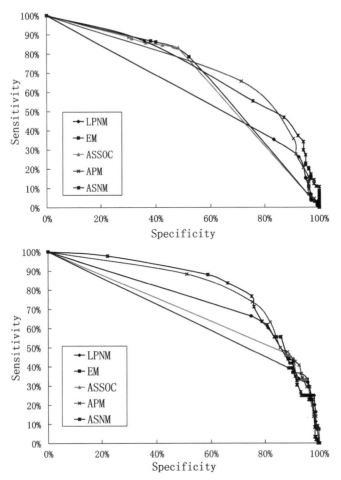

Figure 5.6. Comparison of various methods for specificity and sensitivity on YIP test data with varying reliability [ChL06].

independent, and that two proteins interact if and only if at least one pair of domains in this protein pair interact. The probabilistic model (5.4) was proposed by Deng et al. [Den02] to correlate protein interactions with domain interactions.

Experimental protein interaction data by high-throughput techniques usually have many false positives; specifically, proteins that do not interact in reality are observed to interact in the experiments. On the other hand, because of the incompleteness of an experimental dataset, there may also be false negatives; that is, proteins that interact in reality are not observed to interact in the experiments. Denoting the false-positive rate as *fp* and the false negative rate as *fn*, we obtain

$$fp = \Pr(o_{ij} = 1 | p_{ij} = 0)$$
$$fn = \Pr(o_{ij} = 0 | p_{ij} = 1)$$

TABLE 5.5. Performance of Various Methods in Terms of Correlation Coefficient on YIP

Test of Train	LPNM	EM	ASSOC	ASNM	APM
		Train			
1st	0.8807	0.5343	0.5223	0.6673	0.9052
2nd	0.8532	0.5531	0.5476	0.6643	0.8863
3rd	0.8455	0.5594	0.5552	0.6688	0.9019
4th	0.8595	0.5304	0.5251	0.6808	0.9013
5th	0.8574	0.5510	0.5518	0.6874	0.8983
Average	0.8593	0.5456	0.5404	0.6737	0.8986
		Test			
1st	0.3092	0.3974	0.4017	0.2560	0.4021
2nd	0.4705	0.3086	0.2240	0.2523	0.6463
3rd	0.1946	0.2310	0.2533	0.1638	0.3182
4th	0.3005	0.3428	0.2855	0.1881	0.2410
5th	0.0477	0.1149	0.1162	0.1049	0.0686
Average	0.2645	0.2789	0.2561	0.1931	0.3353

Source: Chen et al. [ChL06].

where $o_{ij} = 1$ if the interaction between proteins P_i and P_j is observed in the dataset and $o_{ij} = 0$ otherwise. The parameters fp and fn can be estimated from the given experimental data and prior knowledge of protein interactions in a species [Den02]:

$$fn = \Pr(o_{ij} = 0 | p_{ij} = 1)$$

$$= 1.0 - \frac{\Pr(o_{ij} = 1, p_{ij} = 1)}{\Pr(p_{ij} = 1)}$$

$$\geq 1.0 - \frac{\Pr(o_{ij} = 1)}{\Pr(p_{ij} = 1)}$$

$$\geq 1.0 - \frac{\text{number of the observed interaction pairs}}{\text{number of real interaction pairs}}, \tag{5.8}$$

$$fp = \Pr(o_{ij} = 1 | p_{ij} = 0)$$

$$= \frac{\Pr(o_{ij} = 1, p_{ij} = 0)}{\Pr(p_{ij} = 0)}$$

$$\leq \frac{\Pr(o_{ij} = 1)}{\Pr(p_{ij} = 0)}$$

$$\leq \frac{\text{number of observed interaction pairs}}{\text{(total protein pairs)} - \text{(number of real interaction pairs)}} \tag{5.9}$$

Hence, the probability for an observed protein interaction is

$$
\begin{aligned}
\Pr(o_{ij} = 1) &= \Pr(o_{ij} = 1, p_{ij} = 1) + \Pr(o_{ij} = 1, p_{ij} = 0) \\
&= \Pr(o_{ij} = 1|p_{ij} = 1)\Pr(p_{ij} = 1) + \Pr(o_{ij} = 1|p_{ij} = 0)\Pr(p_{ij} = 0) \\
&= \Pr(p_{ij} = 1)(1 - fn) + [1 - \Pr(p_{ij} = 1)]\,fp \quad\quad\quad (5.10)
\end{aligned}
$$

The likelihood function for the observed protein interaction data is defined as

$$
L = \prod_{ij} [\Pr(o_{ij} = 1)]^{o_{ij}}[1 - \Pr(o_{ij} = 1)]^{1-o_{ij}} \quad\quad\quad (5.11)
$$

which is a function of $\lambda_{mn} = \Pr(d_{mn} = 1)$ through the probabilistic model (5.4).

The MLE method aims to find a set of domain interaction probabilities as consistent with the observed protein interaction data as possible, that is, to estimate parameters $\theta = (\lambda, fp, fn)$ to maximize the likelihood function L defined above. It is difficult to maximize the likelihood function directly because of the large number of possible interacting domain pairs (the high dimensionality of θ). To solve this problem, the expectation–maximization (EM) algorithm is used to find maximum-likelihood estimates of the unknown parameters θ by maximizing the expectation of the complete data Z consisting of both observed data and missing data in two iterative steps [Den02]. The observed data O represents the protein interaction data and the domain composition of the proteins, whereas the missing data are all putative domain interactions θ. In the expectation (E) step, the expectation of the complete data Z, which includes all domain–domain interactions, is calculated from the observed data O in the following way:

$$
\begin{aligned}
E(d_{mn}^{(ij)}|o_{kl} &= \rho_{kl}, \forall k, l, \theta^{(t-1)}) \\
&= E(d_{mn}^{(ij)}|o_{ij} = \rho_{ij}, \theta^{(t-1)}) \\
&= \frac{\Pr(d_{mn}^{(ij)} = 1, o_{ij} = \rho_{ij}|\theta^{(t-1)})}{\Pr(o_{ij} = \rho_{ij}|\theta^{(t-1)})} \\
&= \frac{\Pr(d_{mn}^{(ij)} = 1|\theta^{(t-1)})\Pr(o_{ij} = \rho_{ij}|d_{mn}^{(ij)} = 1, \theta^{(t-1)})}{\Pr(o_{ij} = \rho_{ij}|\theta^{(t-1)})} \\
&= \frac{\lambda_{mn}^{(t-1)}(1 - fn)^{\rho_{ij}}fn^{1-\rho_{ij}}}{\Pr(o_{ij} = \rho_{ij}|\theta^{(t-1)})}, \quad\quad\quad (5.12)
\end{aligned}
$$

where $\rho_{ij} \in \{0, 1\}$ denotes whether there is an observed interaction between proteins P_i and P_j and $d_{mn}^{(ij)} \in \{0, 1\}$ denotes whether domains D_m and D_n interact in protein pair P_i and P_j. In the maximization (M) step, the parameters λ_{mn} are calculated based on the currently estimated complete data in the following way:

$$
\begin{aligned}
\lambda_{mn}^{(t)} &= \frac{1}{N_{mn}} \sum_{i \in A_m, j \in A_n} E(d_{mn}^{ij} | o_{ij} = \rho_{ij}, \, \theta^{(t-1)}) \\
&= \frac{\lambda_{mn}^{(t-1)}}{N_{mn}} \sum_{i \in A_m, j \in A_n} \frac{(1 - fn)^{\rho_{ij}} fn^{1-\rho_{ij}}}{\Pr(o_{ij} = \rho_{ij} | \theta^{(t-1)})}
\end{aligned}
\tag{5.13}
$$

which means that λ_{mn} is the fraction of $d_{mn}^{(ij)} = 1$ among all $d_{mn}^{(ij)}$; A_m is the set of proteins containing domain D_m, and N_{mn} is the total number of protein pairs between A_m and A_n. With the E and M steps, the whole EM algorithm for inferring domain–domain interactions from experimental protein interactions begins with setting initial values for λ_{mn} and computing $\Pr(p_{ij} = 1)$ by (5.4) and $\Pr(o_{ij} = 1)$ by (5.10). It then updates parameters λ_{mn} by (5.13) and computes the likelihood function by (5.12) repeatedly until the value of the likelihood function converges.

The MLE algorithm has been extended by other authors for predicting protein interactions through integrating high-throughput interaction data from diverse organisms [Liu05]. The idea lying in this kind of integration is that protein pairs from different organisms share some common domain pairs, and thus inferring domain–domain interactions by integrating datasets from multiple organisms will be more reliable and accurate than in the case where a single dataset is used. The MLE for multiple datasets is based on the following extended probabilistic model:

$$
\Pr(p_{ijk} = 1) = 1 - \prod_{D_{mn} \in P_{ijk}} [1 - \Pr(d_{mn} = 1)]
\tag{5.14}
$$

where $\Pr(p_{ijk} = 1)$ represents the interaction probability of proteins P_i and P_j in species k, and $\Pr(d_{mn} = 1)$ represents the probability that domain D_m interacts with D_n. The likelihood function is similarly constructed as

$$
L = \prod_{ij} [\Pr(o_{ijk} = 1)]^{o_{ijk}} [1 - \Pr(o_{ijk} = 1)]^{1-o_{ijk}}
\tag{5.15}
$$

where $\Pr(o_{ijk} = 1) = \Pr(p_{ij} = 1)(1 - fn) + [1 - \Pr(p_{ij} = 1)] fp$. $o_{ijk} = 1$ if proteins P_i and P_j are observed to interact in species k, and $o_{ijk} = 0$ otherwise. The EM algorithm to maximize the likelihood function can be obtained accordingly, which also consists of the expectation (E) step and the maximization (M) step. In the E step, the expectations of the complete data including all the domain–domain interactions for each protein pair P_i and P_j in each species are computed as

$$
E\left(d_{mn}^{(ij)} | o_{ijk} = \rho_{ijk}, \, \forall i, j, k, \, \theta^{(t-1)}\right) = \frac{\lambda_{mn}^{(t-1)} (1 - fn)^{\rho_{ijk}} fn^{1-\rho_{ijk}}}{\Pr(o_{ijk} = \rho_{ijk} | \theta^{(t-1)})}
\tag{5.16}
$$

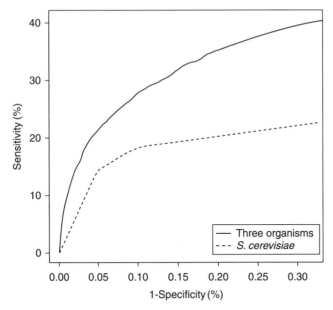

Figure 5.7. ROC curves of prediction results based on multiple organism (three organisms) data and single organism data, respectively. (Reprinted from [Liu05] © 2005 by permission of Oxford University Press.)

where $\theta = \{\lambda_{mn}, fp, fn\}$. With the expectations of the complete data, in the M step, λ_{mn} is updated by

$$\lambda_{mn}^{(t)} = \frac{\lambda_{mn}^{(t-1)}}{N_{mn}} \sum \frac{(1 - fn)^{\rho_{ijk}} fn^{1-\rho_{ijk}}}{\Pr(o_{ijk} = \rho_{ijk} | \theta^{(t-1)})} \tag{5.17}$$

where N_{mn} is the total number of protein pairs containing domain (D_m, D_n) across all species, and the summation is over all protein pairs. Computational results demonstrate that the prediction accuracy employing interaction data from multiple organisms is higher than that employing single-organism data [Liu05] (Fig. 5.7). Figure 5.8 illustrates that interacting protein pairs predicted from multiple organism data have higher gene expression correlation than do those predicted from single organism data.

5.2.3 Deterministic Optimization Approaches

In addition to statistical methods such as Bayesian methods and the MLE algorithm, deterministic optimization approaches, especially linear programming (LP) models, are also efficient for predicting protein interactions from the computational viewpoint.

5.2.3.1 Parsimony Model   A deterministic combinatorial optimization model was developed for predicting interacting protein pairs by Zhang et al. [ZhaX06]. In

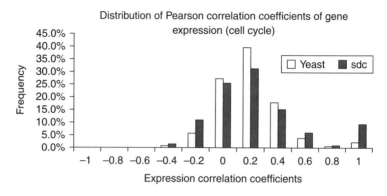

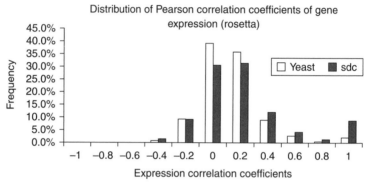

Figure 5.8. Comparison of distributions of Pearson correlation coefficients for top 1000 predicted interacting protein pairs based on multiple organism data and single organism data, respectively. (Reprinted from [Liu05] © 2005 by permission of Oxford University Press.)

the first step, it determines a set of interacting domain pairs that explain the observed protein interaction data. The set of interacting domain pairs is inferred by a combinatorial model based on a parsimony principle, which is formulated exactly into an integer linear programming (ILP). Parsimony principle is widely adopted in a variety of reconstruction problems in biological systems owing to its evolutionary implication. According to Zhang et al. [ZhaX06], the parsimony principle means that the fewest possible interacting domain pairs are used to explain the observed protein–protein interactions, which is biologically plausible. This principle is based on the consideration that, in a pair of interacting proteins, only several domain pairs interact, and domain pairs that appear to multiple interacting protein pairs are more likely to interact with each other, which is consistent with the idea underlying association methods. With the set of interacting domain pairs determined in the first step, all possible domain pairs with interaction scores are used to predict new protein interactions in the second step.

Let $\mathcal{P}$ denote a training set (called a positive dataset); that is, the observed protein interactions and $\mathcal{D}$ denote the set of all possible domain pairs involved in $\mathcal{P}$. A subset of $\mathcal{D}$ is called a *spanning domain pair set* of $\mathcal{P}$ if for each protein pair P_{ij} in $\mathcal{P}$ there is at least a domain pair D_{mn} in this set such that $D_{mn} \in P_{ij}$. In much the same way as we did for the probabilistic model, let an interaction between proteins P_i and P_j or between domains D_m and D_n be represented by a variable p_{ij} or d_{mn}. Then, p_{ij} and d_{mn} are binary variables defined as

$$p_{ij} = \begin{cases} 1 & \text{if } P_i \text{ and } P_j \text{ interact} \\ 0 & \text{otherwise} \end{cases} \tag{5.18}$$

$$d_{mn} = \begin{cases} 1 & \text{if } D_m \text{ and } D_n \text{ interact} \\ 0 & \text{otherwise} \end{cases} \tag{5.19}$$

A basic parsimony model for determining a minimum spanning domain pair set, namely, a spanning set with the minimum number of interacting domain pairs, can be formulated as the following integer linear programming problem (*PM*):

$$\min_{d_{mn}} \quad \sum_{D_{mn} \in D} d_{mn}$$

$$\text{s.t.} \quad \sum_{D_{mn} \in P_{ij}} d_{mn} \geq 1 \quad \text{for} \quad P_{ij} \in \mathcal{P} \tag{5.20}$$

$$d_{mn} \in \{0, 1\} \quad \text{for all} \quad m, n$$

The inequality constraints ensure that every observed interacting protein pair has at least one interacting domain pair to span it. The objective function is to minimize the total number of different interacting domain pairs.

In real protein interaction data, many proteins are single-domain proteins and there are also some proteins whose domains are protein-specific and do not appear in any other protein. To reduce the effect of these domain pairs in the searching for the most active domain pairs, a parameter representing the searching degree (sd), $0 < sd \leq 1$ is introduced to control the proportion of the protein pairs that take an actual role in spanning domain pair set, at the sacrifice of some protein pairs not spanned by the resulting domain pair set. The model in this context is termed PM_{sd} [Eq. (5.21)], which is a refinement of the PM model [Eq. (5.20)] and remains a form of integer linear programming

$$\min_{d_{mn}, e_{ij}} \quad \sum_{D_{mn} \in D} d_{mn}$$

$$\text{s.t.} \quad \sum_{D_{mn} \in P_{ij}} d_{mn} + e_{ij} \geq 1 \quad \text{for} \quad P_{ij} \in \mathcal{P}$$

$$\sum_{P_{ij} \in P} e_{ij} \leq (1 - sd) \cdot |\mathcal{P}| \tag{5.21}$$

$$d_{mn} \in \{0, 1\} \quad \text{for all} \quad m, n$$
$$e_{ij} \in \{0, 1\} \quad \text{for all} \quad P_{ij} \in \mathcal{P}$$

where e_{ij} is an integer variable to exclude the sacrificed protein pairs and $|\mathcal{P}|$ denotes the number of the observed interacting protein pairs.

Note that the two models described above employ only the positive set (interacting protein pairs) to infer domain–domain interactions. If a high-quality negative set (noninteracting protein pairs) is available, the inference accuracy can be improved significantly since many false positives in interacting protein pairs can be excluded. Therefore, except for a given positive training data $\mathcal{P}$, suppose that we also have a negative set of protein pairs $\mathcal{N} = \{N_{ij}\}$, that is, that there are no interactions between these protein pairs. Actually, such data can be collected from multiple sources. For example, proteins with different localizations may not interact. In this case, the parsimony model modified with a negative set (PMN) [Eq. (5.22)], which produces a minimum spanning domain pair set $\mathcal{D}_{\min}$ that spans $\mathcal{P}$ or partial $\mathcal{P}$, and also disintegrates the domain pairs in $\mathcal{N}$ as much as possible, can be formulated as

$$
\begin{aligned}
&\min_{d_{mn}} \quad \sum_{D_{mn}\in D} d_{mn} + M \sum_{D_{mn}\in N_{ij}} d_{mn} \\
&\text{s.t.} \quad \sum_{D_{mn}\in P_{ij}} d_{mn} \geq 1 \quad \text{for} \quad P_{ij} \in \mathcal{P} \\
&\qquad d_{mn} \in \{0, 1\} \quad \text{for all} \quad m, n
\end{aligned}
\tag{5.22}
$$

where M is a large positive number to penalize the use of domain pairs in the negative protein pair dataset.

Finally, models (5.22) and (5.23) can be combined together to form the following model PMN_{sd}

$$
\begin{aligned}
&\min_{d_{mn}, e_{ij}} \quad \sum_{D_{mn}\in D} d_{mn} + M \sum_{D_{mn}\in N_{ij}} d_{mn} \\
&\text{s.t.} \quad \sum_{D_{mn}\in P_{ij}} d_{mn} + e_{ij} \geq 1 \quad \text{for} \quad P_{ij} \in \mathcal{P} \\
&\qquad d_{mn} \in \{0, 1\} \quad \text{for all} \quad m, n \\
&\qquad \sum_{P_{ij}\in P} e_{ij} \leq (1 - sd) \cdot |\mathcal{P}| \\
&\qquad e_{ij} \in \{0, 1\} \quad \text{for all} \quad P_{ij} \in \mathcal{P}
\end{aligned}
\tag{5.23}
$$

which means that we aim to find the solution of (5.22) with parameter sd controlling $\mathcal{P}$.

After obtaining a set of spanning interacting domain pairs, the interaction between proteins P_i and P_j is straightforwardly predicted in the following manner

$$
\text{If} \quad \sum_{D_{mn}\in P_{ij}} d_{mn} \geq 1, \quad \text{then} \quad p_{ij} = 1, \quad \text{else} \quad p_{ij} = 0.
\tag{5.24}
$$

which means that two proteins interact if and only if at least one domain pair in them interacts. This prediction rule plays the same role as the probabilistic rule (5.4) in statistical methods.

On the other hand, from the viewpoint of computational complexity, we can show that inferring protein interactions by the parsimony principle is equivalent to a famous combinatorial optimization problem, namely, the hitting set problem [Gar79]:

- Given a set of subsets $\mathcal{P} = \{P_{ij}\}$ of the universal point set $\mathcal{D} = \{D_{mn}\}$, find the smallest subset $\mathcal{T}$ of $\mathcal{D}$ such that for each P_{ij}, the following relations hold:

$$P_{ij} \cap T \neq \emptyset$$

where D_{mn} is seen as an element and P_{ij} denotes a set of domain pairs that appear in protein pair (P_i, P_j), that is, a subset of $\mathcal{D}$.

Therefore there is no efficient exact algorithm for this model because of its NP-hard nature. Zhang et al. [ZhaX06] relaxed the integer linear programming into a linear programming to solve the problem [ZhX06]. It significantly reduces the computational complexity. An interesting fact is that numerical experiments on almost all the protein interaction datasets resulted in integer solutions by the LP relaxation although it could not be theoretically guaranteed.

The parsimony principle in domain interactions for explaining protein interactions is similar to Occam's razor in that it chooses the shortest explanation for the observed data. According to this principle, although there are many possible domain pairs, only a few of them account for the given protein interactions. To show that there is indeed a parsimony phenomenon in the real protein interaction data, a permutation test is conducted. One permutation method involves shuffling the domain compositions of all the proteins in interacting pairs. Specifically, the domains of each protein are replaced by the ones randomly selected from the domain set while preserving the number of different domains in this protein. In another type of permutation test the domain compositions in all proteins are preserved, but the same number of protein pairs among all possible protein pairs are randomly selected to act as a positive set. The permutation test was conducted on the protein interaction data collected by [Liu05]. After removal of those proteins without domain information, 2118, 2767, and 8073 interacting protein pairs were left as positive sets, respectively, for *Saccharomyces cerevisiae*, *Caenorhabditis elegans*, and *Drosophila melanogaster*. The basic parsimony model (PM) is used to find a minimum spanning domain pair set $D_{\min}$ and the results are listed in Table 5.6, where "Inter" means the number of the observed protein interactions for different species. The numbers in the "Up.B" column are upper bounds of the sizes of minimum spanning domain pair sets for the corresponding protein interaction set, while those in the "Opt." column represent the exact sizes obtained by solving (Eq. 5.20). The "Per.1" and "P.mut.2" columns give the sizes of minimum spanning domain pair sets for the permuted protein interaction sets. This table shows that the size of minimum spanning domain pair sets for real protein interaction sets is much smaller than that of randomly shuffled datasets,

TABLE 5.6. The Results of Permutation Tests on Protein Interaction Data from Three Species

Species	Inter	Up.B	Opt.	Per.1	Per.2
Saccharomyces cerevisiae	2118	2118	1820	2029	2045
Caenorhabditis elegans	2767	2766	2046	2533	2533
Drosophila melanogaster	8073	8073	6020	7720	7060

thereby verifying the parsimony tendency of domain interactions in explaining protein interactions.

iPfam is a resource that describes domain–domain interactions observed in PDB entries. It is widely used as a gold standard for evaluating predicted domain interactions. The parsimonious domain pair sets obtained by PM_{sd} model (5.21) with different searching degrees *sd* overlap with known domain–domain interactions in iPfam. The training set is for yeast, and only the protein interactions in which proteins have domains in iPfam were used. The results are listed in Table 5.7, where *Fold* is defined as

$$Fold = \frac{k_i/K_i}{k_0/K_0}$$

in which K_0 is the total number of the predicted domain pairs by PM model (5.20), that is, PM_{sd} model (5.21) with $sd = 1$ and k_0 is the number of domain interactions in K_0 that appear in iPfam. k_i and K_i are the corresponding quantities by solving (5.21) with different *sd* values. The fold value increases with the decrease of the searching degree parameter *sd*, which indicates that the more parsimonious the minimum spanning domain pair set is, the more reliable the domain interactions are. It also confirms to some extent that domain pairs appearing in more interacting protein pairs are more likely to interact with each other. This is consistent with the evolutionary view that domain pairs appearing in many interacting protein pairs are better conserved, and can survive mutations during evolution.

In order to compare the parsimony models with MLE [Den02] in terms of protein interaction prediction, the protein interaction data and the corresponding domain data

TABLE 5.7. Number of Matched Domain Interactions with iPfam

sd	Total Predictions	iPfam Matching	Percent	*Fold*
1.0	874	85	9.7	1
0.8	657	75	11.4	1.18
0.6	439	63	14.4	1.58
0.4	221	42	19.0	1.96
0.2	60	22	36.7	3.78
0.1	18	11	61.1	6.30
0.05	6	5	83.3	8.59

TABLE 5.8. The Numbers of Matched Protein Pairs to MIPS1 among All Predictions

Models	Predictions	Matching
(5.20)	179171	207
(5.22)	119450	164
$PMN_{0.4}$	55306	131
$PMN_{0.13}$	22113	83
$PMN_{0.11}$	15326	75
$PMN_{0.08}$	12074	70
$PMN_{0.07}$	11893	66
$PMN_{0.05}$	10823	63
$PMN_{0.04}$	9792	55
$PMN_{0.03}$	6657	48
MLE (threshold)		
>0.0	125435	106
≥ 0.20	23182	51
≥ 0.40	16287	47
≥ 0.60	12748	43
≥ 0.80	10441	40
≥ 0.975	9413	35

Source: Zhang et al. [ZhaX06].

once used by [Den02] were employed [ZhaX06]. The training dataset is a combination of protein interaction data obtained by Y2H screens on *S. cerevisiae* [Ito01, Uet00]. The MIPS physical interaction pairs were used as the test dataset. The negative dataset used in this study was derived from protein localization data in yeast cell [Hub03]. Two proteins in different subcellular localization compartments are expected not to interact with each other because the majority of known interactions occur between proteins in the same compartments [Jan04]. Table 5.8 and Figure 5.9 summarize the prediction results of the parsimony models and MLE method, where MIPS1 denotes the set of protein interactions in MIPS after excluding the overlapping with training data. According to Table 5.8 and Figure 5.9, when the numbers of total predictions are comparable to those of MLE, the MIPS1 matching numbers obtained by the parsimony models are always higher than those of MLE. This result further confirms the parsimony phenomenon in the real protein interactions from another perspective, and indicates that domain interactions in the parsimonious domain pair set are reliable and can be used to predict new protein interactions more accurately than MLE.

5.2.3.2 LP for Numerical Interaction Data Although many existing methods assume that protein–protein interaction data are given in binary form, usually multiple experiments are performed for a protein pair in practice and the results are not always the same [Ito01]. Thus the ratio of the number of the observed interactions to the number of experiments is available for each protein pair and it is reasonable to use

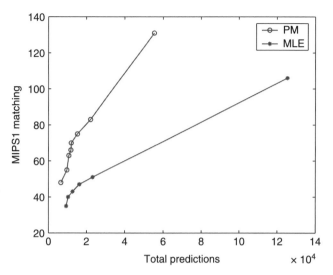

Figure 5.9. Numbers of matched protein pairs to MIPS1 among all predictions by the parsimony model (PM) [Eq. (5.20)] and MLE.

the ratio as input data. The ratio is also referred to as the strength or probability of protein interactions. In addition, in order to improve the quality of protein interactions and remove false positives, confidence scores combining various evidence sources can be assigned to each protein interaction [Den03a, Bad04]. When such weighted protein interaction data are used as a training set for inferring domain–domain interactions, computational methods that are applicable for such data are required.

A method based on linear programming (LP) for inferring domain interactions from strength data of protein interactions has been developed [Hay03]. This method, based on the probabilistic model (5.4), minimizes the errors between the ratios (strength) of the observed interactions and the predicted probabilities by a robust linear programming with a soft margin. The model is sufficiently flexible to incorporate other constraints and can be applied for both binary interaction data and numerical interaction data. The basic version of the LP-based method for binary data is called LPBN. Using the probabilistic model (5.4) with a threshold Θ, protein–protein interactions can be predicted by the following rule

$$P_i \text{ and } P_j \text{ interact} \iff \text{Pr}\,(p_{ij} = 1) = 1 - \prod_{D_{mn} \in P_{ij}} (1 - \lambda_{mn}) \geq \Theta$$

where $\lambda_{mn} = \text{Pr}(d_{mn} = 1)$. This condition can be equivalently rewritten as

$$\prod_{D_{mn} \in P_{ij}} (1 - \lambda_{mn}) \leq 1 - \Theta$$

By taking log transformation on the inequality shown above, it follows that

$$\sum_{D_{mn} \in P_{ij}} \ln(1 - \lambda_{mn}) \leq \ln(1 - \Theta)$$

Letting $\gamma_{mn} = \ln(1 - \lambda_{mn})$, $\beta = \ln(1 - \Theta)$, this condition can be written as

$$\sum_{D_{mn} \in P_{ij}} \gamma_{mn} \leq \beta$$

This is a set of linear inequalities. If γ_{mn} can be found to satisfy

$$o_{ij} = 1 \iff \sum_{D_{mn} \in P_{ij}} \gamma_{mn} \leq \beta \tag{5.25}$$

where $\gamma_{mn} \leq 0$, the parameters consistent with the training data can be obtained. As a result of experimental noise, it is usually impossible to find a set of parameters to satisfy all constraints. In such a case, it is natural and reasonable to minimize the classification error, which can be achieved by the following LP model, where c is an appropriate small constant.

$$\min \sum_{P_{ij}} \xi_{ij}$$

$$\text{s.t} \sum_{D_{mn} \in P_{ij}} \gamma_{mn} \leq \beta - c + \xi_{ij} \quad \text{for} \quad P_{ij} \quad \text{that} \quad o_{ij} = 1$$

$$\sum_{D_{mn} \in P_{ij}} \gamma_{mn} > \beta + c - \xi_{ij} \quad \text{for} \quad P_{ij} \quad \text{that} \quad o_{ij} = 0 \tag{5.26}$$

$$\gamma_{mn} \leq 0 \quad \text{for all} \quad \gamma_{mn}$$
$$\xi_{ij} \geq 0 \quad \text{for all} \quad \xi_{ij}$$

$$\beta < 0$$

The constraints in this LP model correspond to equation (5.25). After γ_{mn} and β are determined through the LP model above, λ_{mn} and Θ can be obtained and correspond to the probability that domains interact and to the threshold of protein interactions, respectively.

As mentioned above, weighted protein interaction data are available in many cases, which can be used as training data. An LP-based method for numerical interaction data (LPNM) is developed by Hayashida [Hay03]. In contrast to using the threshold Θ to predict protein–protein interactions, in LPNM, Θ_{ij} is set as the ratio of interactions between proteins P_i and P_j in a series of experiments $\Theta_{ij} = N(o_{ij})/Z$, where $N(o_{ij})$ is the number of times that P_i and P_j are observed to interact in the experiments and Z is the total number of experiments. Then, the difference between the predicted probability $\Pr(P_{ij} = 1)$ of the interaction through the model (5.4) and the ratio Θ_{ij} of the interaction observed in experiments should be minimized. Specifically, when $\Pr(P_{ij} = 1)$ and Θ_{ij} are equal, the following equation holds for any P_i and P_j:

$$\prod_{D_{mn} \in P_{ij}} (1 - \lambda_{mn}) = 1 - \Theta_{ij}$$

By taking a log transformation, it follows that

$$\sum_{D_{mn} \in P_{ij}} \ln(1 - \lambda_{mn}) = \ln(1 - \Theta_{ij})$$

which is equivalent to

$$\sum_{D_{mn} \in P_{ij}} \gamma_{mn} = \beta_{ij} \tag{5.27}$$

by setting $\gamma_{mn} = \ln(1 - \lambda_{mn})$, $\beta_{ij} = \ln(1 - \Theta_{ij})$.

If we can find γ_{mn} such that these equalities hold, we can obtain the probabilities of domain–domain interactions that are completely consistent with the numerical interaction dataset. However, as a result of experimental noise, many false positives exist in protein interaction data, which means that these equations may not always hold. It is hence natural and reasonable to minimize the sum of the difference $\sum_{P_{ij}} |\sum_{D_{mn} \in P_{ij}} \gamma_{mn} - \beta_{ij}|$, which leads to the following LP model

$$\min \quad \sum_{P_{ij}} \alpha_{ij}$$

$$\text{s.t} \quad \sum_{D_{mn} \in P_{ij}} \gamma_{mn} - \beta_{ij} \leq \alpha_{ij}$$

$$\beta_{ij} - \sum_{D_{mn} \in P_{ij}} \gamma_{mn} \leq \alpha_{ij} \tag{5.28}$$

$$\gamma_{mn} \leq 0 \quad \text{for all} \quad \gamma_{mn}$$
$$\alpha_{ij} \geq 0 \quad \text{for all} \quad \alpha_{ij}$$
$$\beta_{ij} < 0 \quad \text{for all} \quad \beta_{ij}$$

where the constraints correspond to equation (5.27). Experimental results show that LPBN is comparable to existing methods on binary data and LPNM outperforms existing methods on numerical data.

5.2.3.3 Set-Cover Approach

In addition to continuous optimization, combinatorial optimization has also been applied in predicting protein interactions. For example, a well-known set-cover problem was introduced for protein interaction prediction [Hua07]. Similar to the equivalence between parsimony model and hitting set problem in Section 5.2.3.1, the relationship between protein interactions and domain compositions can be described by a generalized weighted set-cover problem. Note that the hitting set problem is equivalent to the set-cover problem [Gar79]. By applying a greedy algorithm, we can obtain a set of domain interactions that explain the presence of protein interactions to the largest degree of specificity [Hua07].

Let X be a finite set and $\mathcal{F}$ be a family of all the subsets of X. The set-cover problem is to find a subset $\mathcal{C}$ of $\mathcal{F}$ to cover X

$$X = \bigcup_{S \in \mathcal{C}} S$$

where $\mathcal{C}$ is required to satisfy certain conditions according to specific problems. The minimum set-cover (MSC) problem is to find a $\mathcal{C}$ with minimum cardinality $|\mathcal{C}|$, while the minimum exact set-cover (MESC) problem requires that $\sum_{S \in \mathcal{C}} |S|$ be minimized. Huang et al. generalized the set-cover problem by enclosing X into a larger set Y [Hua07]. Let Y be a finite set, $X \subseteq Y$, and $\mathcal{F}$ be a family of all subsets of Y. The generalized set-cover problem is to find a subset $\mathcal{C}$ of $\mathcal{F}$ to cover X, and $\mathcal{C}$ is also required to satisfy certain conditions according to different specific problems.

For the protein interaction prediction problem, the set-cover approach [Hua07] maps the relationships between protein interactions and domain compositions to a set-cover problem. Suppose that the experimentally known protein–protein interactions are represented by a graph $\mathcal{G} = (P, E)$, where P is the set of proteins as the vertices of $\mathcal{G}$, and E is the set of interactions as the edges of $\mathcal{G}$. Let $Y = \{(P_i, P_j)|P_i, P_j \in P\}$ denote the set of all protein pairs and $X = \{(P_i, P_j)|P_i, P_j \in P, (P_i, P_j) \in E\}$ denote the set of all interacting protein pairs. Clearly, $X \subset Y$. $\mathcal{F}$ is the set of all domain pairs (D_m, D_n) that can be viewed as subsets of Y since if a protein pair (P_i, P_j) contains (D_m, D_n), then (P_i, P_j) can be seen as belonging to the subset (D_m, D_n). With these defined sets, according to the set-cover problem and protein interaction prediction, a subset $\mathcal{C}$ of $\mathcal{F}$ (a set of domain pairs) is intended to be selected to cover X (the known protein–protein interactions).

After formulated as a set-cover problem, the protein interaction prediction can be solved by finding a set of interacting domain pairs to cover the known protein interactions. There may be several ways to determine such a set of domain pairs. In the parsimony model (Section 5.2.3.1), minimum cardinality acts as a criterion. In the MLE algorithm [Den02], a set of domain pairs maximizing the defined likelihood function is selected. In the set-cover approach [Hua07], a set of domain pairs that allows us to represent the protein interaction network and maximizes both the specificity and sensitivity on the training set is chosen. Such a set-cover problem is called maximum-specificity set cover (MSSC), which is to find a subset $\mathcal{C}$ of $\mathcal{F}$ to cover X such that

$$m(\mathcal{C}) = \sum_{S \in \mathcal{C}} |S - X|$$

is minimized. This criterion indicates that the selected C covers X (maximum sensitivity) and at the same time minimizes its overlap with $Y-X$ (maximum specificity, since false positives are considered to be in $Y-X$). To achieve this goal, a greedy algorithm for solving MSSC is designed:

```
Greedy_MSSC (X,Y,F) {
      U ← X
      E ← F
      C ← Ø
   while U ≠ Ø
         do
             select a S ∈ E with the minimum |S-X/S∩U|

             If there is a tie, it can be broken by |S ∩ U|
             U←U-S
             E ← ε-S
             C ← C∪S
      end do
}
```

where U represents the uncovered part of X and ε is the subset of $\mathcal{F}$ that has not been chosen by the greedy algorithm. Experimental results show that MSSC enables the prediction accuracy comparable to MLE and costs less time than MLE. This algorithm is accessible at http://ppi.cse.nd.edu.

5.3 PROTEIN INTERACTION PREDICTION BASED ON MULTIDOMAIN PAIRS

In the last section, we introduced several domain-based protein interaction prediction methods. We can see that most existing algorithms consider domain pairs as the basic units of protein–protein interactions, and these domain–domain interactions are assumed to be independent. However, such an assumption is actually not biologically reasonable because two or more domains may cooperatively interact with another domain as indicated in the literature [Moz06, Kle96]. Just like proteins in a complex that cooperatively bind with each other to achieve specific functions, domains in a protein pair may also have a cooperation in mediating protein interactions. For example, Klemm and Pabo found that two unlinked polypeptides corresponding to the POU-specific domain and the POU homeodomain in protein Oct-1 bind cooperatively to the octamer site [Kle96]. Moza et al. showed that the binding energetics between different hot regions consisting of interfacial residues in a protein–protein interaction are not strictly additive [Moz06]. Cooperative binding energetics between distinct hot regions is significant. They pointed out that cooperativity between hot regions has significant implications for the prediction of protein–protein interactions. When the hot regions are distributed over different domains in proteins, the cooperativity between different hot regions is actually embodied by multidomain cooperation. In addition, there are superdomains that always appear together in individual proteins to mediate the interactions. Given the close relations and the possible cooperation between domains, the independence assumption of domain–domain interactions does not generally hold.

Furthermore, individual domains in the same multidomain protein may be biologically interrelated as a result of certain evolutionary events. For example, multidomain proteins are formed by gene fusion, domain shuffling, and retrotransposition of exons from the evolutionary viewpoint. These biological mechanisms undergo two operations: domain merge and domain deletion [PrT06]. Domain merge refers to a process that unites two or more separate domains in a single protein, whereas domain deletion refers to a process in which a protein loses one or more of its domains. In addition, multidomain proteins are subject to domain rearrangement. With these biological processes such as domain fusion and domain merge directly arising from the evolution of multidomain proteins, multiple domains in a protein have close biological relations, and cooperativity among domains may play a significant role in facilitating protein interactions. The functions of multidomain proteins are believed to be composites of those of the cooperatively interacting domains in these multidomain proteins. Hence, revealing such domain cooperation may provide deep insight into the essential mechanism of protein interactions at the domain level, and can be further utilized to improve the accuracy of protein interaction prediction.

For the reasons mentioned above, domain combinations in proteins have been studied [Nye05, Api01]. Wang and Caetano-Anolles used the occurrence and abundance of the molecular interactome of domain combinations to construct global phylogenic trees [WaM06]. When a closely correlated domain combination appears in an interactome, domains in this combination may mediate the interaction simultaneously and cooperatively. In particular, Han et al. studied domain combinations in protein interactions, and proposed a probabilistic framework to predict protein interactions based on the interactions of domain combinations [Han04]. In their work, the appearance frequencies of domain combinations in a set of interacting and noninteracting protein pairs are counted to construct appearance probability matrices that provide useful information about the distribution of multidomain interactions. For example, among the listed 300 domain combination pairs with high appearance probability values (top 300) that are counted on the basis of the total 5826 protein interaction pairs in yeast, there are 246 two-domain pairs, 44 three-domain pairs, and 10 pairs containing four or more domains. This statistical result indicates that many domains are closely correlated and tend to appear together in interacting protein pairs. In contrast to such domain combinations, which are characterized purely by coappearance frequency, Wang et al. presented a quantitative method for classifying domain pairs as superdomains, cooperative domains, and strongly cooperative domains [WaR07c], and identified cooperative domains from protein interaction data by a general framework based on linear programming with multidomain pairs (LPM) and an association probabilistic method with multidomain pairs (APMM), which can further predict protein interactions in a more accurate manner. We will introduce this approach in detail in the following subsections.

5.3.1 Cooperative Domains, Strongly Cooperative Domains, Superdomains

Assume that in the protein interactions from the kth species or dataset k, there are N_k proteins respectively denoted by $P_1^k, \ldots, P_{N_k}^k$, $k = 1, \ldots, K$, with M domains in all of these proteins represented by $D_1, \ldots, D_M$. Let P_i^k also denote a set of domains in the protein i of species k. Define P_{ij}^k to represent a protein pair (P_i^k, P_j^k) and $D_{m,n}$ to represent a domain pair (D_m, D_n). A symbol $D_{mr,n}$ is introduced for a three-domain pair (D_m-D_r, D_n) to represent the case that domains D_m and D_r in protein P_i^k cooperatively interact with domain D_n in protein P_j^k. $D_{m,rn}$ denotes a three-domain pair (D_m, D_r-D_n) and has an implication similar to that of $D_{mr,n}$. A multidomain pair usually means a two-domain pair or a three-domain pair. P_{ij}^k is also used to represent the set of domain pairs including all multidomain pairs in P_i^k and P_j^k, that is,

$$\in P_i^k, D_n \in P_j^k\} \cup \{D_{mr,n}|D_m, D_r \in P_i^k, D_n \in P_j^k\} \cup \{D_{m,nr}|D_m \in P_i^k, D_n, D_r \in P_j^k\}$$
$$\in P_i^k, D_n \in P_j^k\} \cup \{D_{mr,n}|D_m, D_r \in P_i^k, D_n \in P_j^k\} \cup \{D_{m,nr}|D_m \in P_i^k, D_n, D_r \in P_j^k\}.$$

Let the interaction between proteins P_i^k and P_j^k or between domains D_m and D_n be represented by a binary random variable p_{ij}^k or $d_{m,n}$. Accordingly, binary random variable $d_{mr,n}$ is introduced to denote whether domains D_m and D_r cooperatively interact with domain D_n. The value $d_{m,rn}$ has a similar implication. Figure 5.10a lists all the multidomain pairs in proteins (P_1, P_2), where $P_1 = \{D_a, D_b, D_c\}$, $P_2 = \{D_e, D_f\}$. Figure 5.10b illustrates domain interactions by considering multidomain pairs. There is one pair of interacting proteins and three pairs of noninteracting proteins. The solid-line arrow is an interacting domain pair, while the dotted-lines arrows indicate the deleted noninteracting domain pairs. Note that theoretically there are high order cooperativity cases with more than three domains, which however are rare and are not considered here, although the methodology described next can be extended in a similar manner.

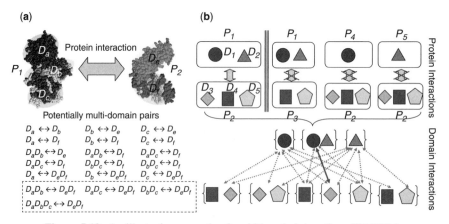

Figure 5.10. An illustrative example of multidomain interactions [WaR07c].

In contrast to domain combinations characterized purely by coappearance frequency [Han04], a quantitative method is used to classify domain pairs as superdomains, cooperative domains, and strongly cooperative domains in [WaR07c]. They can be identified from protein interaction data by extending two-domain interactions to multidomain interactions. Specifically, $\Pr(d_{m,n} = 1)$ represents the probability that domain D_m interacts with D_n. $\Pr(d_{mr,n} = 1)$ represents the probability that domains D_m and D_r cooperatively interact with D_n. $\Pr(d_{m,nr} = 1)$ has a similar meaning. A cooperative-domain pair (cooperative-domain interaction) implies a generalized pair $(D_m - D_r, D_n)$ in which two domains $D_m - D_r$ referred to as cooperative domains coexist in a protein and cooperatively interact with D_n in another protein. The cooperative-domain pair should have a stronger interaction effect than the corresponding two-domain pairs (D_m, D_n) and (D_r, D_n); thus domains D_m and D_r are cooperative domains if $\Pr(d_{m,n} = 1) < \Pr(d_{mr,n} = 1)$ and $\Pr(d_{r,n} = 1) < \Pr(d_{mr,n} = 1)$. A strongly cooperative-domain pair (strongly cooperative-domain interaction) is a cooperative-domain pair $(D_m - D_r, D_n)$, which satisfies the requirement for an interaction effect of D_m or D_r on D_n only if domains D_m and D_r appear together. A superdomain implies two "combined" domains $D_m - D_r$, which are special cooperative domains and always appear together in individual proteins. In contrast to using the interaction strength to determine cooperative domains, the two domains in a superdomain are determined on the basis of their co-occurrence and always appear together in individual proteins to mediate the interactions between them.

With the defined multidomain pairs, the relationship between protein interactions and multidomain interactions is described by an extended probabilistic model

$$\Pr(p_{ij}^k = 1) = 1 - \prod_{D_{m,n} \in P_{ij}^k} [1 - \Pr(d_{m,n} = 1)] \cdot \prod_{D_{mr,n} \in P_{ij}^k} [1 - \Pr(d_{mr,n} = 1)]$$

$$\cdot \prod_{D_{m,nr} \in P_{ij}^k} [1 - \Pr(d_{m,nr} = 1)] \tag{5.29}$$

where $\Pr(p_{ij}^k = 1)$ represents the interaction probability of proteins P_i^k and P_j^k in species k. Like the original probabilistic model (5.4), the extended probabilistic model also requires an independence assumption between different multidomain pairs. For each protein pair in (5.29), if there is a cooperative interaction of domains $D_m - D_r$ with domain D_n in the second multiplying term, then (D_m, D_n) and (D_r, D_n) must be excluded from the first multiplying term in order to maintain the independence assumption of each interaction; otherwise, $(D_m - D_r, D_n)$ needs to be deleted. The third multiplying term for $(D_m, D_r - D_n)$ should be checked in the same way. The first multiplying term represents the effect of two-domain interactions, while the second and third multiplying terms denote the effects of cooperative-domain interactions. Figure 5.10b presents an example for inferring domain interactions from protein interaction and noninteraction data. It shows that the classical probabilistic model fails to give the correct result for this case while the extended model can do it by considering multidomain interactions.

In order to make the variables in model (5.29) independent of each other, a dependent variable deletion strategy is introduced [WaR07c]. Let us define

$$R_{m,n} = \frac{I_{m,n}}{N_{m,n}} \qquad (5.30)$$

where $I_{m,n}$ is the number of interacting protein pairs in the training set that contain domain pair $D_{m,n}$ and $N_{m,n}$ is the total number of protein pairs in the training set that contain $D_{m,n}$. $R_{mr,n}$ and $R_{r,n}$ are similarly defined. For variables $d_{m,n}$, $d_{mr,n}$, and $d_{r,n}$, the variable deletion strategy is described by the following procedure.

1. If $R_{mr,n} < R_{m,n}$ or $R_{mr,n} < R_{r,n}$, this indicates that the appearance frequency of domain pair $D_{mr,n}$ in interacting protein pairs is not higher than those of $D_{m,n}$ and $D_{r,n}$. Hence, it is believed that there is no cooperation between D_m and D_r in their interaction with D_n, and the variables $d_{m,n}$ and $d_{r,n}$ will be retained but the variable $d_{mr,n}$ in (5.25) should be deleted.

2. If $R_{mr,n} \geq R_{m,n}$ and $R_{mr,n} \geq R_{r,n}$, for $D_{m,n}$, then

    • When $R_{mr,n} > R_{m,n}$ and $I_{mr,n} = I_{m,n}$, the appearance frequency of domain pair $D_{mr,n}$ in interacting protein pairs is higher than those of $D_{m,n}$ and $D_{r,n}$; furthermore, $D_{m,n}$ does not appear in any other interacting protein pair without D_r. Hence, it is believed that there is a cooperation between D_m and D_r on interaction with D_n, and thereby the variable $d_{m,n}$ is deleted, but the variable $d_{mr,n}$ is retained in (5.29).

    • When $R_{mr,n} = R_{m,n}$ and $I_{mr,n} = I_{m,n}$, then D_m and D_r always appear together in individual proteins. Hence, D_m and D_r are considered as a superdomain and can be merged into one. For such a case, the variable $d_{m,n}$ is deleted but the variable for the cooperative-domain pair $d_{mr,n}$ is retained.

These operations are performed in the same way for $D_{r,n}$. For the case shown in Figure 5.10b, variables for all domain pairs except $(D_1–D_2, D_3)$ are deleted using this strategy. Note that the operations listed above do not cover all the cases; for example, $R_{mr,n} > R_{m,n}$ and $I_{mr,n} < I_{mn}$ are not considered. For this case, we cannot determine whether there is a cooperative effect between domains D_m and D_r when they interact with domain D_n because $D_{m,n}$ also appears in the interacting pairs without D_r, so all the variables are retained. This manipulation may affect the assumption of independence, but there are few such cases and thereby the assumption can be primarily satisfied [WaR07c]. In the following formulation, all the variables appearing in the formula are those retained after application of the variable deletion strategy, whereas the probabilities of all deleted variables are set to zero.

5.3.2 Inference of Multidomain Interactions

After defining cooperative or strongly cooperative domains, we can identify such domains from protein interaction data using the extended probabilistic model (5.29) and extrapolate the data to predict new protein interactions. Wang et al., inferred the probabilities of multidomain interactions by a linear programming algorithm and an association probabilistic method as follows [WaR07c].

5.3.2.1 Linear Programming with Multidomain Pairs

Before predicting protein interactions, domain interactions, including multidomain interactions, should be inferred by utilizing all available information, for example, from multiple experimental datasets. As a result of existing noise in the experimental data, protein interaction datasets from each organism or each experiment setting have a false-positive rate fp^k and a false-negative rate fn^k for the kth dataset or the kth organism, $fp^k = \Pr(o_{ij}^k = 1 | p_{ij}^k = 0)$, $fn^k = \Pr(o_{ij}^k = 0 | p_{ij}^k = 1)$, where $o_{ij}^k = 1$ if the interaction between proteins P_i^k and P_j^k is observed in the dataset and $o_{ij}^k = 0$ otherwise. Thus the probability that proteins P_i^k and P_j^k in organism k are observed to interact in the experiments is related to the real interaction probability as

$$\Pr(o_{ij}^k = 1) = \Pr(p_{ij}^k = 1)(1 - fn^k) + [1 - \Pr(p_{ij}^k = 1)]fp^k \qquad (5.31)$$

where the parameters fp^k and fn^k can be estimated from experimental data using a procedure similar to that employed by Liu et al. [Liu05]. With the basic probabilistic model (5.29) and formula (5.31), it follows that

$$\frac{\Pr(o_{ij}^k = 1) - fp^k}{1 - fn^k - fp^k} = 1 - \prod_{D_{m,n} \in P_{ij}^k} [1 - \Pr(d_{m,n} = 1)]$$

$$\cdot \prod_{D_{mr,n} \in P_{ij}^k} [1 - \Pr(d_{mr,n} = 1)]$$

$$\cdot \prod_{D_{m,nr} \in P_{ij}^k} [1 - \Pr(d_{m,nr} = 1)] \qquad (5.32)$$

where $\Pr(o_{ij}^k = 1) = 1$ when two proteins (P_i^k, P_j^k) interact and 0 otherwise in the binary interaction data. For numerical interaction data, $\Pr(o_{ij}^k = 1)$ is set as the ratio of interactions between proteins P_i^k and P_j^k in a series of experiments. Normalization can be done on the left side of the equation if $\Pr(o_{ij}^k = 1) > 1$ because of the incomplete interaction information in binary experimental data. Let $x_{m,n} = \ln[1 - \Pr(d_{m,n} = 1)]$, $x_{mr,n} = \ln[1 - \Pr(d_{mr,n} = 1)]$, $x_{m,nr} = \ln[1 - \Pr(d_{m,nr} = 1)]$ and

$$\beta_{ij}^k = \ln\left(1 - \frac{\Pr(o_{ij}^k = 1) - fp^k}{1 - fn^k - fp^k}\right)$$

then the equalities derived above can be equivalently written as

$$\sum_{D_{m,n} \in P_{ij}^k} x_{m,n} + \sum_{D_{mr,n} \in P_{ij}^k} x_{mr,n} + \sum_{D_{m,nr} \in P_{ij}^k} x_{m,nr} = \beta_{ij}^k \qquad (5.33)$$

which can be viewed as an extension of the method used by Hayashida et al. [Hay03]. If $x_{m,n}$, $x_{mr,n}$, and $x_{m,nr}$ ($x_{m,n} \le 0$, $x_{mr,n} \le 0$, and $x_{m,nr} \le 0$) can be found to satisfy (5.33) for all observed protein interaction data, the domain interaction probabilities $\Pr(d_{m,n} = 1)$, $\Pr(d_{mr,n} = 1)$, and $\Pr(d_{m,nr} = 1)$ fully consistent with the training data can be obtained. However, it is seldom possible to satisfy all constraints because of the noise and incompleteness of experimental data. In such a case, it is natural and reasonable to minimize the total error with respect to L_1 norm, which can be achieved through the following linear programming with multidomain pairs (LPM):

$$\min_{\varepsilon, x} \sum_{P_{ij}^k} |\varepsilon_{ij}^k|$$

$$\text{s.t.} \quad \sum_{D_{m,n} \in P_{ij}^k} x_{m,n} + \sum_{D_{mr,n} \in P_{ij}^k} x_{mr,n}$$

$$+ \sum_{D_{m,nr} \in P_{ij}^k} x_{m,nr} = \beta_{ij}^k - \varepsilon_{ij}^k \quad \text{for all} \quad P_{ij}^k \qquad (5.34)$$

$$x_{m,n} \le 0, \ x_{mr,n} \le 0, \ x_{m,nr} \le 0$$

$$i, j = 1, \ldots, N_k, \ k = 1, \ldots, K$$

where $\varepsilon_{i,j}^k$ is the error for each equality in (5.33). This model can be solved by any standard LP solver after removing the absolutes in the objective function by introducing new variables.

5.3.2.2 Association Probabilistic Method with Multidomain Pairs   In addition to LPM, Wang et al. presented another faster probabilistic method based on statistics [WaR07c]. This method is a generalization of APM [ChL06] with multidomain pairs, and therefore is abbreviated APMM. It estimates the interaction probabilities of multidomain pairs in the following way:

$$\Pr(d_{m,n} = 1) = \frac{\sum_{\{P_{ij}^k | D_{m,n} \in P_{ij}^k\}} [1 - (1 - \rho_{ij}^k)^{|P_{ij}^k|}]}{N_{m,n}}$$

$$\Pr(d_{mr,n} = 1) = \frac{\sum_{\{P_{ij}^k | D_{mr,n} \in P_{ij}^k\}} [1 - (1 - \rho_{ij}^k)^{|P_{ij}^k|}]}{N_{mr,n}} \qquad (5.35)$$

$$\Pr(d_{m,nr} = 1) = \frac{\sum_{\{P_{ij}^k | D_{m,nr} \in P_{ij}^k\}} [1 - (1 - \rho_{ij}^k)^{|P_{ij}^k|}]}{N_{m,nr}}$$

where $|P_{ij}^k|$ represents the number of multidomain pairs in P_{ij}^k and ρ_{ij}^k is the observed interaction probability between P_i^k and P_j^k in the experimental data after considering false-positive and false-negative rates. The computation of this method is very simple and highly efficient. In addition, it does not require any parameter tuning.

After the interaction probabilities of multidomain pairs are computed by LPM (5.34) or APMM (5.35), a pair of proteins can be straightforwardly predicted to interact or not interact, by the extended probabilistic model (5.25).

5.3.3 Numerical Validation

Both LPM and APMM were validated using several types of experiments [WaR07c]. First, protein interaction data from MIPS and DIP were used to identify biologically meaningful superdomains, putative cooperative domains, and strongly cooperative domains. The domains in the detected superdomains or strongly cooperative domains were found to have similar biological functions in terms of GO annotation [WaR07c]. In addition, the crystal structures of complexes in PDB can be regarded as a gold standard for verifying protein interactions and domain interactions. Some cooperative domains were verified by checking their physical interactions from the crystal structures of protein complexes in the protein Data Bank PDB, and the essential mechanism of protein interactions was examined at the domain level. Figure 5.11 shows cooperative domains in a complex crystal structure formed by physical interactions of proteins P02994 (ORFs: YBR118W, YPR080W) and P32471 (ORF: YAL003W), where P02994 has three domains and P32471 has one domain, PF00736. Interacting protein pairs and their Pfam domain annotations are described in this figure. In this complex, EF-1 guanine nucleotide exchange domain PF00736 in P32471 has interactions with all of the domains in P02994. These interactions were verified by the binding sites of PF00736 with the domains in P02994. The cartoon image of a crystal structure illustrates that all cooperative-domain interactions in (P02994, P32471) are correctly identified and supported by the interfacial residues involved in the interaction. The interfacial residues are identified using a simple rule that their Cα atoms lie within the distance threshold 10 Å, which is consistent with the more accurate computation given in PROTCOM (a database of protein complexes). This example provides intuitive evidence for the cooperation among domains in the interaction of P02994 and P32471.

In addition to identifying superdomains and cooperative domains, LPM or APMM utilizing the information of both multidomains and multiple organisms has a higher accuracy for protein interaction prediction [WaR07c]. To check this point, Ito's ratio interaction data [Ito01] and Krogan's extended confidence interaction data [Kro06] were used. The cross-validation test confirms the superior performance of LPM and APMM compared with other existing algorithms such as EM, ASSOC, and ASNM mentioned in the last section. The direct comparison results of LPM and APMM based on two-domain pairs and multidomain pairs, respectively, are summarized in Figure 5.12. We can see that LPM based on multidomain pairs in training and testing has less prediction error in each round of fivefold cross-validation than LPM based on only two-domain pairs. APMM also has such a tendency except in

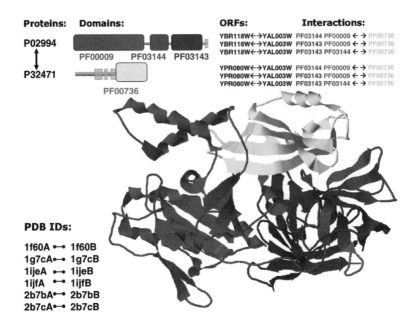

Interfacial residues:

PF03143: THR363 ARG428 GLN429
PF00736: SER1180 ASP1182 ASP1183 ASP1199

PF03144: VAL260 VAL262 SER289 VAL290 GLU291 MET292 HIS293 HIS294 GLU295
GLN296 ASN305 VAL306 GLY307 PHE308 ASN309 ARG320
PF00736: ASP1131 ILE1159 PRO1160 ILE1161 GLY1162 PHE1163 GLY1164 ILE1165
LYS1166 SER1197

PF00009: VAL12 ILE13 VAL16 LYS20 SER21 ARG67 GLU68 ARG69 GLY70 ILE71 THR72
ILE73 ASP74 ILE75 ALA76 LEU77 TRP78 VAL89 ILE90 ASP91 ALA92 PRO93
GLY94 HIS95 ARG96 ASP97 PHE98 ASN101 GLY105 THR106 SER107
PF00736: ALA1119 LYS1120 SER1121 ILE1122 VAL1123 THR1124 LEU1125 LEU1151
THR1152 TRP1153 GLY1154 ALA1155 HIS1156 GLN1157 GLN1169 ILE1170
ASN1171 CYS1172 VAL1173 VAL1174 GLU1175 ASP1176 ASP1177 VAL1179
SER1180 LEU1181 ASP1182 ASP1199 ILE1200 ALA1201 ALA1202 MET1203
GLN1204 LYS1205

Figure 5.11. Cooperative domains in the complex crystal structure formed by proteins P02994 (with ORFs: YBR118W, YPR080W) and P32471 (with ORF: YAL003W) (see color insert) [WaR07c].

the first round in testing. Such results further confirm the benefit of considering multidomain interactions. In addition, the comparison results on binary PPI data also show APMM and LPM with multidomain pairs to have greater accuracy for protein interaction prediction than in the extended EM algorithm employed by Liu et al. [Liu05].

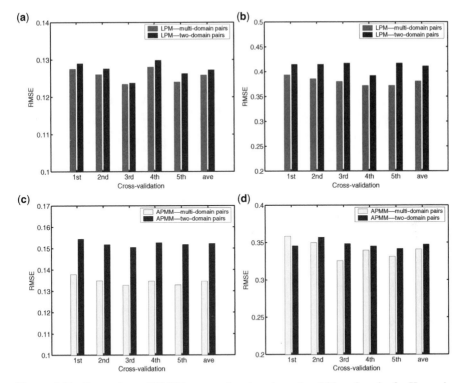

Figure 5.12. Comparison of RMSE on two-domain pairs and multidomain pairs for Krogan's yeast extended datasets: (a) the results of LPM on training; (b) results of LPM on testing; (c) results of APMM on training; (d) results of APMM on testing [WaR07c].

iPfam has been used as a gold standard set to evaluate the predicted domain–domain interactions [Ril05, Gui06]. A comparative experiment for domain interaction prediction was conducted to evaluate the performance of LPM and APMM [WaR07c]. APMM and two other domain interaction prediction methods [domain pair exclusion analysis (DPEA) [Ril05] and PE [Gui06] described in the next section] were applied in the same training set from DIP data, and the overlap of the predicted domain interactions with iPfam by selecting the same number of high-scoring predicted interactions was recorded. The results based on 3005 high-scoring predicted domain interactions [Ril05, Gui06] are listed in Figure 5.13, where PE(1) denotes the parsimony explanation (PE) approach with 60% network reliability (LP-score $\geq$ 0.4, pw-score $\leq$ 0.1) and PE(2) denotes PE approach with 50% network reliability (LP-score $\geq$ 0.4, pw-score $\leq$ 0.1). APMM(1) means APMM based on multidomain pairs, and APMM(2) means APMM based on two-domain pairs. From Figure 5.13a, we can see that APMM has a result comparable to that of PE and better performance than DPEA in terms of domain interaction prediction. Compared with APMM based on two-domain pairs, APMM based on multidomain

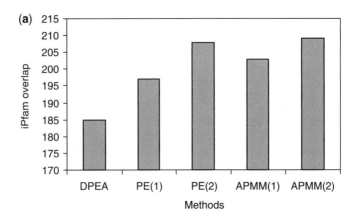

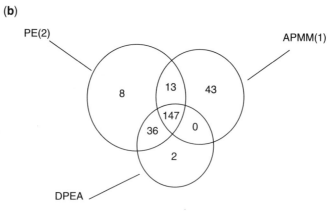

Figure 5.13. Comparison of three methods in terms of domain interaction prediction: (a) overlaps of DDIs predicted by APMM, DPEA, and PE with iPfam. (b) The distribution of the predicted DDI overlaps with iPfam by DPEA, PE, and APMM [WaR07c].

pairs has a slightly smaller iPfam overlap. This is because, according to the definition of cooperative domains and the rule of selecting variables, some two-domain pairs are replaced by cooperative-domain pairs. The distribution of iPfam overlaps is shown in Figure 5.13b, which indicates that APMM can be an important complement since a large portion of the predicted DDIs are not covered by other methods. In addition to two-domain interactions, APMM can also infer cooperative-domain interactions. LPM has similar results, which are not shown here.

5.3.4 Reconstructing Complexes by Multidomain Interactions

Most of the detected cooperative domains with crystal structures are found to be involved in complicated complexes with many proteins. A procedure for reconstructing large protein complexes using the data from multidomain cooperation is described by Wang et al. [WaR07c]. Protein complexes are key molecular entities that integrate multiple gene products to perform cellular functions and the fundamental units of macromolecular organization. Tandem affinity purification coupled to mass spectrometry (TAP-MS) has been applied to find the genomewide screen for complexes so as to investigate the underlying organizational principles of the eukaryotic cellular machinery. However, although many complexes have now been identified, the detailed interacting relationships among the components are beyond our knowledge because 3D structural information is available for only a few of them. X-ray crystallography provides atomic resolution models for proteins and complexes, but it is difficult to obtain sufficient material for the crystallization of large complexes. NMR is generally limited to proteins that have no more than 300 residues. It is therefore necessary to develop new approaches that can reconstruct the structures of complexes on the basis of protein structures and their interaction relationships.

Figure 5.14 shows how to reconstruct the RNA polymerase II-TFIIS complex (PDB ID 1y1v) by LPM or APMM at protein, domain, and atomic levels, respectively, in the following steps:

1. From the available data obtained by TAP-MS, it is known that there are in total 13 different proteins (P04050, P08518, P16370, P20433, P20434, P20435, P34087, P20436, P27999, P22139, P38902, P40422, P07273) in this complex as its subunits (Fig. 5.14a).

2. According to Pfam and protein sequences, all possible domains for each protein in terms of Pfam architectures can be obtained (Fig. 5.14b). There are 30 domains involved in this complex, so it is infeasible to clearly explain the interaction relationships between domains and proteins only by two-domain pairs (total 1435 pairs).

3. By performing APMM or LPM based on protein interaction data, many cooperative-domain interactions can be identified, providing valuable information (Fig. 5.14c).

4. Physical interactions between those 13 proteins in the complex are predicted at the protein level. In Fig. 5.14d, the thick lines denote the physical interactions realized by cooperative-domain pairs and thinner lines indicate those realized by two-domain pairs.

5. Interactions between the protein pairs are further examined at the domain and atomic levels on the basis of structure information using the protein docking procedure.

In step 5 it is easy to estimate the interactions between proteins by considering cooperative domains. For example, proteins P04050 and P08518 probably have the strongest interaction because they have many cooperative-domain interactions. By further combining APMM or LPM with a protein docking procedure, the detailed interactions (e.g., active sites) at atomic level can be identified, which makes it possible to design a stable and coherent complex.

162

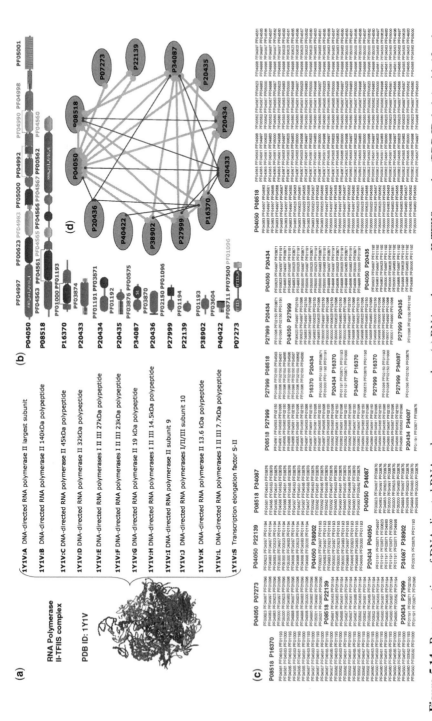

Figure 5.14. Reconstruction of DNA-directed RNA polymerase complex: (a) RNA polymerase II-TFIIS complex (PDB ID 1y1v) with 13 subunits; (b) PfamA domain architecture for every protein; (c) cooperative domains with protein interaction pairs containing them; (d) the complex with two-domain interactions and multidomain interactions (see color insert) [WaR07c].

5.4 DOMAIN INTERACTION PREDICTION METHODS

High-throughput experiments and most interaction prediction methods provide information on whether two proteins interact but give no details on interfaces. Domains are believed to be the fundamental function units of proteins. Protein interaction prediction based on domains often first estimates the interactions of domains and then uses information on the predicted domain–domain interactions for inferring protein interactions [Den02, Liu05, WaR07c, ZhaX06]. Such methods can provide more interaction information since they can determine which domains in a protein pair interact. Some methods have been developed specially for inferring domain–domain interactions from a set of experimental protein interactions [Ril05, Lee06a, Gui06, Ng03] or from phylogenetic profiles [Pag04] and coevolution [Jot06]. In turn, domain interaction networks have been used for analyzing protein interactions [Schu07, Itz06]. We will introduce some domain interaction prediction methods in this section.

5.4.1 Statistical Method

A statistical approach based on p values was proposed to measure the significance of a domain pair accounting for an interacting protein pair [Nye05]. The aim of this method is to predict the most likely pair of domains mediating a given protein interaction instead of predicting new protein interactions. For each domain pair, the null hypothesis that the presence of a superfamily pair in a protein pair does not affect whether the two proteins interact is tested. A global null hypothesis that the interaction is entirely unrelated to the domain architectures of proteins is also tested. To test these hypotheses, a statistic is calculated for each domain pair that takes into account experimental errors represented by the false-positive rate and incompleteness of the dataset represented by the false-negative rate. This statistic is related to the appearance frequency of a domain pair in interacting protein pairs. The reference distribution is simulated by shuffling domains in proteins so that protein interactions and domain frequency are maintained. The resulting p values indicate the possibility of domain interactions and can be used to predict which domains come into contact in an interacting protein pair. Interestingly, this statistical method was shown to outperform other methods such as the association method [Spr01] and the EM method [Den02] when the number of potential contacts of a protein pair increases, which corresponds to a harder prediction case.

5.4.2 Domain Pair Exclusion Analysis

Maximum-likelihood estimation and other methods for inferring domain interactions usually emphasize nonspecific promiscuous domain interactions with high probability scores. Specific and rare interactions between certain members of two-domain families are often neglected. Domain pair exclusion analysis (DPEA) is a method for inferring domain interactions from protein–protein interactions [Ril05]. It extends the previously described MLE method and can detect specific domain interactions. DPEA defines a log odds score E_{ij} reflecting confidence that domains D_i and D_j interact

$$E_{ij} = \sum_{\tau} \sum_{x,y: i \in D(x), j \in D(y)} \log \frac{\Pr(o_{x,y}^{\tau} = 1 | D_i, D_j \text{ interact})}{\Pr(o_{x,y}^{\tau} = 1 | D_i, D_j \text{ do not interact})} \qquad (5.36)$$

$$= \sum_{\tau} \sum_{x,y: i \in D(x), j \in D(y)} \log \frac{1 - \prod_{k \in D(x), l \in D(y)}(1 - \theta_{kl})}{1 - \prod_{k \in D(x), l \in D(y)}(1 - \bar{\theta}_{kl}^{ij})} \qquad (5.37)$$

where $D(x)$ denotes an unordered collection of one or more domains on protein x and θ_{ij} denotes the multispecies probability that domains D_i and D_j interact. For this formula, we can see that E_{ij} is defined as the logarithm of a ratio of two probabilities. The numerator in the ratio corresponds to the probability that two proteins x and y interact given that domains D_i and D_j might interact. The denominator is the probability that proteins x and y interact given that domains D_i and D_j do not interact. The log of the resulting ratio is summed across all organisms τ and all observed interacting protein pairs x and y that potentially interact through domains D_i and D_j. To compute E_{ij}, the probability θ_{kl} in the numerator is estimated by the maximum likelihood L of the observed protein interactions through EM. For the probability in the denominator, EM reruns after setting the probability $\bar{\theta}_{kl}^{ij}$ for domains D_i and D_j as zero, which can help us find competing domain interactions that maximize the likelihood L of the observations under the model that domains D_i and D_j do not interact. Higher E_{ij} implies more instances of domains D_i and D_j potentially interacting. Lower θ_{ij} indicates that competing domains from a protein pair are more likely to be responsible for this interaction. Therefore, domain pairs with θ_{ij} and high E_{ij} can be used to find specific and rare domain–domain interactions.

5.4.3 Parsimony Explanation Approaches

In Section 5.2.3.1, we introduced a protein interaction prediction method based on the parsimony principle which was developed by Zhang et al. [ZhaX06]. In the first step of the method, an integer linear programming (ILP) model is used to infer domain–domain interactions from given protein interaction data. Guimaraes et al. used a parsimony explanation (PE) approach to predict domain–domain interactions from protein interactions [Gui06], in which the model is exactly the same as the basic parsimony model in [ZhaX06] (Section 5.2.3.1), although both models were carried out independently. The difference between these two approaches lies in the fact that Guimaraes et al. did not further predict protein interactions. Rather than extending the model for incorporating negative data, they introduce an concept called network reliability r acting as the right-side parameter of the constraints instead of 1. Such network reliability denotes the interaction possibility of protein interactions. Note that in practice it is heuristically set as 0.5, 0.6, 0.7, and so on. The parameter is less than 1 and thus renders the ILP model as a linear program. The interesting part of their approach is a statistical measure for each domain pair (D_i, D_j), specifically

$$pw\text{-score}(i,j) = \min\{\, p\text{-value}(i,j),\, (1-r)^{w(i,j)}\,\}$$

where $p\text{-value}(i, j)$ is a measure for evaluating the significance of the LP score of (D_i, D_j), which is computed by a separate randomization experiment with a set of 1000 random networks as reference. $w(i, j)$ denotes the number of witnesses (interacting pairs of single-domain proteins supporting it) for (D_i, D_j). $(1-r)^{w(i, j)}$ denotes the probability that all edges corresponding to witnesses are false positives. This term is useful for removing promiscuous domain–domain interactions that are scored high only because of their appearance frequency [Gui06]. With this statistical measure and the LP scores, high-confidence domain–domain interactions can be discovered. More recently, the PE approach was extended by the same authors into the generalized parsimonious explanation (GPE) method [Gui08].

5.4.4 Integrative Approaches

Although large-scale experimental protein interaction data for multiple species are available, such data have a high false-positive rate. To overcome this problem, integrative approaches are often preferred. An integrative approach to computationally derive domain–domain interactions from multiple data sources, such as protein interactions, protein complexes, and rosetta stone sequences, has been developed [Ng03]. All possible domain pairs are generated from interacting protein pairs. Then, the observed frequencies of domain pairs are compared against the corresponding expected frequencies of such domain pairs by random occurrence. The greater the observed frequencies are over the expected frequencies, the higher confidence the inferred domain–domain interactions have. For example, score evidence from protein interactions is defined as

$$O_{\text{int}}(m, n) = \sum_{i=1}^{N} \rho_i \omega_i^{m,n} K_i(m, n)$$

$$E_{\text{int}}(m, n) = 2 \sum_{i=1}^{N} \rho_i \omega_i^{m,n} f(m) f(n)$$

where N is the number of protein–protein interactions used for training; ρ_i denotes the strength of the ith protein interaction (P_k, P_l), which is the total number of distinct experiments observing the ith protein interaction; $\omega_i^{m,n}$ is the weight of the domain pair (D_m, D_n) responsible for the ith protein–protein interaction, which equals $1/(|P_k| \cdot |P_l|)$; $K_i(m, n)$ is the total number of occurrences of the domain pair (D_m, D_n) in the ith protein interaction; and finally $f(m)$ denotes the frequency of domain D_m found in the proteins of the training set. The confidence score of interaction domain pair (D_m, D_n) is defined as an odd ratio:

$$S_{\text{int}}(m, n) = \frac{O_{\text{int}}(m, n)}{E_{\text{int}}(m, n)}$$

The confidence score from protein complexes $S_{cplx}(m, n)$ is defined similarly. The scores from protein interactions and protein complexes are combined with the score from domain fusions $S_{fus}(m, n)$ to form an overall confidence score $S(m, n)$:

$$S(m, n) = \omega_{int}S_{int}(m, n) + \omega_{cplx}S_{cplx}(m, n) + \omega_{fus}S_{fus}(m, n)$$

Putative domain interactions derived using this method are stored in the database InterDom, which is available on http://interdom.lit.org.sg.

Another integrative approach to infer domain–domain interactions from multiple data sources such as protein interactions, molecular sequences, and gene ontology has also been developed [Lee06a]. In this approach, a new measure called the expected number of occurrences of each domain interaction is defined as

$$E(D_{mn}) = \sum N_{mn} \Pr(d_{mn} = 1)$$

where N_{mn} is the number of protein pairs containing domain pair (D_m, D_n). This measure aims to overcome the limitation in using $\Pr(d_{mn} = 1)$ to rank domain–domain interactions [Lee06a]. Interestingly, such a simple measure was shown with performance similar to that of the E score in DPEA [Ril05]. In addition, to employ domain fusion information, another measure, $CE(D_{mn})$, was proposed to characterize the co-existence of domains D_m and D_n, that is, the number of occurrences of domains D_m and D_n coexisting in the same proteins. This measure is based on common knowledge that domains always appearing in the same proteins are more likely to interact. The integration of gene ontology is based on the assumption that two domains in the same GO function are more likely to interact than they do in different functions. Moreover, two domains with a more specific function are more likely to interact than they do with a more general function. Lee et al. considered a function as more specific simply by characterizing it by a smaller number of domains that cover this function [Lee06]. Therefore, assume that domain pair (D_m, D_n) has the same function F_f; then the measure $SG(D_{mn})$ is defined as representing the same gene ontology, which is simply characterized by the number of domains having the function F_f. With the three defined measures, the numbers of evidences supporting domain interactions from protein interactions, domain fusion, and gene ontology are used to score domain pairs for potential interactions. The evidentiary value for a domain pair was set from 0 to 6. Then, a naive Bayesian approach was used to multiple independent data sources by defining a total likelihood ratio as

$$L(d_{mn} = 1) = \prod_{i=1}^{6} \frac{\Pr(d_i|Obs)}{\Pr(d_j|Nobs)}$$

where Obs denotes the set of the observed domain interactions in iPfam, $Nobs$ denotes the set of nonobserved domain interactions in iPfam; $d_1, \dots, d_4$ are the values of $E[\#(d_{mn} = 1)]$ in yeast, worms, fruit flies, and humans, respectively; and d_5 and d_6 are the values of $CE(D_{mn})$ and $SG(D_{mn})$. For each species, the values of $E(D_{mn})$

were split into seven intervals with each interval as a bin. Let $d = E(D_{mn})$ and assume that d falls into the tth bin. $\Pr(d|Obs)$ is the fraction of the observed interactions in the tth bin and $\Pr(d|Nobs)$ is the fraction of the nonobserved interactions in the tth bin. The values of $CE(D_{mn})$ and $SG(D_{mn})$ were similarly split. In addition to the evidence counting method and naive Bayesian approach, a logic regression was designed and compared with these two methods:

$$\log \frac{\Pr(d_{mn}=1)}{1 - \Pr(d_{mn}=1)} = \alpha + \beta_1 E_\gamma(D_{mn}) + \beta_2 E_\omega(D_{mn}) + \beta_3 E_f(D_{mn}) + \beta_4 E_h(D_{mn})$$
$$+ \beta_5 I[CE(D_{mn}) \geq 1] + \beta_6 I[SG(D_{mn}) \geq 1] + \beta_7 EV(D_{mn})$$

$$(5.38)$$

where $E_\gamma(D_{mn})$, $E_\omega(D_{mn})$, $E_f(D_{mn})$, $E_h(D_{mn})$ respectively denote the expected number of occurrences of the domain interactions in yeast, worm, fruit fly, and human protein interactions, and $EV(D_{mn})$ denotes the number of evidences from the evidence counting method. Experimental results show that the naive Bayesian approach outperforms the evidence counting and the logistic regression methods, and integrating multiple data sources indeed increases the coverage and accuracy of the predicted domain interactions [Lee06].

5.5 SUMMARY

High-throughput techniques have resulted in data for large-scale protein interactions that, however, are noisy and incomplete, and thus sophisticated computational methods are required to analyze them. Prediction of new protein interactions based on available data is one of the most important topics in this field. In this chapter, we briefly introduced several experimental techniques for determining protein–protein interactions, and then reviewed prediction methods for these interactions, particularly those based on domain information. In addition, several approaches directly designed for inferring domain–domain interactions from protein interactions were also introduced. The softwares for APMM, and LPM described in this chapter are available from the Websites http://intelligent.eic.osaka-sandai.ac.jp/chenen/software.htm, http://www.isb.shu.edu.cn, and http://www.aporc.org/doc/wiki/BioinformaticsSoftwares. Although these methods can be a valuable complement to experimental techniques, none of them can achieve a satisfactory prediction accuracy, partly because available protein interactions generated by high-throughput techniques contain many false positives. Further exploration could focus on what kind of biological data most essentially support protein interactions, or provide reliable information for protein interactions. In addition, there are some other topics such as predicting interacting sites or interfaces that are also related to the analysis of protein–protein interactions.

CHAPTER 6

TOPOLOGICAL STRUCTURE OF BIOMOLECULAR NETWORKS

6.1 STATISTICAL PROPERTIES OF BIOMOLECULAR NETWORKS

Many systems in real life can be expressed by a network or a graph, in which nodes represent the objects and edges denote the relations between them. For example, in a social system, there are scientific collaboration networks and football team networks. In an ecological system, there are food networks. In particular, in a cellular system, complex interactions between numerous constituents in cells, such as DNA, RNA, proteins, and small molecules, form a variety of biological networks at different levels such as gene regulatory networks, transcriptional regulatory networks, metabolic networks, and signaling networks. More recently, these networks have been revealed to have many interesting topological properties, such as the small-world property and power-law degree distribution [Alb02, Bar04, Alb05], which account for most biological behaviors. Topological analysis of biomolecular networks, as a special type of complex networks, is a topic of great interest in the field of bioinformatics and systems biology, which is expected to provide quantitative insights into biological systems.

Given a network or graph $G = (V, E)$, where V is the node set and E is the edge set, the topological indices for characterizing a network include average degree K, clustering coefficient C, average path length L, and network diameter D [Alb02, YuH04, Zha07]. The topological distributions include degree distribution $P(k)$, cluster coefficient distribution $C(k)$, shortest path distribution $SP(l)$. The most elementary characteristic of a node is its degree or connectivity, which is defined as the number

---

Biomolecular Networks. By Luonan Chen, Rui-Sheng Wang, and Xiang-Sun Zhang
Copyright © 2009 John Wiley & Sons, Inc.

of links that this node has to other nodes. For an undirected network, the average degree of the whole network is the average of the degrees of all individual nodes

$$K = \frac{\sum_{i \in V} k_i}{N}$$

where k_i is the degree of node i, $N = |V|$ is the total number of $= |E|$. In many real-life networks, if node a is connected to node b, and node b is connected to node c, then it is highly probable that node a also has a direct link to node c. This phenomenon can be quantified using the clustering coefficient C, which is defined as the ratio of the number of existing links between a node's neighbors to the maximum number of possible links between them

$$C = \frac{\sum_{i \in V} [e_i / k_i(k_i - 1)]}{N},$$

where e_i is the number of edges existing between the k_i nodes that are connected to node i. $e_i / k_i(k_i - 1)$ quantifies the cohesiveness of the neighborhood of node i. The clustering coefficient of a network is the average of all individual coefficients of the nodes in the network. It reflects the completeness of a network. The shortest path between two nodes is a path with the minimum number of edges that is necessary to traverse from one node to the other. The average path length of a network is an average of the shortest path lengths between every node pair

$$L = \frac{2 \sum_{i,j \in V, i < j} d_{ij}}{N(N - 1)}$$

where d_{ij} is the shortest path length between nodes i and j. It reflects how closely nodes are connected within the network and offers a measure of a network's overall navigability. The diameter of a network is the longest graph-theoretic distance between any two nodes in the graph:

$$D = \max_{i,j \in V} \{d_{ij}\}$$

The degree distribution $P(k)$ gives the fraction of nodes that have degree k and is obtained by counting the number of nodes $N(k)$ that have $k(=1, 2, 3, \ldots)$ edges and dividing it by the total number of nodes N. The degree distribution reflects the probability that a selected node has exactly k links. It quantifies the diversity of the whole network, and allows us to distinguish between different classes of networks. The degree distributions of many types of real-life networks, such as Web networks, scientific collaboration networks, and metabolic networks, follow such a function: $P(k) = Ak^\gamma$, called a power law, where A is a constant ensuring that the $P(k)$ values add up to 1 and γ is a constant usually in the range $2 < \gamma < 3$. A network with such a degree distribution is called scale-free, indicating that there is a high diversity of node degrees and no typical node in the network that could be used to characterize the remaining nodes [Alb05]. A random network has a peaked degree distribution, indicating that the system has a characteristic degree and there are no highly connected nodes

(a)   (b)

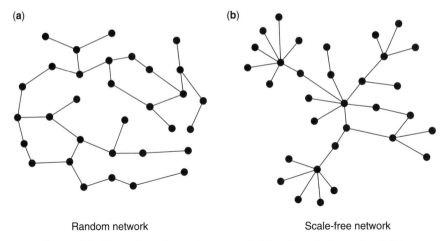

Random network   Scale-free network

Figure 6.1. Illustrations of a random network (a) and a scale-free network (b).

known as hubs (Fig. 6.1). In contrast, a power-law degree distribution indicates that most nodes have only a few connections whereas some nodes are highly connected [Bar04]. Cluster coefficient distribution $C(k)$ is defined by averaging the clustering coefficients of nodes that have the same degree k. It characterizes the diversity of cohesiveness of local neighborhoods and the overall tendency of nodes to form clusters or groups. For many real life networks, $C(k) = k^{-1}$ holds, which implies a network's hierarchical character. Shortest path distribution $SP(l)$ is defined as the proportion of shortest paths with a specified length l in a network and reflects the diversity of the graph distances between two nodes in the network. In most real-life networks, there is a relatively short path between any two nodes, and the length is in the order of logarithm of the network size [Alb02]. This property is known as "small world."

In biological research, high-throughput techniques have generated a tremendous amount of data on cellular networks. Topological analysis of these networks is an important step toward understanding the biological roles and functions of the networks. The topology measures mentioned above can efficiently capture the topological features of cellular networks and provide broad insight into cellular evolution, molecular function, network stability, and dynamic responses, and thereby serve as comprehensive criteria in analyzing cellular networks. For example, many types of biomolecular networks such as protein interaction networks, gene regulatory networks, and metabolic networks have been shown to display scale-free topologies with a hierarchical organization, characterized by a power-law degree distribution that decays more slowly that at an exponential rate [Bar04]. Scale-free network topology is also frequently observed in numerous nonbiological networks and can be generated by simple evolutionary models, where new nodes attach preferentially to sites that are already highly connected, thereby providing the possibility of exploring evolution or growth mechanisms of cellular networks, as indicated by Albert and Barabási [Alb05].

The architectural features of protein interaction networks from different species to a large degree display topological features common to those of other nonbiological complex networks. The graph properties in protein interaction networks directly link to the functional and evolutionary mechanisms in the corresponding biological processes. Studying network nodes and local structures from the topological perspective is helpful in understanding their functions as essential components of cellular interaction networks. Maslov and Sneppen studied the topology of metabolic and signaling pathways shaped by interacting proteins and found that the links between highly connected proteins and lowly connected proteins are favored [Mas02], which indicates a negative correlation between the degrees of two interacting proteins. Yu et al. developed a tool called TopNet to compare the topological characteristics of different subnetworks derived from any given protein network [YuH04]. Yook et al. compared four available databases that approximate the protein interaction network of *S. cerevisiae* and revealed that this network has a scale-free topology with a hierarchical modularity [Yoo04]. Li et al. systematically analyzed the topological structure of the protein interaction networks of *S. cerevisiae*, *C. elegans*, and *D. melanogaster* [LiD06] and also confirmed that these protein interaction networks have a scale-free and high-degree clustering nature as well as hierarchical organization. The analysis also indicates that these networks have the small-world property with similar diameters at 4–5. In addition to protein interaction networks, domain interaction networks and protein domain networks have also been shown to possess the scale-free property [Wuc01]. In a more recent study, Zhu and Qin uncovered topological differences among the metabolic networks of 11 single-cell organisms by comparing their network structures [Zhu05]. They showed that the design principles of the Archaea metabolic network may be fundamentally different from those of bacteria and eukaryotes.

It should be noted that observations of the topological features in cellular networks are subject to the incompleteness and noise of biological data. The architecture of large-scale biological networks is actually determined by sampling the subnetworks of the true networks. Therefore, it is these partial networks that are used to characterize the topology of the underlying true network [Ait06]. It has been shown that it is possible to extrapolate from subnetworks to the properties of the whole network only if the degree distributions of the whole network and randomly sampled subnetworks share the same family of probability distributions [Stu05]. Tanaka et al. argued that some protein interaction networks do not exhibit power-law statistics by evaluating degree sequences [Tan05]. Also, Przulj et al. revealed that the commonly accepted scale-free model for protein interaction networks may fail to fit the data [Prz04b]. Another study suggested that the observed scale-free property of current protein interaction networks cannot be extrapolated to complete interactomes [Han05]. Limited sampling alone may as well give rise to apparent scale-free topologies, irrespective of the original network topology. With these facts and studies, the global properties of the complete network structure based on the current observed networks should be interpreted with caution. On the other hand, while topological measures can efficiently characterize some large-scale attributes of networks, they are only global and rough criteria and may not be able to distinguish more detailed topological structures. For example, it is easy to construct two networks that have identical topological measures including degree distribution and clustering coefficient but display different hierarchical structures [Val06]. Therefore, the local topological features such as modularity, motif, and network clustering are likely to be key concepts in understanding cellular mechanisms and biological functions in biomolecular networks.

6.2 EVOLUTION OF PROTEIN INTERACTION NETWORKS

Researchers have begun to study the topological features of networks from an evolutionary perspective by assuming that the current topology of a network is formed through a series of network assembly events and network evolution events. Understanding how networks evolve is a fundamental issue in real-life complex networks and can provide insights into the structure and function of the networks.

There have been several network growth models developed. One is the Barabási–Albert (BA) model [Bar99], which incorporates two mechanisms: growth (i.e., increasing the number of nodes and edges over time) and preferential attachment (i.e., increasing the chance of high-degree nodes acquiring new edges). In another model for growing network, a network grows by iterative network duplication and integration to its original core [Rav02]. In biological networks, these growth mechanisms correspond to two processes in evolution. The first type of process involves sequence mutations in a gene. Sequence mutations result in modifications of the interface between interacting proteins, and the corresponding proteins may gain new connections (attachment) or lose (detachment) some of the existing connections to other proteins [Sha06]. The second type of evolutionary process consists of gene duplication, followed by either silencing of one of the duplicated genes or by functional divergence of the duplicates. In terms of network structure, a gene duplication corresponds to an addition of a node with links identical to the original node, followed by the divergence of some of the redundant links between the two duplicated nodes [Sha06]. According to the model proposed by Berg et al. [Ber04b], link dynamics is the dominant evolutionary force shaping the statistical structure of the network, while the slower gene duplication dynamics affects mainly the size. Specifically, the model predicts that there is a broad distribution of connectivity of proteins and correlations between the connectivity of interacting proteins. Both features have been observed in the protein interaction network of *S. cerevisiae*. Barabási and Albert suggested gene duplication as the major mechanism for generating the scale-free topology of protein interaction networks [Bar99]. Their network growth model predicts that molecules that appeared early in the network are the most connected ones. This hypothesis has been supported by other work. For example, Eisenberg and Levanon [Eis03] used a cross-genome comparison to show that the older a protein is, the better connected it is, and that the number of interactions that a protein gains during its evolution is proportional to its connectivity. Therefore, preferential attachment governs the evolution of protein interaction networks.

In addition, Qin et al. used network growth theory to model the evolution of a yeast protein interaction network by analyzing the growth pattern of the network [Qin03]. They classified all the proteins into isotemporal categories according to each protein's orthologous hits in several groups of genomes that are informative for the yeast's evolutionary history, and then inferred the main path of the network evolution from six major isotemporal categories. Evlampiev and Isambert proposed a mathematical model to describe the evolution of protein interaction networks under successive genome duplications and domain shuffling [Evl07]. Their model illustrates that scale-free topologies of protein interaction networks appear to be a simple consequence of the conservation of protein-binding domains under asymmetric duplication/divergence dynamics in the course of evolution.

6.3 HUBS, MOTIFS, AND MODULARITY IN BIOMOLECULAR NETWORKS

In the sections above, several global measures were introduced to characterize the topology features of complex networks including protein interaction networks. As indicated earlier, such measures are macrocriteria, and cannot distinguish more detailed topological structures. In this section, in contrast to global network character-istics, we further introduce some concepts related to local topological structure that describe local interconnections and more detailed relationships between nodes.

6.3.1 Network Centralities and Hubs

In a network, different nodes have different levels of connectivity. It is natural to define measures to evaluate which node is the most important according to its topological connection. Network centrality is a local quantitative measure for asses-sing the position of a node relative to the other nodes, and can be used to estimate its importance or role in a global network organization. Different information sources reveal several centrality measures such as degree centrality, closeness centrality, and betweenness centrality. Among them, the degree centrality, possibly the simplest one, is based on the node's connectivity and defined as the degree of a node, or more specifically, the number of edges linking the node. Closeness centrality of a node is based on its shortest paths to other nodes, and betweenness centrality is based on the number of shortest paths going through the node. It measures the extent to which a vertex is in between other vertices, which is calculated as the fraction of shortest paths between node pairs that pass through the node of interest. It is a measure of the influence that a node has over the spread of information through the network.

   Different centralities focus on different features. In biological networks, genes or proteins having many interactions with other genes or proteins are often considered as central and important for the function of the cell. To elucidate the functional roles of components in cellular interaction networks, a high-quality ranking measure of network components is important. Network centrality can be used for this purpose. Actually central elements of molecular networks have been observed to be essential for many biological phenomena, such as viability, evolution, and stability. Fell and Wagner showed that the most central metabolites are evolutionarily conservative in metabolic networks [Fel00]. In yeast protein interaction networks, Jeong et al.

revealed that the centrality of a protein correlates with the essentiality of the encoding gene by the observation that knocking out this gene would lead to a high probability of a lethal effect [Jeo00]. Furthermore, by comparing six centrality measures, Estrada showed that a centrality measures based on graph spectral properties of the network has the best performance in distinguishing essential proteins in the yeast protein interaction network [Est06]. This study may offer a means to select possible targets for drug discovery. A software tool called CentiBiN [Jun06] has been developed for computation and exploration of centralities in molecular networks. The system computes 17 different centralities for directed or undirected networks for numerically evaluating the importance of an element in molecular networks. Hahn and Kern have correlated the rate of evolution of yeast proteins with their degrees in the protein interaction network and showed that a protein's position in the network indicates its centrality to cellular function and evolutionary constraint [Hah05]. By using degree centrality to analyze the metabolic networks of E. coli, S. cerevisiae, and S. aureus, Samal et al. demonstrated that most reactions identified as essential turned out to be those involving the production or consumption of low-degree metabolites [Sam06].

Since biomolecular networks have been shown to have scale-free properties, small-degree nodes are the most abundant. Biologists have a special interest in nodes with high degrees called hubs [Alb02]. Random node disruptions do not lead to a major loss of connectivity, but a loss of the hubs causes the breakdown of the network into isolated clusters [Alb00]. Intuitively, one might expect to find some particularities of such proteins in cellular networks by correlating the severity of a gene knockout with the number of interactions in which the gene products participate. Given the importance of highly connected nodes, one can hypothesize that they are subject to severe selective and evolutionary constraints [Wuc04]. Those hub proteins generally prefer to interact with lowly connected proteins, rather than to interact with other hub proteins in a protein interaction network [Mas02]. For instance, Bergmann et al. showed that high-degree genes tend to be essential and conserved in coexpression networks [BeS04]. Note that all these observations may be affected heavily by the noise in data sources. Batada et al. reevaluated related problems by employing an extensive literature-curated protein interaction datasets, and argued that hubs are likely to be essential, or at least have a larger impact on fitness, but they are not slowly evolving [Bat06a]. He and Zhang proposed an interesting alternative view on essential protein–protein interactions similar to those of essential proteins [HeX06]; thus, a small fraction of randomly distributed interactions are considered essential if each of these interactions is lethal to an organism when disrupted. Another interesting investigation on the so-called date hubs and party hubs was conducted by Han et al. [HanJ04]. In protein interaction networks, party hubs are those hubs coexpressed with many of their neighbors, while date hubs are those not coexpressed with their neighbors (Fig. 6.2). The authors suggested that these two types of hubs dynamically mediate the modularity of networks. In a more recent study, Batada et al. argued, with some contrary observations, that hub–hub interactions are not suppressed and that the biological attributes of a data hub do not differ from those of other hubs, such as different rates of evolution [Bat06b].

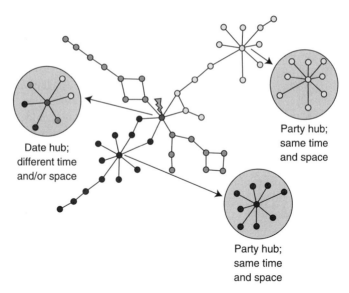

Figure 6.2. Date hubs and party hubs in protein interaction networks. (Reprinted by permission from Macmillan Publishers Ltd: Nature [HaJ04], © 2004.)

Ekman et al. explored the characteristics between hubs and nonhubs, date hubs, and party hubs on the domain level [Eka06]. They pointed that multiple and repeated domains are enriched in hub proteins, and long disordered regions important for flexible binding are statistically significant in date hubs. Kim et al. related 3D structures with protein networks and found that some hubs have many binding interfaces, while some others have only one or a few binding interfaces [Kim06]. This characteristic provides insight into hubs' evolutionary rate and indicates that some additional mechanisms of network growth beyond preferential attachment are active in evolution.

In contrast to hubs, another approach to characterize the importance of individual nodes is based on trees of shortest paths and concepts of bottleneck nodes [Prz04a]. Bottleneck nodes have a high betweenness centrality and low degree. Joy et al. analyzed the betweenness of proteins in a protein interaction network and found that proteins with high betweenness and low connectivity are abundant in yeast interactome [Joy05]. This is mainly because protein interaction networks have a modular organization and low-connectivity proteins usually act as important links between these modules. Yu et al. found that bottleneck proteins are very important [YuH07]. They tend to be essential proteins and key connectors with surprising functional and dynamic properties. In particular, bottleneck proteins correspond to the dynamic components of the interaction network, which are significantly less well coexpressed with their neighbors than are nonbottleneck ones, which implies that expression dynamics are also wired into the network topology. Although many biological phenomena are observed with the assumption of possible cellular mechanisms, we should note that all of those conclusions are not definite and depend on the quality and quantity of available data.

6.3.2 Network Modularity and Motifs

The functions of biomolecular networks are closely related to their topologies and facilitated by characteristic topological patterns. From the theoretical viewpoint, the decomposition of a large network into relatively independent subnetworks is an effective way to understand the basic architecture of the whole network, and has been regarded as a major approach to deal with the complexity of large cellular networks. In fact, many types of cellular networks, including protein interaction networks, have been shown to have a modular organization [Har99, Bar04]. In other words, components of cellular networks including genes, proteins, and other molecules usually act in collaboration to carry out specific biological processes and biochemical activities, by forming relatively isolated functional units called modules. From the topological perspective, a module can be understood as a subnetwork that is densely connected within itself but sparsely connected with the rest of the network. In cellular networks, a module refers to a group of physically or functionally connected biomolecules that work together to achieve some desired cellular function. Revealing modular structure in cellular networks is helpful for understanding biochemical processes and signal pathways. To investigate the modularity of interaction networks, many computational tools and measures have been developed to detect functional modules in protein interaction networks and other cellular networks based on the topological features of the networks (Fig. 6.3), which we will introduce in the later chapters. It is worth noting that modularity does not mean a well-defined subnetwork structure. The modules in cellular networks are often dynamical and hierarchical [HaJ04, Rav02, ZhaZ06]. Moreover, modules are seldom isolated components of the networks. They share nodes, links, and even functions with other modules and also form overlapping modules [Bar04].

A network motif is a subunit of a complex network that appears much more frequently in the given network than expected by chance alone [Mil02, Alo07]. Such subnetworks are considered to be basic building blocks of many real complex

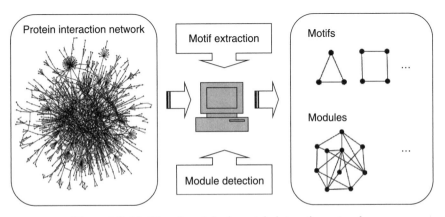

Figure 6.3. Motifs and modules in protein interaction networks.

networks, including biomolecular networks. Elucidating the roles of motifs is of great interest both theoretically and biologically. Figure 6.3 shows a scheme for detecting motifs and modules from protein interaction networks. Generally, the basic steps of motif analysis are

1. Estimating the frequencies of each subgraph in the observed network
2. Grouping them into subgraph classes consisting of topologically equivalent motifs
3. Determining which subgraph classes are displayed at much higher frequencies than in their random counterparts [Ait06]

Obviously, enumerating all subnetworks within a given mode in a large network is practically infeasible. To overcome this difficulty, a probabilistic algorithm based on subnetwork importance sampling strategy has been developed [Kas04]. It can estimate the densities of subnetworks, and detect motifs in a time complexity of asymptotically independent of network size. Moreover, efficient alternatives together with graphical user interfaces for motif detection and visualization in large networks have also been developed [WeS06, Sch05].

Motifs have increasingly been found and studied in a number of biomolecular and nonbiomolecular networks. For example, in biomolecular networks, there are motifs such as feedforward loops and single input motifs in transcriptional regulatory networks, and short cycles in protein interaction networks. The overrepresentation of motifs has been interpreted as manifestations of functional constraints and design principles that have shaped network architecture at the local level [Ait06]. Many representative motifs were found in multiple organisms. For example, several identical motifs and interaction motifs such as autoregulation loops and feedforward loops have been observed in transcription regulatory networks of diverse species. In particular, Zhu and Qin found that *S. cerevisiae* and six bacterial species share identical three-node motifs and 2 four-node motifs in metabolic networks, while four Archaeal species manifest significantly different motifs [Zhu05]. Such a finding implies that Archaeal species may employ different mechanisms to perform biological functions than bacterial species. In protein interaction networks, motifs such as short cycles and small, completely connected subgraphs (or cliques) are both abundant and evolutionarily conserved [Gio03]. By labeling nodes in a protein interaction network with functional attributes, Lee et al. enumerated all recurring patterns of the annotated protein interaction network [LeW06]. They found that evolutionary constraints on the motifs are significantly different from those with functional attributes.

In addition, it has been observed that the frequency of each motif type varies with different condition of the network. Further exploration of structurally dynamical properties by checking the distribution of motifs in different condition-specific cellular networks is necessary and significant. Yeger-Lotem et al. have identified frequent composite transcription/protein interaction motifs, such as interacting transcription factors coregulating a gene or interacting proteins being coregulated by the same transcription factor [Yeg04]. Luscombe et al. modeled a condition-specific transcriptional regulatory network for yeast based on transcription binding data and gene expression data [Lus04]. They observed that different frequencies of various regulatory motifs occurred depending on conditions of the network, which implies structurally dynamical changes in different conditions. By reexamining the datasets of Luscombe et al., Zhang et al. explored how differences in regulatory motif abundance are related to specific transcription hub factors [ZhZ06]. Their studies show that different transcription hubs in a condition-specific network prefer different types of motifs, but variations in motif abundance cannot explain such preferences. They further pointed out that motif preferences of transcription hubs change with variations in molecular networks. Zhang et al. analyzed protein interactions representing signaling pathways and cellular mechanisms in the hippocampal CA1 neuron and found that regulatory motifs, such as positive/negative-feedback/feedforward loops are abundant [Zha05]. They have pointed out that the abundant motifs of integrated mRNA/protein networks are often signatures of higher-order network structures that correspond to biological phenomena. Observing that proteins with common interaction partners tend to interact with these partners through a common interacting motif, Aragues et al. developed a method for delineating the interacting motifs of hub proteins [Ara07]. Their research results show that yeast hubs with multiple interacting motifs are more likely to be essential than hubs with one or two interacting motifs, which is consistent with the observed correlation between essentiality and the number of interacting partners of a protein. As for evolutionary constraint, yeast hubs with multiple interacting motifs are found to evolve more slowly than the average proteins.

These studies and findings regarding motifs not only elucidate the biological implications for network structures but also help us gain insights into biological evolution as well as dynamical behaviors of cellular networks. However, we should also note that motifs are not the sole criterion for analyzing biomolecular networks, and biochemical properties of nodes (molecules) are seldom represented in the motifs. For instance, motifs cannot capture the connection characteristics among nodes. Moreover, Przulj et al. argued that exploring the organization of infrequently appeared subnetworks is also important [Prz04b]. Enumerating all the subnetworks was computationally so intense that they designed efficient sampling heuristics to find small subnetworks in a protein interaction network by focusing only on specific parts of the network [Prz06]. In contrast to network motifs emphasizing statistical significance, one can estimate the distribution of different subnetworks and examine their global properties, such as degree distribution [Vaz04], which can provide valuable information on other aspects of biomolecular networks.

6.4 EXPLORATIVE ROLES OF HUBS AND NETWORK MOTIFS

As described earlier, hubs may correspond to network components with central biological roles because of their topologies. Therefore, biological roles of hubs have been studied. For example, date hubs and party hubs defined by Han et al. [HanJ04] were shown to display diverse spatial distributions and organize network modules in different ways. However, because of the heavy noises in protein interaction data sources, there are controversy and contradicting conclusions regarding the roles of hubs. Batada et al. argued that hubs have a greater impact on fitness but they do not evolve slowly [Bat06a]. On the basis of another filtered yeast interactome data, Batada et al. found that there is no evidence for the coexistence of party hubs and date hubs [Bat06b]. For such a contradiction, Jin et al. combined hubs with network motifs [Jin07] and further revealed their roles in connecting disease pathways [Jin08]. In these studies, they stressed the cellular roles of network motifs in biomolecular networks rather than their topological structures and illustrated the essential functions of hubs with network motifs in organizing network modules. We will discuss these studies in detail next.

6.4.1   Dynamic Modularity Organized by Hubs and Network Motifs

Network motifs are believed to be functional building blocks of biomolecular networks and have important roles in information processing. Generally, a motif is defined as a repeating interconnection pattern of nodes that is highly significant from a statistical standpoint [Alo07, LiC07a]. In order to settle the debate in previous work [HanJ04, Bat06b], by using network motifs, two new types of hubs—the motif party hub (mPHs) and the motif date hub (mDH)—have been defined in terms of the relationship between a hub's network motifs and protein complexes [Jin07]. These two types of hubs have the same characteristics as the party hub and the date hub, respectively. As in previous research work, Jin et al. focused on the important roles of motifs in acting as functional units in organizing network modularity. The motivation for using network motifs is that the main structure of a protein interaction network is composed of network motifs rather than individual proteins and network motifs cover most of proteins and interactions. Another reason is that the appropriate size of network motifs determines their important roles in characterizing both small-size elements (biomolecules) at the low level and large-size elements (modules) at the high level of a network. Jin et al. emphasized the interactions around hubs and network motifs instead of individual proteins and demonstrated that the motifs around an mPH are more likely to remain inside a protein complex and control the local topological structure. They are more likely to be located in the same cellular localizations as the mPH, and coexpressed in microarray data. On the other hand, the motifs around an mDH tend to spread into different complexes and act as the connectors between signal pathways to control the global topological structure. They are more likely to be located in different cellular localizations and expressed differently in microarray data.

6.4.1.1   *Data Sources*   In the study by Jin et al. [Jin07], one filtered yeast interactome (FYI) dataset of 2491 interactions among 1375 proteins was from the paper by Han et al. [HaJ04]. Another FYI dataset HC^{fyi} of 3976 interactions among 1291

proteins was from the Batada et al.'s study [Bat06b]. The protein complex data were extracted from MIPS [Mew06] in September 2006, and the signal pathway data were derived from KEGG in November 2006. Cellular localization data were derived from the Huh et al.'s study [Hub03]. The six microarray datasets are stress response, cell cycle, pheromone treatment, unfolded protein response, sporulation, and compendium, which are the same to those in the studies by Han et al. [HaJ04] and Batada et al. [Bat06b]. The expression measurement for each gene was adjusted to have mean 0 and standard deviation 1 using the original fold change values. Compendium gene expression data are an expression-profiling compendium of 315 data points for most of yeast genes across other five different experimental conditions. The Pearson correlation coefficients of motifs were calculated for the five conditions and the combined set of all conditions. The top 20% proteins with relatively more partners in the protein interaction networks were selected as hubs. The number of their partners is at least 12. There are 103 hubs in the overlap of HC^{fyi} hubs and FYI hubs. Since protein–protein interaction networks are undirected, the motifs in these networks are undoubtedly undirected. Jin et al. detected network motifs using mfinder1.2 [Mil02]. Three-node subnetworks (triangle) and four-node subnetworks (square) were used as network motifs.

6.4.1.2 Definition of Motif Party Hubs and Motif Date Hubs

A hub contained in at least one motif is called motif hub. A motif is called a network motif of a hub if it takes the hub as one of its nodes. Partition of hubs into motif party hubs (mPHs) and motif date hubs (mDHs) is based on the relationship between a hub's network motifs and protein complexes [Jin07]. Assume that a protein H is a hub in a protein interaction network, and $M = \{M_1, M_2, \ldots, M_{|M|}\}$ is a set of the hub's network motifs. For the protein P_j in some network motif M_k, the protein complex set of P_j, denoted by C_j, is composed of those protein complexes containing P_j. $M_{\text{same-complex}}$ is a set of three-protein motifs or four-protein motifs with their proteins contained in same complexes; that is, if $\cap_{j=1}^{|M_k|} C_j > 1$, then $M_k \in M_{\text{same-complex}}$. Then the criterion for distinguishing mPH and mDH is defined as

$$C_{\text{ratio-same}} = \frac{|M_{\text{same-complex}}|}{|M|}$$

By this criterion, a hub with a relatively high $C_{\text{ratio-same}}$ (≥ 0.5) is classified as mPH, and a hub with a relatively low $C_{\text{ratio-same}}$ (<0.5), as mDH.

Let L_j denote the set of cellular localizations that the protein P_j has. The set $M_{\text{same-localization}}$ is composed of those three-protein motifs or four-protein motifs with their proteins located in the same cellular localization; thus, if $\cap_{j=1}^{|M_k|} L_j > 1$, then $M_k \in M_{\text{same-localization}}$. Then the spatial distribution of a hub's network motifs is measured by another quantitative criterion defined as

$$L_{\text{ratio-same}} = \frac{|M_{\text{same-localization}}|}{|M|}$$

The average motif correlation (AMC) for a network motif of a hub is a measure of the average expression level for the encoding genes in the network motif. For each network motif M_i, AMC is constructed as

$$\mathrm{AMC}(M_i) = \frac{\sum_{j=1}^{|M_i|} \sum_{k=1}^{|M_i|} I_{jk} \cdot \mathrm{PCC}(P_j, P_k)}{|M_i|}$$

where P_j and P_k are any two proteins in M_i. $\mathrm{PCC}(P_j, P_k)$ is the Pearson correlation coefficient of the gene expression profiles of P_j and P_k. I_{jk} is an indicator function to denote whether P_j and P_k are linked in M_i. The mean of average motif correlations (MAMC) is the mean of all AMCs for all network motifs of a hub. To analyze the difference between the expression of a hub's network motifs, the standard deviation of average motif correlation (SAMC) is defined [Jin07]. It is the standard deviation of all AMCs for all network motifs of a hub.

6.4.1.3 *Biological Roles of mPHs and mDHs*   According to the data
sources mentioned above, there are 196 motif hubs in HC^{fyi}. According to the relationship between a hub's network motifs and protein complexes, the 196 motif hubs were divided into 98 mPHs and 98 mDHs by using the quantitative criterion $C_{\mathrm{ratio-same}}$. From the definition of mPHs and mDHs, it is clear that the network motifs of an mPH will more likely stay together in the same protein complex as the mPH, while those of an mDH spread outside the protein complex of the mDH. Available mPHs and mDHs were introduced to study hubs at the level of network motifs instead of individual proteins, so as to solve the open debate, namely, whether HC^{fyi} in fact contains date hubs and party hubs. Because of the topological distinction between FYI and HC^{fyi}, 103 hubs were found in the overlap between 199 hubs in FYI and 197 hubs in HC^{fyi}. As a result, among the overlapping 103 hubs, more than 60% of party hubs and date hubs defined by Han et al. have been divided into groups of mPHs and mDHs (see Fig. 6.4).

Party hubs and date hubs have been shown to have different spatial distributions [HaJ04]. Partners of date hubs are significantly more diverse in spatial distribution than are those of party hubs. For mPHs and mDHs, higher $L_{\mathrm{ratio-same}}$ implies that the proteins in more network motifs of a hub are located in the same cellular localization as the hub, and lower $L_{\mathrm{ratio-same}}$ shows that the proteins in more network motifs of a hub are located in different cellular localizations. Figure 6.5 shows that mPHs have significantly higher $L_{\mathrm{ratio-same}}$ than do mDHs. Thus the network motifs of mPHs and mDHs also have significantly different spatial distributions [Jin07]. In addition, mPHs and mDHs have been found to have significant differences in nucleus and cytoplasm cellular localizations (see Fig. 6.6). The cellular localization distribution of hubs and their network motifs implies that mPHs with their network motifs tend to be located in nucleus, while mDHs are more likely located outside the nucleus, and their network motifs have a scattered spatial distribution [Jin07].

Han et al. have shown that the HC^{fyi} network is tolerant to hub deletion, which means that the key components of the HC^{fyi} network still remain after removal of

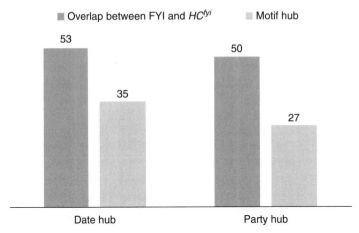

Figure 6.4. Proportions of mPHs and mDHs within the hubs common in FYI and HC^{fyi} [Jin07].

date hubs or/and party hubs [HaJ04]. They believed that hubs have a negligible effect on the network structure. On the other hand, Jin et al. [Jin07] introduced a method of deletion of both mPHs and mDHs with their motifs from the network. Figure 6.7a shows that deleting mPHs and their motifs has little influence on the main network structure, whereas deleting the mDHs and their motifs causes the network to break into many fragments (Fig. 6.7b). Therefore, mDHs and their

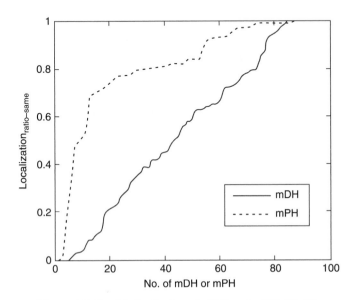

Figure 6.5. Spatial distribution of mDHs and mPHs [Jin07].

(a)

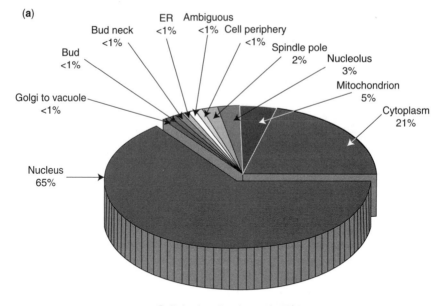

Cellular localizations of mPHs

(b)

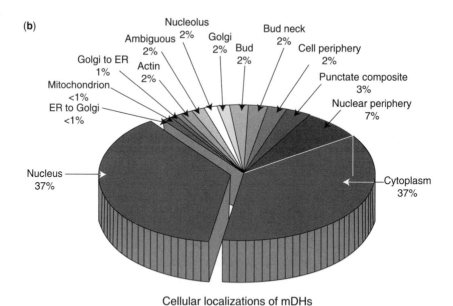

Cellular localizations of mDHs

Figure 6.6. Cellular localizations of mDHs and mPHs [Jin07].

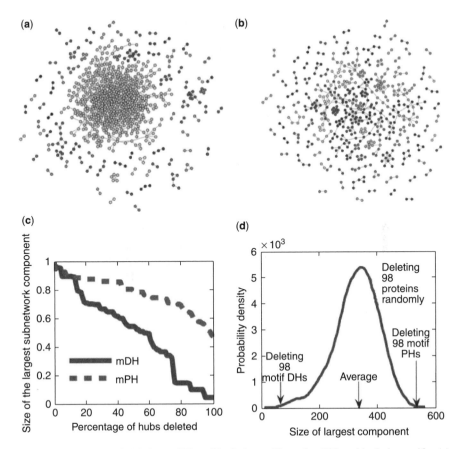

Figure 6.7. Effects of deleting mPHs with their motifs and mDHs with their motifs: (a) the network after deleting mPHs and their motifs; (b) the network after deleting mDHs and their motifs; (c) sizes of the largest connected components by deleting hubs one by one; (d) p values of sizes of the largest connected components by removing mPHs or mDHs with their motifs [Jin07].

motifs have a global effect on network structure. Figure 6.7c illustrates the sizes of the largest connected subnetwork components by deleting hubs with their motifs one by one, which implies that the HC^{fyi} network is tolerant to the deletion of mPHs with their motifs but not tolerant to the deletion of mDHs with their motifs. The largest component after removing mPHs and their motifs contains 50% proteins, while that found after removing mDHs and their motifs contains less than 10% proteins. Figure 6.7d shows the probability density of the size of the largest component by deleting a randomly selected set of 98 hubs with their motifs, namely the p values of the cases by removing mPHs or mDHs with their motifs. Both p values are less than 0.001. Those results demonstrate that mPHs mainly control the local structure by their motifs, while mDHs control the global structure by their motifs.

TABLE 6.1. Statistical Significance of Differences between SAMCs of mDHs and mPHs

Microarray Data	Point	SAMCs			MAMCs		
		mDHs	mPHs	p Value	mDHs	mPHs	p Value
Compendium	315	0.1380	0.1016	8.14e-10	0.2481	0.2972	0.6207
Stress response	174	0.1512	0.1121	1.16e-14	0.2569	0.2940	0.8580
Cell cycle	77	0.1233	0.1101	0.0065	0.1399	0.2080	0.0281
Pheromone treatment	45	0.1511	0.1394	0.0018	0.1100	0.1710	0.0386
Protein response	10	0.2461	0.2392	0.0386	0.1399	0.2080	0.0281
Sporulation	9	0.2391	0.2491	0.7628	0.2044	0.2814	0.2822

Except for their diverse spatial distributions, another distinction between party hubs and date hubs is whether they are coexpressed with their partners [HaJ04]. Han et al. took the average PCC of the hubs and its partners in microarray data as a measure to distinguish party hubs from date hubs. The standard deviation of average motif correlations (SAMC) of a hub was used to measure whether the network motifs of hubs are coexpressed. By adopting the mean of average motif correlations (MAMC), which is similar to average PCC, investigators found that the MAMCs of mPHs are not significantly different from those of mDHs but the SAMCs of mPHs are significantly lower than those of mDHs (see Table 6.1) [Jin07]. Therefore, it can be concluded that the network motifs of mPHs are more likely to be coexpressed than are those of mDHs according to the significant SAMC difference between mPHs and mDHs obtained by the Mann–Whitney U test [Jin07].

6.4.2 Network Motifs Acting as Connectors between Pathways

In the last section, we described the biological roles of hubs with network motifs in terms of spatial distribution, gene coexpression, influence on network architecture, and other properties. In this section, we further introduce the functional roles of network motifs in connecting signaling pathways. It is observed that network motifs are not separated from each other but are highly clustered, in particular for the so-called type I subgraphs [Vaz04]. The distribution of network motifs in biomolecular networks is not uniform. Network motifs are more likely to cluster around the proteins with higher degrees [Vaz04]. Currently, network motifs have been revealed to be basic functional units, but the roles of the clustered network motifs in biomolecular networks are still not clear. In a more recent study, Jin et al. explored the functional roles of clustered network motifs and found that clustered network motifs can act as key connectors between signal pathways [Jin09].

The motivation for the study is that the processes leading to diseases in living organisms are extremely complex because of the interplay between biomolecules and signal pathways. Despite increasing knowledge on pathogenesis, we are still far from the goal of understanding the etiology of most diseases, which should be studied at the system level in contrast to traditional analysis on individual molecules [Kan07]. Jin et al. studied the essential roles of clustered network motifs were in some human diseases such as cancers and type II diabetes mellitus [Jin09]. In particular, the associations of motif clusters with these diseases and their pathogenesis pathways were studied, which is important for deciphering complicated disease mechanisms from a systems biology perspective.

6.4.2.1 *Data Sources*

Although there are several human interaction databases, they still suffer from spurious noise and false positives that result from both experimental and nonexperimental factors. In order to find the causations of human disease accurately, the data were carefully filtered to minimize the errors. Four protein interaction databases—IntAct, DIP, MINT, and MIPS—were used and then the interactions confirmed by at least two methods were gathered. Thus, filtered human interactome (FHI) is composed of 2887 proteins with 3681 interactions, with a main component of 2257 proteins and 3283 interactions (Fig. 6.8a). Signal pathways are extracted from KEGG [Kan00], which is a pathway database including metabolism, genetic information processing, environmental information processing, cellular process, human disease, and drug development pathways. Except for the drug development pathways, all 204 pathways are from KEGG in October 2007. Network motifs were detected by mfinder 1.2 software [Mil02]. Three-node subnetworks (triangle) and four-node subnetworks (square) were used as network motifs.

6.4.2.2 *Characterizing Motif Clusters*

As shown in Figure 6.8b, network motifs in FHI are not randomly distributed, and they are highly clustered. The motif degree of a protein is defined as the number of network motifs sharing this common protein. The network motifs sharing a common protein are known as a motif cluster, and the common protein is called a motif cluster center [Jin09]. Furthermore, each network motif is referred to as an "arm" of the motif cluster. It has been found that there are 451 proteins whose motif degrees are all higher than 2. In order to elucidate the structural and functional roles of the clustered network motifs rather than the individual network motifs, proteins with motif degree higher than 2 were selected. In FHI, there are 451 motif cluster centers. The arms of network motifs may overlap. Except for the degree distribution (Fig. 6.8c) and average cluster coefficient distribution for FHI (Fig. 6.8d), the subgraph distribution of FHI is also described in Figure 6.8e, which is defined as $N_{nm} \sim k^{-[(m-n+1)\alpha-(n-y)]}$, denoting the number ($N_{nm}$) of subgraphs with n nodes and m links of a protein with degree k [Vaz04]. $(m-n+1)\alpha - (n-y)$ is called a subgraph exponent. If the exponent of a subgraph is less than 0, the subgraph is a type I subgraph: otherwise, if it is larger than 0, the subgraph is a type II subgraph.

Jin et al. proposed a method for evaluating the significance of motif clusters and pathways [Jin09]. Let P_1 and P_2 denote two pathways. Simultaneously, they also represent the sets of proteins that they contain. MC is the set of motif clusters composed of $MC_j, j = 1, 2, \ldots, |MC|$. MC_j is the set of network motifs $A_{ji}, i = 1, 2, \ldots, |MC_j|$. For any motif cluster MC_j in MC, those motif clusters located between the pathways P_1 and P_2 are emphasized. Clearly, if a motif cluster MC_j is located between the pathways P_1

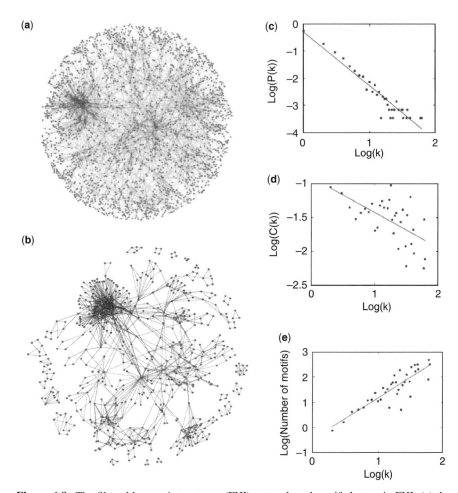

Figure 6.8. The filtered human interactome (FHI) network and motif clusters in FHI: (a) the FHI network; (b) the clustered network motifs in FHI; (c) the degree distribution of FHI, $\gamma = 1.98$; (d) the degree distribution of average cluster coefficients of FHI, $\alpha = 0.91$; (e) the subgraph distribution of FHI with subgraph exponent -1.63 [Jin09].

and P_2, there exist network motifs A_{jk_1} and A_{jk_2} in MC_j such that $A_{jk_1} \cap P_1 \neq \emptyset$ and $A_{jk_2} \cap P_2 \neq \emptyset$. $MC_{P_1P_2} \subset MC$ denotes a subset of motif clusters containing those motif clusters located between P_1 and P_2.

If P_1 and P_2 denote a disease pathway, and a signal pathway, respectively, the number of motif clusters located between these two pathways $|MC_{P_1P_2}|$ can be obtained. A way to evaluate the significance of the enrichment of motif clusters located between the disease pathway P_1 and the signal pathway P_2 was introduced by Jin et al. [Jin09]. Two sets S_1 and S_2 in FHI are randomly sampled to satisfy $|S_1| = |P_1|$, $|S_2| = |P_2|$, and $|S_1 \cap S_2| = |P_1 \cap P_2|$. The number of motif clusters located between S_1 and S_2 is denoted by $|MC_{S_1S_2}|$. By repeating the sampling experiment for 1000 times, a list of the number of motif clusters located between the sampled pair sets can be obtained as follows:

$$L = \{|MC_{S_1 S_2}|_1, |MC_{S_1 S_2}|_2, \ldots, |MC_{S_1 S_2}|_{1000}\}$$

A random distribution f for the number of motif clusters located between sampled pair sets can be constructed from this list. Specifically, the cumulative probability density function $F(|MC_{P_1 P_2}|)$ can be estimated from L as follows

$$F(|MC_{P_1 P_2}|) = \int_{-\infty}^{|MC_{P_1 P_2}|} k(t)dt = \frac{1}{|L|} \sum_{i=1}^{|L|} K\left(\frac{|MC_{P_1 P_2}| - |MC_{S_1 S_2}|_i}{h}\right)$$

where K is defined as the primitive of the kernel function k

$$K(x) = \int_{-\infty}^{x} k(t)dt$$

and $k(t) = (1/\sqrt{2\pi}) \exp\left(-\frac{1}{2}t^2\right)$. h is chosen as the optimal bandwidth $\sigma(4/3|L|)^{1/5}$, where σ is the standard deviation of the observed data. The complementary cumulative probability density $F'(|MC_{P_1 P_2}|)$ can also be derived as

$$F'(|MC_{P_1 P_2}|) = 1 - F(|MC_{P_1 P_2}|)$$

which can be interpreted as the tail p value, where the random variable is equal to or larger than $|MC_{P_1 P_2}|$, assuming that it is drawn from the distribution described by f. Thus, the complementary cumulative probability density $F'(|MC_{P_1 P_2}|)$ is the p value for characterizing the significance of the enrichment of motif clusters $MC_{P_1 P_2}$ located between the disease pathway P_1 and the signal pathway P_2.

6.4.2.3 *Biological Roles of Motif Clusters*

The filtered human interactome (FHI) network was numerically confirmed to be scale-free (Figs. 6.8c, d). Moreover, three-protein motifs and four-protein motifs were detected from FHI, which belong to type I subgraphs, thereby more likely aggregating into clusters in a network. From the distribution of network motifs in Figure 6.8e, it is easy to see that the subgraphs are more likely to take the proteins with higher degrees as their nodes. We can also see that the subgraph exponent for all motifs is less than 0, which is consistent with the fact that the triangles and the squares are type I subgraphs.

As mentioned previously, the network detected motifs in FHI are not isolated but clustered together. There are 451 proteins whose motif degrees are higher than 2, which means that the network motifs are mainly clustered around these 451 proteins. To discover why the network motifs tend to cluster among biomolecular networks or what roles the local topology units play in biological processes, motif clusters around these proteins were analyzed.

The architecture of FHI with highly clustered network motifs reflects the essential functional roles of network motifs in cells. To discover the underlying function principles of network motifs inside living organisms, especially inside humans, Jin et al. studied their biological roles in human diseases extensively and revealed some of the functional roles of motif clusters and identified their correlations with disease and pathogenesis pathways from their special topological structures in FHI [Jin09]. It is natural for a motif cluster linked to a human disease to be located at a specific position near disease pathways and not be scattered randomly in the network. Therefore, a new criterion based on the random sampling method was used to calculate the p values for motif clusters located between cancer pathways and all other signal pathways in KEGG. By comparison with the number of motif clusters located between sampled protein sets, we can determine whether the pathways P_1 and P_2 are the specific positions where motif clusters are usually located in the network. If the p value for P_1 and P_2 is significantly low, there is a statistical enrichment of network motifs located between these two pathways, or these two pathways are the specific positions for motif clusters. All p values for cancers and other signal pathways are shown in Figure 6.9, where the pathways with ID numbers ranging between 1 and 42 on the horizontal axis (abscissa) of each plot (i.e., left of the vertical line) represent two types of pathways belonging to cellular processes and environmental information processing. The line on the vertical axis (ordinate) of each plot represents the cutoff of statistically significance (i.e., p value $= 0.01$). In all cancers except basal cell carcinoma, the p values for the motif clusters are low (there are some points under the horizontal line), which implies that the enrichment of motif clusters is statistically significant for the signal pathways with respect to cancers.

Many pathways belonging to cellular processes and environmental information processing have low p values with respect to all cancers except basal cell carcinoma. Thus, this result suggests that the motif clusters are more likely located near or between some specific pathways and cancers. Such a result is consistent with the findings from previous research work on cancers, namely, that some of the important cellular processes are essential to cell survival, and that environmental factors considerably contribute to the development of cancers. Moreover, by checking the association of cancers and the pathways with significantly low p values, most of those low-p-value pathways have been identified as the pathways of pathogenesis for cancers. Table 6.2 lists the p values for the pathogenesis pathways with respect to cancers, where

CC = colorectal cancer
GC = glioma cancer
MC = melanoma cancer
TC = thyroid cancer
PaC = pancreatic cancer
CML = chronic myeloid leukemia
RC = renal cell carcinoma
EC = endometrial cancer
PrC = prostate cancer

BC = bladder cancer

AML = acute myeloid leukemia

SC = small cell lung cancer

NC = non-small-cell lung cancer

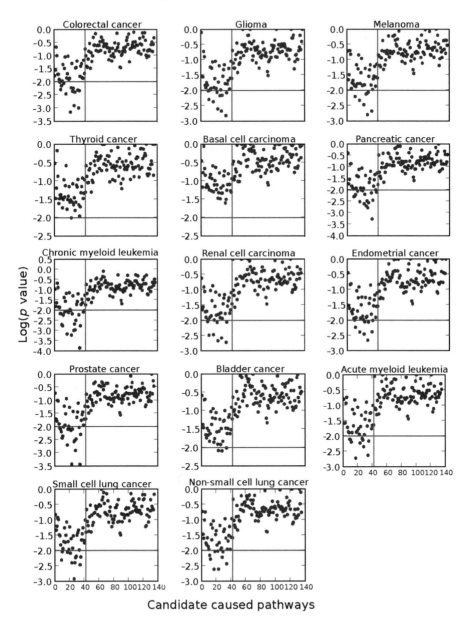

Figure 6.9. p Values of motif clusters located between cancers and other signal pathways [Jin09].

TABLE 6.2. p Values for Pathogenesis Pathways with Respect to Cancers

KEGG ID	CC	GC	MC	TC	PaC	CML	RC	EC	PrC	BC	AML	SC	NC
hsa04662	−2.0				−2.1	−2.3		−2.0	−2.2		−2.0		
hsa04620	−2.1				−2.4	−2.3	−2.2	−2.1	−2.3		−2.2	−2.5	
hsa04660	−2.4	−2.1			−2.4	−2.8	−2.1	−2.0	−2.6		−2.3	−2.2	−2.1
hsa04650	−2.3	−2.5	−2.3		−2.3	−2.9	−2.7	−2.4	−2.5		−2.3		−2.3
hsa04664	−2.1	−2.2	−2.0		−2.0	−2.4	−2.1	−2.1	−2.1		−2.0		−2.4
hsa04670	−2.1	−2.0			−2.1	−2.1							
hsa04910	−2.6	−2.5	−2.5		−2.6	−3.3	−2.7	−2.6	−2.8	−2.0	−3.1	−2.1	−2.8
hsa04510	−3.2	−2.8	−2.6		−2.8	−3.3	−2.8	−2.7	−3.7	−2.2	−2.3	−2.5	−2.8
hsa04520	−2.3			−2.1	−2.3	−2.2		−2.1	−2.2				
hsa04110	−2.4	−2.2	−2.2		−2.7	−3.1			−2.7	−2.0	−2.1	−3.1	−2.0
hsa04210	−2.3	−2.0	−2.2		−2.6	−2.9			−2.7		−2.2	−2.5	
hsa04810	−3.0	−2.8	−2.9		−2.8	−3.1	−2.8	−2.8	−3.1	−2.2	−2.4	−2.3	−2.4
hsa04060	−2.4	−2.2	−2.1		−2.6	−2.5		−2.1	−2.5			−2.2	−2.1
hsa04310	−2.4				−2.2	−2.2			−2.1			−2.0	
hsa04010	−3.1	−3.0	−2.8	−2.1	−3.4	−4.3	−2.8	−2.5	−3.5	−2.2	−2.8	−2.5	−2.6
hsa04630	−2.4	−2.2	−2.0		−2.5	−2.9	−2.2	−2.1	−2.4		−2.2	−2.3	−2.0
hsa04720		−2.1					−2.1	−2.1					
hsa04912		−2.1			−2.0	−2.1	−2.1	−2.1	−2.2				−2.2
hsa04530		−2.0			−2.1	−2.0			−2.2			−2.1	
hsa04540		−2.2				−2.1	−2.3	−2.1	−2.3	−2.1	−2.1		−2.3
hsa04370		−2.1	−2.1		−2.1	−2.2		−2.1	−2.1				−2.2
hsa04730									−2.0				
hsa04920				−2.1	−2.2			−2.1			−2.1		
hsa04350				−2.2	−2.1								

Source: Jin et al. [Jin09].

The identified pathways for cancer pathogenesis include most pathways of cellular processes, such as cell cycle; apoptosis; focal adhesion; natural-killer-cell-mediated cytotoxicity; T-cell receptor signaling pathway; B-cell receptor signaling pathway; Adherens junction; and most pathways of environmental information processing, such as Jak-STAT signaling pathway, Wnt signaling pathway, MAPK signaling pathway, TGF$_\beta$ signaling pathway, and cytokine–cytokine receptor interaction. From the biological perspective, identifying those pathways or modules associated with diseases might be very important in understanding the nature of the disease process, and could also be used in drug design from the computational perspective. The same results on motif clusters have been found in type II diabetes mellitus. In particular, by calculating the p values for all signal pathways with respect to type II diabetes mellitus, a pathogenesis signal pathway with a significantly low p value was identified: an insulin signaling pathway (Fig. 6.10).

The mechanisms of diseases cannot be fully understood by merely analyzing individual proteins. It is the complex interplay or complicated interactions between biomolecules and pathways that ultimately account for the underlying pathogenesis of various human diseases. From these studies, we can see that network-based analysis of pathogenesis can uncover the relationship between disease pathways and their pathogenesis pathways at the network level in contrast to the previous disease studies at the individual protein level. In addition, this method has the potential to identify the specific key proteins (or targets) for a particular disease (e.g., cancer) which may be helpful in medical drug development.

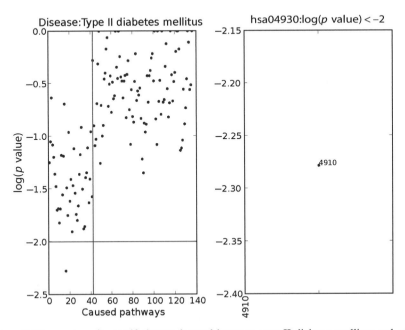

Figure 6.10. p values for motif clusters located between type II diabetes mellitus and other signal pathways [Jin09].

6.5 MODULARITY EVALUATION OF BIOMOLECULAR NETWORKS

As discussed in Section 6.1, driven by the development of information technology, vast amounts of complex network data in the real world are continuously accumulated, and have been revealed to have many interesting topological features such as the small-world property and power-law degree distribution. In addition, modularity is an important common characteristic for many types of networks. A topic of great interest in the area of complex networks is to detect community or modular structure. A community or a module could be roughly described as a collection of vertices in a subgraph that are densely connected among themselves while loosely connected to the vertices outside the subgraph. Since many networks exhibit such modular structure, characterizing and detecting modules or communities have great practical significance. Taking a biomolecular network as an example, dividing a protein interaction network into modular groups provides a strong evidence of independent functions and actions for proteins in different subgraphs [Zha07, Jin07].

More recently, a number of methods from various fields have been developed to detect community structure in a network [New04a, New06]. Actually, the concept of community itself is qualitative rather than quantitative; that is, nodes must be more densely connected within the community than with the rest of the network. Therefore, how to quantitatively measure the modularity of a network is still a subject of debate. A widely used quantitative measure for evaluating the modular structure of a network is the modularity function Q, which was introduced by Newman and Girvan [New04b]. Specifically, given an undirected graph or network $G(V, E)$ consisting of node set $V = \{v_1, v_2, \ldots, v_n\}$ and edge set E, its symmetric adjacency matrix is denoted as $A = [A_{ij}]_{n \times n}$, where $A_{ij} = 1$ if nodes v_i and v_j are connected and otherwise $A_{ij} = 0$. Then the modularity function Q is defined as

$$Q(P_k) = \sum_{i=1}^{k} \left[\frac{L(V_i, V_i)}{L(V, V)} - \left(\frac{L(V_i, V)}{L(V, V)} \right)^2 \right] \tag{6.1}$$

where P_k is a partition of the nodes into k groups and $L(V', V'') = \sum_{i \in V', j \in V''} A_{ij}$. The modularity function provides a way to determine whether a partition is good enough to capture the community structure in networks. Generally, a larger Q corresponds to a more distinct community structure. If one chooses Q as the quantitative function for modular structure, the problem of community detection is equivalent to a modularity optimization problem, that is, searching a k and a partition P_k to maximize the value of Q. Modularity optimization seems to be an effective method to detect communities in both real and artificially generated networks [New06, Gui05].

While widely used in measuring modular structures of networks, Q has been exposed to serious resolution limits. Fortunato and Barthélemy have claimed that Q contains an intrinsic scale that depends on the total size of links in the network. Modules smaller than this scale may not be resolved even in the extreme case that they are complete graphs (i.e., cliques) connected by single bridges [For07]. In a more recent study, Li et al. proposed a novel quantitative measure for evaluating the community structure of networks [LiZ08]. This quantitative measure is based on the concept of average modularity degree and termed modularity density D. It overcomes the resolution limits in Q and improves the quality of module detection. The optimization of modularity density was shown to be equivalent to a special kernel k means [LiZ08]. We will introduce the modularity density D in detail next.

6.5.1 Modularity Density D

Given a network $G = (V, E)$ and a partition of this network $G_1(V_1, E_1), \ldots,$ $G_k(V_k, E_k)$, where V_i and E_i are respectively the node set and the edge set of G_i for $i = 1, \ldots, k$, the well-known modularity function Q is as defined by equation (6.1). Optimizing Q has serious resolution limits, and the size of a detected module depends on the size of the whole network [For07]. This is mainly because the modularity measure does not contain information on the number of nodes in a community, and the choice of partition is highly sensitive to the total number of links in the network [Ros07].

To overcome the limits of Q, a new quantitative function for evaluating the modular structure of a network was proposed by considering the node information of communities [LiZ08]. Specifically, the modularity density of each subgraph $G_i(V_i, E_i)$ is defined as

$$d(G_i) = d_{\text{in}}(G_i) - d_{\text{out}}(G_i)$$
$$= \frac{L(V_i, V_i) - L(V_i, \overline{V}_i)}{|V_i|}$$

where $d_{\text{in}}(G_i)$ is the average inner degree of the subgraph G_i, which equals twice the number of edges in subgraph G_i divided by the number of nodes in set V_i; $d_{\text{out}}(G_i)$ is the average outer degree of the subgraph G_i, which equals the number of edges with one node in V_i and the other node outside V_i divided by the number of nodes in V_i. Then, the modularity density (denoted as D) of a network partition is defined as the sum of the modularity density of all subgraphs G_i for $i = 1, \ldots, k$ as follows:

$$D = \sum_{i=1}^{k} d(G_i) = \sum_{i=1}^{k} \frac{L(V_i, V_i) - L(V_i, \overline{V}_i)}{|V_i|} \tag{6.2}$$

The summation is over all communities G_i of a given partition. The larger value of D corresponds to a more accurate partition or more distinct modular structure. Hence, the community detection problem can be viewed as a problem of finding a partition of the network such that its modularity density D is maximized. In this sense, the role of D is similar to that of the widely used modularity function Q. Generally, searching for a partition with optimal modularity density is an NP-hard problem because the space of possible partitions grows more rapidly than does any power of system size. Therefore, from the computational view, approximate or heuristic algorithms to optimize D are more practical or tractable.

6.5.2   Improving Module Resolution Limits by *D*

By performing tests on the examples from Fortunato and Barthélemy [For07], modularity density D was shown to overcome the resolution limits existing in optimizing Q [LiZ08].

Given a clique G with n nodes, optimization of modularity density D does not divide it into two or more parts. Suppose that P is a partition that divides the clique into G_1 and G_2, and the number of nodes in G_1 and G_2 are n_1 and n_2, respectively, then the number of edges between G_1 and G_2 is n_1n_2. Letting D_0 be the modularity density of G, where D_1 denotes the modularity density of partition P, we obtain

$$D_0 = n - 1$$

$$D_1 = \frac{n_1(n_1 - 1) - n_1n_2}{n_1} + \frac{n_2(n_2 - 1) - n_1n_2}{n_2}$$

$$= -2$$

Since $D_0 > D_1$, optimization of D does not divide the clique into two parts.

To test the quality of modularity density, the schematic example from Fortunato and Barthélemy [For07] is adopted, which is a network consisting of a ring of cliques connected through single links (see Fig. 6.11a). Each clique is a complete graph K_n with $n(n \geq 3)$ nodes and $n(n - 1)/2$ links. Assuming that there are totally m cliques ($m \geq 2$), the network has a clear modular structure where each community corresponds to a single clique. The modularity degree D_{single} of the natural partition can be easily and analytically calculated as follows:

$$D_{\text{single}} = m\frac{n(n - 1) - 2}{n} = m\left(n - 1 - \frac{2}{n}\right)$$

On the other hand, assuming that these m cliques can be exactly divided by k, where $k \geq 2$ is an integer, the network has a total of $N = mn$ nodes and

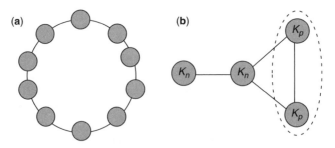

Figure 6.11. Schematic examples of (a) a clique circle network and (b) a network with two pairs of identical cliques. (Reprinted from [For07] © 2007 National Academy of Sciences, U.S.A.)

$L = mn(n-1)/2 + m$ links. The modularity density D_k of the partition in which the k consecutive cliques are considered as single communities is

$$D_k = \frac{m}{k} \frac{kn(n-1) + 2(k-3)}{kn}$$

Supposing $k \geq 2$, $n \geq 3$, $m \geq 2$, we obtain

$$D_{\text{single}} - D_k = m\left(n - 1 - \frac{2}{n}\right) - \frac{m}{k} \frac{kn(n-1) + 2(k-3)}{kn}$$

$$= m\left[(n-1) - \frac{2}{n} - \frac{n-1}{k} - \frac{2(k-3)}{k^2 n}\right]$$

$$> m\left[(n-1) - \frac{2}{n} - \frac{n-1}{k} - \frac{2}{kn}\right]$$

$$\geq m\left[(n-1) - \frac{2}{n} - \frac{n-1}{2} - \frac{1}{n}\right]$$

$$> 0$$

The analysis outlined above is conducted for the special partition where the k consecutive cliques are considered as single communities. By a similar argument, it can be proved that such a result is actually valid for any kind of grouping clique (i.e., with any combination of cliques as communities). Therefore, these results, along with the fact that D does not divide a clique into two parts, lead to a conclusion that optimization of D exactly leads to the correct partition (with each single clique as a community). On the other hand, Q will group several cliques into a community when L is large.

For another example, suppose that there is a network consisting of four cliques, two of which are K_n, and the other two are K_p, for $3 \leq p \leq n$ (see Fig. 6.11b). Fortunato and Barthélemy [For07], observed that optimizing Q tends to group two small modules K_p. In contrast, we show that optimization of D does not have such a restriction [LiZ08a]. Let D_{separate} denote the modularity density of the partition in which the two small cliques are separated, and D_{merge} denote the modularity density of the partition that the two small cliques are merged; then

$$D_{\text{separate}} = \frac{n(n-1) - 1}{n} + \frac{n(n-1) - 3}{n} + 2(p-1) - \frac{4}{p},$$

$$D_{\text{merge}} = \frac{n(n-1) - 1}{n} + \frac{n(n-1) - 3}{n} + (p-1)$$

It is easy to verify that when $p \geq 3$, we obtain

$$D_{\text{separate}} - D_{\text{merge}} = 2(p-1) - \frac{4}{p} - (p-1) > 0$$

This analysis is conducted for the special partition where two small cliques are merged as a community with each other clique as a community. With the fact that D does not partition a clique into two parts, it is easy to see that any other partition has a lower value of D than the one with each clique as a community. Therefore, in contrast to the modularity function Q, optimization of D can more correctly detect communities with heterogeneous sizes.

6.5.3 Equivalence between *D* and Kernel *k* Means

In addition to the tests in the examples given above, the modularity density D has been shown to be equivalent to the objective function of kernel k means [LiZ08a]. Thus, given the number of modules, one can use kernel k means to iteratively optimize D in an efficient manner.

Specifically, given a set of data vectors $V = \{v_1, v_2, \ldots, v_n\}$, the objective of kernel k means is to find a k-way disjoint partition $\{V_c\}$, $c = 1, \ldots, k$ of the data such that the following objective function is minimized

$$F = \sum_{c=1}^{k} \sum_{v_i \in V_c} \| \phi(v_i) - \widetilde{V}_c \|^2 \tag{6.3}$$

where

$$\widetilde{V}_c = \frac{\sum_{v_i \in V_c} \phi(v_i)}{|V_c|}$$

and ϕ is a function mapping the vectors in V onto a generally higher-dimensional space. If ϕ is the identity function, the preceding equation recovers the objective function of k means. By expanding the distance term $\| \phi(v_i) - \widetilde{V}_c \|^2$, it follows that

$$\| \phi(v_i) - \widetilde{V}_c \|^2 = \phi(v_i) \cdot \phi(v_i) - \frac{2 \sum_{v_j \in V_c} \phi(v_i) \cdot \phi(v_j)}{|V_c|}$$
$$+ \frac{\sum_{v_j \in V_c} \sum_{v_l \in V_c} \phi(v_j) \cdot \phi(v_l)}{|V_c|^2}$$

Since only inner products are used in this equation, for a given kernel matrix K (any positive semidefinite matrix can be regarded as a kernel matrix) with $K_{ij} = \phi(v_i) \cdot \phi(v_j)$, the distances between data points and cluster centroid can be computed without knowing the explicit expression of $\phi(\cdot)$; thus equation (6.3) can be rewritten as follows:

$$F = \sum_{c=1}^{k} \sum_{v_i \in V_c} \left(K_{ii} - \frac{2 \sum_{v_j \in V_c} K_{ij}}{|V_c|} + \frac{\sum_{v_j \in V_c} \sum_{v_l \in V_c} K_{jl}}{|V_c|^2} \right) \tag{6.4}$$

On the other hand, given the fixed number of modules k, the objective of detecting communities in complex networks is to efficiently look for a k-way disjoint partition

$\{V_c\}$, $c = 1, \ldots, k$ of V such that D is maximized:

$$D = \sum_{c=1}^{k} \frac{L(V_c, V_c) - L(V_c, \overline{V}_c)}{|V_c|}$$

By defining a diagonal degree matrix C with $C_{ii} = \sum_{j=1}^{n} A_{ij}$, any given network can be associated with an $n \times n$ kernel matrix as follows [LiZ08a]

$$K = \sigma I + 2A - C \tag{6.5}$$

where I is the identity matrix and σ is a real number chosen to be sufficiently large that K is positively definite. For a k-way disjoint partition $\{V_c\}_{c=1}^{k}$ of the network, the modularity density D and the objective function F of kernel k means are related as follows:

$$F = (N - k)\sigma - D$$

Clearly, F reaches its minimum if and only if the maximum of D is achieved since N and σ are constants and k is assumed to be fixed. Therefore, kernel k means can be straightforwardly used to find an optimal k-cluster of the network by using kernel matrix (6.5), which actually consists in maximizing the modularity density D iteratively.

6.5.4 Extension of D to General Criteria: D_λ and D_w

If we use the following kernel matrix K_λ instead of K in equation (6.5)

$$K_\lambda = \sigma I + 2[\lambda A - (1 - \lambda)(C - A)], \quad 0 \leq \lambda \leq 1 \tag{6.6}$$

a more general modularity density measure can be obtained as follows

$$D_\lambda = \sum_{i=1}^{k} \frac{2\lambda L(V_i, V_i) - 2(1 - \lambda)L(V_i, \overline{V}_i)}{|V_i|} \tag{6.7}$$

which can be viewed as the linear combination of well-known ratio association ($\lambda = 1$) and ratio cut ($\lambda = 0$) used in graph partition and image segmentation. When $\lambda = 0.5$, D_λ is equivalent to the modularity density D. Generally, optimization of the ratio association algorithm often divides a network into small communities, while optimization of ratio cut often divides a network into large communities. The general modularity density D_λ can decompose the network into communities at different levels by varying λ. Note that the topological structure of complex networks and biomolecular networks is usually very complicated, so there is no absolutely optimal standard for the community structure of complex networks, which means that we cannot obtain the so-called optimal λ value in a general sense.

For a weighted undirected network $G = (V, E; W)$, assume that there is a partition of G: $G_1(V_1, E_1; W_1), \ldots, G_k(V_k, E_k; W_k)$, where V_i and E_i are respectively the node set and the edge set of G_i for $i = 1, \ldots, k$, and W_i is the weight set for edges in V_i. Then D can be straightforwardly extended to the weighted network as follows:

$$D_w = \sum_{i=1}^{k} d(G_i) = \sum_{i=1}^{k} \frac{L(V_i, V_i; W_i) - L(V_i, \overline{V}_i; W)}{|V_i|} \tag{6.8}$$

The summation is over all communities G_i of a given partition. $L(V', V''; W) = \sum_{i \in V', j \in V''} A_{ij} w_{ij}$, where w_{ij} is the weight on the edge (i, j). By optimizing D_w, the decomposed modules or communities can reflect connection strengths or even attributes of nodes, which are important for analyzing biomolecular networks. Moreover, clearly a combination of D_λ and D_w [i.e., (6.7)–(6.8)] can construct a more general criterion $D_{\lambda w}$ for a weighted undirected network.

6.5.5 Numerical Validation

The community detection problem based on optimizing the modularity density D is formulated into the following integer programming model [LiZ08a]

$$\max \sum_{l=1}^{k} \frac{\sum_{i=1}^{n} \sum_{j=1}^{n} A_{ij} x_{il} x_{jl} - \sum_{i=1}^{n} \sum_{j=1}^{n} A_{ij} x_{il}(1 - x_{jl})}{\sum_{i=1}^{n} x_{il}} \tag{6.9}$$

$$\text{s.t.} \ \ 0 < \sum_{i=1}^{n} x_{il} < n \tag{6.10}$$

$$\sum_{l=1}^{k} x_{il} = 1 \tag{6.11}$$

$$x_{il} \in \{0, 1\}, \quad i = 1, \ldots, n, \ l = 1, \ldots, k \tag{6.12}$$

where x_{il}, $i = 1, \ldots, n, l = 1, \ldots, k$ is a binary variable to denote whether the node v_i belongs to the lth community, and A_{ij} is the element of the adjacency matrix A of the network G. The objective function of this integer programming model is actually the modularity density D. The first constraint denotes that each community is neither an empty set nor the whole network, and the second constraint ensures that the partition of the network is a hard partition, which means that each node can belong to one and only one community. Although the integer nonlinear programming is theoretically difficult to solve, the constraint conditions in the models described above are simple. Hence, the relaxed problem with the continuous variables in [0, 1] are applied and solved using Lingo software [LiZ08]. Note that a more efficient algorithm can be expected if a kernel k-means-based method is exploited for optimization of D.

6.5.5.1 Computer-Generated Networks The first numerical example is a set of the computer-generated networks [Gir02] that has been widely used to test community detection algorithms. Each network has 128 nodes, which are divided into 4 communities containing 32 nodes each. Edges are placed randomly with two fixed expectation values k_{in} and k_{out} so as to keep the average degree of a node at 16. The average edge connection of each node to nodes of other modules is denoted by k_{out}. The computational results of the D optimization method and other algorithms such as the GN algorithm [Gir02] and spectral algorithm [New06] on this set of networks are summarized in Figure 6.12. Note that the spectral algorithm is a method for optimizing the modularity function Q. Figure 6.12 shows the fraction of nodes that are correctly classified into the communities with respect to k_{out} by these three methods. Each point is an average over 100 realizations of the networks. It can be seen that the D optimization method performs much better than other algorithms.

Table 6.3 demonstrates the results of cluster compression algorithm [Ros07], Q optimization algorithm, and D optimization algorithm. From Table 6.3, it can be seen that, when the communities are of equal size and similar total degree, every method performs very well. At the same time, when $k_{out} = 8$, indicating that the corresponding networks are difficult to partition, D has the highest accuracy. When the communities vary in size or total degree, Q optimization is more difficult to resolve for the community structure. In addition, a group of asymmetric networks were also used; three of the four groups in the benchmark test were merged to form a series of test networks, each with one large group of 96 nodes and one small group of 32 nodes. These asymmetrically sized networks are more difficult for both the Q optimization algorithm and the cluster compression algorithm, but the D optimization algorithm

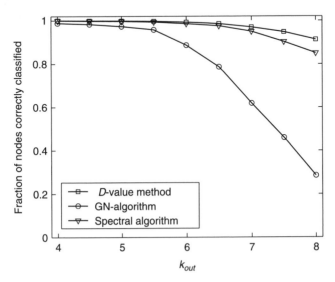

Figure 6.12. Comparison of several methods on computer-generated networks with known community structure. (Reprinted from [LiZ08a] © 2008 by the American Physical Society.)

TABLE 6.3. Performance Comparison of Three Community Detection Methods on Symmetric and Asymmetric Networks[a]

Group	k_{out}	Compression	Q	D
Symmetric	6	0.99 (0.01)	0.99 (0.01)	0.99 (0.01)
	7	0.97 (0.02)	0.97 (0.02)	0.97 (0.02)
	8	0.87 (0.08)	0.89 (0.05)	0.91 (0.03)
Node asymmetric	6	0.99 (0.01)	0.85 (0.04)	0.99 (0.01)
	7	0.96 (0.04)	0.80 (0.03)	0.98 (0.02)
	8	0.82 (0.10)	0.74 (0.05)	0.94 (0.03)
Link asymmetric	2	1.00 (0.00)	1.00 (0.01)	1.00 (0.00)
	3	1.00 (0.00)	0.96 (0.03)	1.00 (0.00)
	4	1.00 (0.01)	0.74 (0.10)	0.99 (0.01)

[a]Standard deviations shown in parentheses.

Source: Li et al. [LiZ08a].

can recover the underlying community structure more often than can the other two methods by a sizable margin. A set of link asymmetric networks used by Rosvall and Bergstrom [Ros07], which acted as another set of benchmark examples, consist of two groups, each with 64 nodes but with different average degrees of 8 and 24 links for each node. For these networks, k_{out} is set as 2, 3, 4, for which the D optimization algorithm has a result comparable to that of the cluster compression algorithm and can recover community structure more often than can the modularity optimization approach.

As discussed previously, the modularity density D has roles similar to those of Q. In general, for a given network, we do not know into how many communities it should be partitioned without prior knowledge. We can determine the number of communities in a network according to the value of D, which means that the maximum value of D corresponds to the correct number of communities. On the other hand, networks in real

TABLE 6.4. Performance Comparison of Three Community Detection Methods for Model Selection[a]

Group	k_{out}	Compression	Q	D
Symmetric	6	1.00 (4.00)	1.00 (4.00)	1.00 (4.00) ($\lambda = 0.65$)
	7	1.00 (4.00)	1.00 (4.00)	1.00 (4.00) ($\lambda = 0.65$)
	8	0.14 (1.93)	0.70 (4.33)	0.82 (4.18) ($\lambda = 0.80$)
Node asymmetric	6	1.00 (2.00)	0.00 (4.95)	1.00 (2.00) ($\lambda = 0.65$)
	7	0.80 (1.80)	0.00 (4.97)	1.00 (2.00) ($\lambda = 0.65$)
	8	0.06 (1.06)	0.00 (5.29)	0.68 (1.70) ($\lambda = 0.65$)
Link asymmetric	2	1.00 (2.00)	0.00 (3.10)	1.00 (2.00) ($\lambda = 0.50$)
	3	1.00 (2.00)	0.00 (4.48)	1.00 (2.00) ($\lambda = 0.50$)
	4	1.00 (2.00)	0.00 (5.55)	1.00 (2.00) ($\lambda = 0.60$)

[a]Average number of assigned modules shown in parentheses.

Source: Li et al. [LiZ08a].

systems are quite complex and may have hierarchical or nesting modularity. Therefore, the extended D_λ is flexible in determining the number of communities, compared with D. To test the performance of D_λ in selecting the number of communities, the abovementioned symmetric and asymmetric networks are used, and the results are listed in Table 6.4. The results demonstrate that by using proper λ, the number of communities can be determined when D_λ is maximum, and the D optimization algorithm again performs much better than the other two methods [LiZ08].

6.5.5.2 Real-World Networks The first example is the famous karate club network. It consists of 34 members of a karate club as nodes and 78 edges representing friendships between members of the club that were observed over a 2-year period. Following a disagreement between the club's administrator and instructor, the club split into two small ones. It is an interesting question as to whether the potential behavior of the network can be recovered. If the number of communities in this network is set as $k = 2$, by solving the corresponding integer programming model, the network is partitioned into two communities exactly consistent with the real partition (Fig. 6.13), where square nodes and circle nodes represent the instructor's faction and the administrator's faction, respectively. However, the optimal partition with $k = 4$ maximizes the value of D, which is also reasonable from the topology of the network.

The journal index network constructed by Rosvall and Bergstrom [Ros07] consists of 40 journals as nodes from four different fields: physics, chemistry, biology, and ecology, and 189 links connecting nodes if at least one article from one journal cites an article in the other journal during 2004. Ten journals with the highest

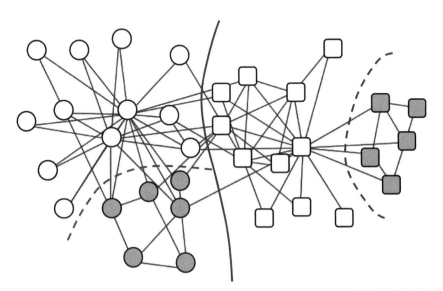

Figure 6.13. Karate club network and optimal partition detected by modularity density D. (Reprinted from [LiZ08a] © 2008 by the American Physical Society.)

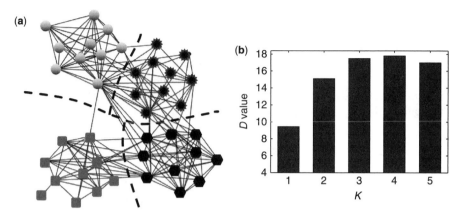

Figure 6.14. Journal index network (a) and D values versus different partitions (b). (Reprinted from [LiZ08a] © 2008 by the American Physical Society.)

impact factor in the four different fields were selected. By optimizing the modularity density D, the number of communities is correctly determined and the network can be partitioned into four communities correctly (Fig. 6.14) [LiZ08]. The network can also be partitioned into two, three, or five modules, but such partitions yield lower values of D.

6.6   SUMMARY

In this chapter, we mainly discussed various topological (both global and local) features common in biomolecular networks such as protein interaction networks, metabolic networks and nonbiomolecular networks such as social networks. Many topological properties such as scale-free feature, small-world characteristic, clustering, hubs and motifs, and modularity were introduced. In particular, we introduced in detail the most recent research work on the biological roles of hubs and motifs in protein interaction networks and human disease signaling pathways. We also described a novel quantitative function, namely, modularity density D, for evaluating the modular structure of biomolecular networks. These theoretical studies indicate that the topological features of nodes and network architectures are indeed related to their biological functions.

CHAPTER 7

ALIGNMENT OF BIOMOLECULAR NETWORKS

7.1 BIOMOLECULAR NETWORKS FROM MULTIPLE SPECIES

A large amount of protein interaction data for multiple species have been generated by high-throughput experimental techniques. For instance, the DIP database [Xen02] contains experimentally determined protein interaction data from *Drosophila melanogaster, Saccharomyces cerevisiae, Escherichia coli, Cuenorhabditis elegans, Homo sapiens, Helicobacter pylori, Mus musculus, Rattus norvegicus*, and other 153 species. Gene expression data from multiple species are also available, which makes it possible to compare cross-species gene expression patterns [Zho04, Stu03]. In addition, the data of gene regulatory networks, transcriptional regulatory networks, and metabolic networks are increasingly deposited for multiple species. Such cross-species data provide unprecedented opportunities to study the function and evolution of biological systems by comparing and analyzing the difference and commonality underlying the networks.

On the other hand, diverse biomolecular networks orchestrate the sophisticated and complex functions of cellular systems. Living organisms differ from each other owing not only to the differences of constituting biomolecules but also to the architectures of interaction networks between them. In other words, the difference and conservation of biomolecular networks account for the diversity and commonality of living organisms from low level to high level. For example, humans and chimpanzees are very similar at the sequence and gene expression levels, but striking differences are observed in the wiring of their coexpression networks [Old06]. Hence, it is important to address the

Biomolecular Networks. By Luonan Chen, Rui-Sheng Wang, and Xiang-Sun Zhang
Copyright © 2009 John Wiley & Sons, Inc.

similarities and differences in the biomolecular networks by comparative network analysis, which can be directly applied for analyzing signaling pathways, finding conserved regions, discovering new biological functions, and understanding the evolution of biomolecular networks. Typical problems related to comparative network analysis include pairwise network alignment, multiple network alignment, and subnetwork query in a given network. Like the important role of genome sequence alignment in genomics, cross-species comparison of biomolecular networks is a promising approach to understand the essential mechanisms of living organisms from the viewpoint of systems biology.

Biomolecular network alignment is a process of comparing two or more networks from different species or under different conditions in terms of node type and topological structure. Figure 7.1 presents a scheme of network alignment. It can be mathematically defined as

- Given k biomolecular networks from different species, find conserved subnetworks (complexes or pathways) within these networks, where the conservation level is measured in terms of molecule sequence (e.g., gene sequence or protein sequence) similarity and network topology similarity.

By comparing multiple networks, we can obtain some profound insights into conserved protein interactions, conserved signaling pathways across species, evolution process of protein interactions, and other phenomena [Sha06]. Compared with the long history of sequence alignment study, research on comparing and aligning

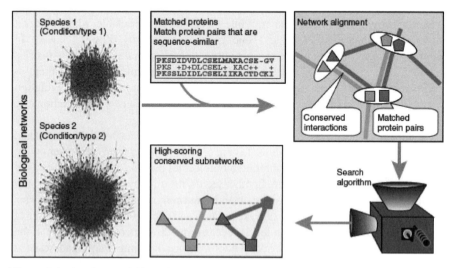

Figure 7.1. A scheme of biomolecular network alignment. Reprinted by permission from Macmillan Publishers Ltd: Nature Biotechnology [Sha06], © 2006.

biomolecular networks is only at its infancy stage. More recently, rapid advancements have been made mainly in computational methodology of network alignment.

In addition to network alignment, a closely related topic is querying a small network (e.g., pathway or functional module) against a large-scale network or network database. The topic is increasingly attracting much attention, and related methods are expected to become a major analytical tool for systems biology. From the computational viewpoint, querying a small network is a problem of local alignment among networks, which in particular requires a highly efficient algorithm because of intense CPU consumption related to querying [Zha08]. The purpose of network querying is to uncover identical or similar subnetworks by mapping the queried network to another network or network database. Therefore, network querying can be mathematically defined as

- Given a biomolecular network G, and a subnetwork or pathway S, find subnetworks in G that are similar to S in terms of sequence similarity and topological similarity.

Such network comparative analysis may reveal biologically or clinically important pathways or regulatory networks.

In this chapter, we survey computational methods for pairwise or multiple alignment of biomolecular networks as well as subnetwork or pathway querying. In particular, we will introduce an approach based on mathematical programming for pairwise network alignment.

7.2 PAIRWISE ALIGNMENT OF BIOMOLECULAR NETWORKS

A number of network alignment or comparison algorithms for biomolecular networks have been proposed in more recent studies. Most of those comparison methods are designed for pairwise alignment, that is, comparing two biomolecular networks. In the pairwise network alignment, usually an objective function reflecting either node similarity or network architecture similarity is defined, and homologous genes or gene products and homologous interactions are often identified by comparing the nodes and edges of two networks. Network alignment problem is computationally difficult since it can be reduced to the subgraph–isomorphism problem under certain formulations, which is known to be NP-hard. Because of the high computational complexity, most of network alignment approaches either restrict comparative analysis to special structures, such as pathways without loops and tree-like networks, or adopt heuristic or approximate algorithms.

Early work on network comparison was contributed by Ogata et al. [Oga00], who developed a heuristic graph comparison algorithm to detect functionally clustered enzymes. Kelley et al. introduced an efficient computational procedure called PathBLAST for aligning two protein interaction networks and identifying conserved interaction pathways within them [Kel03]. It searches for high-scoring pathway alignments involving two paths by combining interaction topology and protein sequence similarity through a score measure. Both gaps and mismatches are allowed to overcome evolutionary variations in module structures. PathBLAST is a heuristic searching algorithm and can detect only short (e.g., three or four nodes) linear paths. The local graph alignment algorithm [Ber04a] is also based on protein sequence similarity. On the other hand, some network alignment methods based on network architecture similarities, such as pairwise local alignment algorithm, were developed [Koy06]. MetaPathwayHunter, based on a graph matching algorithm, is designed for application mainly to relatively small and simple tree-like networks [Pin05]. Given a query pathway and a collection of pathways, it finds and reports all approximate occurrences of the query in the collection, ranked by similarity and statistical significance. Berg and Lässig proposed an evolution-based method for network alignment that estimates relative node weights and link similarity scores systematically by a Bayesian parameter inference model [Ber06]. This Bayesian alignment method can be applied to both weighted and unweighted undirected molecular networks. Li et al. developed an alignment tool MNAligner based on an integer quadratic programming model to align networks [LiZ07]. The method is rather general and can be applied to both weighted undirected and weighted directed networks. Yang and Sze developed algorithms for path matching and graph matching problems [Yan07]. They reduced such problems to find highest-scoring paths or subgraphs and presented algorithms for searching such paths or subgraphs. The method can extract biologically meaningful pathways from protein interaction networks or metabolic networks. Another method based on graph matching for comparing two protein interaction networks and identifying matching subgraphs is given by Narayanan and Karp [Nar07]. A global network alignment approach analogous to Google's PageRank method was also proposed [Sin08], where a protein is matched with a protein in the other network if and only if the neighbors of the two proteins can also be well matched. Table 7.1 lists a number of representative online software tool for network alignment or pathway query. A more comprehensive survey can be found in a review [Sha06] for biomolecular network comparison problems and potential applications. In this section, we will introduce several network alignment methods.

7.2.1 Score-Based Algorithms

Network alignment involves a score or measure evaluating the quality of possible alignments and a search procedure for finding high-scoring pathways or complexes. The scoring function measures the similarity of each subnetwork to a predefined structure of interest in terms of sequence similarity and subnetwork topology. Searching the conserved subnetworks of interest is often done by a greedy search or by the optimization/graph approach such as dynamic programming (DP) or color coding. Therefore, algorithms based on a defined score are common on this problem to find conserved pathways or complexes across multiple species. For example, PathBLAST [Kel03], first constructs a global alignment graph in which each vertex v represents a pair of proteins (one from each network) with sequence similarity expressed as a BLAST E value and each edge e represents a conserved interaction,

TABLE 7.1. Software Tools for Network Alignment or Pathway Querying

Tools	Description
PathBLAST	A dynamical programming algorithm is applied to search high-scoring paths in the alignment graph of two interaction networks
NetworkBLAST	A multinetwork alignment framework that extends likelihood-based scoring scheme and searches a network alignment graph of multiple networks
QPath	A network querying framework for identifying biologically significant pathways and inferring their function in protein interaction networks
Græin	With an evolution-based probabilistic scoring scheme, this method is capable of searching a large set of dense networks for conserved subnetworks; the algorithm attempts to align multiple networks
MNAligner	By employing both molecule similarity and architecture similarity, this method is based on an integer quadratic programming model to find the conserved substructures of two networks
MaWISH	This method is based on an evolution-based scoring scheme to detect conserved protein clusters
MetaPathwayHunter	The pathway alignment method is based on a subtree comparison algorithm; it has been developed into a network query procedure
MetaPAT	A tool for finding alignments of metabolic pathways; for a given pattern and a host pathway, it finds all high-scoring homeomorphisms between the pattern and a subgraph of the host, using a scoring scheme introduced by Tohsato et al. [Toh00]
QNet	A tool for tree queries
GraphMatch	A network alignment method based on graph matching, that is, finding the highest-scoring subgraphs in a graph
PathMatch	A path querying method, that is, finding the longest weighted path in a directed acyclic graph
SAGA	A substructure index-based approximate graph alignment

gap, or mismatch. Figure 7.2 illustrates these concepts. A gap occurs when a protein interaction in one path skips over a protein in the other, whereas a mismatch occurs when aligned proteins do not share sequence similarity [Kel03]. A path in such an alignment graph corresponds to a pathway alignment between the two networks whose quality is characterized by the following log probability score

$$S(P) = \sum_{v \in P} \log_{10} \frac{p(v)}{p_{\text{random}}} + \sum_{e \in P} \log_{10} \frac{q(e)}{q_{\text{random}}}$$

where $p(v)$ is the probability of true homology of the protein pair v and $q(e)$ is the probability of the real interaction e between a protein pair. The background probabilities p_{random} and q_{random} are the expected values of $p(v)$ and $q(e)$ over all vertices and edges in the global alignment graph. With the defined score, for acyclic alignment graphs, a procedure based on dynamic programming (DP) is used to find

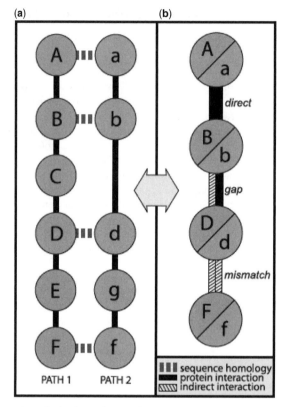

Figure 7.2. Illustration of pairwise pathway alignment and merged alignment graph. (Reprinted from [Kel03] © 2003 National Academy of Sciences, U.S.A.)

the highest-scoring path of length L, in which the highest-scoring path of length $l = 2, \ldots, L$ ending in vertex v has the score

$$S(v, l) = \arg \max_{u \in pa[v]} \left[S(u, l-1) + \log_{10} \frac{p(v)}{p_{\text{random}}} + \log_{10} \frac{q(e_{u \to v})}{q_{\text{random}}} \right]$$

$$S(v, 1) = \log_{10} \frac{p(v)}{p_{\text{random}}}$$

where $pa[v]$ is the set of parents of v. This DP algorithm can be done in linear time relative to problem size. Since the alignment graphs are seldom acyclic, a sufficient number $5L!$ of acyclic subgraphs are generated by randomly removing edges from the global alignment graph and then the results of running DP are aggregated. PathBLAST is available at www.pathblast.org. This approach was applied to protein interaction networks from *S. cerevisiae* and *H. pylori* and revealed a large complement of conserved pathways and a large number of yeast-specific pathways.

Another scoring scheme is based on maximum likelihood [Sha05a], where a probabilistic model for the conservation of protein complexes between two species was developed. This approach requires specifying a null model and a protein complex model for vertex pairs. For each of two aligned subnetworks, a loglikelihood ratio is computed to measure the fit of the subnetworks to the desired structure versus the chance that the subnetwork is observed at random. First, a simple model of a protein complex is constructed. The model is additive over the edges and non-edges of protein interaction networks with the assumption that each protein pair within a complex interacts with a high probability β, independently of all other information. The null model assumes that every two proteins u, v interact with probability $p(u, v)$, which depends on their node degrees. The likelihood ratio for a protein complex model is thus

$$L(C) = \sum_{(u,v) \in E(C)} \log \frac{\beta}{p(u, v)} + \sum_{(u,v) \notin E(C)} \log \frac{1 - \beta}{1 - p(u, v)}$$

where C is a protein complex and $E(C)$ is a set of interactions in C. For the conserved protein complex model of two species, the likelihood score consists of two parts: The first part is the simple summation of scores of two aligned subnetworks with the assumption that the interaction networks of the two species are independent of each other; The second part is accounting for the degree of sequence conservation among the pairs of proteins associated with a possible alignment and defined as the ratio of the probability that protein pairs in the alignment are orthologous to the probability that two independently chosen proteins are orthologous. To allow efficient search for conserved protein complexes, Sharan et al. formulated the problem of finding conserved complexes as a search for heavy subgraphs in an edge–node-weighted orthology graph, and a bottom–up heuristic procedure based on a local search scheme was adopted [Sha05a].

7.2.2 Evolution-Guided Method

Among all network alignment methods, Koyutürk et al.'s evolution-guide model is most similar to the idea of sequence alignment [Koy06]. They developed a mathematical model that extends the concepts of match, mismatch, and gap in sequence alignment to those of match, mismatch, and duplication in network alignment, and evaluated the similarity between graph structures through a scoring function. This evolution-based network alignment model can interpret the conservation and divergence of interactions, as well as the resulting alignments. In their study [Koy06], a duplication of a protein interaction is a duplication of the two corresponding genes in the course of evolution, which is associated with a score δ estimated from sequence similarity reflecting the divergence of functions between two proteins. Let $\mathcal{D}$ denote the set of the duplicated protein pairs within each subnetwork. A match implies a conserved interaction between two orthologous protein pairs in the protein interaction networks from two species, which is associated with a match score μ reflecting the confidence in both protein pairs being orthologous. Let $\mathcal{M}$ be the set of interologs (matches) among two subnetworks. A mismatch means two pairs of proteins with orthology relations between them but with only one interacting pair. Mismatches are penalized to account for the divergence from the common ancestor by score v. Let $\mathcal{N}$ denote the set of mismatched interactions. For comparison of two protein inter- action networks $G(U, E)$ and $H(V, F)$, where U, V are the sets of proteins and E, F are the sets of edges for the two networks G, H, respectively, let $P = \{U', V'\}$ be defined as a pair of protein subsets of U and V, respectively, which induces a local alignment $A(G, H, S, P) = \{\mathcal{M}, \mathcal{N}, \mathcal{D}\}$ of G and H with respect to a node similarity function S, and evolutionary events $\mathcal{D}$, $\mathcal{M}$, and $\mathcal{N}$ in two protein interaction networks. In the duplication–divergence model [Koy06], the overall score of alignment $A(G, H, S, P)$ is defined as follows:

$$\sigma(A) = \sum_{M \in \mathcal{M}} \mu(M) + \sum_{N \in \mathcal{N}} v(N) + \sum_{D \in \mathcal{D}} \delta(D)$$

With such a score, the network alignment problem is to find all maximal protein subset pairs P such that $\sigma(A(G, H, S, P))$ is locally maximal.

To find locally maximal protein subset pairs, a weighted network alignment graph is created to denote a merged representation of the two networks being compared, where the nodes denote the orthologous protein pairs and the edges denote dupli- cations, matches, or mismatches associated with the corresponding scores. A greedy algorithm for detecting heaviest subgraphs (subgraphs with maximal total weight) in the network alignment graph is adopted for identifying the conserved subnetworks. The software for this evolution-based network alignment is available at www.cs. purdue.edu/homes/koyuturk/mawish/.

7.2.3 Graph Matching Algorithm

A new pairwise network alignment method based on graph matching has been devel- oped to find functionally similar or conserved protein modules between the protein interaction networks from two species [Nar07]. The term *graphmatching problems* refers to a class of problems that find similar subgraphs between two graphs, most of which are NP-hard. In contrast to most existing network alignment methods, this algorithm can guarantee provable correctness in a polynomial running time. To detect conserved functional modules, a conserved protein module, which is intuitively a pair of protein modules that share cross-species similarity at the node level and net- work structure level, is imposed on two additional criteria: connectedness and local matching. Connectedness means that a function module should be a connected subnet- work, which makes it likely for a subset of proteins to be functionally homogeneous. Local matching for two proteins within two networks indicates that both sequences and neighborhoods are similar, which makes it likely for two protein subsets in cross-species interaction networks to be functionally similar.

Given two networks G and H, and a node similarity function S as inputs, a local- match function $LM_{G',H'}(u, v)$ for any subgraph pair G' and H' of the input graphs is defined to use node similarity function S. Several possible local structures can be used to define the local-match function LM, such as similar length-p paths and s-similar neighborhoods around nodes. This new function captures local or contextual match between the nodes u in G' and v in H' by using such local structures present around these nodes in G' and H'. With the defined local matching function, the network alignment problem can be described as follows. Given two input graphs G and H, a node similarity function $S(u, v)$, and a local-match function $LM_{G',H'}(u, v)$, find all maximal induced subgraph pairs $G' \subset G, H' \subset H$ such that G' and H' are connected and each node u in G' locally matches at least one node v in H' according to the local-match function $LM_{G',H'}(u, v)$, and vice versa. The detailed algorithm for each step is as follows:

```
Procedure
  Match-and-Split(G,H)
    Input G, H, S,
LM: Two graphs, the node similarity function and local-
match function
    Output: the maximal subgraph pairs of (G,H)
    [Match]Compute induced subgraph:
        find G' in G and H' in H over the locally
matching nodes lm(G,H)
    [Split] Find connected components:
        find G₁,...,G_c in G', and H₁,...,H_d in H'
    [Recurse] if (c=1; d=1 and G'=G, H'=H)
            Output the maximal solution G,H
        else
            for i=1 to c, j=1 to d
                Match-and-Split(G_i,H_j)
End procedure
```

The algorithm runs in time $O(n_G n_H + (n_G + n_H) m_G m_H)$ on graphs G and H, where n_F and m_F denote the number of nodes and edges, respectively, in a graph F. The software of this approach is available at http://www.cs.berkeley.edu/nmani/M-and-S/.

7.3 NETWORK ALIGNMENT BY MATHEMATICAL PROGRAMMING

Most network alignment methods introduced in Section 7.2 require heuristically searching for high-scoring subnetworks. These methods have different features, depending on specific network structures. For example, PathBLAST evaluates the link similarity along the path of connected nodes by adopting a sequence alignment algorithm [Kel03, Kel04], while MetaPathwayHunter analyzes metabolic pathways with no cycles by a subtree comparison algorithm [Pin05]. In contrast, an efficient and exact optimization approach for aligning general biomolecular networks based on both node similarity and network architecture similarity has been developed [LiZ07]. In this method, the network alignment problem is formulated as an integer quadratic programming (IQP) model with a logprobability-like criterion as an objective function [Kel03]. The IQP model can be relaxed into quadratic programming (QP), which always results in integer optimal solutions although without theoretical proof, thereby making the computation of network alignment tractable in terms of computational complexity. In contrast to PathBLAST and MetaPathHunter, which focus on the search of pathways without a loop, the IQP approach can handle general networks without any restriction. This method can be applied to both unweighted undirected networks and weighted directed networks. In addition to simple topological substructures such as chains and trees, it can reveal biologically meaningful local structures or subnetworks with loops, which is significant since many studies indicate that general subnetworks such as feedforward loop network motifs appear frequently in biomolecular networks and play important roles in biological systems. In the following subsections, we will introduce this method.

7.3.1 Integer Programming Formulation

A biomolecular network can be represented by a graph $G(V, E)$, where each node v in the node set V represents a biomolecule, such as protein, gene, or RNA, and each edge (u, v) in the edge set E represents an interaction or relation between nodes $u \in V$ and $v \in V$. For example, a protein interaction network is represented as an undirected graph $G(V, E)$, in which each node represents a protein and each edge represents a binary interaction (binary value) or an interaction with a confidence value (continuous value) between two proteins. A metabolic pathway or network is represented as a directed graph $G(V, E)$, in which nodes correspond to enzymes that catalyze the pathway's reactions, and edges connect nodes if the product of one enzyme serves as the substrate of the other. We define two biomolecular networks (directed or undirected) as $G_1 = (V_1, E_1)$ and $G_2 = (V_2, E_2)$, where $V_1 = \{v_1^1, \ldots, v_m^1\}$ and $V_2 = \{v_1^2, \ldots, v_n^2\}$. The adjacency matrices of G_1 and G_2 for unweighted networks are respectively $A = (a_{ij})_{m \times m}$ and $B = (b_{ij})_{n \times n}$, where $a_{ij} = 1$ if there is an interaction between biomolecules i and j, and $a_{ij} = 0$ otherwise; b_{ij} has similar implications. Besides binary values, a_{ij} and b_{ij} can also be straightforwardly extended to real numbers between 0 and 1 to represent the confidence scores of the interactions for weighted networks. Actually, several studies have presented useful methods for estimating the reliability or confidence of protein interactions [Den03a]. In this case, a biomolecular network can be formulated as a weighted graph. As in other network alignment methods, a node similarity function is required. Li et al. defined a similarity score to measure the similarities between two proteins or genes according to their sequences or other information [LiZ07]. Specifically, the similarity score is defined as a function $S: V_1 \times V_2 \to [0, 1]$. For any $v_i^1 \in V_1$ and $v_j^2 \in V_2$, $s_{ij} = S(v_i^1, v_j^2)$ measures the similarity between molecules v_i^1 and v_j^2. In particular, $s_{ij} = 1$ implies that the sequences of v_i^1 and v_j^2 are identical, whereas $s_{ij} = 0$ indicates no similarity of the sequences between v_i^1 and v_j^2.

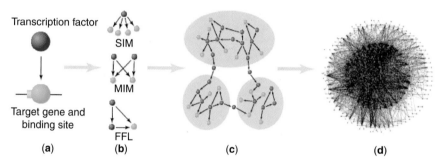

Figure 2.7. Structural organization of transcription regulatory networks: (a) basic unit; (b) motifs; (c) modules; (d) transcriptional regulatory network. (Reprinted from [Bab04], © 2004, with permission from Elsevier.)

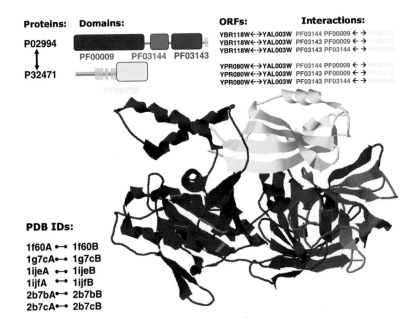

Proteins: **Domains:**

P02994

P32471

PF00009   PF03144   PF03143

PF00736

ORFs: **Interactions:**

YBR118W←→YAL003W   PF03144 PF00009 ← →
YBR118W←→YAL003W   PF03143 PF00009 ← →
YBR118W←→YAL003W   PF03143 PF03144 ← →

YPR080W←→YAL003W   PF03144 PF00009 ← →
YPR080W←→YAL003W   PF03143 PF00009 ← →
YPR080W←→YAL003W   PF03143 PF03144 ← →

PDB IDs:

1f60A •—• 1f60B
1g7cA•—• 1g7cB
1ijeA •—• 1ijeB
1ijfA •—• 1ijfB
2b7bA•—• 2b7bB
2b7cA•—• 2b7cB

Interfacial residues:

PF03143: THR363 ARG428 GLN429

PF00736: SER1180 ASP1182 ASP1183 ASP1199

PF03144: VAL260 VAL262 SER289 VAL290 GLU291 MET292 HIS293 HIS294 GLU295
GLN296 ASN305 VAL306 GLY307 PHE308 ASN309 ARG320

PF00736: ASP1131 ILE1159 PRO1160 ILE1161 GLY1162 PHE1163 GLY1164 ILE1165
LYS1166 SER1197

PF00009: VAL12 ILE13 VAL16 LYS20 SER21 ARG67 GLU68 ARG69 GLY70 ILE71 THR72
ILE73 ASP74 ILE75 ALA76 LEU77 TRP78 VAL89 ILE90 ASP91 ALA92 PRO93
GLY94 HIS95 ARG96 ASP97 PHE98 ASN101 GLY105 THR106 SER107

PF00736: ALA1119 LYS1120 SER1121 ILE1122 VAL1123 THR1124 LEU1125 LEU1151
THR1152 TRP1153 GLY1154 ALA1155 HIS1156 GLN1157 GLN1169 ILE1170
ASN1171 CYS1172 VAL1173 VAL1174 GLU1175 ASP1176 ASP1177 VAL1179
SER1180 LEU1181 ASP1182 ASP1199 ILE1200 ALA1201 ALA1202 MET1203
GLN1204 LYS1205

Figure 5.11. Cooperative domains in the complex crystal structure formed by proteins P02994
(with ORFs: YBR118W, YPR080W) and P32471 (with ORF: YAL003W) [WaR07c].

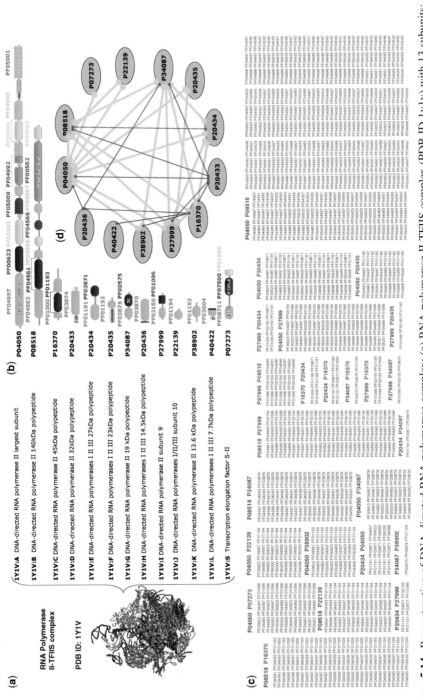

Figure 5.14. Reconstruction of DNA-directed RNA polymerase complex: (a) RNA polymerase II-TFIIS complex (PDB ID 1y1v) with 13 subunits; (b) PfamA domain architecture for every protein; (c) cooperative domains with protein interaction pairs containing them; (d) the complex with two-domain interactions and multidomain interactions [WaR07c].

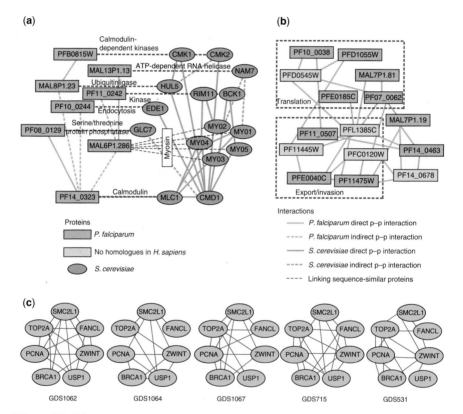

Figure 7.9. Biomolecular network querying examples for multiple species and conditions: (a) endocytosis—a conserved complex identified between *Plasmodium falciparum* and *Saccharomyces cerevisiae*; (b) translation/invasion—a representative complex uncovered within the *P. falciparum* network only; (c) a potential transcription module that appeared in five leukemia gene coexpression networks under different conditions [Zha08].

To perform the alignment of two networks, a series of binary variables are introduced to represent the detailed matching among nodes between two networks [LiZ07]:

$$x_{ij} = \begin{cases} 1 & \text{if } v_i^1 \in V_1 \text{ matches } v_j^2 \in V_2, \\ 0 & \text{otherwise} \end{cases}$$

The optimal matching $X = \{x_{ij}\}$ determined by the IQP model represents an optimal alignment in terms of node similarity and network structure. The similarity between two biomolecular networks G_1 and G_2 with respect to a given matching matrix X of nodes is first defined by summing scores, including both node and edge matching scores in the objective function [LiZ07], which is similar to the form of the logprobability score used in previous work. Then, the network alignment problem actually consists in finding an alignment with maximum similarity between two networks G_1 and G_2 among all feasible alignments X, which can be formulated as the following integer quadratic programming (IQP)

$$\max_X \lambda \sum_{i=1}^{m} \sum_{j=1}^{n} s_{ij} x_{ij} + (1 - \lambda) \sum_{i=1}^{m} \sum_{j=1}^{n} \sum_{k=1}^{m} \sum_{l=1}^{n} a_{ik} b_{jl} x_{ij} x_{kl} \qquad (7.1)$$

$$\text{s.t.} \quad \sum_{j=1}^{n} x_{ij} \leq 1, \quad i = 1, 2, \ldots, m \qquad (7.2)$$

$$\sum_{i=1}^{m} x_{ij} \leq 1, \quad j = 1, 2, \ldots, n \qquad (7.3)$$

$$x_{ij} \in \{0, 1\}, \quad i = 1, 2, \ldots, m; j = 1, 2, \ldots, n \qquad (7.4)$$

where the coefficient λ is a scalar parameter between 0 and 1 to control the balance between node similarity and edge scores. For instance, only the node scores are considered in the alignment if $\lambda = 1$, while only the edge scores are included if $\lambda = 0$. The first constraint, (7.2), implies that one node in G_1 can correspond to at most one node in G_2, while the second constraint, (7.3), means that each node in G_2 can match at most one node in G_1. The last constraint, (7.4), is the integer constraint for variable X. Depending on the parameter λ, different optimal alignment solutions can be obtained. A large λ emphasizes the node matching score, and the aligned substructures generally have fewer edges but with more related nodes, such as homologous proteins or consistent enzyme labels. On the other hand, a small λ emphasizes the edge matching score, and the aligned substructures generally have more edges and are also larger in size. Similar to the loglikelihood score in the probabilistic model, the objective function in the deterministic IQP model is also a summation over all the aligned nodes and edges. s_{ij} can be sequence similarity or function similarity, and the second term represents network structure similarity. The summation of these two terms together is able to provide a significant evidence of orthology between two species [LiZ07], although network structure similarity and node similarity are both weak.

Actually, the IQP model can be equivalently transformed into an integer linear programming (ILP) model by introducing additional variables. Specifically, we introduce matching variables $y_{ij,kl} \in \{0, 1\}$ for two edges $(v_i^1, v_k^1) \in E_1$ and $(v_j^2, v_l^2) \in E_2$ to denote whether these two edges actually match. $y_{ij,kl} = 1$ indicates that (v_i^1, v_k^1) and (v_j^2, v_l^2) are matched, that is, that two pairs of nodes on these two edges are respectively matched; otherwise $y_{ij,kl} = 0$. Therefore, the original IQP can be rewritten as the following ILP model

$$\max_{X,Y} \lambda \sum_{i=1}^{m} \sum_{j=1}^{n} s_{ij} x_{ij} + (1 - \lambda) \sum_{i=1}^{m} \sum_{j=1}^{n} \sum_{k=1}^{m} \sum_{l=1}^{n} a_{ik} b_{jl} y_{ij,kl} \qquad (7.5)$$

$$\text{s.t.} \quad \sum_{j=1}^{n} x_{ij} \leq 1, \qquad i = 1, 2, \ldots, m \qquad (7.6)$$

$$\sum_{i=1}^{m} x_{ij} \leq 1, \qquad j = 1, 2, \ldots, n \qquad (7.7)$$

$$x_{ij} \geq y_{ij,kl}, \qquad i, k = 1, 2, \ldots, m; \ j, l = 1, 2, \ldots, n \qquad (7.8)$$

$$x_{kl} \geq y_{ij,kl}, \qquad i, k = 1, 2, \ldots, m; \ j, l = 1, 2, \ldots, n \qquad (7.9)$$

$$x_{ij} \in \{0, 1\}, \qquad i = 1, 2, \ldots, m; \quad j = 1, 2, \ldots, n \qquad (7.10)$$

$$y_{ij,kl} \in \{0, 1\}, \qquad i, k = 1, 2, \ldots, m; \ j, l = 1, 2, \ldots, n \qquad (7.11)$$

where the newly added constraints (7.8) and (7.9) mean that two edges $(v_i^1, v_k^1) \in E_1$ and $(v_j^2, v_l^2) \in E_2$ match ($y_{ij,kl} = 1$) if and only if the nodes on these two edges are respectively matched (i.e., $x_{ij} = 1$ and $x_{kl} = 1$).

7.3.2 Components of the Integer Quadratic Programming Approach

Network alignment requires a similarity function S to characterize the similarity between the nodes in two networks. In other words, before aligning networks, we should define s_{ij} in the IQP model. The similarity score S between a protein pair from two networks can be defined by several methods. One of them is by detecting orthologs and in-paralogs using InParanoid [Rem01], which was developed to find disjoint ortholog clusters in two species. Each ortholog cluster is characterized by two main orthologs, one from each species, and possibly several other in-paralogs from both species. The main orthologs are assigned to a confidence value between 0 and 1, while the in-paralogs are assigned to confidence scores on the basis of their relative similarity to the main ortholog in their own species. The similarity between two proteins u and v is defined as $S(u, v) = \text{confidence}(u) \times \text{confidence}(v)$.

Besides InParanoid, the similarity score can also be defined by the following formula [LiZ07]:

$$S(u, v) = \log \frac{p_{uv}}{q_u q_v} = \log(p_{uv}) - \log(q_u q_v)$$

When a common ancestor exists between proteins u and v, the numerator p_{uv} is the probability that u is replaced by v, and the denominator expresses the product of the probabilities of obtaining u and v by substitution randomly. This score reflects the degree to which u and v are evolutionarily related in terms of a log–odds ratio. Except for the definitions given above, the similarity can be determined from the information of the sequence similarity by using BLAST [Kel03]. For metabolic networks, each enzyme is associated with its Enzyme Commission (EC) number, which consists of four sets of numbers and categories the types of the catalyzed chemical reactions. In the study by Li et al. [LiZ07], a simple rule is adopted: $S(e_i, e_j) = 0.25 \times r(e_i, e_j)$, where r denotes the class number of the lowest common upper class. For example, $r([1.2.3.4], [1.2.3.5]) = 3$ and $r([1.2.3.4], [2.1.3.4]) = 0$. In contrast to sequence similarity, enzymes with similar EC classification represent functional homologs for functionality of EC classification.

In addition, the statistical significance of an alignment was evaluated by a p value calculated from the t test [LiZ07], which was computed by comparing an alignment with an objective score f^* and that of 100 random networks. Here, the random networks are generated by containing the same set of nodes and the same number of edges as in the original one. The program used to generate the randomized undirected or directed networks was developed by Maslov and Sneppen [Mas02]. It generates randomized networks by randomly reshuffling links, while keeping the in- and out-degree of each node constant. Since it is time-consuming to apply the QP or IQP algorithm directly to align two large networks, a network partition method MCODE was used to detect network modules. Li et al. computed network modules using the MCODE algorithm in a fly protein interaction network, and then determined the corresponding subnetworks in yeast protein interaction network on the basis of the nodes' interspecies homologous mapping [LiZ07]. Finally, IQP was applied in aligning such network modules.

7.3.3 Numerical Validation

Both protein interaction networks and metabolic networks were used to test the IQP approach for network alignment [LiZ07]. The protein interaction networks for yeast and fly, and data for protein similarities between yeast and fly were obtained from a study by Bandyopadhyay et al. [Ban06]. Two protein interaction networks were formed from 14,319 interactions among 4389 proteins in yeast and 20,720 interactions among 7038 proteins in fly. In total, 2244 clusters covering 2836 yeast proteins and 3828 fly proteins were generated by the InParanoid algorithm. In addition, metabolic pathways of *E. coli* and *S. cerevisiae* were obtained from a study by Pinter et al.

[Pin05]. With those available databases, the IQP approach was compiled as an alignment tool called MNAligner (molecular network aligner) and tested on both undirected and directed networks, which represent a variety of biomolecular networks, such as protein interaction networks, gene regulatory networks, coexpression networks, and metabolic networks. Note that the elements of adjacency matrices may be symmetric or asymmetric, depending on whether it is a directed or undirected network. The software for MNAligner is available from http://intelligent.eic.osaka-sandai.ac.jp/chenen/MNAligner.htm, http://www.isb.shu.edu.cn, or http://www.aporc.org/doc/wiki/MNAligner.

7.3.3.1 Aligning Undirected Networks

A small undirected synthesized network taken from the tutorial files provided in the PathBLAST plugin of software Cytoscape 1.1 was used to test MNAligner [LiZ07]. Meanwhile, PathBLAST was implemented by software Cytoscape 1.1 with the same data for comparison with MNAligner. Both methods follow similar network alignment procedures. In the first step, a global alignment graph is formed to consider node similarity and edge similarity together. Then, conserved pathways are identified by considering the local acyclic structures with high scores. Computational results show that the performance of MNAligner is similar to that of PathBLAST in terms of the ability to find conserved pathways in the two networks but outperforms PathBLAST in the ability to find the most conserved pathways. An optimal solution with the objective function 3.57 for $\lambda = 0.5$ was obtained by MNAligner. The protein matching is illustrated in Figure 7.3, where upper and lower nodes represent the nodes from the two networks, respectively. The thicker lines indicate that the corresponding edges are matched, whereas the thinner lines indicate that an edge from one network without matching with the one from another network. For this small example, the t-test score is 5.83, and p value is 1.96×10^{-78}.

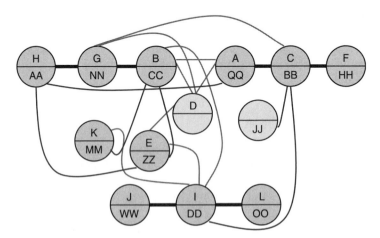

Figure 7.3. A tutorial network alignment example from PathBLAST plugin of Cytoscape software with $\lambda = 0.5$ by MNAligner. (Reprinted from [LiZ07] © 2007 by permission of Oxford University Press.)

MNAligner found three conserved pathways, all with length 3, that is, $A|QQ \leftrightarrow C|BB \leftrightarrow F|HH$, $J|WW \leftrightarrow I|DD \leftrightarrow L|OO$, and $H|AA \leftrightarrow G|NN \leftrightarrow B|CC$. The results from PathBLAST indicate that the pathway $A|QQ \leftrightarrow C|BB \leftrightarrow F|HH$ has the highest probability score, and $J|WW \leftrightarrow I|DD \leftrightarrow L|OO$ is ranked second by probability score. In some cases, PathBLAST and MNAligner identify the same elements of pathway but organize them differently. For example, the best pathway identified by PathBLAST, $C|QQ \leftrightarrow A|BB \leftrightarrow F|HH$, and the best pathway identified by MNAligner, $A|QQ \leftrightarrow C|BB \leftrightarrow F|HH$, contain the same elements (nodes and edges). PathBLAST inserts a gap between C and A and forms an indirect link. The MNAligner retains the natural sequence order $C \leftrightarrow A \leftrightarrow F$ and $QQ \leftrightarrow BB \leftrightarrow HH$ in the original network. In addition, some pathways identified by MNAligner do not show up in the PathBLAST results. The comparison results support the assumption that MNAligner can find the best matched subnetworks between two biomolecular networks in terms of optimization, while PathBLAST is a heuristic approach that can list many feasible solutions.

7.3.3.2 *Aligning Directed Networks*

MNAligner can also be used for aligning directed networks, such as gene regulatory networks [LiZ07]. A small synthesized directed network, shown in Figure 7.4, was used to verify the effectiveness of MNAligner. MNAligner obtained the optimal objective function value 9.22 by parameter $\lambda = 0.5$, where the optimal matching is as follows: (u_1, v_1), (u_2, v_2), (u_3, v_3), (u_4, v_4), (u_5, v_5), (u_6, v_6), (u_7, v_7), (u_8, v_{11}), (u_9, v_9), (u_{11}, v_8), and (u_{12}, v_{12}). For this example, the t-test score is 5.06 and the p value is 1.60×10^{-72}. A significant advantage of MNAligner is that it can find more complex substructures, including loops, such as $(u_1, v_1) \mapsto (u_7, v_7) \mapsto (u_8, v_{11}) \mapsto (u_6, v_6) \mapsto (u_1, v_1)$.

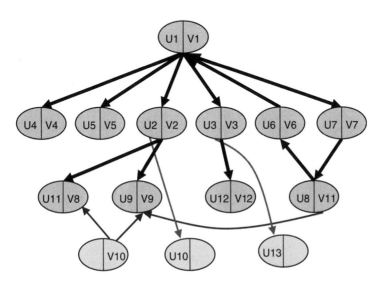

Figure 7.4. A simulated alignment example of two directed networks with $\lambda = 0.5$ by MNAligner. (Reprinted from [LiZ07] © 2007 by permission of Oxford University Press.)

The results presented above show that MNAligner can be applied to both undirected and directed networks with or without loops, in contrast to PathBLAST, which is appropriate mainly for undirected networks without loops. Generally, PathBLAST performs a heuristic search for global alignment graphs and lists many short paths on the basis of statistical scores, whereas MNAligner obtains optimal alignments on the basis of both node similarity and edge similarity.

7.3.3.3 Aligning Biomolecular Networks MNAligner was also used to align protein interaction networks from yeast and fly, and metabolic pathways from yeast and bacterium [LiZ07]. Alignment of protein interaction networks incorporates sequence homology and network structure, and thus can be a powerful tool for predicting protein functions, uncovering true functional orthologs, and revealing biologically significant pathways. Li et al. partitioned yeast and fly protein interaction networks into network modules, and then MNAligner aligned those module pairs from two protein interaction networks to discover conserved subnetworks [LiZ07]. Figure 7.5

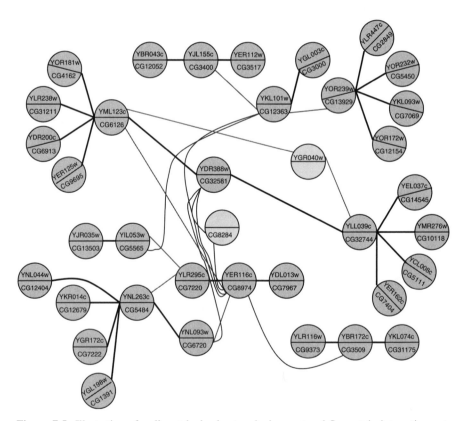

Figure 7.5. Illustration of well-matched subnetworks in yeast and fly protein interaction networks with $\lambda = 0.9$. (Reprinted from [LiZ07] © 2007 by permission of Oxford University Press.)

shows an example in which several well-matched subnetworks were found. Each circle represents a match. The nodes in these subnetworks of yeast correspond to two basic functions: DNA processing and transport routines. Naturally, the corresponding subnetworks in fly can be predicted to have these two functions. In addition, MNAligner can be applied to identify functional orthologs in protein interaction networks [Ban06].

In addition to the alignment of protein interaction networks, MNAligner was applied to align metabolic pathways [LiZ07]. All the possible pairs between 113 *E. coli* pathways and 151 *S. cerevisiae* pathways [Pin05] were aligned by MNAligner. The results show that about half of those pathways from one species match well with the corresponding ones in another species. Such results demonstrate the presence of abundant conserved pathways among species, although *E. coli* and *S. cerevisiae* come from prokaryotic and eukaryotic, respectively. Figure 7.6 illustrates four aligned metabolic pathways, which demonstrate the effectiveness of MNAligner in uncovering interesting biological conservative units. The arginine biosynth2 pathway and the arginine metabolism pathway, respectively, from *E. coli* and *S. cerevisiae* form a well-matched linear path, except for a nonidentical match where the nonmatch may

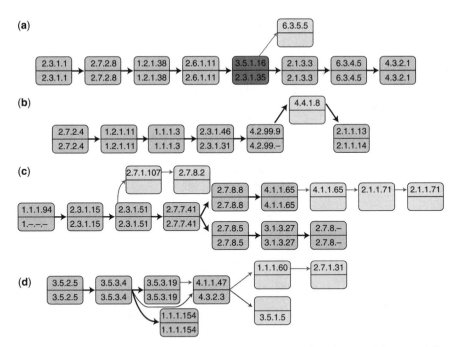

Figure 7.6. Three matched interspecies metabolic pathway pairs with $\lambda = 0.9$: (a) arginine biosynth2 pathway and arginine metabolism pathway; (b) homoserine methionine biosynth pathway and methionine biosynth pathway; (c) phospholipid biosynth1 pathway and phosphatidic acid phospholipid biosynth pathway; (d) allantoine degradation pathway and ureide degradation pathway. (Reprinted from [LiZ07] © 2007 by permission of Oxford University Press.)

hint to interesting evolutionary information. The mismatch in Figure 7.6a is between AreE in *E. coli* and Ecm40 in *S. cerevisiae*. Actually, the two enzymes catalyze different reactions, but produce the same compound L-ornithine. Moreover, these two proteins have no significant sequence similarity. This indicates that nonhomologous proteins that carry out different intermediate processes may mediate same subsequent processes.

Figure 7.6b illustrates an alignment of the homoserine methionine biosynth pathway and the methionine biosynth pathway, respectively. These two pathways have only minor differences between two matched pairs, including EC 2.3.1.46 versus EC 2.3.1.31 and EC 2.1.1.13 versus EC 2.1.1.14. An enzyme (4.4.1.8) is embedded into ethionine biosynth pathway from *S. cerevisiae*, which implies the possible existence of more complex biochemical reactions in *E. coli*. Although biochemical reactions are the same in the first three products (compound : homoserine; after enzyme : EC 1.1.1.3), they differ in the subsequent chain reactions, but have the same final compound, L-methionine. Biologically, the reactions catalyzed by metA, metB, metC, and metE in *E. coli* can be viewed to play the same role as the reactions catalyzed by met2, met17, and met6 in *S. cerevisiae*. More interestingly, three among all the seven enzymes, met17, metB, and metC, are sequence homologs, which may imply either gene duplication in *E. coli* or gene fusion in *S. cerevisiae*.

Figure 7.6c illustrates the third aligned pathway pair, in which the phosphatidic acid phospholipid biosynth pathway from *S. cerevisiae* can be considered as a subnetwork of phospholipid biosynth1 pathway from *E. coli*. Figure 7.6d illustrates the fourth aligned pathway pair. Although the two pathways (allantoine degradation pathway from *E. coli* and ureide degradation pathway from *S. cerevisiae*) have different final compounds, they have very similar initiative subpathways. All examples illustrate strong evolutionary trace between the distant organisms from the viewpoint of topological structure, which may not be recognized simply by analyzing sequences or structures of individual molecules.

In addition, MNAligner can be employed to carry out intraspecies alignment, which may provide interesting duplication and divergence information within a species. Figure 7.7 illustrates two statistically significant examples from all-against-all

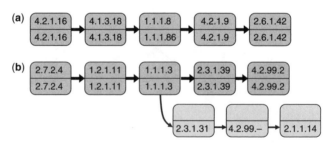

Figure 7.7. Two matched intra-species pairs with $\lambda = 0.9$: (a) isoleucine biosynth1 pathway and NAD dephosphorylation pathway from *E. coli*; (b) threonine biosynth pathway and threonine methionine biosynth pathway from *S. cerevisiae*. (Reprinted from [LiZ07] © 2007 by permission of Oxford University Press.)

alignments in *E. coli* and *S. cerevisiae*, respectively. MNAligner can also as a network query tool [Pin05]. For example, there are many biologically significant complexes known in yeast but very few known in other species such as fly. By applying MNAligner to querying a known complex from yeast in the biomolecular network from another species, a conserved complex may be identified.

7.4 MULTIPLE ALIGNMENT OF BIOMOLECULAR NETWORKS

Although most of the existing network alignment methods aim to compare two networks, multi-network alignment also has important applications since it can provide conserved information across more than two species. With the availability of hundreds of protein interaction networks and other kinds of biomolecular networks from different species, generalization of the network alignment process to more than two networks is necessary and imperative. Multiple network alignment entails devising an appropriate scoring scheme, defining a proper alignment graph, and locating conserved network topologies, as in pairwise network alignment (Fig. 7.8). The earliest attempt for multi-network alignment can be tracked to the paper by Tohsato et al. [Toh00]. The scenario that they deal with is relatively simple since the compared networks are linear paths, multiple sequence alignment techniques can be easily adopted to solve it. Another early work is that by Stuart et al. [Stu03], which compared cross-species coexpression networks by forcing a consistent one-to-one mapping across all the networks and constructed an alignment graph in which each gene was a member of at most one node. Sharan et al. described a framework for multiple network alignment that can handle general correspondence relationships across multiple networks [Sha05b]. They extended the likelihood-based scoring scheme and the notion of a network alignment graph [Sha05a] to multiple networks. By using this method, they identified conserved protein subnetworks across yeast, worm, and fly, and found 71 conserved network regions that fall into well-defined functional categories. The approach was complied as an online software called NetworkBLAST available at www.cs.tau.ac.il/networkblast.htm. Although NetworkBLAST extends a likelihood-based scoring scheme, it scales poorly with the number of networks increasing. Flannick et al. developed a robust and fast alignment tool called Grælin for multiple large interaction networks [Fla06], which is a great breakthrough in scalable multi-network alignment. In Grælin, functional evolution allows both the generalization of existing alignment scoring schemes and the location of conserved network topologies other than protein complexes and metabolic pathways. This approach employs an objective function of probabilistic formulation for topology matching, and can be applied to search conserved functional modules among multiple protein interaction networks. In addition, Dutkowski and Tiuryn developed a multiple network alignment framework based on protein network evolution [Dut07], which takes into account the phylogenetic history of the proteins and the evolution of their interactions. By constructing an ancestral protein interaction network, they identified many conserved ancestral modules. Singh et al. extended their PageRank-based algorithm to multiple protein network alignment [Sin08]. Also, a new algorithm for multi-network

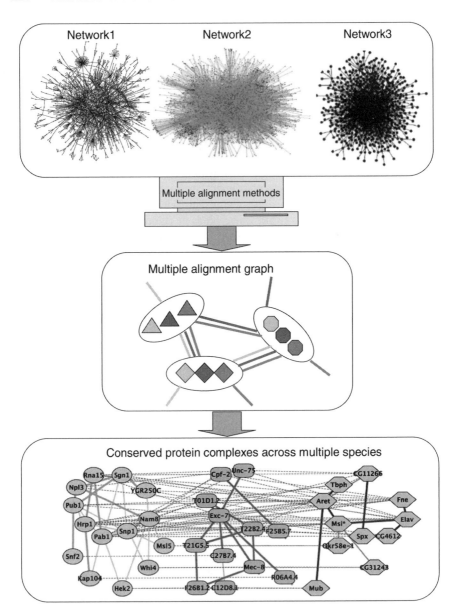

Figure 7.8. Illustration of the scheme for multi-network alignment.

alignment based on a novel representation of the network data has been proposed [Kal08]. The algorithm does not need the explicit representation of every set of potentially orthologous proteins and thus dramatically saves time and memory requirements.

As does multiple sequence alignment, multiple alignment of biomolecular networks is important but quite difficult since the network topologies to be aligned may be very diverse. The key and critical point is how to design a scoring scheme that can effectively characterize the cross-species evolution and conservation. Although great progresses have been gained, more sophisticated approaches that can efficiently and accurately analyze multiple networks are still required.

7.5 SUBNETWORK AND PATHWAY QUERYING

Network alignment aims at discovering biologically significant regions in multiple networks, based on an assumption that some regions are functionally and evolutionarily conserved. It can be viewed as a kind of unsupervised learning for detecting conserved protein complexes or functional modules. In some cases, we need to query a subnetwork or pathway that was previously known to be functional from a given large network or database. Such module detection approaches are known as network querying and belong to supervised learning. Their goal is to identify subnetworks in a given network, similar to sequence querying [Sha06]. Biomolecular network querying is defined as a computational problem that maps the components of one interesting subnetwork (e.g., complex, pathway, functional module) to a given large network for uncovering similar subnetworks. It is closely related to a graph matching problem that finds similar subgraphs between two graphs. Automated querying tools for implementing such network comparison are important for harnessing the information hiding in multiple networks across different species or conditions. So far, the network querying problem has been studied by several groups with only a few search tools available (see Table 7.1).

Actually, in the PathBLAST network alignment algorithm [Kel03, Kel04], network querying is adopted since the alignment of two networks is achieved by designating one of the networks as the query. When PathBLAST is applied in this setting, it identifies all matches to the query from the network under study. Nevertheless, the queries can only take the form of a linear path of interacting proteins. By using PathBLAST to compare multiple networks across different species, Suthram et al. explored the possibility of whether the divergence of *Plasmodium* at the sequence level can be embodied at the level of the structure of its protein interaction network [Sut06]. They found that *Plasmodium* has only three conserved complexes against yeast, and no conserved complexes against fly, worm, and bacteria. But yeast, fly, and worm share abundant conserved complexes with each other [Zha08]. Figure 7.9a shows one of those three conserved complexes, which has a conserved counterpart in yeast, whereas Figure 7.9b shows an example of a complex in *Plasmodium* with no conserved subnetworks to other organisms. Among the three conserved complexes, it has also been found that one protein in *Plasmodium* often has multiple homologous proteins in yeast, such as MAL6P1.286 in Figure 7.9a. All these comparative results show that although there are a few similar substructures, the protein interaction networks between *Plasmodium* and the other four eukaryotes are considerably different, which implies that *Plasmodium* may have evolutionary processes quite different from those of other four organisms. On the other hand, based on microarray data from multiple conditions and multiple species, a variety of

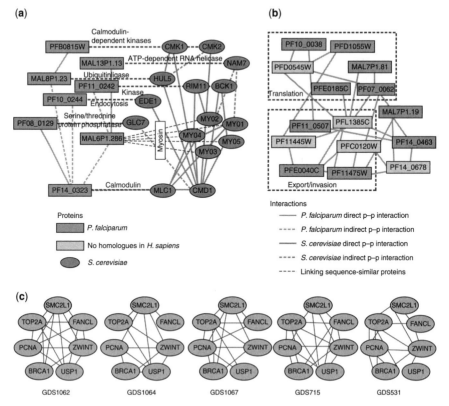

Figure 7.9. Biomolecular network querying examples for multiple species and conditions: (a) endocytosis—a conserved complex identified between *Plasmodium falciparum* and *Saccharomyces cerevisiae*; (b) translation/invasion—a representative complex uncovered within the *P. falciparum* network only; (c) a potential transcription module that appeared in five leukemia gene coexpression networks under different conditions (see color insert) [Zha08].

comparative studies have been comprehensively conducted for revealing transcriptional regulatory modules, predicting gene functions, and uncovering evolutionary mechanisms [Zho04]. Figure 7.9c illustrates a condition-specific module that appears in five leukemia coexpression networks across different conditions. Moreover, its member genes were identified as being involved in the cell cycle and DNA repair process, which is consistent with the nature of leukemia and thereby confirms the effectiveness of such an analysis.

Pinter et al. devised an algorithm called MetaPathwayHunter for querying metabolic networks [Pin05]. On the basis of an efficient graph matching algorithm, the method can find and report all approximate occurrences of the query in the collection, ranked by similarity and statistical significance for a given query pathway and a collection of pathways. Their algorithm allows metabolic pathways to take the form of a tree only within a collection of such pathways. Compared with PathBLAST, the MetaPathwayHunter enables fast queries for more general pathways. However, its searching is limited within a collection of subnetworks without cycles. In addition, a pathway querying tool, QPath [Shl06], has been developed for a linear query pathway with respect to a network of interest. Rather than finding networks with possible feedback loops, the algorithm mainly searches efficiently for homologous pathways, allowing both insertions and deletions of proteins in the identified pathways. In contrast to the subnetwork querying methods limited to linear paths, a tree queries called QNet was developed to extend the class of pathways that can be efficiently queried to the case of trees, and graphs of bounded tree width [Dos07]. QNet exploits a color-coding technique and allows the identification of nonexact (homeomorphic) matches. NetMatch was also based on a graph matching algorithm [Fer07]. The queried results by NetMatch are subgraphs of the original graph connected in the same way as the querying graph, and therefore they can be viewed as candidate network motifs because of their similar topological features. NetMatch can also handle multiple attributes per node and edge, but is impeded by the restricted match criterion. An approximation graph matching technique called SAGA has been used to query biological pathways [Tia07]. This technique employs a flexible model for computing graph similarity, which allows for node gaps, node mismatches, and graph structural differences. SAGA employs an indexing technique that enables it to efficiently evaluate queries even against large graph datasets. Yang and Sze formally defined path matching and graph matching problems respectively [Yan07] as

- Given a query path p and a graph G, find a path p' that is most similar to p in G.
- Given a query graph G_0 and a graph G, find a graph G_0' that is most similar to G_0 in G.

In path matching and graph matching problems, p and G_0 represent a given substructure of interest to a biologist such as pathways, protein complexes, or functional modules. G represents a large network in which biologists desire to find a related substructure such as a protein interaction network or a metabolic network. Yang and Sze [Yan07] reduced the path matching problem to find a longest weighted path in a directed acyclic graph that can be exactly solved in polynomial time. This is in contrast with most previous approaches that use exponential time algorithms to find simple paths and are practical only when the paths are short. On the other hand, since it is an exact algorithm to find the highest-scoring subgraphs in a graph, it is also superior to most existing heuristic or randomized algorithms. Software programs implementing PathMatch and GraphMatch are available at http://faculty.cs.tamu.edu/shsze.

Although many methods have been developed for querying, they are far from perfect in contrast to the demand from the field of systems biology. Network querying tools are still at an early stage, and most of tools are limited to sparse special topological structures and suffer from the problem of computational complexity. On the other hand, with the increasing accumulation of huge network datasets, it is imperative to develop user-friendly, systems biology tools for biomolecular network querying. As do the developments in sequence/structure alignments and their essential roles in the areas of sequence and structure researches, network querying

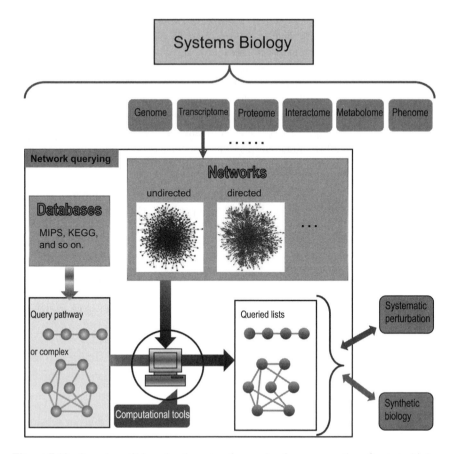

Figure 7.10. Overview of biomolecular network querying from perspective of systems biology [Zha08].

or alignment demonstrates the great potential in elucidating network organization, function, and evolution and will greatly enhance the research activity of systems biology (see Fig. 7.10). The querying problem should be extended to uncover more informative cellular machineries. For example, by constructing a portion of a pathway related to an disease of interest based on analysis and integration of experimental data, we are able to uncover the disease-related biological processes by querying the pathway in a pathway database. Therefore, similar to the querying methods of sequences, a universal querying system that can search interesting small subnetworks with complex substructures efficiently from a variety of biomolecular networks is of high demand in the area of both bioinformatics and systems biology.

7.6 SUMMARY

In this chapter, we introduced several network alignment methods, including pairwise network alignment, multiple network alignment, and network querying. In particular, we described an integer quadratic programming approach for pairwise network alignment. Comprehensive review literature for this area can be found in the literature [Sha06; Zha07, Zha08]. Intuitively, in contrast to sequence alignment, which can be viewed as a one-dimensional problem, and structure alignment, which can be viewed as a three-dimensional problem, network alignment is a multi-dimensional problem that generally requires more sophisticated theoretical techniques to develop the efficient computational tools. Although great progress has been achieved in these areas, there is still much room for further investigation such as improving computational complexity and accuracy, and extending the alignment to general networks from simple pathways and subtrees. Like sequence alignment and subsequence querying tools, which have been indispensable for biological research, with the increasing accumulation of network data, efficient network alignment techniques and subnetwork query tools are expected to play critical roles in the advance of bioinformatics and systems biology.

CHAPTER 8

NETWORK-BASED PREDICTION OF PROTEIN FUNCTION

8.1 PROTEIN FUNCTION AND ANNOTATION

Almost all the activities of living organisms are achieved by proteins with diverse functions. Modern experimental techniques have resulted in a large amount of data that reflect the function information of proteins at different levels. In such a functional genomic era, we are able to make use of the vast wealth of protein knowledge to decipher the rich but complicated behaviors of living organisms.

What is protein function? Actually, this is not a well-defined concept since protein function is highly context-sensitive such as species-specificity, tissue, and so on. Generally, it implies all types of activities that a protein is involved in. For instance, the activities may be cellular, molecular, physiological, or biological in nature. Bork et al. suggested that protein function can be categorized as follows [Bor98]:

- *Molecular Function.* Each protein has molecular elementary functions such as ligand binding, catalysis of biochemical reactions, conformational changes, and transporting.
- *Cellular Function.* Some proteins also have a physiological cellular function. Usually many proteins come together to form metabolic pathways, signal transduction networks, or protein complexes to keep the cellular systems

Biomolecular Networks. By Luonan Chen, Rui-Sheng Wang, and Xiang-Sun Zhang
Copyright © 2009 John Wiley & Sons, Inc.

working well. The cellular function of a protein is often context-dependent and characterized by taxon, organ, tissue, and so on.

- *Phenotypic Function.* The totality of the physiological subsystems and their interplay with environmental stimuli determine phenotypic function, morphology and physiology of an organism.

Actually, biological function for proteins is defined in terms of subjectivity, hierarchy, and dimension. Subjectivity means that a protein function is often described by human language, and different researchers may denote the functions of a protein diversely. Hierarchy means that protein functions can be defined at different levels. The lower levels correspond to the general functions and the higher levels, to the specific functions. For example, we can say that a protein has the function of cellular process at a low level. More specifically, this protein is involved in cell communication. If we describe its function in more detail at higher levels, we can respectively say that the protein is involved in signal transduction, cell surface receptor linked signal transduction, G-protein-coupled receptor signaling pathway, signal transduction during conjugation with cellular fusion, and so on. Dimension means that functional attributes themselves have different categories.

With the characteristics of the function described above, the naming systems of protein functions should ensure necessary and desirable properties such as a wide coverage, a standardized format, a hierarchical structure, disjoint categories, multiple functions, and dynamic nature. The earliest systematic scheme for naming protein function was the Enzyme Commission (EC) [Web92]. It mainly categorizes enzymes, and divides them into six classes on the basis of their chemical composition. These classes are then further subdivided into three hierarchical levels that further specify the precise reaction that a particular enzyme is involved in. Nowadays, many functional schemes have been proposed for standardizing and classifying protein functions. The Gene Ontology (GO) database and the MIPS Functional Catalogue Database, FunCat, are currently two of the most popular annotation schemes. In particular, FunCat involves the functional description of proteins from prokaryotes, unicellular eukaryotes, plants, and animals [Rue04], and consists of 28 main functional categories that cover general fields such as cellular transport, metabolism, and cellular communication/signal transduction. It has been widely used as standards for validating function prediction techniques because of its wide coverage and standardized hierarchical structure. There are also other databases with function annotations, such as SwissProt, KEGG, and TIGRFAMs, which are listed and described in Table 8.1.

The Gene Ontology (GO) project is a collaborative effort to address the need for consistent descriptions of gene products in different databases, resulting in a function database intended to provide controlled vocabularies that can be used to describe any organism [GO08]. The controlled vocabularies are hierarchically structured so that they can be queried at different levels. GO is based on solid computer science and biological principles, and has been rapidly recognized as the most general scheme for functional annotation techniques across a wide variety of biological data. GO

TABLE 8.1. Gene and Protein Function Annotation Databases

Databases	Description
GO	Gene ontology database, a controlled vocabulary for describing gene and gene product attributes
COG	Clusters of orthologous groups
EC	Enzyme Commission; mainly categorizes enzymes into different hierarchical classes
EGAD	Nonredundant set of human transcript (HT) sequences and non-human-transcript (ET) sequences
ECOLI	Functions encoded by the *E. coli* K-12 (strain MG1655) genome
HAMAP	High-quality automated and manual annotation of microbial proteomes
Uniprot	The most comprehensive catalog of information on proteins including sequence, function, etc.
FunCat	An annotation scheme for the functional description of proteins from prokaryotes, unicellular eukaryotes, plants, and animals
TIGRFAMs	Protein families based on hidden Markov models
EXProt	A database for experimentally verified protein functions
EFICAz	A genomewide enzyme function annotation database

describes a protein's function from molecular, biological, or cellular perspectives. Each of them represents a key concept in molecular biology:

- *Molecular Function.* GO describes the activities of gene products at the molecular level such as catalytic activity, binding activity, and transporting activity.
- *Biological Process.* A biological process is a recognized series of events or molecular functions. Biological process ontology describes the role of gene products in multistep biological processes, involving more than one activity.
- *Cellular Component.* GO describes the protein locations of cellular components at the levels of subcellular structures and macromolecular complexes.

The building blocks of the Gene Ontology are terms. Each entry in GO has a unique numerical identifier of a form such as GO:0007165 with a term name, such as "signal transduction." Each term is also assigned to one of the three ontologs: molecular function, cellular component, or biological process. Terms from the Gene Ontology can be applied in the annotation of gene products in biological databases.

The process of determining biological functions through experimental techniques, such as gene knockout and mass spectrometry, is laborious and time-consuming. Hence, computational function annotation for genes and proteins by employing genomic data has become popular. Function annotation is a process of making associations between gene products and function categories that describe them. Function prediction is an important topic in bioinformatics and systems biology. More recently, a large number of methods have been developed for protein function annotation based on different types of biological information such as sequences, 3D structures, sequence or structure motifs, gene expression data, comparative genomics, and phylogenomics. The earliest methods for protein function prediction are based mainly on primary sequences, which usually apply the well-known sequence alignment tools such as PSI-BLAST and FASTA to find homologous proteins since proteins with similar sequences are assumed to carry out similar functions. However, sequence-alignment-based methods may not work well when the sequence similarity between a known protein and the query protein is very low. Machine learning techniques employing sequence features provide an alternative approach to this problem. Also, 3D structures can be used to assign functions for uncharacterized proteins. The folding patterns of proteins are often better preserved than are the corresponding sequences during evolution, and hence structure alignment can identify homologs where sequence alignment becomes futile. The basic idea of these traditional function prediction methods is that if protein P_a has function f and protein P_b possesses sequence similarity, structure similarity, or common motifs with protein P_a, then protein P_b might have a similar function related to f. Moreover, comparative genomics is one of the most powerful methods for analyzing the function relationships between proteins from different species [Pel99]. This method is based on the assumption that proteins with similar functions are expected to evolve together. All such functionally linked proteins tend to be either preserved or eliminated in a new species during evolution. In addition to these approaches, there are also methods for predicting gene product functions on the basis of gene expression data, phylogenomics, or other data.

Generally, a biological function is facilitated not by individual proteins but by a concerted effect of those proteins through their interactions. Furthermore, it has been observed that interacting proteins are often involved in the same biological processes and have similar functions. On the other hand, the high-throughput techniques for determining protein interaction patterns have attracted the attention of researchers from the study of individual proteins to that of the entire interactome, which makes it possible to annotate a protein function according to its neighbors in a protein interaction network [Den03a]. Actually, it has been realized that genomic information is not sufficient for accurate function annotation, and system-based approaches may work well. Annotating protein functions on the basis of protein interaction networks can be categorized into three classes: detecting functional modules, creating functional linkages, and direct function prediction. In this chapter, we will introduce some of these function annotation methods.

8.2   PROTEIN FUNCTIONAL MODULE DETECTION

The organization of biological networks has long been considered modular in nature. A functional module is regarded as a group of genes or gene products that are related by genetic or cellular interactions, such as co-regulation, co-expression, or comembership of a protein complex, a metabolic pathway, a signaling pathway, or a cellular aggregate (e.g., chaperone, ribosome, protein transport facilitator). In particular, protein interaction networks often contain functionally relatively isolated subnetworks corresponding to specific biological units that lead to extensive use of modules in prediction of molecular functions. In terms of topology, a functional module can be typically understood as a group of cellular components that are densely interconnected and contribute together to a specific biological function [Har99]. An important property of a module is that its function is separable from those of other modules and its members are related more to one another than to members of other modules, which is reflected in network topology. The separability may stem from, for example, cellular localization, special interactions of proteins, or special regulation of genes. Revealing modular structures in cellular networks is very helpful for understanding biochemical processes and signal pathways. It is also related to community structure detection in the field of complex system theory. Unlike conventional methods that predict functions for individual genes or proteins, detecting functional modules attempts to first identify coherent groups of proteins and then assign functions to all the proteins in each group. A large number of methods can be adopted for module detection techniques. Once a module is obtained, the function prediction within the module [Sha07] is usually conducted in a straightforward way by simple methods. For module detection techniques, clustering is a popular unsupervised learning algorithm and plays an important role in this field, since detecting functional modules in protein interaction networks is closely related to the data clustering problem without the information on network structure. In addition, network analysis is closely related to the graph theory in combinatorics. Hence, graph-theoretic methods are also widely used in this field. The main purpose of those algorithms is to detect functional modules, but many of them can also detect protein complexes.

8.2.1 Distance-Based Clustering Methods

Many partition and local search methods have been proposed to decompose a whole network into functional units. Specifically, hierarchical clustering methods have proved to be an effective strategy for detecting functional modules in protein interaction networks. A key problem in using hierarchical clustering for module detection is how to select a similarity measure between two proteins. The distance between two nodes in a network is usually defined as the number of edges on the shortest path between them. The ties in the proximity problem are serious when using the shortest-path distance in a hierarchical clustering setting since the distances between many protein pairs are identical. Ravasz et al. defined a simple similarity relationship between two nodes to cluster nodes and analyzed the hierarchical structure of modularity in metabolic networks [Rav02]. Rives and Galitski developed a network clustering method to identify modules in cellular networks on the basis of the fact that each vertex in a network has a unique profile of shortest-path distances to every other vertex, and that module comembers are likely to have similar shortest-path distance profiles [Riv03]. They used hierarchical clustering on the all-pair shortest-path distances matrix, and outlined modules by manual inspection. Arnau et al. applied the hierarchical clustering method with the shortest path length between proteins as a distance measure [Arn05], where the strategy of randomly resampling hierarchical clustering solutions is adopted to overcome the ties in the proximity problem. Lu et al. suggested a simple measure, $S = A + wA^2$, to depict the link relationship between any two nodes [LuH04], where w is a very small number and A is the adjacency matrix of the network. The second term in this measure is intended to ensure that the interacting protein pair that shares more neighbors should be clustered first. In addition, the Czekanowski–Dice distance has been used for calculating the distance between two proteins in a hierarchical clustering setting [Bru04]. Samanta and Liang used the statistical significance of the number of common interaction partners as a measure of similarity to hierarchically clustering proteins in protein interaction networks [Sam03]. In another application of clustering [Dun05], Girvan and Newman's edge-betweenness algorithm [Gir02] was used to cluster the Lehner dataset of human protein interactions to derive protein clusters.

Although many similarity measures have been proposed so far for hierarchical clustering, a reliable way to evaluate them is still lacking. For this purpose, two evaluation schemes based on the depth of a hierarchical tree and width of the ordered adjacency matrix suggested by Lu et al. may be useful [LuH04]. A systematic evaluation of various distance measures should be conducted in a comprehensive manner. In addition, since different types of biomolecular networks have different modularity characteristics, network-specific measures would be preferred.

8.2.2   Graph Clustering Methods

Detecting functional modules in protein interaction networks is closely related to graph partition and graph clustering. So far, numerous graph clustering algorithms have been applied in this field. Bader and Hogue proposed a molecular complex detection algorithm (MCODE) to predict complexes in protein interaction networks [Bad03]. In their method, firstly the vertices of the network are weighted by their core clustering coefficients (the density of the largest k core of its immediate neighborhood), and then densely connected modules are detected in a greedy fashion. Spirin and Mirny presented two algorithms to find complexes and functional modules [Spi03]. One is based on superparamagnetic clustering (SPC), which uses an analogy to the physical properties of an inhomogenous ferromagnetic model to find tightly connected clusters in a large graph. Another is a Monte Carlo algorithm that aims to maximize the density of the predicted clusters. The highly connected subgraph (HCS) method is a graph-theoretic algorithm that separates a graph into several subgraphs using minimum cuts [Prz04a]. Although the objective of this method is to find a subgraph with a high density, this method differs from those approaches that seek to directly identify the densest subgraphs. In contrast, it exploits the inherent connectivity of the graph and cuts the most unimportant edges to find highly connected subgraphs. In this sense, this method is similar to edge-betweenness-based clustering [Dun05]. King et al. proposed a cost-based local search algorithm based on a tabu search called the restricted neighborhood search clustering (RNSC) algorithm to partition a protein interaction network into clusters [Kin04]. The algorithm begins with an initial random cluster assignment and then proceeds by reassigning nodes to maximize the partition's score. The authors show that the RNSC algorithm outperforms the MCODE algorithm. A spectral method derived from graph theory was introduced [Bu03] to uncover hidden topological structures such as quasicliques and quasibipartites in protein interaction networks. These hidden topological structures were found to consist of biologically relevant functional groups.

The Markov clustering algorithm (MCL), invented by [Don00], is a fast and scalable unsupervised clustering algorithm for graphs based on simulation of stochastic flow in graphs. The algorithm starts by computing the graph of random walks of an input graph, yielding a stochastic matrix. Then it simulates random walks within a graph by an alternation of the expansion operation, which takes the squared power of the matrix, and the inflation operation, which takes the Hadamard power of a matrix, followed by a scaling step, so that the resulting matrix is again stochastic. This process continues until there is no further change in the matrix. The final matrix is interpreted as graph clusters with some postprocessing. This clustering procedure can handle weighted graphs and works efficiently on large dense graphs, where it displays good convergence and robustness. Pereira-Leal et al. used a software of the Markov clustering algorithm called TribeMCL to conduct a clustering-based analysis of the yeast interaction network [Per04]. In a study for detecting complexes in protein interaction data, Krogan et al. also applied the MCL algorithm to find complexes in protein interaction networks [Kro06], where the strengths of protein interactions are estimated in advance. When applied in protein interaction networks, the MCL algorithm simulates a flow on the network by constructing its adjacency matrix and computing its successive powers to increase the contrast between regions with a high flow and regions with a low flow. This process converges to a final matrix that demonstrates a partition of the network into high-flow regions corresponding to protein complexes, separated by regions of no flow.

It is worth noting that most of proteins are observed to have multiple functions. The multiple functionality of proteins usually causes different modules to overlap. Therefore, it is not reasonable to transform a hard partition of protein interaction networks into separated functional modules. However, most current methods are hard-partition algorithms, meaning that each protein can belong to only one specific module. Although some local search methods can detect modules with overlap, there is no detailed discussion on the possible significance and biological implication of overlapping nodes. A graph-theoretic method called CFinder has been applied to find overlapping functional modules in molecular networks [Ada06]. It is based on the clique percolation method (CPM) [Pal05]. However, the CFinder method is too restrictive since its basic element is a 3-clique, and thus it can only detect few modules and discard many proteins in sparse protein interaction networks such as fly and worm interactomes. Integrating semantic similarity between GO function terms, Cho et al. proposed an information-flow-based modularization algorithm to efficiently identify overlapping modules in weighted interaction networks [Cho07]. Although a large number of module detection methods have been developed, only a few of them can detect such overlapping modules, with different degrees of limitation. Therefore, efficient module detection algorithms that can not only detect abundant modules but also uncover meaningful overlapping components are imperative so as to further improve the accuracy. In addition, protein interaction networks are generally very sparse, but most methods only identify strongly connected subgraphs as modules. Hence, only a few modules can be detected with many proteins discarded. This problem may be alleviated by integrating other information sources such as gene expression measurements or deletion phenotypes [Zho02].

8.2.3   Validation of Module Detection

With various module identification tools available, disparate results can be generated using different approaches. Therefore, validation of the detected modules by using biological evidence is important. A straightforward way to validate the clustering results is to examine the homogeneity of clusters in terms of the function similarity of proteins e.g., comparing the clustering results with ground true function categories from protein function annotation databases, such as FunCat and the GO database. In general, functional homogeneity of proteins in a module with known function annotation from MIPS or GO can be evaluated with the following hypergeometric distribution [Bu03]:

$$P = 1 - \sum_{i=0}^{k-1} \frac{\binom{C}{i}\binom{G-C}{n-i}}{\binom{G}{n}} \tag{8.1}$$

which denotes the probability of observing at least k proteins from a functional module with size n by chance in a function category containing C proteins from the total number of proteins G within the network. Obviously, it characterizes the significance of a functional module. In addition, the match between detected modules and experimental complexes can be efficiently used to validate the biological significance of modules and evaluate different detection algorithms [Bad03, Spi03, Kin04, Dun05, Per04]. The proteins included in the same module generally tend to share similar temporal expression profiles, subcellular localizations, and gene phenotypes, which support the functional relevance of the modular organization of protein interaction networks.

Although many module detection methods have been developed for biomolecular networks, there are still many challenging problems in this field. Specifically, the detected modules are often differ from one method to another because of the unclear boundaries between modules or within the hierarchical architecture of the networks. Generally speaking, most methods introduce some parameters that are usually sensitive to the local density of networks. Although we can learn the so-called optimal parameters related to known function annotation or other genomic information, the results heavily depend on parameter tuning and the datasets employed. Evaluation of the algorithms for detecting a functional module entails intricate work. Brohée and van Helden performed a comparative assessment of four algorithms: MCODE, SPC,

RNSC, and MCL [Bro06]. With a set of known complexes in a protein interaction network, they compared the performance levels of the four methods in detecting complexes in perturbed networks. They showed that MCL is remarkably robust for graphing alterations and effective for the extraction of complexes. But it is only a small scale evaluation. A further comprehensive assessment of existing methods with more reasonable validations is required.

8.3 FUNCTIONAL LINKAGE FOR PROTEIN FUNCTION ANNOTATION

In addition to functional modules, another way for indirect function prediction is to create functional linkage. Usually, such approaches create functional assocations or linkages of protein pairs according to their positions in a protein interaction network. Some of them also incorporate the function evidences from other information such as gene expression correlation. The functional associations form a function linkage network with weighted edges representing the possibility that protein pairs have the same functions. Creating functional linkage networks is a promising step toward obtaining a detailed understanding of the functional relationships between proteins. Although such links reveal important clues for relating proteins by their function similarities, they rarely provide detailed information on which specific functional annotation the proteins share. Therefore, these methods usually need a second step, in which uncharacterized proteins are assigned certain functions according to their relationships with local or global neighbors within the functional linkage network. Some methods also explore clustering algorithms to group proteins on the basis of linkage information.

8.3.1 Bayesian Approach

One way to create functional linkage is to integrate biological experimental data and then extract the evidences contributed to functional relationships. For instance, two proteins might be functionally linked if they share similar sequences, structures, or gene ontology annotations, or if they test positive in a yeast two-hybrid screen, appear in the same protein complex, or their gene expression patterns are correlated in several experiment conditions. In addition, incorporating phylogenetic information can also improve the prediction of functional linkages [Jot06].

Chen and Xu developed a Bayesian statistical method combined with Boltzmann machine and simulated annealing for protein functional annotation in the yeast *S. cerevisiae* through integrating a variety of high-throughput biological data, including Y2H data, protein complexes, and microarray gene expression profiles [ChY04]. Specifically, in their approach, they first quantified the relationship between functional similarity and high-throughput data, and coded the relationship into a functional linkage network, where each node represents one protein and the weight of each edge is characterized by the probability of function similarity between two proteins. The probabilities for two genes (or proteins) to share the same function on the basis of different types of high-throughput data (i.e., microarray data, protein binary interaction data, and protein complex data) are calculated and combined by a Bayesian method. Given two genes correlated in gene expression with the Pearson correlation coefficient r in microarray data M_r, the posterior probability $\Pr(S|M_r)$ that two genes have the same function is computed by the Bayes formula in the following way

$$\Pr(S|M_r) = \frac{\Pr(M_r|S)\,\Pr(S)}{\Pr(M_r)}$$

where S represents the event that two genes have the same function at a given level of GO INDEX (according to GO database hierarchy), $\Pr(M_r|S)$ is the a priori probability that two genes are correlated in their expression profiles with correlation coefficient r, given that both genes have the same level of GO INDEX. $\Pr(S)$ is the probability for proteins having similar functions at the given level of GO INDEX by chance. $\Pr(M_r)$ is the frequency of gene expression correlated with coefficient r over all gene pairs in yeast, which is calculated from the genomewide gene expression profiles. For protein binary interaction B, the probability $\Pr(S|B)$ that two proteins have the same function is computed in the following way

$$\Pr(S|B) = \frac{\Pr(B|S)\,\Pr(S)}{\Pr(B)}$$

where $\Pr(B|S)$ is the probability for two proteins to have a binary interaction given the knowledge that they share the same function. The probability $\Pr(B)$ is the relative frequency of two proteins having a known binary interaction over all possible pairs in yeast. Similarly, given two proteins in the same complex C, the probability $\Pr(S|C)$ of two proteins having the same function is calculated as

$$\Pr(S|C) = \frac{\Pr(C|S)\,\Pr(S)}{\Pr(C)}$$

where $\Pr(C|S)$ is the probability for two proteins to be in the same complex given that they share the same function. The probability $\Pr(C)$ is the relative frequency of two proteins having a complex interaction over all protein pairs in yeast.

To integrate the probability scores from three data sources, a likelihood score G_k is defined as

$$G_k = 1 - [1 - \Pr(S|M_r)][1 - \Pr(S|B)][1 - \Pr(S|C)]$$

which combines the evidences from the gene expression correlation, protein binary interactions, and protein complex interactions, and represents the probability for two proteins sharing the same function. Therefore, G_k forms a functional linkage network, in which the Boltzmann machine is used to characterize the global stochastic behavior of the network. Each node has a binary state $Z \in \{0, 1\}$ to denote whether it has the given function. Then, the functional annotation of uncharacterized proteins is iteratively determined by their direct neighbors, which have true annotations or the predicted annotations

$$\Pr(Z_{t,i} = 1 | Z_{t-1, j \neq i}) = \frac{1}{1 + e^{-\beta \sum_{j \neq i} W_{ij} Z_{t-1, j \neq i}}}$$

which indicates that for the state at time t, node i has the probability for $Z_{t,i}$ to be 1, and $\Pr(Z_{t,i} = 1 | Z_{t-1, j \neq i})$ is given by the inputs from all the other nodes at time $t - 1$. β is a parameter reversely proportional to the annealing temperature, and W_{ij} is the weight of the edge connecting proteins i and j calculated from G_k in the functional linkage network. The system undergoes a dynamic process from a nonequilibrium to an equilibrium, which corresponds to the optimization process for the function prediction. Based on this method, 1802 out of 2280 unannotated proteins in yeast were assigned functions systematically [ChY04].

8.3.2 Hopfield Network Method

Karaoz et al. presented an effective methodology for combining evidentiary biological data obtained in several high-throughput experiments to achieve the agreement between annotations of neighbors in interaction networks [Kar04]. Their approach models the functional linkage graph into a variant of a discrete-state Hopfield network, which is a neural architecture often used in computational neuroscience [Hop86]. The nodes and edges of the functional linkage graph have a one-to-one correspondence to those of the constructed Hopfield network.

In the constructed network, each node (protein) has three discrete states. Given a particular GO function f, each node has a trinary state $s \in \{1, 0, -1\}$. The state of a node is 1 if the protein is annotated with f and -1 if the protein is annotated with a different function. The state of already annotated nodes will no longer be changed in the execution of the algorithm. Those proteins that have an unknown functional role are labeled as hypothetical proteins. The initial states of all hypothetical proteins are set as 0, which means that their functions have not been determined yet. Each edge e_{ij} connecting proteins i and j in the network has a real-valued weight w_{ij} that is derived by integrating available biological evidentiary data and represents a noisy putative functional relationship between the corresponding proteins. Intuitively, two nodes connected by an edge should receive the same functional assignment. Since it is not always possible to ensure that every edge is consistent, an energy function is defined for a certain function f in terms of the weights of the edges in the network and the functional annotations of all proteins to measure the consistency degree of a functional assignment as follows [Kar04]:

$$E = -\frac{1}{2} \sum_{i=1}^{n} \sum_{j=1, j \neq i}^{n} w_{ij} s_i s_j$$

where n is the number of nodes in the network and s_i is the state assigned to protein i. It is desirable to compute a maximally consistent state assignment, which is equivalent to maximizing the weighted sum of consistent edges and can be achieved by minimizing E. However, since the computation for identifying maximally consistent assignments is intractable in terms of computational complexity, an iterative gradient descent procedure is adopted. As an activation function in standard neural networks, the following activation rule

$$s_i = \text{sgn}\left(\sum_{j=1}^{n_i} w_{ij}s_j - \theta\right)$$

is iteratively applied to each node of the network until the states converge. Such an iteration process ensures that energy function E always decreases, and reflects the dynamic behavior of the network. This procedure was run for each function in GO, and the results were evaluated in terms of the F measure [Kar04]. This study showed that this integrated network gives more accurate predictions for many proteins compared to those using only protein–protein interaction networks. New functional annotations were also suggested for some proteins, which confirms the merit in integrating multiple information sources.

8.3.3 *p*-Value Method

Instead of integrating biological experimental data, another way to create a functional linkage network is to retrieve reliable protein interactions by considering the topology of protein interaction networks. Many methods have been proposed to redefine the reliable interaction relationship between two proteins, such as shortest path, alternative path, or diffusion kernel [Chu06, Zho02]. They all show that global topology information in a protein–protein interaction network is useful for identifying reliable protein interactions. Samanta and Liang presented a network-based statistical algorithm to derive functional relationships of proteins from large-scale interaction data [Sam03]. They hypothesized that if two proteins have a number of common interaction partners in the measured dataset significantly larger than what is expected from a random network, this would suggest close functional linkages between the proteins. Therefore, by ranking all possible protein pairs in the order of their probabilities for having a certain measured number of common interaction partners by chance, those protein pairs with an unusually large number of common partners will be considered for further analysis. Specifically, to calculate such probabilities, the number of distinct ways in which two proteins with n_1 and n_2 interaction partners share m in common is counted. Assume that there are m common protein partners that interact with both protein 1 and protein 2, there are $n_1 - m$ partners interacting only with protein 1, and that there are $n_2 - m$ partners that interact only with protein 2. Thus, the total number of distinct ways of assigning these three groups to N proteins is given by

$$\binom{N}{m}\binom{N-m}{n_1-m}\binom{N-n_1}{n_2-m}$$

Therefore, the p value of two proteins with m common interaction partners is defined as follows:

$$P(N, n_1, n_2, m) = \frac{\binom{N}{m}\binom{N-m}{n_1-m}\binom{N-n_1}{n_2-m}}{\binom{N}{n_1}\binom{N}{n_2}} \quad (8.2)$$

$$= \frac{(N-n_1)!(N-n_2)!n_1!n_2!}{N!m!(n_1-m)!(n_2-m)!(N-n_1-n_2+m)!} \quad (8.3)$$

The denominator of (8.2) is the total number of ways for the two proteins to have n_1 and n_2 interaction partners regardless of how many are shared in common. The numerator in (8.2) characterizes the number of ways for the protein pair to have m common interaction partners. This p value reflects the significance of a protein pair having m common interaction partners. The larger the p value is, the closer functional linkage the protein pair has. The p values for all possible protein pairs are stored in a matrix, and then a hierarchical clustering algorithm is used to group proteins with similar functions [Sam03]. According to their cluster groups, unannotated proteins can be assigned one or several functions.

8.3.4 Statistical Framework

In the p-value method, only local neighbors of a protein are considered, and thus the method may suffer from the noise problem caused by high-throughput experimental techniques. As indicated by a rigorous comparative analysis and performance assessment [Sut06], current technologies such as Y2H and TAP suffer from high false-positive rate. Therefore, it is necessary to associate confidence scores with protein interactions. On the other hand, it is often difficult to formulate the long-range relationships of a protein with other proteins. Therefore, efficient methods for determining the transitive functional relationships by defining remote neighborhoods are required such as shortest-path profiles, domain interaction neighborhoods, and diffusion kernel-based neighborhoods. Zhou et al. use shortest-path analysis to identify transitive genes between two given genes from the same biological process [Zho02]. By computing shortest paths, they could not only identify functionally related genes with correlated expression profiles but also detect those without significant expression correlation if they are transitively correlated.

Wang et al. established a unified statistical framework to explore the functional relationships of protein pairs by analyzing the significance of protein pairs sharing similar global partnerships in protein interaction networks [WaY07]. Many techniques that globally bridge protein pairs on the basis of interaction data can be incorporated into this framework, such as shortest-path profiles, domain interaction relationships [ChL06], and similarity measures derived from the diffusion kernel. Furthermore, this framework can deal with weighted interaction data instead of binary data. In other words, the interaction or relationship between two proteins is assessed by a probabilistic score, which enables interaction. Similar to other methods discussed earlier, this statistical framework represents the evidences of protein functional relationships by a functional linkage graph in which an edge between two nodes (proteins) represents the possibility that they share the same function. If two proteins share similar neighbor profiles globally rather than randomly, they have close functional associations. Taking shortest-path profiles as an example, we introduce a technique for describing the global neighborhood profile for each protein in a protein interaction network and then describe the statistical framework for significance analysis.

8.3.4.1 Global Neighborhood Profile   The functional linkage network is an undirected graph, $G = (V, E, W)$ where the node set $V = \{P_1, P_2, \ldots, P_n\}$ consists of all the proteins concerned. The edge set is $E = \{e_{ij}; i, j = 1, 2, \ldots, n\}$, and the weight w_{ij} on the edge e_{ij} denotes the strength of the functional relationship between proteins P_i and P_j. According to Wang et al. [WaY07], to construct such a functional linkage network, each protein is first assigned with a vector representing all its global neighbor relationships with other proteins in a protein interaction network, and then a statistical method is applied to derive the score to assess the strength of the functional relationship between two proteins. Given a protein, it is logical to extract functional information by considering its neighbors, because a protein facilitates its functions by the interconnected macromolecules. A protein interaction network provides a natural neighborhood structure owing to its graph representation. In such a graph, a set of proteins physically interacting with the appointed protein is defined as neighbors. Most of the previous methods for protein function prediction are based on this neighborhood structure [Sam03, ChY04]. Instead of using direct interaction partners, nondirectly interacting neighbors at different levels have also been incorporated to give more clues for functional linkage [Vaz03, Chu06, LeH06]. Such global topology information is expected to effectively represent the functional relationships of the protein with other proteins.

The Floyd–Warshall algorithm is an algorithm for solving the all-pair shortest-path problem on weighted graphs in the time complexity $O(n^3)$, where n is the number of nodes in the network. Wang et al. used the Floyd–Warshall algorithm to identify the shortest paths between a source protein to all other proteins in the protein–protein interaction network [WaY07]. For all, $(P_i, P_i) \in V \times V$, the similarity measure is denoted by d_{ij}, which represents the length of shortest paths between proteins P_i and P_j. By computing the shortest paths of all protein pairs, we can assign a protein with a shortest-path neighborhood profile. For example, protein P_i is represented by a vector of the lengths of its shortest paths to other proteins in the network, which is denoted as $P_i = (d_{i,1}, d_{i,2}, \ldots, d_{i,i-1}, d_{i,i+1}, \ldots, d_{i,n})$.

8.3.4.2 Statistical Significance Analysis   With the first step for creating global neighborhood profiles based on the shortest paths, each protein is assigned a vector in which each element denotes the relationships of the protein to other proteins. For a pair of proteins $(P_i, P_j) \in V \times V$, $i < j$, of their global neighborhood profiles are represented as follows:

$$(p_{i,1}, p_{i,2}, \ldots, p_{i,i-1}, p_{i,i+1}, \ldots, p_{i,j-1}, p_{i,j+1}, \ldots, p_{i,n}, p_{ij})$$
$$(p_{j,1}, p_{j,2}, \ldots, p_{j,i-1}, p_{j,i+1}, \ldots, p_{j,j-1}, p_{j,j+1}, \ldots, p_{j,n}, p_{ji})$$

where p_{ij} can be the length of the shortest path between P_i and P_j, or similarity value computed in other ways. The similarity between two vectors is computed by their inner product as follows:

$$S_{ij} = \sum_{k=1, k \neq i,j}^{n} p_{ik} p_{jk}$$

As stated by the central-limit theorem in probability theory, if $X_1, X_2, \ldots, X_N$ are N independent random variables and each X_i has an arbitrary probability distribution $\Pr(\cdot)$ with mean μ_i and a finite variance σ_i^2, then the random variable

$$X_{\text{norm}} = \frac{\sum_{i=1}^{N} X_i - \sum_{i=1}^{N} \mu_i}{\sqrt{\sum_{i=1}^{N} \sigma_i^2}}$$

has a cumulative function with near-normal distribution, provided that N is sufficiently large. Since protein interaction networks in living organisms are generally large in scale and involve many proteins, score S_{ij} approximately follows a normal distribution. In the paper by Wang et al., a Z score for the assessment of statistical significance of function similarity between two proteins P_i and P_j is defined by $Z_{ij} = (S_{ij} - \mu)/\sigma$, where μ and σ are respectively the average and standard deviation of the normal distribution obtained by the central-limit theorem [WaY07]. A negative Z score indicates that it is less possible for the protein pair to have similar functions than that expected by random chance. A positive Z score indicates that two proteins are more likely to share similar functions than that expected at random. A score near zero indicates that the possibility is at a level near that expected by random.

8.3.4.3 *Numerical Validation*

The statistical framework presented above establishes the functional relationships between proteins from their global neighbor profiles in a protein interaction network. This method is applied to the yeast *S. cerevisiae* protein–protein interaction network [WaY07]. Effectiveness and efficiency are assessed by showing the correlation with GO function similarity and by identifying meaningful functional modules.

The protein interaction data from the paper by Gavin et al. [Gav06] are used, which is the first genomewide screen data for complexes in model organism budding yeast using affinity purification and mass spectrometry. In this study, Gavin et al. explicitly avoided defining protein relationships as binary interactions. They derived a socioaffinity score that quantifies the propensity of proteins to form partnerships. It measures the log–odds ratio of the number of times that two proteins are observed together, relative to what would be expected from their frequency in the dataset. Generally, pairs with socioaffinity indices below 5 should be considered with caution and protein pairs with high socioaffinity indices are more likely to be in direct contact as measured by either 3D structures or the yeast two-hybrid system. Gavin's core dataset has 1507 nodes with 70,647 strength links. A functional linkage network is established by the

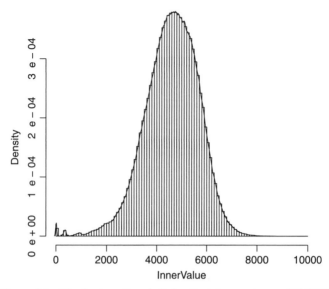

Figure 8.1. Distribution of score S_{ij} for Gavin's core dataset [WaY07].

statistical method described above. If the Z-score threshold is set as 1.65, which means that the p value is 0.05, then there are 40,419 functional links. However, if the Z-score threshold is set 3.08 and the p value is 0.01, 5909 links are left. To show that the central-limit theorem is appropriately used in this work, the distribution of the score S_{ij} of Gavin's core dataset is shown in Figure 8.1, which clearly verifies the assumption of normal distribution of the score S_{ij}.

The Z scores derived from Gavin's protein interaction data correlate well with GO function similarity and can be used as similarity measures to identify meaningful functional modules [WaY07]. Several novel measures can be used to assess the similarity of two gene products on the basis of the GO terms describing them. One of them is a simple and easy method used successfully by Chen and Xu [ChY04]. When quantifying the similarity between two GO terms, it is desired that both their commonality and individual specificities be captured simultaneously. Let G_s and G_t be the hierarchical subgraphs induced from two GO terms T_s and T_t, and let R_s and R_t be the set of GO terms that form the paths of G_s and G_t, respectively. The similarity of two GO terms $s(T_s, T_t)$ is defined as follows [ChY04]:

$$s(T_s, T_t) \equiv \max_{R_s \in G_s, R_t \in G_t} |R_s \cap R_t|$$

This score means that the more terms shared by T_s and T_t, the more similar are the two GO terms that describe proteins. Since a protein may be involved in more than one biological process, it may be assigned multiple GO terms. Let $T(P_i)$ denote the set of all the GO terms assigned to a protein P_i. Thus the functional similarity between two proteins P_i and P_j is defined as the maximum similarity of all possible combinations of $T(P_i)$ and $T(P_j)$:

$$S_{GO}(P_i, P_j) \equiv \max_{T_s \in T(P_i), T_t \in T(P_j)} s(T_s, T_t)$$

To make the measurement of protein function similarity biologically meaningful, the functional annotation of the biological process for the known proteins is assigned a GO Identification (ID). A numerical GO INDEX represents the hierarchical structure of the functional classification [ChY04]. Detailed GO INDEX levels correspond to specific functions for a protein. The maximum level of GO INDEX is 14. In general, the function similarity between proteins P_x and P_y is defined by the maximum number of index levels from the top shared by P_x and P_y. The smaller is the value of function similarity, the less specific is the functional category shared by the two proteins.

In Figure 8.2, the correlation relationships between Z score and GO similarity are shown. To highlight the advantage of using global neighborhood structure instead of local interaction information in the protein interaction network, the correlation between the socioaffinity score and GO similarity is also shown and compared with that of the Z score. We can see that Z score correlates better with the functional similarity score in general. In particular, when Z score ranges from -0.5 to 4.32, the GO similarity score increases from 8 to 14 linearly. On the other hand, the socioaffinity score does not correlate well when it is higher than 5, which demonstrates the effect of false positives in high-throughput protein interaction data. The detailed Pearson correlation coefficient of the socioaffinity score with GO similarity is 0.54 (1408 random samples), whereas the Pearson correlation coefficient between the Z score and GO similarity is improved to 0.67 (1000 random samples).

If the Z score accurately reflects the functional similarity of two proteins, it can be used as a vertex similarity criterion to detect functional modules from the functional linkage network. Wang et al. used Newman's modularity optimization approach [New06] to decompose the constructed network into modules and reveal the modularity patterns of the functional linkage network [WaY07]. As a result, eight modules—whose cellular components, with their dense interrelationships, are attributed to a specific biological function—are identified using the Z score as a vertex similarity measure. One module contains 18 proteins and 69 functional links is shown in Figure 8.3. All the proteins in this module are annotated by the protein biosynthesis function. The biological functional modules can be used to predict or annotate the functions of unknown proteins, usually by simple methods. For example, every function shared by the majority of the module's genes is assigned to all the genes in the module. Alternatively, a hypergeometric enrichment p value is computed for every function. The functions enriched within the module are then predicted for all the genes in the module. For example, the protein YDL115C is predicted to have the transcription function because it belongs to a 25-protein functional module and other group members within this module all have the transcription function. In the same manner, proteins YPL181W and YMR075W are annotated by the DNA repair function.

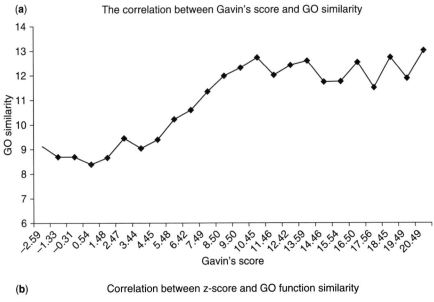

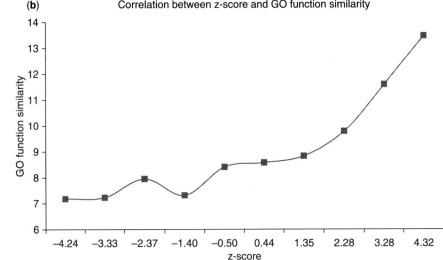

Figure 8.2. Correlation analysis of Z score with GO similarity: (a) correlation of Gavin's socioaffinity score with GO similarity; (b) correlation of Z score with GO similarity [WaY07].

We can see that protein functional linkage networks provide a good basis for functional annotation. The availability of functional linkage networks instead of raw interaction networks will drive the development of computational methods to elucidate protein functions in a more accurate way. Usually protein functional linkage map is denser than raw protein interaction networks. This is quite reasonable. Except for the direct physical protein interaction, functional links can be formed by genetic

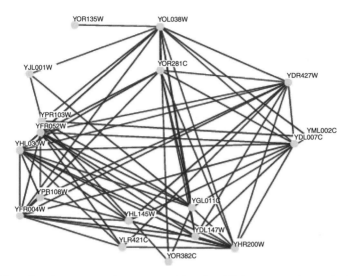

Figure 8.3. A functional module in constructed functional linkage network revealed by statistical framework [WaY07].

interaction or comembership in the same protein complex. Furthermore, there is a transitive phenomenon in functional linkage networks. This implies situations in which two proteins do not interact, but carry out similar functions in the biological process. In the simplest case, proteins P_a and P_b strongly interact in the same way as proteins P_b and P_c do. However, proteins P_a and P_c may not have strong interactions. For such a case, we say that proteins P_a and P_c transitively interact and the protein P_b serves as a transitive protein. Such transitivity makes protein functional linkages more information-abundant than direct interactions. In addition, a functional linkage network can integrate other biological experimental data besides protein interaction data, such as sequence or structure similarity data, ChIP-chip data, microarray gene expression data, and protein subcellar localization data, which will provide more accurate functional relationships between proteins.

8.4 PROTEIN FUNCTION PREDICTION FROM HIGH-THROUGHPUT DATA

After introducing the "functional module detection" and the "functional linkage establishment" concepts in this section, we will describe some methods that can be applied directly for function prediction. As mentioned earlier, different types of methods based on sequences, structures, phylogenic profiles, gene expression data, protein complexes, and other properties have been developed for this problem. Again, we will focus on those approaches employing protein interaction data. This class of methods is based on the topological structure of protein interaction networks, or on integration of multiple data sources. Protein interaction data are directly related to

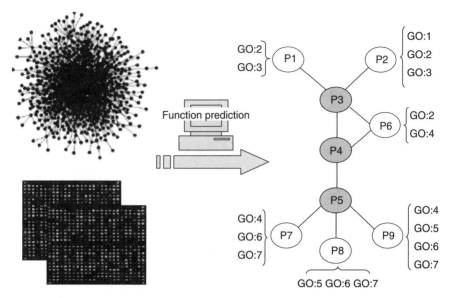

Figure 8.4. Illustration of protein function prediction based on protein interaction data and other data sources.

network structures, thereby not only enlarging the information bases but also enabling the application of new techniques of systems biology to function prediction. Now, systematic protein function classification databases with a specifically designed complex scheme have been constructed, such as FunCat and GO, which provide detailed annotations for a growing number of proteins within a hierarchical organization. Naturally, how to exploit the global structure of protein interaction networks and comprehensive function information for predicting unannotated proteins becomes an attracting topic. Figure 8.4 illustrates an example of function prediction from protein interaction data and other data sources, where five proteins (white nodes) have known function annotations and the other three (gray nodes) are unknown proteins.

8.4.1 Neighborhood Approaches

Given the natural neighborhood relationships for proteins provided by protein interaction networks, a simple direct method for function prediction is to annotate a protein according to the functions of its immediate neighborhood. In an early paper adopting this method [Schw00], a protein interaction network was assembled from a variety of sources, and then the functions of a protein were assigned as the three most frequent functions among its neighbors. Despite the simplicity of the prediction method, an accuracy of 72% was achieved. However, this method only exploited the local connection information and did not use the global topology of the network in the annotation process. Furthermore, it lacked significance evaluation for any function assignment. Nevertheless, it did confirm the effectiveness of protein interaction networks for function prediction.

Hishigaki et al. developed a strategy to improve the statistical significance of the abovementioned function prediction by using χ^2-like scores [HiS01]. Instead of using the immediate neighbors, the n neighborhood of a protein that consists of proteins with distances of n links to the protein is considered. In addition, the frequencies of all the functions in this neighborhood are recorded. For a protein P_i, each function f is assigned a score

$$S_i(f) = \frac{[n_i(f) - e_i(f)]^2}{e_i(f)}$$

where $n_i(f)$ is the number of proteins in the n neighborhood of P_i that have the function f, and $e_i(f)$ is the expected number of the proteins with the function f in this neighborhood on the basis of the frequency of f among all proteins in the network. According to the defined score, for a fixed k, an unannotated protein with k functions having the top k χ^2 statistics can be assigned. The two methods described above treat all n neighbors equally in their analysis, although proteins with different distances from P_i may have different contributions to the function assignment of P_i.

In contrast to these methods based on experimental protein interaction data, McDermott et al. proposed the use of predicted protein interaction networks for function prediction using neighborhood-based approaches [McD05]. They defined neighborhood weights by a majority-rule method and annotated a protein according to the functional annotation quality score from each of its neighbors. In this way, they made functional predictions for over 50 organisms. Chua et al. made a statistical study on interaction data to find the relation between network distance and functional similarity [Chu06]. They found that a substantial number of proteins are observed to share functions with level 2 neighbors but not with level 1 neighbors. A functional similarity score, called the FS-weight measure, has been designed, and the score gives different weights to proteins according to their distances from the target protein [Chu06]. This method employs the indirect functional association, which has shown relative superiority over other methods.

8.4.2 Optimization Methods

Neighborhood approaches are attractive and effective for those proteins with enough neighbors. However, if a protein has an insufficient number of neighbors in the network, or its neighbors are not sufficiently annotated, such methods are questionable in terms of reliability and accuracy. This problem is especially obvious in a sparse protein interaction network such as fly interactome and worm interactome. To address these issues, the global connection pattern or long-range indirect functional association should be taken into account in function annotation. In fact, several approaches that employ the full topology of the network have been proposed. Usually these approaches optimize an objective function representing some global topology property that the network should possess on the basis of function assignment.

The first optimization approach employing global topology for function prediction was developed by [Vaz03], who adopted a graph cut idea and performed function assignment to minimize the number of connections among different functional categories. Specifically, they minimize the following objective function

$$E = -\sum_{i=1}^{N} \sum_{j=1}^{N} A_{ij}\delta(\sigma_i, \sigma_j) - \sum_{i=1}^{N} h_i(\sigma_i)$$

where N is the number of unannotated proteins in the network, and A is the adjacency matrix on unannotated proteins. $\delta(x, y)$ is the discrete δ function that equals 1 if $x = y$ and 0 otherwise. σ_i is a functional variable whose value is assigned to the unannotated protein P_i. $h_i(\sigma_i)$ denotes the number of neighbors of P_i previously annotated with function σ_i. The major difference of this approach lies in the assumption that interaction leads to similar function and is also applied to unannotated proteins, which is achieved by the first term in E. The second term is the same to the well-known majority rule [Ito01, Uet00]. It also makes use of interactions between unannotated and previously annotated proteins. In view of the exponential number of function assignments, the optimization problem is heuristically solved by a simulated annealing algorithm. As expected, this approach was shown to outperform the majority-rule strategy in the study by Schwikowski et al. [Sch00].

This approach and the one in the paper by Karaoz et al. [Kar04] are referred to as GenMultiCut [Nab05]. These approaches exploit the global topological structure of protein interaction networks and annotate proteins to minimize the cost of edges connecting proteins with different function assignments. In the study [Nab05], they uniformly formulated the function annotation problem as a generalization of the minimum multiway k-cut problem (GenMultiCut) in computer science and proposed an integer linear programming (ILP) model to solve the problem in practice by CPLEX. Let $x_{i,f}$ be a binary variable that indicates whether the protein P_i has function f. If protein u has been functionally annotated, then $x_{i,f}$ is fixed as 1 or 0, depending on its known annotations. $x_{i,j,f}$ is also a binary variable that indicates whether the adjacent proteins P_i and P_j are annotated with function f. According to the goal of minimizing the weighted number of neighboring proteins with different annotations, the function annotation problem can be formulated as the following ILP

$$\max_{x_{i,f}, x_{i,j,f}} \sum_{(P_i,P_j)\in E} x_{i,j,f} w_{i,j} \tag{8.4}$$

$$\text{s.t.} \quad \sum_f x_{i,f} = 1 \qquad \text{if } \text{annot}(i) = \varnothing \tag{8.5}$$

$$x_{i,f} = 1 \qquad \text{if } f \in \text{annot}(i) \tag{8.6}$$

$$x_{i,f} = 0 \qquad \text{if } f \notin \text{annot}(i), \text{annot}(i) \neq \varnothing \tag{8.7}$$

$$x_{i,j,f} \leq x_{i,f} \qquad \text{if } (P_i, P_j) \in E \tag{8.8}$$

$$x_{i,j,f} \leq x_{j,f} \qquad \text{if } (P_i, P_j) \in E \tag{8.9}$$

$$x_{i,f}, x_{i,j,f} \in \{0, 1\} \qquad \text{if all } P_i, P_j, f \tag{8.10}$$

where $\text{annot}(i)$ is the set of known annotations for protein P_i, $\text{FUNC} = \cup_i \text{annot}(i)$ is the set of all functional annotations, and $f \in \text{FUNC}$. E is the set of all protein interactions of interest. The first constraint of the model indicates that exactly one function should be assigned to any unannotated protein to ensure that every protein in the network has a function. The second and third constraints are set for previously annotated proteins. The third and fourth constraints indicate that a particular function is selected for an edge only if it is also chosen for the corresponding proteins.

Besides the ILP model for GenMultiCut, Nabieva et al. introduced a network-flow-based algorithm that simulates functional flow between proteins [Nab05]. The functional flow algorithm is modified from the traditional max-flow min-cut algorithm for directed graphs, and simulates the spread of functional flow by an iterative procedure using discrete timesteps. Each protein is associated with a "reservoir" that represents the amount of functional flow that the node can pass on to its neighbors at the next iteration. Capacities of the edges are interaction reliabilities of protein interactions estimated by experimental or computational techniques. Each protein with function annotations acts as the source of a functional flow. After a certain number of iterations based on several simple update rules, each unannotated protein receives a certain amount of functional flow from both local and global connections.

More recently, a modified and faster global optimization (MFGO) method [SuS06] was designed to avoid the high-intensity computation of the repeated process of Monte Carlo simulated annealing (MCSA) [Vaz03]. Let n denote the number of proteins in a dataset, and m denote the number of protein functions. In MFGO, the protein P_i is assigned with a functional vector $w_i = (w_{i1}, w_{i2}, \ldots, w_{im})$ satisfying $\sum_{s=1}^{m} w_{is}^2 = 1$, where $w_{is}, 0 \leq w_{is} \leq 1$, measures the tendency for protein i to possess the sth function. For each protein P_i, let Nei(i) be the set of all proteins adjacent to protein P_i. The goal of MFGO is to maximize the following objective function

$$E = \sum_{i=1}^{n} \sum_{j=1}^{n} \sum_{s=1}^{m} \rho_{ij} w_{is} w_{js} + \sum_{i=1}^{n} \sum_{j=1}^{n} \sum_{s=1}^{m} \lambda_{ij} w_{is} w_{js}$$

where for each adjacent protein pair (P_i, P_j), $\rho_{ij} = 1$, $\lambda_{ij} = 0$, and for each non-adjacent pair (P_i, P_j), $\rho_{ij} = 0$ and

$$\lambda_{ij} = \frac{\left| \text{Nei}(i) \cap \text{Nei}(j) \right|}{\left| \text{Nei}(i) \cup \text{Nei}(j) \right|}$$

The first term of this objective function is similar to that in the paper by Vazquez et al. [Vaz03], while the second term accounts for those proteins without direct interactions but sharing the same interaction partners. Hence, MFGO takes into account indirect interactions of proteins. An iterative local optimization algorithm is adopted to optimize the abovementioned objective function [SuS06]. However, the iterative local optimization algorithm for MFGO can give only a local optimal solution because of the NP-hard nature of the problem. The authors also stated that MFGO can be used to predict multiple functions. However, this is in fact a very difficult problem because there is no knowledge or technique to determine an appropriate threshold on w_{is}. As expected, experiments on four datasets show that MFGO saves much computational time but with the accuracy remaining nearly at the same level as that of other methods.

8.4.3 Probabilistic Methods

Like the successful applications of optimization techniques, a number of probabilistic methods for the function annotation problem have been developed. One of them is the Markov random-field (MRF) approach, which provides a probabilistic framework for simulating the mutual influence of random variables via a neighborhood system. It borrows the Markovian assumption that the state of any variable is independent of the states of all other random variables given those of its immediate neighbors. Deng et al. used an MRF approach to infer the function of unannotated proteins [Den03b]. For a function of interest, X_i is a random variable with 1 to denote the ith protein having the function, and 0 otherwise. Let $X = (X_1, X_2, \ldots, X_{n+m})$ be a configuration of the functional labeling of the proteins, where $X_1 = \lambda_1, \ldots, X_n = \lambda_n$ are unknown and $X_{n+1} = \lambda_{n+1}, \ldots, X_{n+m} = \lambda_{n+m}$ are annotated. The protein interaction dataset is denoted by E. It has been shown that a pair of interacting proteins tend to have the same function. Hence, the probability of the network conditional on the functional labeling modeled as a MRF is

$$\frac{1}{Z}\exp\{\beta N_{10} + \gamma N_{11} + \delta N_{00})$$

where Z is a normalizing constant and $N_{ll'}$ is the number of protein pairs in the dataset with one protein labeled l and the other labeled l', $l, l' \in \{0, 1\}$. Therefore, the total probability of the functional labeling is

$$\Pr(X|\theta) = \frac{1}{Z(\theta)}\exp\{-U(x)\} \tag{8.11}$$

$$= \frac{1}{Z(\theta)}\exp\{-\alpha N_1 - \beta N_{10} - \gamma N_{11} - \delta N_{00}) \tag{8.12}$$

where N_1 is the number of proteins having the function of interest; $\alpha, \beta, \gamma, \delta$ are parameters for weighting the contributions of the different terms; and $\theta = (\alpha, \beta, \gamma, \delta)$. Then, we can obtain

$$\log\frac{\Pr(X_i = 1|X_{[-i]}, \theta)}{1 - \Pr(X_i = 1|X_{[-i]}, \theta)} = \alpha + (\beta - \delta)N_0(i) + (\gamma - \beta)N_1(i) \tag{8.13}$$

where $X_{[-i]} = (X_1, X_2, \ldots, X_{i-1}, X_{i+1}, \ldots, X_{n+m})$ and $N_l(i)$ denotes the number of interaction partners labeled with l for protein P_i. A quasilikelihood estimation method based on the standard linear logistic model and the functions of the annotated proteins is used to estimate the parameters θ [Den03b], and then the Gibbs sampling strategy is adopted on the conditional probability $\Pr[\Pr(X_i = 1|X_{[-i]}, \theta)]$ to infer the functional annotations with probabilities for unknown proteins.

Letovsky and Kasif also used an MRF model [Let03]. Their main assumption is that the number of neighbors of a protein that are annotated with a given term is binomially distributed, where the distribution's parameter depends on whether the protein has that function. They employed loopy belief propagation to perform inference in their model. Instead of using only immediate neighbors, Lee et al. introduced a diffusion kernel technique into the MRF approach [Lee06b]. The diffusion kernel K that calculates the similarity distance between any two nodes in the network is defined as follows

$$K = e^{\tau L} = \lim_{n \to \infty} \left(1 + \frac{\tau L}{n}\right)^n$$

where L is the Laplacian matrix of the protein interaction network with entries defined as

$$L(i, j) = \begin{cases} 1 & \text{if } (P_i, P_j) \in E \\ -d_i & \text{if } i = j \\ 0 & \text{otherwise} \end{cases}$$

where d_i is the number of interaction partners for protein P_i, τ is a diffusion constant, and e^L represents the matrix exponential of L. It is clear that $K(i, j)$ decreases as the shortest distance between protein P_i and protein P_j increases. Therefore, $K(i, j)$ can be regarded as a similarity measure not only for pairs of interacting proteins but also for protein pairs separated through several interactions. Similar to the idea of the MRF approach [Den03b], Lee et al. modeled the total probability of the functional labeling $X = (X_1, X_2, \ldots, X_{n+m})$ in an MRF procedure [Lee06b]

$$Pr(X|\theta) = \frac{1}{Z(\theta)} \exp\{-U(x)\} \qquad (8.14)$$

$$= \frac{1}{Z(\theta)} \exp(-\alpha N_1 - \beta D_{10} - \gamma D_{11} - \delta D_{00}) \qquad (8.15)$$

where all the notations have the same implications except that

$$D_{11} = \sum_{i<j} K(i, j) I\{x_i = 1, x_j = 1\}$$

$$D_{10} = \sum_{i<j} K(i, j) I\{(x_i = 1, x_j = 0) \text{ or } (x_i = 0, x_j = 1)\}$$

$$D_{00} = \sum_{i<j} K(i, j) I\{x_i = 0, x_j = 0\}$$

where x_i is the observed value of the random variable X_i. Obviously, D_{11}, D_{10}, D_{00} are respectively the extensions of N_{11}, N_{10}, N_{00}. The logistic linear regression model (8.13) is extended as

$$\log \frac{\Pr(X_i = 1 | X_{[-i]}, \theta)}{1 - \Pr(X_i = 1 | X_{[-i]}, \theta)} = \alpha + (\beta - \delta)K_0(i) + (\gamma - \beta)K_1(i)$$

where $K_0(i) = \Sigma_{i \neq j} K(i,j) I\{x_j = 0\}$ and $K_1(i) = \Sigma_{i \neq j} K(i,j) I\{x_j = 1\}$. Again, $K_0(i)$ and $K_1(i)$ are respectively the extensions of $N_0(i)$ and $N_i(i)$. When $K(i,j)$ is directly the adjacency matrix of the protein interaction network, the model is same as the MRF model of Deng et al. [Den03b]. Since K measures the similarity between each pair of proteins regardless of whether they have a direct physical interaction, we can see that Lee et al.'s approach exploits not only the information of immediate neighbors but also that of long-range neighbors [Lee06b]. This is the core reason why the extended MRF has a higher prediction accuracy.

8.4.4 Machine Learning Techniques

Protein function annotation is closely related to classification problems. Therefore, machine learning techniques have wide applications in this field. In particular, support vector machines (SVMs) have been used for predicting gene functions and showed promising results [Lan04, BaZ06]. For example, Lanckriet et al. introduced an integrated SVM classifier to integrate multiple sources of biological experimental data for function prediction [Lan04], in which a kernel method is used for data fusion and protein interaction data are used to derive one of the kernels.

Despite the good performance of the machine learning techniques, there are some limitations lying in existing methods if protein function prediction is formulated as a classification problem. Generally, to construct a classifier for function prediction, one needs a number of training samples with known category membership. In this case, positive samples are those proteins with known function annotations, which are relatively easy to obtain. However, it is difficult to find representative negative samples since function annotation databases, such as GO and MIPS, provide only positive samples. In other words, we know which proteins belong to which functional class but we have no knowledge about which proteins do not belong to a particular class. Furthermore, many proteins have multiple functions; thus it is inappropriate to use all the other proteins outside the target function class as negative samples. The sample imbalance problem will arise if all the proteins outside the target function family are seen as negative samples, given the fact that usually only a small number of genes or proteins are annotated with the function, while the number of negative samples may be hundreds or even thousands times that of positive samples. To address these issues underlying machine learning techniques for function annotation, Zhao et al. proposed an effective technique function prediction [ZhaX08a]. In this approach, a functional linkage network is first constructed to integrate heterogeneous information sources such as protein interaction data, gene expression data, and protein complex data, and then the singular value decomposition (SVD) technique is employed to reduce data dimensionality and remove noise from the data. Finally, the "annotating genes with positive samples" (AGPS) algorithm is presented to define negative samples and predict functions of unknown genes.

Zhao et al. [ZhaX08a] denoted genes annotated with the target function as labeled data; and those annotated with other functions, as unlabeled data [ZhX08a]. The unlabeled data imply that the genes without the target annotation may possess the function even though they are currently not annotated with that function. The conventional one-class learning algorithms are usually trained only on positive samples, and the conventional binary classifiers need both definite positive and negative samples [ZhX08a]. The AGPS algorithm aims to define representative negative samples from unlabeled data automatically in the learning procedure. With the negative samples available, it is straightforward to predict the functions of unknown genes by utilizing both the positive samples and the defined negative samples, which is achieved by SVM as a core learning algorithm. Experimental results indicate that the AGPS algorithm can predict the functions of unknown genes effectively [ZhX08a]. Next we will introduce the process of AGPS for function annotation.

8.4.4.1 *Integration of Heterogeneous Data*   Zhao et al. [ZhaX08a] obtained the functional annotation data of *S. cerevisiae* genes from FunCat 2.0 [Rue04]. The annotation data in FunCat are organized as a hierarchical and tree-like structure with up to six levels of increasing specificity. In total, FunCat includes 1307 functional categories. A protein annotated by one function in the functional tree is also annotated by all the parents of the functional node. Then 13 general functional classes are selected, and consequently 4049 genes have been annotated in total. Table 8.2 shows some selected functional classes and the numbers of annotated genes that they contain.

TABLE 8.2. Selected Functional Categories and Numbers of Annotated Genes

Functional Categories	Number of Annotated Genes
01 Metabolism	967
02 Energy	241
10 Cell cycle and DNA processing	727
11 Transcription	829
12 Protein synthesis	364
14 Protein fate	680
20 Cellular transport	726
30 Cellular communication	86
32 Cell rescue, defense, and virulence	307
34 Interaction with the environment	332
40 Cell fate	201
42 Biogenesis of cellular components	471
43 Cell type differentiation	354

Source: Zhao et al. [ZhaX08a].

The protein interaction data are obtained from the 2.0.20 version of BioGRID database, which contains 82,633 interactions among 5299 yeast genes. Among them, 4049 genes are annotated by the 13 functional classes. The gene expression dataset is downloaded from the Stanford Gene expression Database (SGD). The missing values in the gene expression profiles are estimated by the KNNimpute algorithm with k set to 15. The dataset contains 6012 common genes, including 5132 genes among the 5299 genes in the protein interaction dataset. Consequently, the final dataset contains 5132 genes with 278 real-value features for gene expression data. The protein complex data are from the MIPS database. Although the direct interaction relationships among some genes in complexes are not observed, the genes occurring in the same complex are generally considered to have functional correlations. Hence, functional relationships are assigned to genes occurring in the same complex, where an edge is constructed for a pair of genes occurring in the same complex [ZhaX08a]. Finally, 62,042 functional edges are obtained.

To construct functional linkage networks by integrating multiple sources of heterogeneous data, the functional similarity between a pair of genes should be defined first. Zhao et al. [ZhaX08a] employed the Czekanowski–Dice (CD) distance between genes P_i and P_j in a network

$$D(i, j) = \frac{|\text{Nei}(i)\Delta\text{Nei}(j)|}{|\text{Nei}(i) \cup \text{Nei}(j)| + |\text{Nei}(i) \cap \text{Nei}(j)|} \tag{8.16}$$

where Nei_i denotes a set containing gene P_i and its neighbors in the network [ZhX08a]. $\text{Nei}(i) \cup \text{Nei}(j)$ denotes the union of $\text{Nei}(i)$ and $\text{Nei}(j)$, $\text{Nei}(i) \cap \text{Nei}(j)$ indicates the intersection of $\text{Nei}(i)$ and $\text{Nei}(j)$, and $\text{Nei}(i)\Delta\text{Nei}(j)$ denotes the symmetric difference between two datasets $\text{Nei}(i)$ and $\text{Nei}(j)$. The relationship between any pair of genes in the protein interaction and complex datasets is expressed as a binary variable to denote whether two genes interact or occur in the same complex, which can be further represented by a network. Therefore, it is straightforward to apply the CD distance. After that, the functional similarity between any pair of genes is represented as a real value between 0 and 1. The smaller the value, the more likely that the pair of genes have the similar function. The functional linkage networks obtained from protein interaction data and protein complex data are respectively denoted as G_1 and G_3. For gene expression data, the Pearson correlation coefficients are first calculated for each pair of genes, and a binary network is then constructed by setting a threshold on correlation coefficients (say, 0.7). Subsequently, the CD distance is applied to the binary network and the functional linkage network obtained is denoted as G_2. Finally, the three functional linkage networks are merged into one integrated functional network in the way as $G = \alpha G_1 + \beta G_2 + \gamma G_3$, where G is an $n \times n$ matrix and n is the number of genes. A simple rule $\alpha : \beta : \gamma = 1 : 1 : 1$ was employed in the numerical experiments. The idea behind the simple rule is that all three data sources contain functional relationships among genes, and integrating them into one functional network can complement each of them.

8.4.4.2 *Dimensionality Reduction*   The singular value decomposition (SVD) technique is employed to uncover the dominant structure of the functional linkage graph and extract informative features described by Zhao et al. [ZhaX08a]. In SVD, given a matrix A of size $m \times n$, A can be decomposed into three matrices

$$A = S\Sigma V^T \tag{8.17}$$

where S is the left singular matrix of size $m \times k$, V is the right singular matrix of size $n \times k$, and Σ is the diagonal matrix of size $k \times k$ with nonnegative eigenvalues $\lambda_1 > \lambda_2 > \cdots > \lambda_k > 0$. After applying SVD to the matrix G, one can express G as follows:

$$G = \sum_{t=1}^{k} \lambda_t s_t v_t^T \tag{8.18}$$

where s_t and v_t respectively represent the tth column of S and V, corresponding to the tth eigenvalue. It can be seen from equation (8.18) that the larger the eigenvalue, the more it contributes to matrix G. Hence, to reduce the dimensionality, one can simply discard the smaller values in the diagonal matrix Σ and keep the top r eigenvalues ($r \leq k$). Accordingly, using the first r columns of S and V, the sizes of the three matrices S, Σ, and V are reduced to $m \times r$, $r \times r$, and $m \times r$, respectively. Therefore, the number of features is reduced to r. Note that $S\Sigma$ gives coordinates of rows of G in the space of r principal components, and rows of V^T are eigenvectors of $G^T G$. Given a new gene vector $G_i = (G_{i1}, \ldots, G_{im})$, G_i can be projected into the R-dimensional subspace as $G_i' = G_i V$, where G_i' is a new vector with dimensionality $r(r \ll m)$.

8.4.4.3 *Annotating Genes with Positive Samples*   As described in previous sections, negative samples are seldom found in practice for gene function prediction because function annotation databases provide only positive samples. The one-class SVM can avoid the imbalance problem by learning from only the positive set, where it draws a decision boundary to cover most positive samples in the feature space. However, a small number of genes are usually annotated in each class. Therefore, without a negative set, one-class SVM tends to overfit easily. The AGPS algorithm can overcome these problems [ZhaX08a].

Genes with target annotation are denoted as the positive set P, genes without target annotation are denoted as the unlabeled data Ku, and genes without any annotation are denoted as Ug. For a specific biological function, genes without target annotation are regarded as unlabeled data instead of negative samples. The goal of AGPS is to predict the functions of unknown genes on the basis of P and Ku. Its goal is to find a subset of negative samples from unlabeled data that can best recover the positive samples hidden in the unlabeled data. The extracted negative set may be a small part of the true negative set, but it should represent the whole negative set well and alleviate the sample imbalance problem. To achieve this goal, the positive set is divided into positive training set $P1$ and validation set $P2$, where $P2$ is put into Ku to form a new unlabeled data U (i.e., $U = P2 + Ku$). The set of representative negative samples is denoted by RN, which belongs to U and can help us obtain best prediction results on validation set $P2$:

```
Annotating Genes with Positive Samples (AGPS)
Input: P1, P2, Ku, and Ug
Output:
Prediction results Stage 1: Learning
        U = Ku ∪ P2
    Stage 1.1: Initial negative set generation
    Construct classifier f₁ based on P1 and U with one-class SVM
            Classify U using f₁. Obtain a predicted negative set N₁, and let
            U = U \ N₁
    Stage 1.2: Negative set expansion
            Classifier set FC, negative set NS, i = 1
            repeat
                    i = i + 1
                    Construct classifier fᵢ based on P1 and N₁ with two-class SVM
                    FC(i - 1) = fᵢ, NS(i - 1) = N1
                    Classify U by fᵢ, N₂ is the predicted negative set, |N₂| ≤ k|P1|
                    N₁ = [ N₂; Nₛᵥ] , Nₛᵥ is the set of negative SVs of fᵢ
                    U = U - N2
            until |U| < k|P1|
    Stage 1.3: Classifier and negative set selection
            Classify U by classifiers from FC
            Select FC(i) that has the best accuracy
            Return negative set RN ← NS(i)
    Stage 2: classification
    Classify Ug with P and RN, where P = P1+P2
```

The AGPS algorithm consists of two stages: (1) learning and (2) classification. A flowchart of the AGPS algorithm is printed out above. In the first stage, one-class SVM is utilized to draw an initial decision boundary to cover most of the whole dataset, including positive and unlabeled data. The data points not covered by the generated decision boundary are regarded as negative data points because they are far from the positive set in the feature space. With the generated initial negative dataset, the two-class SVM is then employed to expand and refine the negative set from unlabeled data, where each classifier is trained on the positive training set and the negative set generated in the previous iteration, and the trained classifier is subsequently used to classify the remaining unlabeled data. The classifier and negative set generated in each step are recorded. This procedure continues until the stop criterion is satisfied. It can be seen that the error in the previous step would affect the current step. To reduce the cumulative error and alleviate the imbalance problem, the size of the extracted negative samples in the current step is set to $|N_{\text{cur}}| \leq k|P|$, where N_{cur} is the predicted negative genes corresponding to the top $n(n \leq k|P|)$ smallest decision values by SVM and k is set to 3 so that the false negatives can be reduced to some extent. The negative training set is then set to $N = [N_{cur}; N_{sv}]$, where N_{sv} denotes the set of negative support vectors (SVs) and N_{cur} is N_2. The idea behind this is that the negative SVs represent well the previous negative training set, and it is not necessary to merge the previous negative set into the current extracted negative set. Thus, the size of the negative set is controlled. After obtaining the negative set and the trained classifiers, one needs to find the best classifier that can recover the largest number of positive samples underlying the unlabeled data because the classifiers trained above have different discriminative powers on the left unlabeled data. The discrimination ability of the trained classifiers is evaluated with $F1$ as defined in the next subsection. Accordingly, the negative set corresponding to the best classifier is returned as representative negative samples, and the selection of negative samples in this way can help reduce the false negatives to some extent. With the positive and negative samples available, it is straightforward to predict the function of unknown genes in the same way as the conventional two-class SVM does.

8.4.4.4 *Numerical Validation*
Precision measure, recall measure, and F measures are used to evaluate the performance of the classifiers, which are respectively defined as

$$\text{Precision} = \frac{\text{TP}}{\text{TP} + \text{FP}} \times 100\% \tag{8.19}$$

$$\text{Recall} = \frac{\text{TP}}{\text{RP}} \times 100\% \tag{8.20}$$

$$F_1 = \frac{2 \cdot \text{precision} \cdot \text{recall}}{\text{precision} + \text{recall}} \times 100\% \tag{8.21}$$

where TP is the number of genes with function f that are predicted correctly, FP is the number of genes incorrectly predicted to have function f, and RP is the total number of genes that have function f. For each target function f, AGPS defines the negative samples and then predicts the potential genes that may be annotated with f from the unknown genes. Gene function prediction is formalized as a multi-class classification problem, which is then reduced to a set of binary classification problems solved by SVM.

The training set consists of genes annotated in the MIPS annotation of March 2004, where 3663 genes were annotated by the selected 13 functional classes (Table 8.2). AGPS is compared against four other methods, including conventional two-class SVM method, one-class SVM method, PSoL method [WaC06], and kernel integration method, which is a simplified version of the one described by Lanckriet et al. [Lan04]. Tenfold cross-validation was adopted to determine the number of components that should be retained in SVD dimensionality reduction. For fair comparison, dimensionality reduction is performed for all the methods except kernel integration to find the informative components. No dimensionality

TABLE 8.3. Results of Tenfold Cross-Validation Using Five Methods Averaged over 13 Classes

Methods	Precision (%)	Recall (%)	F_1 (%)
AGPS	68	61	61
PSoL	68	37	47
Two-class SVMs	45	24	33
Two-class SVMs_balanced	61	70	69
One-class SVMs	50	21	31
Kernel integration	58	28	37
Kernel integration_balanced	64	47	52

Source: Zhao et al. [ZhaX08a].

reduction is performed for the kernel integration method because of its specific data structure. All the methods adopted the radial basis function (RBF) kernel. For each of the four methods, tenfold cross-validation is employed to find the optimal parameters for kernel function.

The results of tenfold cross-validation by the five methods are shown in Table 8.3, where two-class SVMs_balanced means the results by two-class SVMs trained on balanced data and the same for kernel integration. It can be seen that the AGPS algorithm performs well compared with other methods. Furthermore, all the methods utilizing the negative samples outperform the one-class SVM that was trained only on positive samples. The poor performance of the one-class SVM is due to the relatively few positive training samples. For the two-class SVM and kernel integration, it can be clearly seen that with balanced data, performance levels of both classifiers are considerably improved. On the other hand, we can learn that the imbalanced data can indeed degrade the performance of the classifiers. Furthermore, the results on imbalanced and balanced data demonstrate the importance of selecting negative samples in gene function prediction. Compared with PSoL, the AGPS algorithm achieves a higher recall; it can recognize more positive samples hidden in the unknown data because it defines better representative negative samples in the learning procedure.

In total, 386 previous unknown yeast genes have been annotated by the selected 13 functional classes (in 2006) since March 2004. To validate AGPS and other methods, these 386 genes are collectively regarded as a test set. For the test data, the AGPS algorithm works as a conventional two-class SVMs here with parameters and negative set defined above. For PSoL, the unlabeled data are defined to include unknown genes and those genes outside the target functional class. Note that the test data were included in unknown genes in PSoL. With the best parameters determined in the training procedure and all positive samples, PSoL is applied to identify putative positive samples from unknown genes. For other three methods, the classifiers trained above are utilized only to predict the functions of unknown genes. Specifically, the two-class SVMs and kernel integration trained on imbalanced and balanced data are separately applied to predict gene functions. Furthermore, the ROC score (i.e., the area under the ROC curve) is utilized to evaluate the overall performance of the classifiers. The results are shown in Table 8.4, where the figures in parentheses are

TABLE 8.4. Prediction Results Using Five Methods Averaged over 13 Classes

Methods	Precision (%)	Recall (%)	F_1 (%)	ROC Score	Coverage
AGPS	15	66	22	0.61	13 (13)
PSoL	20	18	19	0.55	12 (13)
Two-class SVMs	28	10	16	0.53	11 (13)
Two-class SVMs_balanced	18	36	29	0.57	10 (13)
One-class SVMs	10	42	15	0.53	13 (13)
Kernel integration	39	16	23	0.56	11 (13)
Kernel integration_balanced	11	32	24	0.59	6 (13)

Source: Zhao et al. [ZhaX08a].

the true number of functional classes, whereas the other figures in this column represent classes that can be predicted by the corresponding method.

It can be seen from Table 8.4 that the AGPS algorithm outperforms all the other methods with respect to ROC scores. The poor performance of one-class SVMs is caused by the relatively small number of positive training samples, resulting in underfitting. The PSoL algorithm performs well because it defines the negative samples like the AGPS algorithm. However, the selected negative samples and the predicted positive samples by PSoL may not be true. On the other hand, the AGPS algorithm defines the representative negative samples that can best recognize the positive samples from the unlabeled data instead of predicting positive samples from the unlabeled data directly, which also partly explains why the AGPS algorithm can achieve a much higher recall rate. The results on balanced and imbalanced data demonstrate again that the two-class SVMs and kernel integration can be degraded by the imbalance problem. On the other hand, the differences between results from balanced and imbalanced data also demonstrates the importance of selecting negative samples in gene function prediction. Although the two-class SVMs and kernel integration can achieve a higher $F1$ score, they obtain a lower recall rate compared with AGPS, whereas the higher recall is more important because biologists are interested mainly in genes with the target function instead of those that do not. Although the imbalance problem is avoided, both two-class SVMs and kernel integration trained on balanced data do not perform as well as the AGPS algorithm because the randomly selected negative training samples cannot capture the true distribution of negative samples very well.

To see the ability of these methods to recover positive genes from unknown data, the numbers of genes that they predict correctly from unknown genes on each functional class are compared and the results are summarized in Figure 8.5a. It can be easily seen that the AGPS algorithm can recover most of the unknown genes for nearly each functional class. Furthermore, AGPS is compared against other methods class by class. The number of classes versus one ROC score threshold is counted, and a higher curve indicates a better result. Figure 8.5b shows the results. It can be seen from the results that the AGPS method outperforms all the other methods in this case.

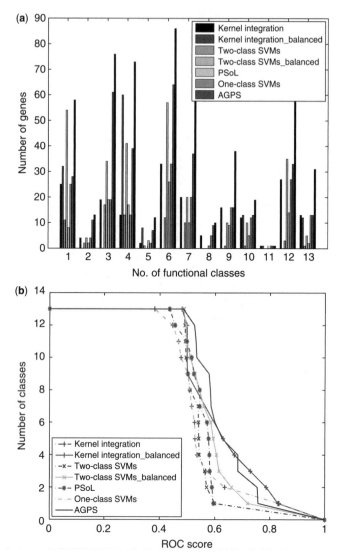

Figure 8.5. Comparison of five methods for function prediction: (a) number of genes correctly predicted for the 13 functional classes; (b) ROC scores of the five methods class by class [ZhaX08a].

The AGPS algorithm provides a general framework to learn and predict based mainly on positive samples. With explicit positive samples, it can define representative negative samples automatically in the learning procedure. Utilizing the defined negative samples, the AGPS algorithm performs well with the existing methods in terms of prediction accuracy. Therefore, applications of the AGPS algorithm can be expected in other fields in bioinformatics in addition to gene function prediction.

8.5 FUNCTION ANNOTATION METHODS FOR DOMAINS

In the previous sections, we introduced some protein function prediction methods, including direct and indirect methods. It is well known that domains and peptide motifs act as units of both structure and function of proteins. It has been shown that proteins interact with each other through domain interactions [Den02, Lee06a, ChL06], where a domain in one protein binds to a domain or smaller peptide motif in the other protein. In other words, domains are building blocks of all proteins and provide an alternative means to understand protein functions. Domains are more conserved than proteins, and the number of available domains is finite and much smaller than that of proteins. Therefore, domain composition can provide key clues to protein functions. It is a promising way to infer the functions of proteins by the functions of their constituent domains.

InterPro2GO and Pfam2GO provide GO function annotations respectively for InterPro domains and Pfam domains. However, only a small number of domains have been annotated until now. Few studies have been performed effectively to predict the functions of domains automatically from biological data. In the literature, several methods have been proposed for domain function prediction. Schug et al. developed a heuristic algorithm for associating GO molecular functions to domains in two domain databases, namely, ProDom and CDD [Schu02]. In this method, domains are first searched against the sequence database, and the algorithm generates rules for function–domain associations based on the intersection of functions assigned to the top hit protein sequences. Despite the promising results obtained on the selected dataset, this method cannot be used widely because of the restrictive assumption that each protein is annotated by only one GO term.

Conserved protein sequence motifs are short stretches of amino acid sequence patterns that potentially encode the function of proteins. Lu et al. presented a method for predicting the functions of novel protein motifs automatically [LuX04]. They treated the task of assigning GO terms to protein motifs as both a binary classification problem and an information retrieval problem. Specifically, GO term–motif associations are first established by a mutual information-based measure that evaluates the correlation between two discrete random variables X and Y:

$$I(X; Y) = \sum_{x,y} \Pr(X = x, Y = y) \log \frac{\Pr(X = x, Y = y)}{\Pr(X = x)\Pr(Y = y)}$$

Mutual information compares the observed joint distribution with an expected joint distribution under the hypothesis that X and Y are independent. A larger amount of mutual information indicates a stronger association between X and Y. The probabilities in the mutual information measure can be empirically estimated from the data by counting occurrence/cooccurrence followed by normalization. In establishing GO term–motif associations, the assignment of a GO term T to a sequence and the matching of a sequence with a motif M are described as two binary random variables. The probabilities involved can be empirically estimated according to the number of sequences matching motif M, the number of sequences assigned with term T, the number of sequences both matching M and also assigned with T, and the total number of sequences in the database. A simple threshold method based on mutual information can be used to assign a GO term to a motif. Lu et al. constructed a more sophisticated method based on the logistic linear regression model to establish the association rules between motifs and GO terms [LuX04]. This sophisticated method has good performance in terms of prediction accuracy. However, both the mutual information measure and the logistic regression model require protein–motif mapping features and protein functions. Since the functional annotation of proteins is still incomplete, the coverage of domains that can be annotated is highly limited.

In a more recent study, Zhao et al. presented a framework to annotate domain functions by integrating several heterogeneous data sources, including domain–domain interactions, protein–domain mapping features, and domain coexisting features [ZhX08b]. The motivation for using domain–domain interactions is that much research work has been performed on domain interaction predictions by exploiting protein interactions, with the assumption that proteins interact with each other through domain interactions [Den02, Ril05, Gui06]. Similar to protein–protein interactions, which are used widely for predicting protein functions, domain interaction information can also provide a way to infer domain functions. Since domains are functional units of proteins, it is reasonable to assume that interacting domains have a high probability of having similar functions. Therefore the majority-rule method used widely by protein function prediction through protein interactions can be applied to domain function annotation in the same manner [Nab05, Chu06]. In addition, protein–domain mappings along with protein functional annotations can provide important clues for domain function [ScJ02, LuX04]. Although the functions of many domains are unknown, the proteins containing these domains may have been annotated. By studying the functions of proteins that contain the target domain, the functions of the target domain can be inferred to a certain extent. Assuming that the protein function is encoded by the domain function, protein annotations can be transferred to the target domain directly if the functions of all the proteins containing the target domain are known and consistent. However, proteins containing the target domain may be annotated with multiple and inconsistent functions, and many proteins consist of more than one domain. Therefore, each domain has an equal possibility of possessing the functions that have been assigned to those proteins. Hence, it is necessary to establish certain rules to assign the functions of proteins to domains. Moreover, most proteins are composed of multiple domains that are either repeated or combined. Despite the large number of combinations of domains, the number of domain combinations in proteins is finite [Api01], which is similar to the phenomenon of domain fusion. More recently, domain coexisting features have been used for domain interaction prediction [LeH06]. Similarly, this hypothesis can be extended to domain function prediction, where a pair of domains is more likely to have the same function if both domains occur in the same protein. Statistically, it is reasonable to proportionally allocate a rate to each domain on the basis of the function of the protein when there is no other information available. With the integration of these sources of heterogeneous data, two methods—a threshold-based classification method and the support vector machine (SVM) method—have been used for domain function prediction [ZhX08b]. Compared with the existing methods using a single data source, this approach can improve both annotation coverage and prediction accuracy. We will introduce this method in this section.

8.5.1 Domain Sources

Two domain datasets from databases InterPro and Pfam-A are investigated and functionally annotated by the integration approach described above. The annotations for InterPro domains are downloaded from InterPro2GO in the GO database. In general, only a few domains are annotated by GO terms. To derive rules for associating GO terms with domains, some informative GO terms were selected. Here, "informative" means that each selected GO term should have a sufficient number of annotations and represent reasonable specific biological functions, so that association rules can be derived from the learning set. GO terms are stored in a hierarchical directed acyclic graph in the database. Each GO term has a GO INDEX indicating its position in the graph [ChY04]. The informative GO terms are selected according to their depths with the following requirements: (1) each selected GO term has no less than 30 annotations and (2) the descendants of the term have annotations no more than 30. Table 8.5 shows the selected 20 GO terms and their definitions for the InterPro domains. InterPro domains, which appear in the protein interaction data

TABLE 8.5. Selected GO Terms for InterPro Domains

GO ID	Definition
GO:0005524	ATP binding
GO:0046872	Metal ion binding
GO:0043169	Cation binding
GO:0042623	ATPase activity, coupled
GO:0005386	Transmembrane transporter activity
GO:0016301	Kinase activity
GO:0008324	Cation transmembrane transporter activity
GO:0010264	Myoinositol hexakisphosphate biosynthetic process
GO:0043412	Biopolymer modification
GO:0051234	Establishment of localization
GO:0009987	Cellular process
GO:0009719	Response to endogenous stimulus
GO:0044238	Primary metabolic process
GO:0048519	Negative regulation of biological process
GO:0009056	Catabolic process
GO:0008104	Protein localization
GO:0006807	Nitrogen compound metabolism
GO:0043228	Non-membrane-bound organelle
GO:0043227	Membrane-bound organelle
GO:0019814	Immunoglobulin complex

Source: Zhao et al. [ZhX08b].

TABLE 8.6. Selected GO Terms for Pfam-A Domains

GO ID	Definition
GO:0016301	Kinase activity
GO:0010264	Myoinositol hexakisphosphate biosynthetic process
GO:0043412	Biopolymer modification
GO:0051234	Establishment of localization
GO:0009719	Response to endogenous stimulus
GO:0043228	Nonmembrane-bound organelle
GO:0043227	Membrane-bound organelle
GO:0019814	Immunoglobulin complex
GO:0048519	Negative regulation of biological process
GO:0009056	Catabolic process

Source: Zhao et al. [ZhX08b].

used, are selected. Among 2305 domains, 1218 domains have been annotated by the selected GO terms.

The domain annotation for the Pfam domain is downloaded from Pfam2GO in the GO database. Ten informative GO terms are selected and shown in Table 8.6. Of a total 1751 Pfam domains, 563 have been annotated by the informative GO terms. The minimum depth of the selected GO terms is 4, while the maximum depth is 8, and the average depth of the selected GO terms is 4.9.

8.5.2 Integration of Heterogeneous Data

Some domain interaction databases such as iPfam are currently available, but only a small number of domain–domain interactions are deposited, which are not sufficient for domain function prediction. On the other hand, there are many domain interaction prediction methods available [Den02, Ril05, ChL06]. To predict domain–domain interactions, protein interactions for yeast from the DIP database are used. Only proteins that have at least one InterPro domain are considered, and domains contained in these proteins are extracted for further analysis. Finally, 2822 proteins, 2305 domains, and 9048 protein interactions are left for further analysis. As another test set based on Pfam domains, proteins with at least one Pfam-A domain are considered. Domains contained in the selected proteins are extracted. Finally, 3280 proteins, 1751 domains, and 11,363 protein interactions are extracted for further analysis. In this study, APM, introduced in Chapter 5, is adopted to predict domain–domain interactions from protein interaction data. In total, 37,937 InterPro domain interactions and 16,242 Pfam domain interactions are predicted, with each domain pair having an interaction probability to denote interaction strength hereafter.

Zhao et al. extended the majority-rule method for protein function prediction to deal with domain–domain interactions under the assumption that interacting domains tend to have similar functions [ZhX08b]. Assume that domain D_i interacts with m domains, which are annotated by n functions. Among the n functions, k ($k < n$) functions occur with the highest frequency. Therefore, from the statistical viewpoint, the k functions of the m interaction partners can be transferred to domain

D_i to a certain extent. Specifically, given a domain–domain interaction (DDI) network and a target domain D_i, D_i can be annotated by the function T_j with the following probability (denoted as DDI hereinafter)

$$\Pr(T_j|D_i, \text{DDI}) = \frac{\sum_k \lambda_{ik} I_{kj}}{\sum_k \lambda_{ik}} \tag{8.22}$$

where $\Pr(T_j|D_i, \text{DDI})$ denotes the probability that domain D_i is annotated by the function T_j, given the predicted domain–domain interactions. λ_{ik} denotes the interaction strength between domains D_i and D_k, and I_{kj} is an indicator of whether domain D_k is annotated with function T_j; $I_{kj} = 1$ if domain D_k is annotated by the function T_j, and $I_{kj} = 0$ otherwise.

Protein–domain mapping information is used to identify domain pairs occurring in the same protein. Furthermore, the known domains are assigned functions by using annotations from InterPro2GO and Pfam2GO in the GO database. Two domains may cooperatively exert certain biological functions if they are in the same protein. For example, if domains A and B occur in the same protein, and domain A is annotated by the GO term T while B is unknown, it is possible that domain B also possesses the function of the term T or related to T. Actually, from the statistical viewpoint, it is reasonable to proportionally allocate a function rate to each domain in the protein, although cooccurring domains seldom have the same functions. Therefore, the number of domains cooccurring with the target domain in the same protein is counted, and the probability that the target domain D_i is annotated by the GO term T_j can be expressed as follows (denoted as CDD hereinafter)

$$\Pr(T_j|D_i, \text{CDD}) = \frac{\sum_k N_{ik} I_{kj}}{\sum_k N_{ik}} \tag{8.23}$$

where $\Pr(T_j|D_i, \text{CDD})$ denotes the probability that domain D_i is annotated by the function T_j, given the domain coexisting relationships. N_{ik} denotes the number of times that domain D_i cooccurs with domain d_k. I_{kj} has the same meaning as before.

The protein–domain mapping information obtained from InterPro and Pfam is used to associate proteins with domains. Furthermore, annotations to proteins are downloaded from the GO database and mapped to the GO terms that have been selected for domains as described above. The protein annotations are used to infer the domain functions with the assumption that domains are the functional units of proteins. Given proteins with domains, the functions of proteins can be transferred to domains with the following probability (denoted as P2D hereinafter)

$$\Pr(T_j|D_i, \text{P2D}) = \frac{NP(D_i, T_j)}{NP(D_i)} \tag{8.24}$$

where $\Pr(T_j|D_i, \text{P2D})$ denotes the probability that domain D_i is annotated by the function T_j, given the protein–domain mapping. $NP(D_i, T_j)$ is the number of proteins with function T_j and containing D_i, and $NP(D_i)$ is the number of proteins containing D_i.

8.5.3 Domain Function Prediction

To predict the functions of domains, a simple method is to set a threshold on the probabilities described above. For example, if the threshold is set to θ, then domain D_i will be annotated with the function T_j by using domain–domain interactions if $\Pr(T_j|D_i, \mathrm{DDI}) > \theta$. Hence, to predict whether domain D_i has function T_j, one can compare evidences from domain–domain interaction $[\Pr(T_j|D_i, \mathrm{DDI})]$, protein–domain association $[\Pr(T_j|D_i, \mathrm{P2D})]$, and domain coexisting $[\Pr(T_j|D_i, \mathrm{CDD})]$ against the preset threshold θ, respectively. Each score from the three evidence sources provides a way to determine whether the target domain has the function of interest. Generally, with the assumption that data sources are independent, three information sources can be integrated in the following way

$$\Pr(T_j|D_i) = 1 - [1 - \Pr(T_j|D_i, \mathrm{DDI})][1 - \Pr(T_j|D_i, \mathrm{P2D})][1 - \Pr(T_j|D_i, \mathrm{CDD})]$$

where $\Pr(T_j|D_i)$ denotes the probability that domain D_i is annotated with the function T_j by the integrated data sources. Furthermore, various combinations for one, two, or three data sources can be done in the same way, such as CDD, P2D, DDI, CDD + P2D, DDI + CDD, DDI + P2D, and CDD + P2D + DDI.

Zhao et al. described another method that formulates function prediction as a classification problem to predict domain functions [ZhX08b]. For classification, each domain is constructed as a fixed-length feature vector. Features from the three information sources are constructed in a manner similar to that described by Lu et al. [LuX04]. For P2D, the following five features are extracted for the domain–function pair (M, T):

- Number of proteins with function T that contain domain M
- Number of proteins annotated by function T
- Number of proteins containing domain M
- Number of distinct domains annotated by function T
- Mutual information between function T and domain M

For CDD, the following four features with (M, T) are extracted:

- Number of domains with function T that cooccur with domain M
- Number of domains cooccurring with domain M
- Number of distinct domains annotated by function T
- Mutual information between function T and domain M

For DDI, the following four features are extracted for (M, T):

- Number of domains with function T that interact with domain M
- Number of domains interacting with domain M
- Number of distinct domains annotated by function T
- Mutual information between function T and domain M

Of the 13 features extracted above, some of them are common for all three information sources. After constructing the feature vectors for domains, domain function prediction can be regarded as a multiclass classification problem, where domain vectors are used as inputs for SVMs. In SVM, the matrix computed by kernel functions is normalized in the following way:

$$K(x, y) = \frac{K(x, y)}{\sqrt{K(x, x)K(y, y)}} \tag{8.25}$$

For each function, the trained SVM classifier provides a decision value as output for each target domain D_i. Consequently, domain D_i will be annotated by the function whose corresponding SVM classifier provides the largest decision value.

8.5.4 Numerical Validation

To evaluate the performance of domain function prediction, indices such as sensitivity, specificity, ROC score, and accuracy are adopted. The definitions of all measures except for accuracy have been given in previous chapters. The accuracy measure is defined as follows

$$\text{Accuracy} = \frac{\text{TP} + \text{TN}}{\text{TP} + \text{FP} + \text{FN} + \text{TN}} \tag{8.26}$$

where TP is the number of domains correctly predicted to have the target function term T, FP is the number of domains incorrectly predicted to have function T, TN is the number of domains correctly predicted to lack function T, and FN is the number of domains incorrectly predicted to lack function T.

8.5.4.1 Experiments on InterPro Domains
To evaluate the performance of the integration method and confirm the advantage of using multiple data sources, tenfold cross-validation is utilized on those annotated InterPro domains. The threshold-based classification method is applied on three heterogeneous data sources separately and then integratively to predict domain function, where the threshold is set from 0.1 to 1 with the interval as 0.1. The results are summarized in Table 8.7 and Figure 8.6, where "All" implies CDD + DDI + P2D. The results show that each of three information sources can contribute to domain function prediction with reasonably good results. However, using the integration of all information sources can yield better overall results than using any single data source. Among the three data sources, DDI performs worst and P2D performs best. The DDI method performs worst because the domain–domain interactions are predictively derived from protein–protein interactions, which have many false positives. The CDD method performs worse because many of the proteins contain only one domain. On the other hand, the annotations of proteins are more reliable, and therefore P2D performs better. The results demonstrate that the three information sources are useful for domain function prediction and complement each other. Therefore, the integration of heterogeneous information sources can improve the accuracy of domain function prediction.

TABLE 8.7. Tenfold Cross-Validation Results Averaged over 20 Classes by Threshold-Based Classification Method on InterPro Domains

Information	TP	TN	FP	FN	ROC
DDI	8.36	91.91	11.84	9.70	0.65
CDD	9.71	100.51	3.23	8.35	0.74
P2D	13.82	94.40	9.34	4.25	0.78
DDI + CDD	12.24	91.95	11.80	5.83	0.80
P2D + DDI	14.43	90.23	13.51	3.64	0.79
CDD + P2D	15.50	92.92	10.83	2.56	0.84
All	15.74	90.25	13.50	2.34	0.84

Source: Zhao et al. [ZhX08b].

The SVM method with the RBF kernel is also applied to predict the functions of domains on the same dataset, and tenfold cross-validation is used to evaluate the performance of the classifier. The contribution of each information source and various combinations of the three information sources to domain function prediction are investigated through SVM method. The results are listed in Table 8.8, which shows that the SVM method yields results similar to those obtained by the threshold-based classification method. The integration of heterogeneous information sources yields the best results, and the DDI method yields the worst results. This again confirms that the

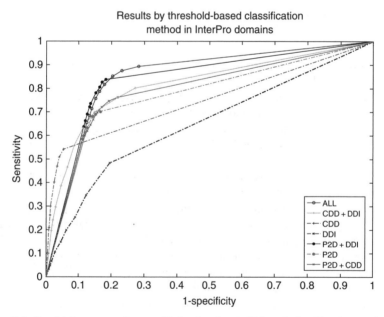

Figure 8.6. Sensitivity versus $1 -$ specificity for threshold-based classification method on InterPro domains [ZhX08b].

TABLE 8.8. **Tenfold Cross-Validation Results Averaged over 20 Classes by SVMs on InterPro Domains**

Information	TP	TN	FP	FN	ROC
DDI	10.61	99.30	4.44	7.45	0.60
CDD	10.61	100.88	2.86	7.46	0.62
P2D	12.06	100.13	3.62	6.00	0.69
DDI + CDD	11.92	100.04	3.70	6.14	0.70
CDD + P2D	13.94	100.21	3.49	4.13	0.76
P2D + DDI	13.03	99.36	4.39	5.03	0.73
All	14.18	100.07	3.68	3.89	0.79

Source: Zhao et al. [ZhX08b].

integration of heterogeneous information sources can indeed improve the accuracy of domain function prediction.

In addition, the threshold-based classification method and SVM method based on all data sources are compared with the logistic regression model for domain function prediction [LuX04]. The logistic regression approach integrates the following six features, with five of them identical to the features used in P2D and one additional feature:

- Number of distinct functions associated with domain M

This additional feature is not considered here because it is impossible to derive this feature for unannotated domains. Figure 8.7 illustrates the comparison results in terms of sensitivity, specificity, accuracy, and ROC score, all of which indicate

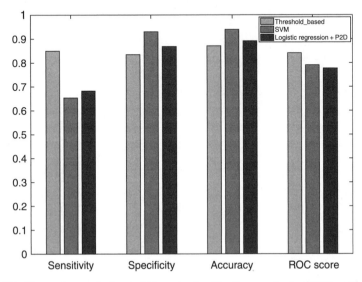

Figure 8.7. Comparison of threshold-based classification method, SVM, and logistic regression for InterPro domains [ZhX08b].

that the method that utilizes the integration of heterogeneous information sources outperforms the logistic regression model [LuX04].

8.5.4.2 Experiments on Pfam-A Domains
To further confirm the benefit of integrated data sources, the abovementioned methods are also applied to predict the functions of Pfam-A domains [ZhX08b]. The threshold-based classification method is applied to predict the functions of Pfam-A domains using the same procedure as that applied for InterPro domains. The results are summarized in Table 8.9 and Figure 8.8, which illustrate trends similar to those obtained on InterPro domains. Meanwhile, P2D performs best among the three information sources. Among the

TABLE 8.9. Tenfold Cross-Validation Results Averaged over 10 Classes by Threshold-Based Classification Method on Pfam-A Domains

Information	TP	TN	FP	FN	ROC
DDI	4.47	41.49	6.16	4.18	0.68
CDD	1.81	47.21	0.44	6.84	0.62
P2D	7.67	42.25	5.40	0.98	0.87
DDI + CDD	5.26	41.77	5.88	3.39	0.74
P2D + DDI	7.87	40.92	6.73	0.78	0.88
CDD + P2D	7.74	42.11	5.54	0.91	0.88
All	7.92	40.75	6.90	0.73	0.88

Source: Zhao et al. [ZhX08b].

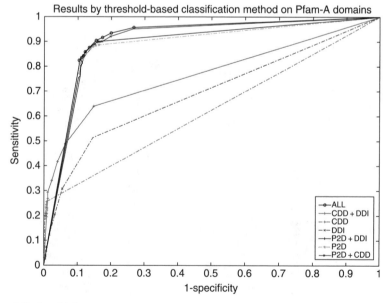

Figure 8.8. Sensitivity versus $1 -$ specificity for threshold-based classification method on Pfam-A domains [ZhX08b].

TABLE 8.10. Tenfold Cross-Validation Results Averaged over 10 Classes by SVMs on Pfam-A Domains

Information Sources	TP	TN	FP	FN	ROC Scores
DDI	3.02	45.84	1.81	5.63	0.62
CDD	1.20	47.43	0.22	7.45	0.58
P2D	4.96	46.02	1.63	3.69	0.77
DDI + CDD	3.76	45.55	2.10	4.89	0.67
CDD + P2D	5.70	45.34	2.31	2.95	0.79
P2D + DDI	6.13	45.59	2.06	2.52	0.83
All	6.34	45.53	2.12	2.31	0.84

Source: Zhao et al. [ZhX08b].

three data sources, CDD performs worst because few of the proteins used here contain more than one Pfam-A domain. In this experiment, the integration of all the three data sources again yields the best results, as indicated in Figure 8.8, where we can see that the combination of P2D and DDI can yield results comparable to those obtained by integrating all information sources. On the other hand, the results show that integration of heterogeneous information sources at least does not degrade the performance even though some information sources do not contribute much to the performance, such as CDD in this case.

The SVM method is applied to Pfam-A domains in the same manner as it was applied to InterPro domains. Table 8.10 shows that the SVM method yields results similar to those obtained by the threshold-based classification method. Once more, the integration of heterogeneous information sources yields the best results, and the CDD method has the worst performance. Figure 8.9 compares results of the study with Lu's logistic regression method and the SVM method with respect to sensitivity, specificity, accuracy, and ROC score. As indicated in Figure 8.9, the

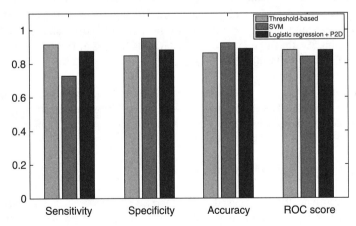

Figure 8.9. Comparison of SVM method, threshold-based classification method, and logistic regression on Pfam-A Domains [ZhX08b].

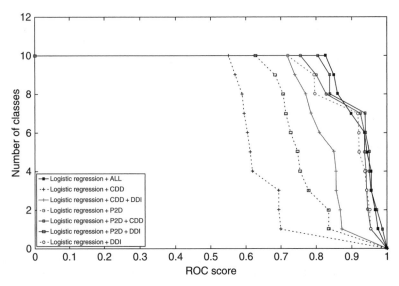

Figure 8.10. Results obtained by logistic regression model with various combinations of information sources for Pfam-A domains [ZhX08b].

threshold-based method outperforms Lu's method but Lu's method outperforms SVM. Although Lu's method outperforms SVM, the advantage of integration of heterogeneous information sources is again demonstrated by applying the logistic regression model to various combinations of the three information sources for domain annotation (Fig. 8.10).

8.5.4.3 Functional Annotations for Unknown Domains

In addition to cross-validation, the threshold-based method in this study is applied to predict the functions of InterPro domains with the selected GO terms. Table 8.11 shows the top five domains assigned to each class with the highest probabilities. Many of these functional annotations are biologically meaningful. For example, one of the top hit domains for the functional class of GO:0044238 is IPR006379, which has been annotated with GO:0008152 defined as

> Processes that cause many of the chemical changes in living organisms, including anabolism and catabolism. Metabolic processes typically transform small molecules, but also include macromolecular processes such as DNA repair and replication, and protein synthesis and degradation.

On the other hand, GO:0044238 is defined as

> Reactions involving those compounds that are formed as a part of the normal anabolic and catabolic processes. These processes take place in most, if not all, cells of the organism

in the GO database, which is a descendant of GO:0008152.

TABLE 8.11. **Top Five Domains Assigned to Each GO Function Class with Highest Probabilities**

GO ID	Top Five Hit Domains				
GO:0005524	IPR009077	IPR013134	IPR006863	IPR004776	IPR013253
GO:0046872	IPR001374	IPR004388	IPR005145	IPR006070	IPR010923
GO:0043169	IPR001374	IPR004388	IPR005145	IPR006070	IPR010923
GO:0042623	IPR013748	IPR005045	IPR008946	IPR009110	IPR003006
GO:0005386	IPR005045	IPR009110	IPR003006	IPR003586	IPR003587
GO:0016301	IPR006567	IPR006828	IPR012993	IPR011072	IPR011026
GO:0008324	IPR008217	IPR010256	IPR005045	IPR004923	IPR005217
GO:0010264	IPR006379	IPR005097	IPR005109	IPR008630	IPR003135
GO:0043412	IPR006567	IPR006828	IPR005109	IPR008630	IPR013915
GO:0051234	IPR013598	IPR008672	IPR013805	IPR006590	IPR000225
GO:0009987	IPR013890	IPR013598	IPR002086	IPR012999	IPR013027
GO:0009719	IPR013194	IPR012993	IPR014016	IPR014017	IPR003583
GO:0044238	IPR013890	IPR006379	IPR013105	IPR012295	IPR013150
GO:0048519	IPR013890	IPR008672	IPR001858	IPR013194	IPR013724
GO:0009056	IPR013915	IPR007716	IPR007717	IPR013882	IPR001232
GO:0008104	IPR012971	IPR007134	IPR007135	IPR006285	IPR007681
GO:0006807	IPR005097	IPR001498	IPR006575	IPR002912	IPR002547
GO:0043228	IPR012295	IPR003008	IPR000533	IPR013252	IPR012971
GO:0043227	IPR013890	IPR013598	IPR002086	IPR012999	IPR001017
GO:0019814	IPR006379	IPR003008	IPR008672	IPR013805	IPR013252

Source: Zhao et al. [ZhX08b].

Another example is the domain IPR006567 PUG, which is defined as follows: "PUG is a domain in protein kinases, *N*-glycanases, and other nuclear proteins found in eukaryotes in the InterPro database." It is annotated with GO:0016301, where GO:0016301 is defined as "kinase activity" and "catalysis of the transfer of a phosphate group, usually from ATP, to a substrate molecule in the GO database." It can be seen that the predicted result is also consistent with the description of the InterPro database.

8.6 SUMMARY

In this chapter, we comprehensively surveyed a variety of function prediction methods by exploiting protein interaction networks and integration of multiple data sources. Some of them are indirect methods such as functional module detection and functional linkage establishment, and direct function prediction methods are also introduced. These approaches demonstrate the successful applications of machine learning, probabilistic approaches, and global optimization techniques. Further materials can be found in some review papers [Zha07, ZhaX08d]. Most of them are based on the basic assumption that the interaction partners of a protein are likely to share similar functions. Although the topological link (direct or indirect) relationship between proteins implies their functional similarity, the results may be biased by the noise and incompleteness in experimental data. More recently, phenotype data have demonstrated a very informative gene function. Future exploration of these types of data in the function prediction is promising. In addition, with further progress in domain interaction predictions, domain–domain interactions will become an invaluable resource for function prediction.

PART III

METABOLIC NETWORKS AND SIGNALING NETWORKS

CHAPTER 9

METABOLIC NETWORKS: ANALYSIS, RECONSTRUCTION, AND APPLICATION

9.1 CELLULAR METABOLISM AND METABOLIC PATHWAYS

Cellular functions are accomplished by interactions of their chemical constituents. Cellular metabolism is the total set of all biochemical reactions that occur in a cell, such as the reactions involved in degrading food molecules, in synthesizing macromolecules, and in generating small precursor molecules. It also includes all reactions involving electron transfer. Metabolism processes are usually classified into two broad categories, which are the phases of intermediate metabolism. One is catabolism, which breaks down various substrates into common metabolites, involves removing electrons from nutrients, and harvests energy in cellular respiration. In other words, catabolism encompasses degradation and energy-yielding reactions, in which complex substances and macromolecules are broken down to low molecular weight compounds. In general, the reactions in catabolism are oxidative and produce reducing potential. The other is anabolism, which synthesizes complex molecules such as amino acids, fatty acids, and nucleic acids, uses energy to enrich molecules in electrons, and requires the cell to expend energy obtained from nutrient catabolism. In other words, anabolism encompasses biosynthetic and energy-requiring reactions, in which complex substances and macromolecules are synthesized from low-molecular-weight precursors. In general, the reactions of anabolism are reductive and consume reducing potential. During catabolism and anabolism processes, an intricate exchange of chemical groups and reduction–oxidation (redox) potentials

Biomolecular Networks. By Luonan Chen, Rui-Sheng Wang, and Xiang-Sun Zhang
Copyright © 2009 John Wiley & Sons, Inc.

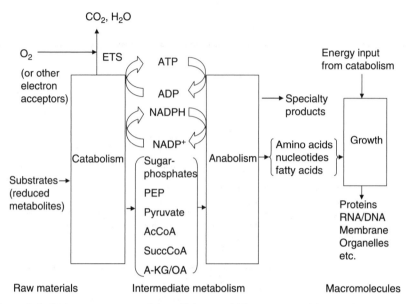

Figure 9.1. Major components of the cellular metabolism. (Adapted from Palsson [Pal06].)

takes place through a set of carrier molecules such as ATP, GTP, NADH, and NADPH. These carrier molecules and what they transfer consist of the whole metabolism in a cell. Figure 9.1 illustrates the major parts of cellular metabolism, where intermediate metabolism converts raw materials into energy as well as building blocks of a cell such as proteins and membranes.

All biochemical reactions in a cell are catalyzed by a kind of specialized protein called enzymes, which often require dietary minerals, vitamins, and other co-factors in order to function properly. These biochemical reactions allow organisms to grow, reproduce, maintain their structures, and respond to their environments. In a biological system full of different types of chemical reactions, energy, which is defined as the capacity to do work, is indispensable. The two fundamental types of energy in biological systems are potential energy and kinetic energy. Potential energy is the energy of state or position that matter has because of its structure or location. It is the stored energy waiting to do work. For example, chemical bonds have potential energy because of their structure. Kinetic energy is the energy of motion. It is the type of energy that can do work. Both kinetic and potential energy can be found in many forms, such as electrical, light, chemical, thermal, and mechanical forms. Under certain conditions, energy can be transformed or converted from one form to another, obeying the laws of thermodynamics. The usable energy is called free energy (G). The unusable energy is entropy, which measures the disorder of the system. Exergonic chemical reactions release free energy and have a negative change in free energy ($\Delta G < 0$). Endergonic chemical reactions consume free energy and have a positive change in free energy ($\Delta G > 0$). Adenosine triphosphate (ATP) serves as an energy currency in biological systems. One important exergonic reaction is the breaking of the bonds of ATP, in which ATP releases a relatively large amount of free energy after undergoing hydrolysis. The ATP cycle couples exergonic and endergonic reactions. It captures the free energy released in an exergonic chemical reaction and transfers that captured energy to the reactants of an endergonic reaction.

Enzymes are the catalysts of biological systems that affect the rates of biochemical reactions by lowering the energy barrier, supplying the activation energy needed to initiate a reaction [Sad07]. Nearly all known enzymes are proteins. The most striking characteristics of enzymes are their catalytic power and specificity. Enzymes not only determine the patterns of chemical transformations but also mediate the transformation of one form of energy into another. Most reactions in biological systems do not take place at perceptible rates in the absence of enzymes. Usually enzymes are classified according to the types of reactions that they catalyze. The International Union of Biochemistry established an Enzyme Commission (EC) to develop a nomenclature for enzymes, in which reactions are divided into six major groups numbered 1–6 (Table 9.1). These groups were subdivided and further subdivided, so that a four-digit number preceded by the letters EC (for Enzyme Commission) could precisely identify all enzymes.

Metabolic pathway is a series of chemical reactions occurring within a cell, in which one chemical is transformed into another through chemical reactions catalyzed by a sequence of enzymes. Metabolic pathways can be simple linear sequences of a few reactions, or extensively branched with reactions converging on or diverging from a central main pathway. There are a large number of metabolic pathways in biological systems. Some of them are common to many living organisms. For example, glycolysis metabolism is involved in glucose oxidation in order to obtain ATP, and it is an energy-conversion pathway in many organisms. The citric acid cycle involves acetyl–CoA oxidation in order to obtain GTP and valuable intermediates. It is usually regulated by substrate availability, by product inhibition, and by some cycle intermediates. The oxidative phosphorylation pathway disposes of the electrons released by glycolysis and citric acid cycle. The pentose phosphate pathway is involved in the synthesis of pentose and the release of the reducing power needed for anabolic reactions. Other main metabolic pathways include fatty acid metabolism, glycogen metabolism, and amino acid metabolism. Many chemicals may participate in multiple pathways existing within a cell. This collection of pathways is quite elaborate and forms a complicated metabolic network, which is the complete set of metabolic and physical

TABLE 9.1. Six Major Classes of Enzymes According to Enzyme Commission

Class	Type of Reaction
Oxidoreductases	Oxidation–reduction
Transferases	Chemical group transfer
Hydrolases	Hydrolysis reactions
Lyases	Addition or removal of chemical groups to form double bonds
Isomerases	Isomerization
Ligases	Ligation of two substrates at the expense of ATP hydrolysis

processes that determine the physiological and biochemical properties of a cell (see Fig. 9.2). These networks comprise the chemical reactions of metabolism as well as the regulatory interactions that guide these reactions and become powerful tools to elucidate the cellular machinery and modeling metabolism. With the advance of genomic techniques, metabolic networks in many organisms can be reconstructed from biochemical reactions [Ree03].

Table 9.2 lists some main metabolic network databases. The Kyoto Encyclopedia of Genes and Genomes (KEGG) Pathways is a database containing information on the

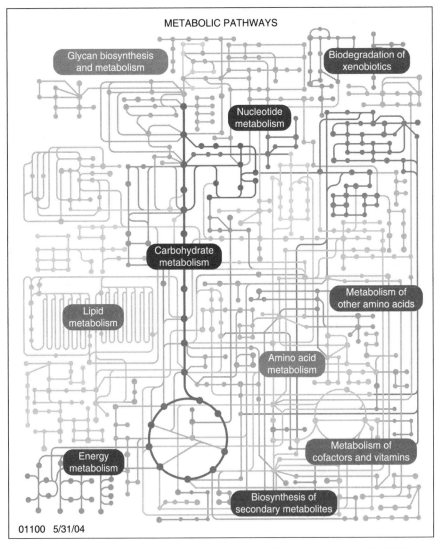

Figure 9.2. Overview of the main metabolic pathways. [The figure is from KEGG Website with permission.]

TABLE 9.2. Some Databases of Metabolic Pathways

Databases	Websites
KEGG	http://www.genome.ad.jp/kegg
BioCyc	http://www.biocyc.org
EcoCyc	http://www.ecocyc.org
MetaCyc	http://metacyc.org
AraCyc	http://www.arabidopsis.org/biocyc/index.jsp
RiceCyc	http://www.gramene.org/pathway
PseudoCyc	http://v2.pseudomonas.com:1555
MPB	http://www.gwu.edu/mpb
MRAD	http://capb.dbi.udel.edu/whisler
EMP	http://empproject.com
MAlARIA	http://sites.huji.ac.il/malaria
PUMA2	http://compbio.mcs.anl.gov/puma2
PathCase	http://nashua.cwru.edu/PathwaysWeb
BRENDA	http://www.brenda-enzymes.info

molecular interactions and reaction networks of genes and proteins. It includes graphical pathway maps for all known metabolic pathways from various organisms. BioCyc is a collection of 371 pathway databases, containing whole databases dedicated to certain organisms. Each pathway database in the BioCyc collection describes the genome and metabolic pathways of a single organism. For example, EcoCyc, which belongs to BioCyc, is a highly detailed bioinformatics database on the entire genome of *E. coli*. EcoCyc contains literature-based information on transcriptional regulation, protein complexes, enzymes, transporters, and metabolic pathways. Additionally, MetaCyc, an encyclopedia of metabolic pathways, is a metabolic pathway and enzyme database that contains 1100 metabolic pathways elucidated from 1500 organisms. Most metabolic pathways in MetaCyc are compiled from scientific experimental literature. MetaCyc contains pathways involved in both primary and secondary metabolism, as well as associated compounds, enzymes, and genes. BRENDA is an enzyme database containing comprehensive information on enzymes and enzymatic reactions. It is one of several databases nested within the metabolic pathway database set of the SRS5 sequence retrieval system at the European Bioinformatics Institute (EBI).

Metabolic networks have some common properties shared with other biological networks and also have unique characteristics. To elucidate the organizational and biological principles of the metabolism of living organisms, more recent studies have adopted graph-theoretic approaches to analyze large metabolic networks. Unlike isolated functional module organization of other cellular networks, Ravasz et al. studied metabolic networks of many organisms and found them to be organized into many highly connected topological modules that combine larger, less cohesive units in a hierarchical manner [Rav02]. The number and degree of such units generally follow a power-law distribution. Jeong et al. systematically compared mathematical analysis of the metabolic networks from 43 organisms [Jeo00] and found that these metabolic networks have the same topological scaling properties and show striking similarities to the inherent organization of complex nonbiological systems. In contrast, Arita indicated that metabolic networks have flux distributions with an average path length that is longer than that observed in network structure and that their functional states may not have scale-free characteristics [Ari04]. Mahadevan and Palsson studied the relations between structure and function of metabolic networks [Mah05]. They found that, unlike the scenario in other influence-type biological networks such as protein–protein interaction networks or regulatory networks, in flow-type metabolic networks, the essentiality of reactions in a node is not correlated with node centrality. Such results suggest that fundamental differences exist among different biological networks owing to network representation and functional constraints. Their study indicates that even the least connected nodes in metabolic networks are just likely to be critical to the overall network function as those highly connected nodes.

9.2 METABOLIC NETWORK ANALYSIS AND MODELING

Dynamic simulation and analysis of metabolic networks enables us to elucidate the underlying mechanisms of metabolic processes. Both signaling networks and metabolic networks consist of many biochemical reactions. Hence, naturally metabolic networks can also be modeled by ordinary differential equations (ODE) or Petri net. However, despite the similarity to signaling networks, they have some different properties that should be taken into account in mathematical modeling. In signaling pathways, we focus not on substance flow but on signal flow, which is performed by phosphorylated and dephosphorylated protein forms [Sac06]. In contrast, in metabolic networks, stoichiometric reaction equations govern the dynamics of metabolism, which stresses substance flow. In particular, the activity dynamics of enzymes has special kinetics. These factors lead to special features of metabolic network simulation, which differ from those of other biomolecular networks.

9.2.1 Flux Balance Analysis

Flux balance analysis (FBA), a mathematical analysis of the metabolism according to chemistry laws, has been shown to be a very useful technique for analysis of metabolic capabilities of cellular systems. For instance, using FBA, we can know which metabolic fluxes maximize the growth rate of an organism, provided that some nutrients are known to be available. The fundamentals of FBA have been reviewed in the literature [LeM06, Kau03]. Here, we give only a brief introduction.

Figure 9.3 illustrates a reaction network and FBA. Stoichiometry is the calculation of quantitative relationships of the reactants and products in chemical reactions. Metabolic networks can be represented by a stoichiometric matrix S with the rows corresponding to metabolites and the columns corresponding to reactions. The elements in S are stoichiometric coefficients of the associated reactions. Metabolic flux, usually denoted by v, is the rate of turnover of molecules through a reaction or an enzyme. Regulation of flux is vital for all metabolic pathways to regulate their

I. Reaction network and stoichiometric matrix

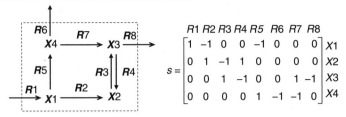

II. Dynamic mass balance at steady state

$$\frac{dX}{dt} = Sv \quad \Longrightarrow \quad Sv = 0$$

$$\begin{bmatrix} 1 & -1 & 0 & 0 & -1 & 0 & 0 & 0 \\ 0 & 1 & -1 & 1 & 0 & 0 & 0 & 0 \\ 0 & 0 & 1 & -1 & 0 & 0 & 1 & -1 \\ 0 & 0 & 0 & 0 & 1 & -1 & -1 & 0 \end{bmatrix} \begin{bmatrix} v_1 \\ v_2 \\ \vdots \\ v_8 \end{bmatrix} = 0$$

III. Flux balance analysis

Optimization criterion: max $c^T v$

Constraints: $Sv = 0$

$v \geq 0$

Figure 9.3. Illustration of a reaction network and flux balance analysis.

activity under different conditions. Let the flux vector be $v = (v_1, v_2, \ldots, v_n)^T$ and the concentration vector of reactants be $x = (x_1, x_2, \ldots, x_m)^T$. Then, according to the mass balance law in biochemistry, the following equation governs the dynamics of the metabolic network:

$$\frac{dx}{dt} = Sv \qquad (9.1)$$

Generally, v is a function of x. At a steady state, the change of the concentrations of all reactants and products over time t across all reactions within the metabolic system becomes zero. The steady-state assumption leads to the following flux balance equation:

$$Sv = 0 \qquad (9.2)$$

This mass balance represents the principal constraints for analyzing the metabolism of an organism, and is the core content of flux balance analysis. Actually, the reactions of many metabolic systems are so fast that the quasi-steady-state assumption (9.2) approximately holds.

All possible solutions to the linear system described above can be described by a set of basis vectors, which can be generated through convex analysis and the inequality constraints on the flux values of the irreversible reactions, specifically, $v \geq 0$. However, usually as a result of $m < n$, the linear system is still underdetermined. In other words, there may be many solutions for it. Hence, some optimization criteria or additional biological constraints are needed to obtain a unique biological solution, such as maximizing the growth rate (biomass production) of an organism. Linear programming is generally used to find such solutions owing to the linear relationship between the stoichiometric matrix S and the flux rates of the reactions

$$\text{max} \quad c^T v \tag{9.3}$$

$$\text{s.t.} \quad Sv = 0 \tag{9.4}$$

$$v \geq 0 \tag{9.5}$$

where c represents the coefficients of the linear objective function. Objective functions can take many forms. Common objective functions include maximizing biomass or cell growth, maximizing/minimizing ATP production in order to determine conditions of optimal metabolic energy efficiency, maximizing the rate of synthesis of a particular product, or minimizing nutrient uptake in order to evaluate the conditions under which a cell will perform its metabolic functions while consuming the minimum amount of nutrients [LeM06, Kau03]. The linear programming described above derives a feasible set of steady-state fluxes that optimizes a certain biological objective subject to a set of constraints on mass balance. This type of method for analyzing the metabolism of an organism constitutes the core content of FBA.

Flux balance analysis can accurately check whether the reaction stoichiometry is consistent with predictions by calculating fluxes for the balanced reactions. It can also be used to determine the most effective and efficient pathway in a metabolic network by optimizing a particular objective function. In addition, FBA has already been applied to gene knockout studies, perturbation studies, and drug target discovery [Seq02, Edw00, Ver07]. By comparing the flux distribution of a mutant metabolic pathway with an enzyme removed and the wild one, we can evaluate the importance of enzymes, which may be correlated with the essentiality of genes.

9.2.2   Elementary Mode and Extreme Pathway Analysis

From the description of flux balance analysis, we see that metabolic networks can be represented by stoichiometric matrices that relate to reactions and metabolites. These matrices are usually analyzed by algorithms that compute particular sets of routes satisfying specified conditions. For example, a minimal set of reactions that can operate in a steady state forms an elementary mode, while the systemically independent subset of the elementary modes constitutes an extreme pathway. Elementary mode analysis and extreme pathway analysis of metabolic pathways have proved to be valuable tools for assessing the properties and functions of biochemical systems [Pap02, Pap04, ScJ06].

The concept of elementary modes was introduced by Schuster et al. [ScS00]. Generally, a set of linear pathways does not capture the full range of behaviors of a metabolic network. But a set of elementary modes can comprehensively describe all metabolic routes that are both stoichiometrically and thermodynamically feasible for a group of enzymes. Mathematically, an elementary mode is defined as a flux vector $v = (v_1, v_2, \ldots, v_n)^T$ derived from the stoichiometric matrix of a biochemical network by using convex analysis. A flux distribution v determines a pathway in the metabolic network according to the used reactions, namely, those reactions with $v_i \neq 0$, denoted by $P(v)$. An elementary mode should satisfy the quasi-steady-state assumption (9.2). If a reaction i is irreversible, v_i should satisfy the nonnegative constraint $v_i \geq 0$. In particular, an elementary mode v should not be decomposable. In other words, the reaction set that v corresponds to is a minimal set. There is no vector $v'(v' \neq 0, v' \neq v)$ fulfilling the quasi steady-state assumption and nonnegative constraint such that $P(v') \subset P(v)$. These properties uniquely define an elementary mode that can be generated by the convex analysis [ScS00]. For any given network, there is a unique set of elementary modes. According to the nondecomposability of elementary modes, each elementary mode consists of a minimum number of reactions that it needs as a functional unit. If any reaction in an elementary mode were removed, the whole elementary mode could not operate as a functional unit [Pap04, ScS00]. Therefore, there is a set of the smallest subnetworks determined by elementary modes that allows a metabolic network to function in the steady state. Elementary modes can be used to understand cellular objectives for the overall metabolic network, such as by maximizing product yield in amino acid and antibiotic synthesis. Furthermore, elementary mode analysis can be used for reconstruction and consistency checks of metabolism from genome data, analysis of enzyme deficiencies, and drug target identification in metabolic networks [ScS00].

Extreme pathway is a concept similar to elementary mode. In addition to the conditions that an elementary mode should satisfy, an extreme pathway must meet the following two criteria:

1. Flux vectors of extreme pathways are convex basic vectors in the feasible solution space. Therefore, extreme pathways describe all possible steady-state flux distributions that the network can achieve by nonnegative linear combinations of their flux vectors.

2. Each reaction in an extreme pathway must be classified either as exchange flux or as internal reaction. All reversible internal reactions must be split up into two separate, irreversible reactions. Hence, no internal reaction can have a negative flux. This condition ensures that the set of extreme pathways is unique for a given network. Therefore, for any given metabolic network, there is a unique set of extreme pathways.

Figure 9.4 gives examples of elementary modes and extreme pathways in a reaction network. Note that ElMo 1 (ExPa 1) and ElMo 2 (ExPa 2) can be combined to form ElMo 4, so that ELMo 4 is an elementary mode but not an extreme pathway. In conclusion, extreme pathways are a unique and minimal set of convex basis vectors derived from the stoichiometric matrix that completely characterizes the steady-state capabilities of a metabolic network [Pap02]. No extreme pathway can be represented

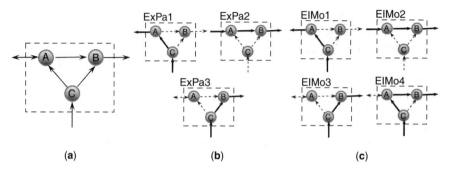

Figure 9.4. Elementary modes and extreme pathways in a reaction network: (a) reaction network; (b) extreme pathways; (c) elementary modes. (Reprinted from [Pap03], © 2003, with permission from Elsevier.)

as a nonnegative linear combination of any other extreme pathways [Pap04]. There are already many methods for studying extreme pathways of metabolic networks. The calculation of extreme pathways is computationally challenging for large networks.

In extreme pathway analysis, singular value decomposition (SVD) works as an efficient technique for extracting information from the stoichiometric matrices of metabolic networks. Famili and Palsson used SVD to define the underlying modes that characterize the overall biochemical conversions in a metabolic network and rank the importance of elementary reactions [Fam03]. For a stoichiometric matrix $S_{m \times n}$, SVD states that there are orthogonal matrices $U_{m \times m}$, $W_{n \times n}$, and a diagonal matrix $\Sigma_{m \times n} = \text{diag}(\sigma_1, \ldots, \sigma_r, 0, \ldots, 0), \sigma_1 \geq \sigma_2 \geq \cdots \geq \sigma_r > 0$ such that $S = U \Sigma W^T$, where the columns of U and W are the left and right singular vectors of matrix S that represent the modes of S. With this decomposition, the dynamic mass balance equation (9.1) has the following form

$$U^T \frac{dx}{dt} = \Sigma W^T v$$

which is equivalent to

$$\frac{du_k^T x}{dt} = \sigma_k w_k^T v \qquad (9.6)$$

where u_k and w_k are the kth left and right singular vectors of S, respectively. Equation (9.6) indicates that a linear combination of metabolites $u_k^T x$ is uniquely moved by a linear combination of metabolic fluxes $w_k^T v$ with the extent of the σ_k. Since the singular vectors of SVD are orthogonal to each other, each of the kth motions in (9.6) is independent from the others. $u_k^T x$ is interpreted as a systemic reaction driven by the linear combination of the reactions $w_k^T v$. These systemic metabolic reactions can be used to describe the function of the metabolic network as a whole and are useful concepts in studying the systems biology of metabolism [Fam03]. Instead of decomposing the stoichiometric matrices of metabolic networks, Price et al. used the SVD of matrices of extreme pathways to develop a conceptual framework for the interpretation of large sets of extreme pathways and the steady-state flux solution space that they defined [Pri03a], and applied the approach to understand regulation of a human red blood cell metabolism [Pri03b].

The common objective of elementary mode and extreme pathway analyses is to extract functionally independent units of a whole metabolic network. We already know that each steady-state flux distribution can be expressed as a linear combination of elementary modes or extreme pathways. However, not all steady states may actually be attainable in a real biological organism. An inverse problem of elementary mode analysis is to study how physiological steady states can be reconstructed from a metabolic network's extreme pathways. A first attempt to solve this problem is the so-called α spectrum [Wib03]. For a given steady-state flux distribution v and a set of n_p extreme pathways whose flux vectors are $p_1, p_2, \ldots, p_{n_p}$, the α-spectrum approach determines the range of possible weights of a particular mode by using linear programming to maximize or minimize the weight of a particular extreme pathway:

$$\text{max} \quad \alpha_i \tag{9.7}$$

$$\text{s.t.} \quad P\alpha = v \tag{9.8}$$

$$0 \le \alpha_j \le 1 \tag{9.9}$$

$$j = 1, 2, \ldots, n_p \tag{9.10}$$

and

$$\text{min} \quad \alpha_i \tag{9.11}$$

$$\text{s.t.} \quad P\alpha = v \tag{9.12}$$

$$0 \le \alpha_j \le 1 \tag{9.13}$$

$$j = 1, 2, \ldots, n_p \tag{9.14}$$

where P is the matrix of $p_1, p_2, \ldots, p_{n_p}$ and α is a vector of weights on the pathway. The ranges of weights reflect to some extent the possibility that an extreme pathway is utilized in a particular flux distribution. A drawback of the α spectrum is that the range of allowable weights for a given extreme pathway is computed separately. This may not be so reasonable since the range of allowable weights for a given extreme pathway is not necessarily independent of the weight value taken by any other extreme pathway [ScJ06]. Wiback et al. presented another approach based on mixed integer linear programming (MILP) to find a minimum number of extreme pathways that are needed to reconstruct a particular flux distribution [Wib03]:

$$\text{min} \quad \sum_{i=1}^{n_p} \beta_i \tag{9.15}$$

$$\text{s.t.} \quad P\alpha = v \tag{9.16}$$

$$0 \le \alpha_i \le \beta_i \tag{9.17}$$

$$\beta_i \in \{0, 1\} \tag{9.18}$$

$$i = 1, 2, \ldots, n_p \tag{9.19}$$

The solution of this MILP model is a set of weights such that a minimum number of extreme pathways are used to obtain the desired flux distribution. It should be noted that this MILP model may not have a unique solution. It may give one of many possible minimum pathway combinations. To overcome these limitations, a quadratic programming is proposed to decompose steady-state flux distributions [ScJ06]:

$$\min \ \sum_{i=1}^{n_p} \alpha_i^2 \tag{9.20}$$

$$\text{s.t.} \quad P\alpha = v \tag{9.21}$$

$$\alpha_i \geq 0 \tag{9.22}$$

$$i = 1, 2, \ldots, n_p \tag{9.23}$$

This model can assign each extreme pathway a unique weight and has been used to study yeast glycolysis metabolism [ScJ06].

9.2.3   Modeling Metabolic Networks

Modeling of biochemical reaction networks has gained much success in the field of metabolic pathways. In addition to FBA and extreme pathway analysis, many other techniques have been developed for studying metabolic systems. Like signaling pathway modeling, metabolic network modeling also contains a set of biochemical reactions including binding, dissociation, complex formation, transfer of molecule groups, phosphorylation, and dephosphorylation. Despite these similarities, there are major differences between signaling and metabolism that lead to some special features in metabolic network modeling. For example, in metabolism, the amount of enzyme and substrate often differs by several orders of magnitude, which makes Michaelis–Menten kinetics suitable for modeling metabolic networks [Kli06]. In contrast, in signaling pathway modeling, mass action kinetics is usually adopted since the numbers of catalyst and substrate molecules are in the same order of magnitude.

Although FBA and extreme pathway analysis are widely used to study metabolic networks, they are actually based on the topological analysis of metabolic networks. There are several public-domain biochemical reaction databases available such as BRENDA, which provides enzymatic reaction kinetics but is insufficient in comparison with a large amount of reaction data. Kinetic modeling is still challenging because of the insufficient number of kinetic parameters. A method that allows quantitative account of the possible dynamics of metabolic systems without prior knowledge of the underlying rate equations and parameters has been proposed [Ste06]. This approach builds on metabolic fluxes and concentrations of metabolic intermediates by using local linear models. Each steady metabolic state is associated with a unique spectrum of dynamic properties, which is defined by the ensemble of all possible kinetic models consistent with the respective state. This strategy represents an intermediate step from flux balance analysis to explicit kinetic models of metabolic systems [Ste06].

The Petri net has widely been used to model the time evolution of metabolite concentrations in a metabolic pathway. In Petri net modeling of metabolic networks, places are generally used to represent reactants, products, or enzymes whereas transitions represent reactions. This formulation gives a simple and intuitive representation of a metabolic network, with the stoichiometric coefficients of the reactions denoted by the arc weights. Figure 9.5 illustrates the Petri net modeling of five types of reactions, where the markings in place nodes represent distribution of the species in the network. The first attempt to use Petri nets for modeling metabolic pathways was made by Reddy et al. [Red93]. Since then, much effort has contributed to further exploration of this approach [Hof94, Vos03, Koc05]. Extensions of the Petri net method, such as colored Petri nets, stochastic Petri nets, and hybrid Petri nets, have also been applied to model a variety of biological pathways. A comprehensive review of Petri net modeling of biological network is given by Chaouiya [Cha07].

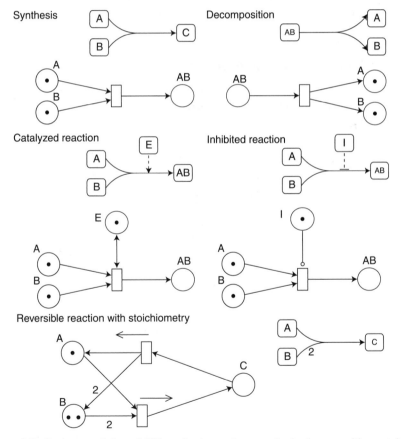

Figure 9.5. Petri net modeling of different basic reactions: synthesis, decomposition, catalysis, inhibition, and a reversible reaction. (Reprinted from [Cha07] © 2007 by permission of Oxford University Press.)

9.3   RECONSTRUCTION OF METABOLIC NETWORKS

Understanding the relationship between the genome and the physiology of an organism is important for elucidating cellular metabolism. Primary metabolic networks can be obtained from available genomic, biochemical, and physiological information [For03]. High-throughput technologies have resulted in a large amount of component data, including metabolites and enzymes, which make it also possible to recover metabolic pathways from this collection [Bea01]. In addition, metabolite profiles, experimental flux profiles, and other types of timecourse data facilitate the reconstruction of metabolic networks by computational methods. Integration of knowledge at different levels in the cascade from genes to proteins and further to metabolic fluxes will be pivotal for understanding how the individual components in the metabolic system interact and influence overall cell functions. Hence, reconstructing metabolic pathways of fully sequenced organisms is a task of major importance. Figure 9.6 gives a general flowchart for reconstruction of genome-scale metabolic networks from available data. In this section, we will introduce several metabolic network reconstruction methods.

9.3.1   Pathfinding Based on Reactions and Compounds

Most approaches for reconstructing metabolic networks rely on databases of already characterized metabolic pathways, enzymes, compounds, reactions, and so on, with the objective to find active metabolic pathways that convert one compound into

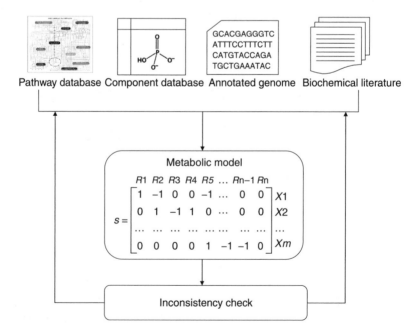

Figure 9.6. Flow chart of reconstruction of a genome-scale metabolic network.

another on the basis of information in these databases. Boyer and Viari formulated the problem of metabolic pathway reconstruction as follows [Boy03]:

> Given a set of biochemical reactions together with their substrates and products, find a sequence of reactions transferring a maximal (or preset) number of atoms between given source compound and sink compound, where the reactions are taken as transfers of atoms between the chemical compounds.

They studied the theoretical complexity of this problem and gave a practical algorithm for solving it. A similar formulation of reconstructing metabolic pathways presented later is as follows: Given a database of reactions and compounds, recover a specific set of reactions and compounds that have been experimentally determined to be active in a metabolic pathway [Bea01]. McShan et al. built a biochemical state space using data from known enzyme-catalyzed transformations, where compounds define the states and transformations between compounds define the state transitions [McS03]. Then, a heuristic search algorithm is designed for searching active metabolic pathways in the biochemical state space. King et al. presented a qualitative reasoning method based on ODE for identifying metabolic pathways [Kin05]. These approaches typically enumerate possible paths satisfying various constraints from the source compound to the target compound and have an underlying problem caused by traversing irrelevant shortcuts through highly connected nodes such as H_2O and NADP. Croes et al. represented a metabolic network as a weighted graph [Cro06], in which compounds are the nodes with a weight denoting the number of reactions that the compound participates in. They proposed a pathway finding procedure to identify the k paths with minimal weight sum between a pair of source and target reaction. This approach circumvents the problem of shortcuts by introducing weights for compounds.

More recently, an efficient optimization model was developed for recovering active metabolic pathways from a source compound to a target compound [Bea01]. Unlike most of other existing methods, this approach does not need to enumerate individual possible paths, and can identify the expected pathway according to some biochemical constraints and certain objective functions. Specifically, assume that there are N_R reactions that totally involve N_C different compounds. The problem is to seek a pathway that transforms Q_S molecules of source compound S into Q_T molecules of target compound T. A binary variable x_r, $r = 1, 2, \ldots, N_R$ is introduced for each reaction to represent if the reaction is active in the pathway. If reaction r is active in the pathway, then $x_r = 1$; otherwise $x_r = 0$. y_r, $r = 1, 2, \ldots, N_R$ is a nonnegative integer variable denoting the number of ticks of reaction r. It is related to x_r in the following way

$$x_r \leq y_r \leq M_1 x_r \qquad (9.24)$$

which indicates that the reaction ticks if and only if it is active in the pathway. M_1 is a large positive constant that represents the maximum number of ticks of any reaction. Let u_{cr} be the number of molecules of compound c used as input in one tick of reaction r, and let p_{cr} be the number of molecules of compound c produced by output of one tick of reaction r. A binary variable b_c is introduced to denote whether compound c

is balanced. Obviously, if $\sum_{r=1}^{N_R} u_{cr} y_r = \sum_{r=1}^{N_R} p_{cr} y_r$, then $b_c = 1$ and 0 otherwise. Similarly, e_c and f_c are binary variables that help determine whether, for the compound c, the number of molecules used is less or more than the number produced. For compound c, it must hold that $b_c + e_c + f_c = 1$. Thus, the following constraints can be formulated:

$$b_c \left(\sum_{r=1}^{N_R} p_{cr} y_r - \sum_{r=1}^{N_R} u_{cr} y_r \right) = 0 \qquad (9.25)$$

$$\frac{\sum_{r=1}^{N_R} p_{cr} y_r - \sum_{r=1}^{N_R} u_{cr} y_r}{M_2} \le e_c \le 1 + \frac{\sum_{r=1}^{N_R} p_{cr} y_r - \sum_{r=1}^{N_R} u_{cr} y_r - 1}{M_2} \qquad (9.26)$$

$$\frac{\sum_{r=1}^{N_R} u_{cr} y_r - \sum_{r=1}^{N_R} p_{cr} y_r}{M_2} \le e_c \le 1 + \frac{\sum_{r=1}^{N_R} u_{cr} y_r - \sum_{r=1}^{N_R} p_{cr} y_r - 1}{M_2} \qquad (9.27)$$

where M_2 is a large positive constant.

These constraints are based on reaction variables and compound variables. In addition, metabolic constraints are needed. To specify the number of molecules of the source compound S and the target compound T, the following constraints are required:

$$\sum_{r=1}^{N_R} u_{Sr} t_r = Q_S, \qquad \sum_{r=1}^{N_R} p_{Tr} t_r = Q_T \qquad (9.28)$$

If the source compound and target compound are different, that is, the pathway is not a cycle, then

$$\sum_{r=1}^{N_R} p_{Sr} t_r = \sum_{r=1}^{N_R} u_{Tr} t_r = 0 \qquad (9.29)$$

which means that none of the source compound is produced and none of the target compound is consumed. In order to distinguish high-presence compounds with low-presence compounds, a measure δ_c is introduced to define the presence percentage of a compound c. It is believed that low-presence compounds correspond to internal reactions and must be balanced, and that high-presence compounds correspond to external reactions and can be produced to excess or balanced [Bea01]. Therefore, it follows that

$$b_c = 1 \quad \text{if } \delta_c < \delta_0, \, c \ne S, T \qquad (9.30)$$

In addition, each reaction active in the pathway is required to have at least one active balance compound as an output, except the reactions producing the target compound T:

$$\sum_{c=1, p_{cr} > 1}^{N_C} b_c \ge x_r \quad \text{for } r \text{ satisfying } p_{Tr} = 0 \qquad (9.31)$$

An additional constraint $x_\alpha + x_\beta \le 1$ is provided for reversible reactions α and β.

There may be more than one feasible solution to these constraints, and therefore an optimization criterion is needed. In the study by Beasley and Planes [Bea01], the total number of reactions involved in the pathway and the number of excess molecules of ATP are combined into two objective functions with different priorities

$$\min M_3 \sum_{r=1}^{N_R} x_r - \left(\sum_{r=1}^{N_R} p_{1r}y_r - \sum_{r=1}^{N_R} u_{1r}y_r \right) \tag{9.32}$$

$$\max M_3 \left(\sum_{r=1}^{N_R} p_{1r}y_r - \sum_{r=1}^{N_R} u_{1r}y_r \right) - \sum_{r=1}^{N_R} x_r \tag{9.33}$$

where M_3 is a large positive constant. Equations (9.32) and (9.33) have the same form, but clearly stress different priorities when M_3 is far from 1. With objective (9.32) or objective (9.33), and all constraints described above, a linear integer optimization model is obtained for recovering a metabolic pathway. Experimental results show that a number of experimentally determined metabolic pathways can be recovered by this optimization model [Bea01].

9.3.2 Stoichiometric Approaches Based on Flux Profiles

Initial metabolic networks can be extracted from available knowledge such as biochemical literature, pathway databases, reaction databases, and genome sequence. However, such initial reconstruction is certainly not flawless. After the initial stage of the reconstruction, a systematic verification should be made in order to ensure that no inconsistencies are present and that all the entries listed are correct and accurate. Manual correction of the imperfections is laborious, and in many cases incorrect predictions cannot be identified by intuitive deduction. There is a clear need for computational methods to reconstruct metabolic networks more accurately according to experimentally measured data. Therefore, another, stoichiometry-based, class of metabolic network reconstruction methods has been developed to check consistency within the metabolic models [Her06a]. Burgard and Maranas introduced an optimization-based framework based on FBA for testing whether experimental flux data are consistent with different objective functions [Bur03a]. Another computational problem for consistency check is to identify the correct active reactions to be included in the metabolic model from a larger set of possible enzymatic reactions by comparing model predictions and experimental data [Her06b]. Herrgard et al. used a bilevel mixed-integer optimization model, adopted from the bilevel programming based gene knockout approach [Bur03b], to identify the optimal network structure given a limited number of experimentally measured metabolic flux profiles:

$$\min_{y} \sum_{i \in M} w_i \left| v_i^{\text{opt}} - v_i^{\text{exp}} \right| \tag{9.34}$$

$$\text{s.t.} \begin{cases} v^{\text{opt}} = \arg \max_v c^T v \\ \quad \text{s.t.} \quad Sv = 0 \\ \qquad\qquad 0 \leq v_j \leq v_j^{\text{max}}, \; j \in F \\ \qquad\qquad 0 \leq v_k \leq v_k^{\text{max}} y_k, \; k \in D \\ \qquad\qquad v_l = v^{\text{exp}}, \; l \in E \end{cases} \qquad (9.35)$$

$$v_{\text{biomass}}^{\text{opt}} \geq v_{\text{biomass}}^{\text{exp}} \qquad (9.36)$$

$$y_k \in \{0, 1\}, \; k \in D \qquad (9.37)$$

$$\sum_{k \in D} (1 - y_k) = K \qquad (9.38)$$

where D is a set of reactions that can be deleted, E is a set of reactions with experimentally measured exchange fluxes, F is a set of all collected reactions, and M is a set of reactions with intracellular fluxes. y_k, $k \in D$ is a binary variable to indicate whether the reaction k is included in the metabolic model. K is the number of allowable deletions. This method is applied to flux data for evolved strains, which provides insights into mechanisms that limit the ability of microbial strains to evolve towards their predicted optimal growth phenotypes [Her06b].

9.3.3 Inferring Biochemical Networks from Timecourse Data

The inference of biochemical networks from timecourse data is one of the main challenges in systems biology. It is based on experimentally measured timecourse data that reflect the dynamic behavior of a metabolic system. Usually a prior biochemical equation is assumed known according to certain kinetics such as the Michaelis–Menten equation, and then kinetic parameters are inferred by minimizing the error between model prediction and experimental observation. The ultimate goal is to quantitatively understand every detail and the principle of metabolic systems. For example, Liu and Wang assume that biochemical networks have a realizable S-system structure and use a multiobjective optimization technique to minimize simultaneously the concentration error, slope error, and interaction measure in order to find a suitable S-system model structure and its corresponding model parameters [LiP08]. Srividhya et al. used mass action kinetics to model biochemical networks and adopted a global nonlinear modeling technique to infer biochemical pathway mechanisms from timecourse data [SrJ07]. Nemenman et al. investigated the ability of reverse-engineering algorithms of transcriptional regulatory networks to reconstruct metabolic networks from high-throughput metabolite profiling data [Nem07]. Although biochemical reactions are believed to reflect certain kinetics, those kinetic equations may not always represent the real phenomena. Sugimoto et al. presented a genetic programming technique to predict both biochemical equations and kinetic parameters from timecourse data [Sug05]. A major advantage of this approach is that it can search network topology and numerical parameters simultaneously, which greatly improves the limit of the required prior knowledge of biochemical equations. For a comprehensive review of inferring biochemical reaction mechanism, one can refer to Crampina's article [Cra04]. As an example, we will introduce the Srividahya et al. approach in detail next.

In contrast to the chemical equilibrium assumption in flux balance analysis, timecourse data from biochemical reactions reveal the transient behavior of the meta-bolic system and contain information on the dynamic interactions among reacting components [SrJ07]. Currently, there are several powerful experimental techniques available to allow the simultaneous measurements of the abundance of multiple metabolites such as NMR, MS, protein kinase phosphorylation, and tissue arrays, which, in turn, can be used for determining the structure of metabolic pathways, specifically, the reaction diagram relating reactants and products. The kinetic model for a metabolic pathway describes the change rate of the concentration x_i of each species

$$\frac{dx_i}{dt} = F_i(x, a_i) \tag{9.39}$$

where a_i is a parameter associated with a specific process. Srividhya et al. modeled a biochemical system by a complete set of polynomial basis functions Φ_j generated from the elementary reactions based on the law of mass action [SrJ07]

$$F_i(x, a_i) = \sum_{j=1}^{K} a_{ij} \Phi_j(x, b) \tag{9.40}$$

where a_{ij} are model parameters denoting the weights of different basis functions. If the parameter b is assumed to be known and the basis functions are kept fixed, the weights a_{ij} can be obtained by using the least-squares method and SVD. However, this approach will encounter too many nonzero weights, which are not biologically plaus-ible. In genuine situations, only a subset of potential reactions (basis functions) are required to model the timecourse data [SrJ07]. Exhaustive search over all combi-nations of K basis functions is clearly impossible as the number of species increases. Srividhya et al. used two model construction approaches to determine basis functions: a specific-to-general approach and a general-to-specific approach [SrJ07].

Any biochemical pathway is composed of a number of elementary reaction steps. Consider a general elementary biochemical reaction

$$n^A A + n^B B \xrightarrow{\lambda} n^C C + n^D D$$

where λ is the rate constant of the reaction and n^A, n^B, n^C, and n^D are the numbers of molecules of reactants A, B, C, and D, respectively. The law of mass action states that the velocity or rate of the reaction shown above is proportional to the product of the concentrations of its reactants

$$v = \lambda(x_A)^{n^A}(x_B)^{n^B} = \lambda\phi(x_A, x_B)$$

where x_A and x_B are the concentrations of the species A and B. Therefore, the change rate of each species is given as follows:

$$\frac{dx_A}{dt} = -n^A v(t), \quad \frac{dx_B}{dt} = -n^B v(t), \quad \frac{dx_C}{dt} = n^C v(t), \quad \frac{dx_D}{dt} = n^D v(t)$$

Assume that in a pathway to be inferred there are K possible elementary reactions. Then, each species k corresponds to a model design matrix of $N \times K$, where N is the number of timepoints

$$\Phi^k = \begin{bmatrix} \sigma_1^k n_1^k \Phi_1(t_1) & \sigma_2^k n_2^k \Phi_2(t_1) & \cdots & \sigma_K^k n_K^k \Phi_K(t_1) \\ \sigma_1^k n_1^k \Phi_1(t_2) & \sigma_2^k n_2^k \Phi_2(t_2) & \cdots & \sigma_K^k n_K^k \Phi_K(t_2) \\ \vdots & \vdots & \vdots & \vdots \\ \sigma_1^k n_1^k \Phi_1(t_N) & \sigma_2^k n_2^k \Phi_2(t_N) & \cdots & \sigma_K^k n_K^k \Phi_K(t_N) \end{bmatrix} \quad (9.41)$$

where n_i^k is the number of molecules of species k in the ith reaction (only for those reactions in which species k takes part, n_i^k is nonzero). $\sigma_i^k \in \{-1, 1\}$ depending on the species k is a reactant or product. The overall matrix for a biochemical pathway is a concatenation of such matrices for each M species, which represents a complete dictionary of basis functions. However, the connectivity of a genuine pathway involves only a small subset of this complete dictionary. The next step of the approach is to apply the iterative model selection method to deduce the biochemical mechanism [SrJ07]. The methodology described above has been applied to reconstruct the chemical reaction steps and connectivity of the glycolytic pathway of *Lactococcus lactis* from timecourse experimental data.

9.4 DRUG TARGET DETECTION IN METABOLIC NETWORKS

High-throughput techniques produce massive data on a genomewide scale, which has pushed pharmaceutical research into a rapid development phase. Drug target discovery, which aims to rapidly and accurately identify drug targets, is a crucial step in the drug discovery process and also plays a vital role in new therapeutics. It is generally believed that most drugs are inhibitors that block the action of particular target proteins or enzymes. Since proteins or enzymes often interact with each other together and with other compounds in cells to form a metabolic network, the systems biology approach or network-based analysis is essential to gain insight into key biomedical processes [Cas02, Gui07, Yil07]. There have already been some efforts to rank the essentiality of enzymes to uncover drug targets by analyzing the topology structures of metabolic networks [Jeo01, Pal05, Gui07]. However, all of these studies have yielded only modest results. On the other hand, if some components other than the intended targets are affected in a metabolic network, toxicity or lack of efficacy will arise. In other words, a good drug should be potent and specific; that is, it must have powerful effects on specific compounds or biological pathways with minimal effects on all other components of the network. Drug research in post-genomic-era stresses on the identification of specific biological targets or gene products, such as enzymes or proteins for drugs, which can be manipulated to produce the desired effect of curing a disease with minimal disruptive side effects.

Sridhar et al. proposed a drug target detection model [Sri07, Sri08], in which a set of enzymes (drug targets) can be found to inhibit the target compounds and meanwhile reduce the side effects (nontarget compounds). In 2007 they presented a scalable iterative algorithm that computes a suboptimal solution in a heuristic manner within reasonable timebounds [Sri07]; in 2008 they developed a branch-and-bound algorithm named OPMET to explore the search space dynamically [Sri08], but this algorithm requires intense computation for large-scale metabolic systems. In order to solve the drug target discovery problem more accurately and efficiently, Li et al. proposed a novel approach to exactly formulate this problem as an integer linear programming (ILP) model [LiZ09], which ensures that optimal solutions can be easily found without any heuristic manipulations. Numerical results show that the ILP approach can identify the optimal drug targets in an exact and efficient manner [LiZ09]. The running time of the ILP is almost at the same level as that of its LP relaxation. Therefore, it can be applied to large-scale systems, including the whole metabolic networks from various organisms. We will introduce this approach in the following section.

9.4.1 Drug Target Detection Problem

It is well known that enzymes play important roles in the whole metabolism system of a living organism. However, the malfunctions of some enzymes may lead to an accumulation of certain undesired compounds, and thereby may result in diseases [Cas02]. Such compounds are generally considered as target compounds because they are directly related to the diseases. On the other hand, those enzymes are considered as drug targets because undesired compounds will not be produced if they are inhibited by drugs. The remaining compounds in the metabolic system are all considered as nontarget compounds. Hence, the drug target detection problem is to identify an enzyme set that can be manipulated by drugs to prevent the excess production of all target compounds, while nontarget compounds are affected minimally [Sri07, Sri08]. The number of nontarget compounds whose production is stopped by the inhibition of the enzyme set is defined as a "damage" of the corresponding enzyme set.

In order to facilitate the identification of drug targets, a metabolic network can be reformulated as a Boolean directed graph [Sri07]. The node set of this graph consists of all reactions (R), compounds (C), and enzymes (E), whereas edges represent the relationships between them. There is a directed edge from an enzyme to a reaction if and only if this enzyme catalyzes the reaction. Similarly, a directed edge links a chemical compound to a reaction if and only if the compound is the reactant of the reaction. A directed edge from a reaction to a compound denotes that the compound is produced by the reaction. As an illustrative example of such a model, consider a set of reactions as follows

$$R1: \quad C5 \xrightarrow{E1} C1 + C2 \tag{9.42}$$

$$R2: \quad C6 \xrightarrow{E1} C2 + C3 + C4 \tag{9.43}$$

$$R3: \quad C8 \xrightarrow{\text{E2}} C5 \tag{9.44}$$

$$R4: \quad C9 \xrightarrow{\text{E3}} C5 \tag{9.45}$$

$$R5: \quad C9 \xrightarrow{\text{E1}} C6 + C7 \tag{9.46}$$

whose reformulated metabolic network along with its adjacency matrix is shown in Figure 9.7. In this figure, circles, rectangles, and triangles denote compounds, reactions, and enzymes, respectively. C1 is the target compound. In order to stop the production of C1, R1 must be prevented from taking place. R1 has two reactants, E1 and C5, and therefore there are two possible solutions to inhibit R1. One is to disrupt its catalyzing enzyme E1, which incurs a damage of 5 (i.e., C2, C3, C4, C6, C7) (see Fig. 9.7b). The dotted lines indicate removal of the subgraph because of inhibition of enzyme E1. The other lines indicate that production of its reactant compound C5 should stop. To stop the production of C5, the enzyme combination that is indirectly responsible for its production (E2 and E3) should be inhibited. The combined damage of E2 and E3 is one compound, namely, C2. The optimal solution is the enzyme combination whose disruption causes minimum damage to the network (E2 and E3 in this case).

9.4.2   Integer Linear Programming Model

Define R, C, and E to be the sets of reactions, compounds and enzymes in a metabolic network, respectively. Let T be the set of target compounds, $T \subset C$. The reformulated network is denoted by $G(V, \bar{E})$, where $V = R + E + C$, and $\bar{E}$ is defined by the adjacency matrix $A = [A(v_i, v_j)]$, where $A(v_i, v_j) = 1$ denotes that there is a directed edge from vertex v_i to vertex v_j, and $A(v_i, v_j) = 0$ otherwise, where $v_i, v_j \in V$. The drug

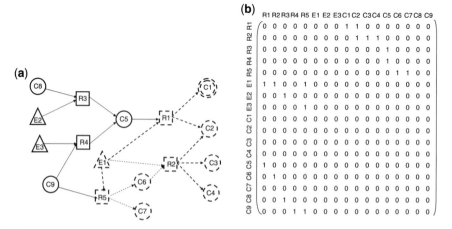

Figure 9.7. An illustrative metabolic network: (a) a small hypothetical metabolic network; (b) the adjacency matrix of the reformulated metabolic network.

target identification in a metabolic network is such an optimization problem, that is, given a metabolic network $G(V, \bar{E})$ and a set of target compounds T $(T \subset C)$, find a set of enzymes in E such that the inhibition of these enzymes will halt the production of all the compounds in T while stopping the production of the least compounds not in T.

Let x_{R_i} be a binary variable, where $x_{R_i} = 0$ indicates that the ith reaction is inhibited, and $x_{R_i} = 1$ otherwise. Similarly, binary variable x_{E_j} denotes whether the jth enzyme is inhibited, and x_{C_k} denotes whether the kth compound is inhibited. According to the goal of the drug target detection problem described above, from the viewpoint of optimization, the problem can be formulated as an integer linear programming (ILP) as follows [LiZ09]:

$$\max_{x_{R_i}, x_{E_j}, x_{C_k}} z = \sum_{k=1}^{N_C} x_{C_k} \qquad (9.47)$$

$$\text{s.t.} \quad x_{R_i} \leq x_{E_j} \quad \text{for } A(E_j, R_i) = 1 \qquad (9.48)$$

$$x_{R_i} \leq x_{C_k} \quad \text{for } A(C_k, R_i) = 1 \qquad (9.49)$$

$$1 - x_{R_i} \leq \sum_{j=1}^{N_E} A(E_j, R_i)(1 - x_{E_j}) + \sum_{k=1}^{N_C} A(C_k, R_i)(1 - x_{C_k}) \qquad (9.50)$$

$$x_{C_k} \leq \sum_{i=1}^{N_R} A(R_i, C_k) x_{R_i} \quad \text{for } \sum_{i=1}^{N_R} A(R_i, C_k) \geq 1 \qquad (9.51)$$

$$x_{R_i} \leq x_{C_k} \qquad \qquad \text{for } A(R_i, C_k) = 1 \qquad (9.52)$$

$$x_{C_k} = 0 \qquad \qquad \text{for } C_k \in T \qquad (9.53)$$

$$x_{C_k} = 1 \qquad \qquad \text{for } \sum_{i=1}^{N_R} A(R_i, C_k) = 0 \qquad (9.54)$$

$$x_{R_i}, x_{E_j}, x_{C_k} \in \{0, 1\} \qquad (9.55)$$

$$i = 1, 2, \ldots, N_R, \quad j = 1, 2, \ldots, N_E, \quad k = 1, 2, \ldots, N_C \qquad (9.56)$$

Here, N_R, N_E, and N_C denote the numbers of reactions, enzymes, and compounds in the metabolic network, respectively. The objective in this model is to maximize the number of noninhibited compounds, or equivalently, minimize the damage. Constraints (9.48) and (9.49) mean that for every reactant compound or enzyme in the reaction R_i, if that reaction is active, all of its reactant compounds and enzymes must not be inhibited. Constraint (9.50) implies that if reaction R_i is inhibited, then at least one of its reactant compounds or enzymes is inhibited. Constraint (9.51) means that if a compound is not inhibited, then at least one reaction producing this compound is active. Constraint (9.52) indicates that if a compound is inhibited, then all reactions producing this compound must be inhibited. Constraint (9.53) implies

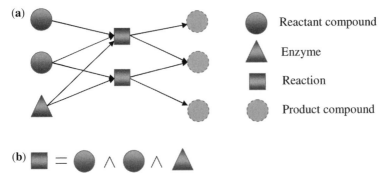

(b)

It corresponds to constraints (7), (8), (9), implying that a reaction is inhibited if and only if at least one of its reactant compounds is inhibited

(c)

It corresponds to constraints (10), (11), implying that a product compound is inhibited if and only if all the reactions producing it are inhibited

Figure 9.8. Graphical illustration of the integer linear programming model: (a) a hypothetical metabolic network; (b) relationship between reactant compounds, enzymes, and reactions; (c) relationship between one product compound and all the reactions producing it.

that all target compounds must be inhibited, whereas constraint (9.54) indicates that all compounds without reaction producing them must not be inhibited. Figure 9.8b illustrates the logical relationships between a reaction and its reactant compounds [i.e., constraints (9.48)–(9.50)], and Figure 9.8c illustrates the logical relationships between a product compound and the reactions producing it [i.e., constraints (9.51) and (9.52)].

The ILP model described above works in reverse (or backward) to detect drug targets. In order to inhibit the target compounds [constraint (9.53)], the model inhibits all the reactions producing these compounds by using constraint (9.52). To inhibit the reactions, the model searches an enzyme or a set of enzymes that must be inhibited. Through the biochemical logic relationships between reactions, enzymes, and compounds, a set of enzymes that incur minimal damage is determined, along with the routes from the drug targets to target compounds. It is believed that the potential of an enzyme to be an effective drug target is related to its essentiality in the corresponding metabolic network [Jeo01]. The essentiality of an enzyme can be reflected to some extent by the enzyme's topological centrality in the network. Actually, the damage of inhibiting an enzyme has been used as an indicator of enzyme essentiality [PaM05], which means that the enzymes with larger damages tend to be essential. The model described above can also be used to predict essential enzymes by determining their damage. This is achieved by replacing constraint (9.53) with $x_{E_j} = 0$ to compute the damage of the jth enzymes. For this case, the model works in a forward way.

Inhibiting the enzyme stops some reactions, which in turn inhibit some compounds. By optimizing the ILP model, a damage is calculated for the enzyme. In order to evaluate the running time and solution nature of the ILP model (9.47)–(9.56), its LP relaxation with $x \in [0, 1]$, deduced from the ILP by dropping integer constraints, is adopted.

9.4.3 Numerical Validation

The ILP approach was tested on both *E. coli* and *H. sapiens* metabolic networks [LiZ09]. *E. coli* metabolic network information was extracted from KEGG Pathway [Kan00]. Drugs were extracted from KEGG Drug, and the corresponding *H. sapiens* metabolic pathways were also from KEGG Pathway. The test data consist of both simulated target compound data and real target compound data. For the simulated data, as in the paper by Sridhar et al. [Sri07], for each *E. coli* metabolic pathway, query sets with sizes of one, two and four target compounds are constructed by randomly choosing compounds from those pathways. Each query set contains 10 queries, and the computational results are averaged on 10 queries. For real target compounds, drug entries in KEGG Drug that provide drug targets, metabolic pathways and expected target compounds are selected. Note that only entries that provide all of the required information can be used as test examples.

9.4.3.1 Escherichia coli *Pathways*
To basically evaluate the efficiency of ILP algorithm, experiments on simulated target compound data were first conducted [LiZ09]. The *E. coli* pathway datasets in the paper by Sridhar et al. [Sri07] were used to perform experiments. Specifically, for each pathway, target compound sets with sizes of one, two and four target compounds are constructed, by randomly choosing compounds from that network. Then, the ILP algorithm is used to determine the optimal enzyme set (drug targets) to eliminate the given set of target compounds with minimal damage. In addition to directly solving the ILP model, the LP relaxation is also used to identify drug targets. The comparison results between ILP and its relaxation are shown in Figure 9.9.

The experimental results in Figure 9.9 show that the ILP algorithm is an efficient, exact algorithm and can always find global optimal solutions in less than 1 s for the networks with no more than 1000 nodes. Furthermore, the computation was also conducted on the entire metabolic network (pathway ID: 22), which has 537 enzymes, 988 compounds, and 1970 reactions. The ILP algorithm obtained optimal solutions in no more than 3 s for this network with more than 3000 nodes. Figure 9.9a depicts the average CPU time of solving LP and ILP, respectively. Interestingly, the running time of the ILP model and its LP relaxation are almost the same. The reason underlying this phenomenon is that an optimal solution obtained by the LP is an integer solution in most cases. Hence, not many branching implementations are needed in the branch-and-bound process to solve the ILP. Such numerical results demonstrate that the ILP algorithm is a very efficient, exact algorithm for the drug target detection problem. The average damages returned by the ILP and the LP are compared and shown in Figure 9.9b. We can see that the average damages computed by LP and ILP have

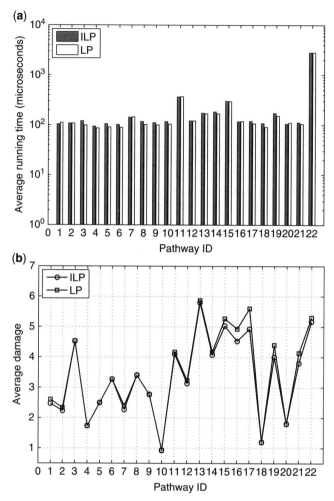

Figure 9.9. Comparison of LP and ILP on various metabolic pathways in terms of implementing CPU time and average damage.

no distinct differences, which means that the LP relaxation is also an exact algorithm in most cases and can be used for solving drug target detection problems efficiently without sacrificing the accuracy [LiZ09].

In addition, in order to test the running time of the ILP with the increased number of target compounds, some target compound sets are generated with the number of target compounds ranging from 10 to 100 by using the entire *E. coli* metabolic network. Figure 9.10 depicts the experiment results of both LP and ILP. Figure 9.10a shows that the average running time of LP decreases as the number of target compounds increase, while the running time of the ILP does not have this tendency. On the other hand, Figure 9.10b shows that the average damages computed by LP and ILP

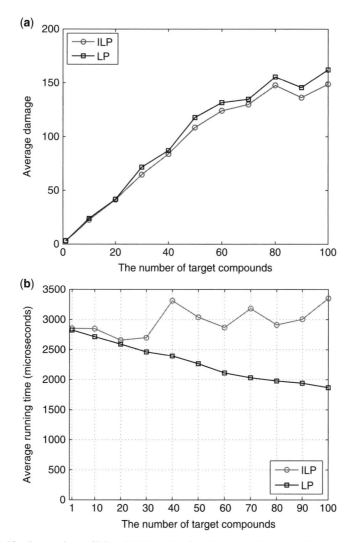

Figure 9.10. Comparison of LP and ILP on *E. coli* entire metabolic network in terms of implementing CPU time and average damage.

both increase with the number of target compounds, which means that the inhibition of more target compounds may result in elimination of more nontarget compounds. This explains that the drugs for complex diseases may have more side effects.

9.4.3.2 Homo sapiens *Pathways* KEGG Drug contains known drug molecules along with the enzymes that they inhibit and their therapeutic categories. In KEGG, each drug, compound, or enzyme is assigned to a unique identifier with the letter D, C, or E, respectively. Benoxaprofen (D03080) and rasagiline mesylate (D02562) have been used as benchmarks [Sri08]. Besides these drugs, some other drugs and metabolic pathways are selected as test examples to evaluate whether the ILP model can correctly recognize the drug targets [LiZ09].

Benoxaprofen (D03080) is a drug that inhibits arachidonate-5-lipoxygenase (EC 1.13.11.34). This enzyme appears in several metabolic pathways, including arachidonic acid metabolism (hsa00590). In pharmacology, the biosynthesis of LTB4, LTC4, LTD4, and LTE4 will decrease when 5-lipoxygenase is inhibited. According to the ILP model, removal of 5-lipoxygenase eliminates eight compounds, including three target compounds: LTB4, LTC4, and LTD4. The other five compounds are 5(S)-HPETE, 5-HETE, LTA4, 20-OH-LTB4, and 9(S)-HPOD. In other words, the damage of drug target 5-lipoxygenase is 5. When LTB4, LTC4, LTD4, and LTE4 are selected as the target compound set, LTA4H (EC 3.3.2.6) and LTC4 synthase (EC 4.4.1.20) consist of the optimal enzyme set. The inhibition of these enzymes eliminates only one nontarget compound, 20-OH-LTB4, which means that the damage of enzymes LTA4H (EC 3.3.2.6) and LTC4 synthase (EC 4.4.1.20) is 1, that is, one compound. This drug target is better than that of the existing drug target set. More recent research revealed that the levels of LTA4H and LTC4 really affect the antiinflammatory drug [Sri08].

Rasagiline mesylate (D02562) is an antiparkinsonian drug that inhibits monoamine oxidase B (MAO-B) (EC 1.4.3.4). In the histidine metabolism network (hsa00340), the removal of amine oxidase eliminates the compounds methylimidazole acetaldehyde and methylimidazoleacetic acid according to the ILP model. Levels of pros-methylimidazoleacetic acid affect the severity of Parkinson's disease in patients. When selecting methylimidazoleacetic acid and methylimidazole acetaldehyde as the target compounds, the ILP algorithm can find amine oxidase as the optimal target. This implies that rasagiline mesylate targets the optimal enzyme EC 1.4.3.4. In addition, the drug micafungin sodium (D02465) is β-1,3-glucan synthesis inhibitor, and its therapeutic activity is treatment of *Aspergillus* and *Candida* fungal infections. In the starch–sucrose metabolic pathway, the ILP model correctly detected EC 2.4.1.34 as the drug target of micafungin sodium [LiZ09].

The drug febuxostat (D01206) is a xanthine dehydrogenase (EC 1.17.1.4) and xanthine oxidase (EC 1.17.3.2) inhibitor. Its therapeutic activity is management of hyperuricemia in patients with gout. Urate is a compound whose excess causes hyperuricemia. In the purine metabolism network (hsa00230), there are chemical reactions that produce urate. By selecting urate as the target compound, the ILP model identified three enzymes as a target enzyme set (EC 1.17.1.4, EC 1.17.3.2, and EC 2.4.2.16) which consist of two real targets and one additional target, EC 2.4.2.16. The urate–ribonucleotide phosphorylase EC 2.4.2.16 is an enzyme that also catalyzes a chemical reaction producing urate. Hence, in order to entirely inhibit urate, the model also selected EC 2.4.2.16 as a drug target.

In addition to the drugs mentioned above, other drugs were used as test examples [LiZ09]. The ID of these drugs, corresponding metabolic pathways, drug targets, and intended target compounds are listed in Table 9.3, where in the last column, "No" implies that the ILP model identified a drug target set different from that in KEGG. "Yes" indicates that the model identified a drug target set identical to the real one; "Part" denotes that the detected target set includes the real one but with additional

TABLE 9.3. List of Drug Targets for Some Drugs Detected by ILP Approach with Validation (Vd) Status

Drugs	Pathways	Drug Targets	Target Compounds	Vd
D00155	hsa00230	EC 3.5.4.4	Deoxyinosine	Yes
D00222	hsa00240	EC 2.7.7.7	DNA polymerase	Yes
D00285	hsa00670, hsa00790	EC 1.5.1.3	Folate	Yes
D00321	hsa00150	EC 1.3.99.5	5α-Dihydrotestosterone	Yes
D00401	hsa00350	EC 1.11.1.8	L-Thyroxine	Yes
D00410	hsa00150	EC 1.1.1.146	Adrenosterone	Yes
D00939	hsa00900	EC 2.5.1.21	Squalene	Yes
D01064	hsa00240	EC 2.1.1.45	dTMP	Part
D01206	hsa00230	EC 1.17.1.4 EC 1.17.3.2	Urate	Part
D01683	hsa00590	EC 5.3.99.5	Thromboxane A2 (TXA2)	Yes
D02418	hsa00564	EC 3.1.1.7	Choline	Part
D02465	hsa00500	EC 2.4.1.34	β-1,3-Glucan	Yes
D02562	hsa00340	EC 1.4.3.4	Methylimidazoleacetaldehyde, methylimidazoleacetic acid	Yes
D02755	hsa00430	EC 2.3.2.2	5-Glutamyltaurine	Yes
D03010	hsa00591	EC 1.13.11.34	9-HpODE	Yes
D03080	hsa00590	EC 3.3.2.6, EC 4.4.1.20	LTB4, LTC4, LTD4, LTE4	No
D04498	hsa00120	EC 1.3.99.5	7α,12α-Dihydroxy-5-α-cholestan-3-one	Yes
D04793	hsa00330	EC 1.14.11.2	*trans*-4-Hydroxy-D-proline	Part
D05032	hsa00600	EC 2.4.1.80	Glucosylceramide	Part
D05292	hsa00071	EC 2.3.1.21	L-Palmitoylcarnitine	Yes

Source: Li et al. [LiZ09].

drug targets. For most drugs that can act as test examples, the ILP algorithm found the same target enzymes and actual drug targets.

9.4.3.3 Damage and Essentiality of Enzymes
The potential of an enzyme to be an effective drug target is related to its essentiality in the corresponding metabolic network [Jeo01], which, in turn, can be reflected to some extent by its topological centrality in the network. The importance of enzyme is examined in the entire *E. coli* metabolic network by using the ILP model to determine the damage of each enzyme [LiZ09]. The enzymes are sorted according to the degree of damage and the fraction of essential enzymes in each group is determined, as is summarized in Figure 9.11. The result demonstrates that with the increasing damage of enzymes, their fraction in essential category also increases, which indicates that the damage can be a quantitative measure of enzyme importance to some extent and used for identifying novel potential targets. A widely used p-value formula is

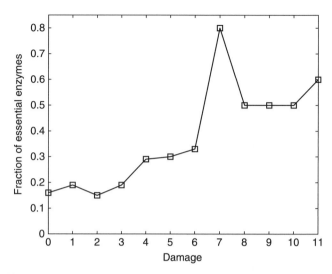

Figure 9.11. Fraction of essential enzymes plotted against enzymes with certain damage.

employed to evaluate the significance of the correlation between damage and essentiality of enzyme [LiZ09]

$$P = 1 - \sum_{k=0}^{N} \binom{n}{k} p^k (1 - p)^{n-k} \tag{9.57}$$

where n is the number of enzymes with certain damage, N is the number of essential enzymes in this set, and p is the probability that a randomly selected enzyme is essential. This formula reflects the probability of finding at least N essential enzymes in an enzyme set of size n by chance. Obviously, the smaller the p value is, the more significant the correlation between damage and essentiality. The p value of the number of essential enzymes in the group of enzymes with damage no less than 7 is 1.21×10^{-5}, which indicates that the result is significant.

The goal of the drug target identification problem discussed above is to minimize the damage brought by the inhibition of a set of enzymes. However, it does not consider how many targets the drug needs. In other words, even two enzyme combinations with different numbers of enzymes may perform in the same way on the target compounds. Actually, an integer goal linear programming model can handle such a case, by minimizing the damage as the goal with the highest priority and the number of enzymes as the lower priority. In addition, the drug target problem discussed in this section may be ideal without detailed structural information on drugs and targets. The model can be further incorporated with flux balance analysis, 3D structure of drugs and enzymes, and other metabolism information to solve the problem from a pharmaceutical perspective.

9.5 SUMMARY

Compared with other types of biomolecular networks, the structure of metabolic networks is quite complex and diverse since it involves various heterogeneous compounds, proteins, and reactions. In this chapter, we introduced some elementary concepts of metabolic networks and related topics including metabolic network analysis, modeling, identification, and applications. Nowadays, owing to rapid progress on biotechnology, huge amounts of biological data are increasingly available, and thus it becomes realistic to determine genome-scale biochemical reactions in many living organisms. Therefore, more sophisticated computational methods and efficient tools are needed in the field of metabolic networks to analyze the metabolism mechanism in a more accurate and detailed manner. In addition, we introduced a drug target detection method. Although that method gives an archetypal model, it can act as a basis for more refined practical models, which are expected to play critical roles in pharmaceutics.

CHAPTER 10

SIGNALING NETWORKS: MODELING AND INFERENCE

10.1 SIGNAL TRANSDUCTION IN CELLULAR SYSTEMS

Living cells utilize a complex collection of interacting chemicals and molecules to receive different signals from the cellular environment and other cells. Such processes are known collectively as signal transduction. Signal transduction is an important part of cell system communication that governs basic cellular activities and coordinates cell actions [ChL05, Zho05]. It is a primary mechanism for maintaining equilibrium between the cell and its surroundings, and allows a cell to react to events outside the cell membrane. Many cellular decisions such as proliferation, differentiation, development, and other responses to external stimuli are achieved by signal transduction. The ability of cells to sense and respond to their microenvironment is crucial for adaptation, survival, and immunity. Abnormality in cellular signal transduction is responsible for diseases such as cancer, autoimmunity, and diabetes. Therefore, understanding cell signaling is very helpful for treating complex diseases effectively [Kra99, Fin03].

Signal transduction processes are activated by multiple extracellular factors as well as cell membrane receptors. Most processes of signal transduction involve the ordered sequences of biochemical reactions inside the cell, which result in a signal transduction pathway. Generally, it consists of a set of chemical reactions carried out by enzymes and activated by second messengers, which transfer a chemical or an external signal from outside the cell to produce a response in the cell. This

---

Biomolecular Networks. By Luonan Chen, Rui-Sheng Wang, and Xiang-Sun Zhang
Copyright © 2009 John Wiley & Sons, Inc.

process involves an interaction between a signaling molecule and a receptor, the transduction of the signal via a responder within the cell, and an effect on the function of the cell [Sad07]. Figure 10.1 gives a coarse-grained view of a signal transduction process, which demonstrates that signaling transduction has three principal stages: (1) signaling molecules bind to an extracellular receptor—these events occur around the membrane; (2) intracellular enzymes are autophosphorylated, and the signal is amplified and passed to the cytoplasm, then to the nucleus and further to genes through a series of biochemical reactions that link submembrane events; and (3) cells respond to the signal by changing cellular function, which is often manifested by increased expression of some genes. These events lead to gene transcription by activated transcription factors.

Although various signaling mechanisms account for different cellular functions, many signal transduction pathways share common essential components such as membrane receptors, G proteins, small G proteins, signal-regulated kinase (ERK), and mitogen-activated protein kinase (MAPK). Cells respond to signals by specific receptor proteins that can bind those signals. Most receptors of signaling pathways are transmembrane proteins. In some cases, receptor activation caused by ligand binding to a receptor is directly coupled to the cell's response to the ligand. Such direct transduction is a function of the receptor itself and occurs at the plasma membrane. However, for many cell surface receptors, ligand–receptor interactions are not directly linked to the cell's response. Such indirect transduction involves a second messenger. The activated receptor must first interact with other proteins inside the cell before the ultimate physiological effect of the ligand on the cell's behavior is produced. Depending on the nature of its signaling ligand, a receptor may be located in the plasma membrane or in the cytoplasm of the target cell [Sad07]. Receptors located in the

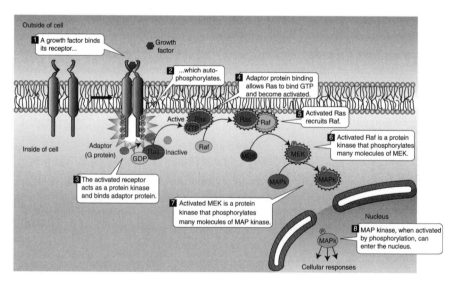

Figure 10.1. Coarse-grained view of signal transduction. (Reprinted from [Sad06] © (2006), with permission of Sinauer Associates, Inc.)

plasma membrane include ion channels, protein kinases, and G-protein-linked receptors. Receptors that are solely intracellular include those for steroid hormones, thyroid hormone, retinoic acid, and derivatives of vitamin D_3. Cells can regulate the number and activity of specific receptors when they respond to a signal by production, degradation, and phosphorylation of serine/threonine.

After the binding of signaling molecules to a receptor, the next step in signal transduction is often the activation of G proteins. G-protein-coupled receptors are important components of signal transduction pathways. The G-protein complex is a heterotrimer and consists of subunits α, β, γ. In the inactive state of G proteins, the α subunit is bound to guanosine diphosphate (GDP). On activation, the G protein exchanges GDP for a guanosine triphosphate (GTP), which causes the G protein to dissociate from the receptor and split into two subunits: a β, γ complex and a GDP-bound α subunit. These subunits can transmit the signal to downstream processes. As soon as the GTP is hydrolyzed to GDP, the subunits can reassociate to form the initial heterotrimeric G protein. These are all the chemical transformations for G-protein signaling. There are also small G proteins such as Ras, Rho, Rab, Ran, and Arf, which belong to the Ras superfamily of small GTPases. They also bind GTP and GDP and are involved in signal transduction. Guanine exchange factor (GEF) catalyzes the transformation from the GDP state to the GTP state, while the reverse process is facilitated by a GTPase-activating protein (GAP), which induces hydrolysis of the bound GTP. In addition, extracellular signal-regulated kinase (ERK) and classical mitogen-activated protein kinase (MAPK) are the most widely expressed protein kinase intracellular signaling molecules. MAPK is involved in the action of most nonnuclear oncogenes and responsible for cell response to growth factors such as BDNF or nerve growth factor. MAPK cascades consist of three or four different proteins that specifically catalyze the phosphorylation of the subsequent kinases under consumption of ATP. Extracellular stimuli lead to activation of a MAP kinase via MAPK cascade composed of MAPK, MAP kinase kinase (MKK or MAP2K), and MAP kinase kinase kinase (MKKK or MAP3K). In some cases, the members of a signaling cascade form complexes with scaffold proteins that bring together various other proteins in a signaling pathway and allow for their interactions. By binding the kinases, scaffolds can ensure the physical vicinity or even the correct molecular orientation, recruit downstream effectors in a pathway and enhance specificity of the signal. In other words, although signaling pathways contain common components, they often appear to be separated in transferring signals with speciality.

Signaling pathways interact and communicate with one another to form complex networks in living systems known as signaling networks. Such networks are complex systems in their organization and often too complicated to be assimilated, organized, and analyzed by the human mind. Analysis of cellular signaling networks requires a combination of experimental and theoretical approaches, including the development of proper models and the generation of quantitative data. Traditional work in biology has focused on studying individual parts of cell signaling pathways. Systems biology research helps us understand the underlying structure of signaling networks and how changes in these networks may affect the transmission and flow of information from a system-level perspective [Kra99, Gom02]. In particular, with the large amount of

TABLE 10.1. List of Signal Transduction Databases

Databases	Websites
SPAD	http://www.grt.kyushu-u.ac.jp/spad/index.html
KEGG	http://www.genome.jp/kegg
DOQCS	http://doqcs.ncbs.res.in/doqcs
BBID	http://bbid.grc.nia.nih.gov
BioCarta	http://www.biocarta.com
NetPath	http://www.netpath.org
MiST	http://genomics.ornl.gov/mist
TRANSPATH	http://www.biobase-international.com
STCDB	http://bibiserv.techfak.uni-bielefeld.de/stcdb
aMAZE	http://www.scmbb.ulb.ac.be/amaze
BioModels	www.ebi.ac.uk/biomodels
DOQCS	doqcs.ncbs.res.in
CellML	www.cellml.org/models

high-throughput data available, "omic" approaches are popular for the global analysis of cell signaling, such as gene expression profiling, protein–protein interaction screening, protein microarrays, mass spectroscopy, and gene disruption [ZhuH02]. For example, Roberts et al. used yeast expression microarrays to monitor signal transduction during the yeast pheromone response [Rob00]. By analyzing genes expressed during the yeast mating response and comparing expression profiles of many different mutants in the MAPK signaling pathways, they precisely identified signaling components required for pheromone response and/or filamentous pathways.

Table 10.1 lists some signal transduction databases depositing experimentally determined signaling molecules and signaling pathways. Despite the success of experimental methods in detecting components involved in signaling networks, they can generate only specific linear signaling pathways. The functions and mechanisms of complex signaling networks and their internal interactions still remain unclear. Therefore, it is necessary to develop new computational methods to capture the details of signaling pathways by exploiting high-throughput genomic and proteomic data. In contrast to experimental approaches, in the remaining sections, we will mainly introduce mathematical and computational methods for modeling signaling pathways and inferring signal transduction networks from available experimental data.

10.2 MODELING OF SIGNAL TRANSDUCTION PATHWAYS

Cells are dynamic systems consisting of a large set of dynamic processes. It is the dynamic interactions of gene products and other molecules, rather than individual components, that give rise to biological functions. Signal transduction is also achieved by such dynamic protein interactions and ligand–receptor interactions. There are several ways to monitor the activity of signal transduction pathways. For instance, at the genetic level, large-scale timecourse experimental data for mRNAs can be obtained using microarrays, which form the basis for dynamic pathway modeling; whereas at the protein level, the concentrations for proteins can be measured from proteomics technologies and are able to provide detailed information on the dynamical behavior of each functional component in the signaling network. Modeling of signal transduction pathways is an important topic in systems biology that is attracting increasing attention of researchers from both experimental and theoretical fields. It helps integrate experimental knowledge into a raw model used to test the hypothesis regarding the underlying biological mechanisms [Kli06]. The raw model is, in turn, improved because of new experimentation. In this way, model development and experimental design are synergistically improved and iteratively refined.

So far, there have been many contributions to research on modeling signal transduction networks from a variety of viewpoints. To simulate the dynamic interactions and transient behavior in signal transduction, most of the mathematical models have been based on preexisting data such as concentrations, reaction kinetics, flux measurements, and microscopic images. Changes in these factors reflect the behavior of signal transduction indirectly. Different mathematical models are used to describe such changes. A model can be deterministic, such as ordinary differential equations (ODEs), or probabilistic, such as stochastic differential equations [ChL05, Zho05]. It can be discrete with respect to component abundance such as stochastic process with molecule numbers as dynamic variables, or continuous with compound concentrations as states [ChL05, Zho05]. In addition the Petri net, Boolean networks [LiS06], Bayesian methods, and partial differential equations have also been used to model signaling pathways. The choice of a model depends on the system, the available information, and the specific questions to be studied [Kli06]. The model parameters are usually estimated from available experimental data or obtained by information from the literature. Signal transduction is a complex process, which makes exact modeling or complete reconstruction of a signaling network almost impossible in many cases. In order to retrieve its cellular dynamics, there are still numerous hurdles such as identifying network topologies, and estimating model parameters [Cho03]. Scarcity of available data sets makes the problem even more difficult. In this section, we introduce some research studies on modeling signaling pathways, with the main focus on ODE and Petri net models.

10.2.1 Differential Equation Models

As mentioned in Chapter 4, biochemical reaction systems can be described in a deterministic and continuous manner by rate equations with the concentrations of reactants as variables. Signal transduction is actually a biochemical reaction system that includes binding, dissociation, complex formation, transfer of molecules, phosphorylation, and dephosphorylation. In addition to its applications in modeling gene regulatory networks and transcription regulatory networks, ODE is one of the most popular approaches to model signaling networks. A signaling network whose biochemical reaction system consists of m biochemical species (signaling components) and r

reactions (interactions) can be represented by a set of ODEs as

$$\frac{dx_i(t)}{dt} = P_i(t) - C_i(t) \tag{10.1}$$

$$= \sum_{j=1}^{r} s_{ij} v_j(t) \tag{10.2}$$

where $i = 1, \ldots, m$, P_i and C_i are respectively the production rate and the consumption rate of the ith species; x_i is the concentration of the ith signaling component, v_j is the velocity rate of the jth reaction, and s_{ij} denotes the stoichiometric coefficients. The equations above state that the rate of change in concentration of a signaling component is equal to the combination of the rates at which that component is being produced and consumed in all reactions that it involves. According to sophisticated kinetic laws such as mass action kinetics or Michaelis–Menten kinetics, the rates of reactions can be represented by the concentrations of species with some parameters.

Among the research on dynamic pathway modeling, the mitogen-activated protein kinase (MAPK) pathway is one of the most important and intensively studied signaling pathways. There are a wide variety of mathematical models of the MAPK pathway that have led to some novel insights and predictions about how this system functions. An early study on dynamic modeling of signaling pathways was contributed by Huang and Ferrell, who developed an ODE model of MAPK cascade and showed that the simulated response curve of MAPK with regard to MAPK kinase follows the experimental characteristic of p42 MAPK/ERK2 from *Xenopus oocyte* [Hua96]. Asthagiri and Lauffenburger studied a negative-feedback mechanism of MAPK pathway through mathematical modeling, and identified conditions for ultra-desensitization [Ast01]. Bhalla and Iyengar proposed a computational model of MAPK1,2/protein kinase C signaling network and analyzed its stability for growth factor stimulation [Bha99]. Schoeberl et al. presented a computational model integrating quantitative, dynamic, and topological representation of intracellular signal networks, based on known components of epidermal growth factor (EGF) receptor signal pathways [Sch02]. Orton et al. took the MAPK pathway as an example and presented an overview of the processes involved in modeling a biological system using the popular approach of ODEs [Ort05]. They introduced the features and functions of the pathway, compared the available models, and described new biological insights from the analysis of pathways.

In addition to the MAPK pathway, ODE-based mathematical models also have been applied widely in other signaling pathways. For example, Sedaghat et al. developed a mathematical model for metabolic insulin signaling pathways to gain insight into the complexities of the pathway [Sed02]. Bhalla and Iyengar have studied the platelet-derived growth factor (PDGF)-stimulated Ras and phospholipase-C γ pathways, which interact to form a positive-feedback loop and function as a bistable switch [Bha99]. Their simulation results have been verified by biological experiments. Cheong et al. reviewed a variety of mathematical models of NF-κB which is an important component in mammalian inflammatory signaling pathways, and stated that mathematical and computational models play instrumental roles in enhancing our understanding of the control of NF-κB signaling [ChR08]. Comprehensive reviews for mathematical modeling of signaling pathways can be found in papers by Klipp and Liebermeister [Kli06] and Eungdamrong and Iyengar [Eun04].

It should be noted that different signaling pathways usually require different types of mathematical models. ODE-based modeling implies that concentration is a function of only time, not space. A pathway in which spatial effects are minimal can be modeled by ODE. However, for pathways that involve specific signaling events in different subcellular compartments, to understand the rich dynamics that arises from variation in both space and time, spatial distribution of compounds can be described by compartmental models or partial differential equations (PDEs). The spatiotemporal dynamics of any signaling component in a signaling pathway can be generally described by the diffusion–reaction equation [Eun04]

$$\frac{\partial x_i(t, s)}{\partial t} = D\frac{\partial^2 x_i(t, s)}{\partial s^2} - v\frac{\partial x_i(t, s)}{\partial s} + R$$

where $x_i(t, s)$ is the concentration of the ith signaling component, t represents time, s is a spatial variable, D is the diffusion coefficient, v is the convective velocity, and R is the rate of production and consumption. Note that generally D, v, and R are functions of x, s, and t. This equation is a typical PDE since the concentration of a species depends on multiple independent variables: both time and space in this case. It states that the rate of change of concentration of a signaling component at any particular location depends on diffusion, active transport or convection, and biochemical reactions [Eun04]. In addition, to account for the stochastic effects in signal transduction, reaction events can be simulated by stochastic ODEs. Signaling systems that are discrete with respect to time and values of variables can be modeled by Boolean networks [LiS06], Petri nets [Gil06], and other methods.

10.2.2 Petri Net Models

Although signal transduction pathways are modeled mostly by ODEs and PDEs, there are some underlying difficulties in the modeling. The major disadvantage of these quantitative methods is that the kinetic parameters in the biochemical reactions are often unknown. One has to resort to sophisticated learning algorithms to estimate such kinetic parameters, which becomes more difficult with the increasing size and complexity of signaling pathways. At the same time, much fragmentary knowledge of the components and reactions in a biological process can be collected from experimental literature as qualitative data. Therefore, some qualitative techniques such as Boolean networks and the Petri net have been developed for modeling signal transduction pathway [LiS06, Gil06], which are more suitable for inducing dynamical properties of complex systems when few data are available, and thereby these qualitative techniques are important complements to quantitative approaches.

The Petri net is one of the mathematical representations of concurrent systems with independent and causally dependent components, in which several processes can occur at the same time. It is widely used to analyze biochemical networks. A Petri net consists of places, transitions, and directed arcs. Arcs run only between places and transitions. Therefore, Petri nets actually use a directed bipartite graph to describe the structure of a distributed concurrent system. The bipartite graph has two types of nodes, place nodes and transition nodes, connected by directed arcs (Fig. 10.2). Many extensions of the simple Petri net model have been developed for different modeling and simulation purposes, such as hierarchical Petri nets, timed Petri nets, stochastic Petri nets, and colored Petri nets [Pin03], which have sufficient descriptive power to execute sophisticated logic programs. In addition to their wide applications to manufacture systems and distributed systems, different kinds of Petri nets, including qualitative and quantitative models, have also been widely used in the area of systems biology.

In modeling biochemical pathways using Petri nets, place nodes usually represent biochemical entities (genes, mRNAs, proteins, protein complexes, enzymes, compounds, ions, etc.) and transition nodes represent biochemical reactions between them. The first attempt to use Petri nets for modeling biological pathways was by Reddy et al., who proposed a method for representing metabolic pathways [Red93]. Since then, Petri net applications have been mainly for metabolic pathways and metabolic networks [Hof94, Vos03, Koc05]. Lee et al. used Petri nets to model the molecular mechanisms of cell signaling and to describe their pathological implications [Lee04]. They established a framework for reconstructing and analyzing signal transduction networks and applied their approach to model the IL-1β and TNFα-induced signaling system. A novel notion of the Petri net, the hybrid functional Petri net, was defined by Matsuno et al. [Mat03]. A software tool, Genomic Object Net, was also introduced for representing and simulating gene regulation networks and signal transduction pathways. Gilbert and Heiner investigated the integration of Petri nets and ODEs for modeling and analyzing biochemical networks [Gil06a] and applied their approach to a Petri net model of the influence of the Raf kinase inhibitor protein (RKIP) on the extracellular signal regulated kinase (ERK) signaling pathway [Gil06b, Hei04]. Li et al. presented basic Petri net components representing molecular interactions and mechanisms of signaling pathways and used a timed Petri net to model and simulate an apoptosis signaling pathway [LiG07].

Both qualitative and quantitative methods have their own advantages and disadvantages. Figure 10.3 gives an illustration of an enzyme-catalyzed reaction represented by

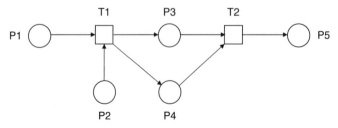

Figure 10.2. Example of a Petri net, where circles represent place nodes and boxes denote transition nodes.

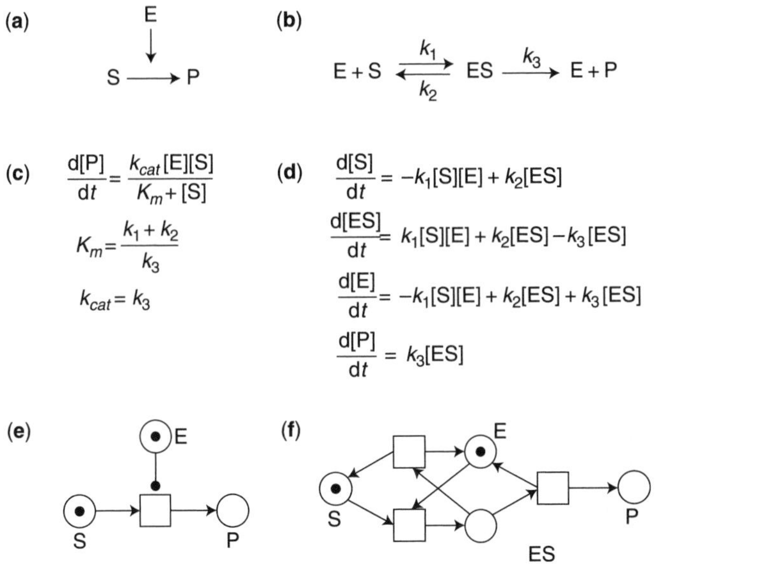

Figure 10.3. An enzyme-catalyzed reaction formulated using various models. (Reprinted from [Gil06b] © 2006 by permission of Oxford University Press.)

various mathematical models [Gil06b], where the left column shows Michaelis–Menten approximations, and the right column shows mass-action kinetics. Diagrams (a) and (b) are conventional notations of the chemical reactions and kinetic constants; (c) and (d) are possible ODE representations based on different kinetics that mathematically describe the temporal change of each molecular species. Diagrams (e) and (f) are discrete Petri net descriptions of the enzyme–substrate complex, where circular nodes represent biochemical entities and boxes represent reactions. Qualitative methods only require information about the stoichiometry and reversibility of the constituent reactions. They do not rely on the availability of measurements of kinetic parameters. However, overcoming the combinatorial explosion associated with large networks is recognized as a difficult challenge [Pin03]. A comprehensive and critical review of modeling techniques for analyzing and simulating signaling networks is given by Gilbert et al. [Gil06b].

10.3 INFERRING SIGNALING NETWORKS FROM HIGH-THROUGHPUT DATA

In the previous section, we described several approaches for modeling signal transduction pathways. These approaches require some basic knowledge about a certain pathway, such as signal components and possible interactions. Biological experiments can provide fragmented knowledge about a signaling pathway, but it is quite difficult to completely know its true state. Experimental identification of every reaction and component, even in a relatively simple signaling pathway, requires a concerted and even decades-long effort. Many signaling components and mechanisms are unknown, and there is not much kinetic data available to create models of pathway component interactions. On the other hand, high-throughput techniques result in a large amount of biological data such as protein interaction data and gene expression data, which can provide indirect evidence for signaling pathways. Therefore, many researchers turn their attention to recover signal transduction pathways and identify key components from multiple high-throughput data sources. We introduce some of these methods in this section.

10.3.1 NetSearch Method

The first purely computational approach for extracting signal transduction pathways from protein interaction maps and gene expression profiles was the NetSearch method [Ste02]. It was inspired by the fact that signal transduction is usually achieved by interactions of proteins and small molecules in the same or similar biological processes. In principle, this approach is to extract subnetworks from protein interaction data whose members have the most correlated expression profiles. Since signaling pathways usually start from membrane proteins and end at transcription factors, the first step of NetSearch is to query all paths up to length 8 that begin at membrane proteins and end at transcription factors. Of course, the number 8 here is somewhat empirically set. Then the biological plausibility of these paths is evaluated by gene expression profiles.

In NetSearch, the k-means algorithm is first used to group all yeast genes into clusters according to their expression profiles, and then a statistical score is assigned to each possible pathway according to the number of pathway members that are clustered together. The more the members of a path are clustered together, the higher the score is. The underlying principle is that the components of a signaling pathway should be involved in the same biological process, and thus they are more likely to be coexpressed. Assume that there are totally N proteins in the network and these proteins are partitioned into k clusters $C_1, C_2, \ldots, C_k$ according to their expression correlations. The k clusters have $N_1, N_2, \ldots, N_k$ members, respectively. p is a pathway with L proteins (i.e., $p_1 \rightarrow p_2 \rightarrow \cdots \rightarrow p_L$), and $c_p(i)$ is the number of proteins in pathway p that are clustered into C_i. NetSearch statistically scores a pathway for a cluster C_i such that pathways that have more components clustered into C_i have higher scores:

$$\text{Prob}_p(i) = -\log_{10}\left[\sum_{h=c_p(i)}^{L} \frac{\binom{N_i}{h}\binom{N - N_i}{L - h}}{\binom{N}{L}}\right] \tag{10.3}$$

This score computes the cumulative hypergeometric probability of pathway p containing $c_p(i)$ or more members of C_i. It assesses coclustering of pathway members in the single cluster C_i. Then, $\text{Prob}_p(i)$ values are summed over all clusters for which $c_p(i) \geq 2$ as follows:

$$\text{SumProb}(p) = \sum_{i,c_p(i)\geq2}^{k} \text{Prob}_p(i) \qquad (10.4)$$

It is a simple measure of coclustering across the entire collection of available clusters. In practical application of NetSearch, high-scoring linear pathways are assembled into signaling networks, with each component assigned a weight proportional to the sum of scores of the paths in which that component is found. In order to make the inference more reasonable and reduce computational complexity, NetSearch adopts a reprocessing of protein interaction data by eliminating highly connected proteins. NetSearch has demonstrated the ability to accurately reconstruct MAPK signaling networks in *S. cerevisiae* [Ste02]. The advantage of this inference method is that it does not require prior knowledge about signaling components. However, many explicit parameters and the scoring–assembling strategy interrogate the robustness of NetSearch. Furthermore, the predicted signaling pathways are highly dependent on the clustering method used and the number of clusters into which genes are grouped.

10.3.2 Ordering Signaling Components

Another interesting approach to determine signal transduction pathways is presented by Liu and Zhao [Liu04]. The basic principle is similar; they hypothesize that the genes encoding the proteins in same signaling pathways, especially the adjacent components in the pathways, have similar gene expression profiles. This approach assumes that the components of signal transduction pathways are known, and attempts to determine the correct order of the components in the pathways. Therefore, this method can only find linear signal transduction pathways, with complex signaling networks ruled out.

To infer the correct order of pathway components, all possible orders (candidate pathways) are considered. First, a score function in terms of protein interaction is designed to evaluate each candidate pathway p (i.e., $p_1 \to p_2 \to \cdots \to p_L$)

$$S_{\text{PPI}}(p) = \sum_{i=1}^{L-1} \log\left[(1 - fn)^{x_{i,i+1}} fn^{1-x_{i,i+1}}\right] \qquad (10.5)$$

where L is the total number of proteins on the pathway and $x_{i,i+1} = 1$ if there is an observed interaction between the ith and the $(i + 1)$th proteins on the pathway and $x_{i,i+1}=0$ otherwise. fn represents the false-negative rate of the interaction data. In order to increase the accuracy of the inference, another score function in terms of gene expression profile is also defined for each pathway p

$$S_{\text{EXP}}(p) = \sum_{i}^{L-1} r_{i,i+1} \qquad (10.6)$$

where $r_{i,i+1}$ represents the correlation coefficient between the ith and the $(i+1)$th proteins in the pathway. Although the contribution of protein interactions and gene expression profiles may be different, the two data sources are assigned with equal importance [Liu04]. The scores from each data source are rescaled over all the possible pathways to [0, 1] by

$$S_{i,\text{rescale}} = \frac{S_i - S_{\min}}{S_{\max} - S_{\min}} \tag{10.7}$$

where $S_{\min}$ and $S_{\max}$ are the minimum and the maximum scores of all the possible pathways, respectively. The integrated score is the sum of the rescaled scores for each individual dataset:

$$S(p) = S_{\text{PPI}}(p) + S_{\text{EXP}}(p)$$

Liu and Zhao conducted experiments to test each kind of scores S_{PP1}, S_{EXP}, and S, and found that, although the score function is straightforward, it can provide evidence that both data sources have information for inferring correct signaling pathways. Protein–protein interaction data can provide key information to reveal the relationships between components in a signal transduction pathway, but they are not so reliable and subject to many biases such as high false-positive and false-negative rates. Furthermore, they cannot capture the dynamic nature of the pathways. On the other hand, gene expression profiles can provide information about whole-cell responses in different conditions, but they cannot provide direct information on the ordering of genes in a pathway. Hence, the integration of these two data types can significantly increase the ability for the reliable inference of ordering pathway components.

Although Liu and Zhao's approach is straightforward and interesting, it requires prior knowledge about the signaling components that a pathway has. In addition, their approach can only infer linear signaling pathways and is not able to deal with more complex cases such as signaling networks. In particular, many kinds of nonnumerical meta-information such as published literature, public databases, and biologist expert knowledge, are difficult to include in the model. The computational complexity of this approach is exponentially increased with the length of candidate pathways since it requires a permutation search of all signal components [Liu04].

10.3.3 Color-Coding Methods

NetSearch and ordering component approaches both are scoring methods based on integrated data, and assume that all protein interactions are equally reliable. Scott et al. formulated the problem of finding signaling pathways as detecting minimum-weight simple paths with certain lengths in a weighted protein interaction network [Sco06]. They presented linear time algorithms as biologically motivated extensions of the color-coding technique in graph theory, which allow computation of optimal paths within acceptable timeframes.

In a weighted protein interaction network $G = (V, E)$ with n proteins in V and m interactions in E, an edge (u, v) denotes an interaction of proteins u and v with a numerical value $p(u, v)$ assigned as the probability with which u and v interact. Each simple path in this network can be assigned a score. Among paths of a given length, those with the highest scores are considered to be plausible candidates for being identified as linear signal transduction pathways. Let the weight of each edge (u, v) be $w(u, v) = -\log p(u, v)$, and define the weight of a path as the sum of the weights of its edges. Then, detecting signaling pathways is actually to find a minimum-weight simple path of certain length starting and ending at given vertices, which is an NP-hard problem [Sco06]. Given a set I of possible start vertices (receptor proteins), for each vertex $v \in V$, a minimum-weight simple path of length k that starts within I and ends at v can be found by a standard dynamic programming (DP) algorithm. For each nonempty set $S \subseteq V$ of cardinality at most k, and each vertex $v \in S$, let $W(v, S)$ be the minimum weight of a simple path with length $|S|$ that starts at some vertex in I, visits each vertex in S, and ends at v. The following recurrence can be used to tabulate this function by generating the values $W(v, S)$ in increasing order of the cardinality of S

$$W(v, S) = \min_{u \in S - \{v\}} W(u, S - \{v\}) + w(u, v), \quad |S| > 1 \qquad (10.8)$$

where $W(v, v) = 0$ if $v \in I$ and ∞ otherwise. Therefore, the weight of the optimal path to v is the minimum of $W(v, S)$ over all pairs v, S such that $|S| = k$, and the optimal path can be recovered successively in a reverse order by a backtracking procedure.

Although the DP algorithm can theoretically solve the problem, the search space is very large, which makes the complexity of DP high from a computational perspective. The idea of color coding is to reduce the search space by a random sampling approach. It assigns each vertex a random color between 1 and k, and then, instead of searching for paths with distinct vertices, searches for paths with distinct colors (called "colorful paths"). Therefore, the solution space is greatly reduced. However, color coding will miss some paths containing two vertices with the same color. Hence, the algorithm needs repeated trials by random colorings. In each trial, every vertex $v \in V$ is randomly assigned a color $c(v) \in \{1, 2, \ldots, k\}$. Finding a minimum-weight colorful path of length k that starts within I and ends at v can also be achieved by a DP algorithm. For each nonempty set $S \in \{1, 2, \ldots, k\}$ and each vertex v such that $c(v) \in S$, let $W(v, S)$ be the minimum weight of a simple path of length $|S|$ that starts within I, visits a vertex of each color in S, and ends at v. Then, the following recurrence can be used to tabulate this function

$$W(v, S) = \min_{u:c(u) \in S - \{c(v)\}} W(u, S - \{c(v)\}) + w(u, v), |S| > 1 \qquad (10.9)$$

where again $W(v, \{c(v)\}) = 0$ if $v \in I$ and ∞ otherwise. A minimum-weight colorful path ending at v can be retrieved by backtracking in DP, and its weight is $W(v, 1, \ldots, k)$. Since color coding is a randomized algorithm, it cannot guarantee finding a minimum-weight simple path in G. However, it can guarantee finding an optimal path with a certain probability by certain times of trials.

The original color-coding algorithm introduced above can only detect linear signaling pathways. Scott et al. made extensions of the color-coding algorithms by adding some biological constraints [Sco06]. For example, some signaling components are known to be involved in a signal cascade. In this case, color-coding solutions should have a constraint on the set of proteins in a path to incorporate known components. In addition, many signaling pathways start from membrane proteins and end at transcription factors. To incorporate such a case, color-coding solutions should have a constraint on the order of occurrence of the proteins in a path. In particular, Scott et al. extended the color-coding algorithm to find more general pathway structures such as subtrees. Although trees are more general than linear pathways, in practice, it is the simple signaling networks that represent signal transduction processes. In their approach, to form a signaling network, all the optimal pathways need to be assembled in the same way as in NetSearch and the ordering component method.

10.4 INFERRING SIGNALING NETWORKS BY LINEAR PROGRAMMING

In the last section, we introduced several methods for recovering signal transduction pathways or signaling networks from protein interaction networks along with gene expression data. A common characteristic of these methods is that they can only detect linear signaling pathways by a scoring scheme. In order to identify complex signaling networks, they have to assemble individual high-scoring linear pathways. Some other approaches have been developed for this problem more recently. For example, Arga et al. proposed a selective permissibility algorithm (SPA) for recovering signaling networks from protein interaction networks and gene expression profiles along with functional information [Arg07]. Bebek and Yang presented a new framework called Pathfinder for identifying signaling pathways by integrating protein interaction networks with microarray expression profiles, protein subcellular localization and sequence information [Beb07]. Despite their technical differences, only a few of the existing approaches can directly find a signaling network as a whole entity. They are either iterative or multistaged. Usually they first identify separate linear pathways and then heuristically assemble them into a signaling network. Therefore, the solutions may be inconsistent and make some important components missing.

Zhao et al. presented a novel computational method for detecting a signal transduction network (STN) in an accurate manner by integrating PPI data with gene expression profiles [ZhaX08c]. This approach is based on an integer linear programming (ILP) model. In this approach, signaling network detection is formulated as an optimization problem that aims to find an optimal subnetwork starting from membrane proteins and ending at transcription factors. Unlike most existing methods that heuristically rank and assemble individual linear pathways, the ILP approach identifies a signaling network as a whole entity. In particular, it is flexible for additional constraints and can detect signaling pathways with general network structures. Therefore, it is able to extract and utilize prior information from experimental results or the literature. Since a linear programming (LP) relaxation algorithm is adopted to solve the optimization problem, it is efficient and able to handle a large-scale problem without numerical difficulty. The numerical experiments on yeast MAPK signaling pathways demonstrate the superiority of the ILP model. In particular, the prediction results are found to be in close agreement with current biological knowledge and available information from the literature. We will introduce this method in this section.

10.4.1 Integer Linear Programming Model

Most signaling pathways start from membrane proteins as receptors and end at transcription factors (TFs) as targets. The ILP approach aims to detect a signal transduction network (STN) starting from membrane proteins and ending at TFs [ZhX08c]. A protein interaction network is represented as a weighted undirected graph $G(V, E, W)$, where the vertex $v_i \in V$ is a protein and the edge $E(i, j) \in E$ denotes the experimentally observed interaction between proteins i and j. Weight $w_{ij} \in W$ of an edge $E(i, j)$ is the confidence score of interaction or the expression correlation coefficient between the encoding genes i and j. In literature, many methods have been proposed for estimating the reliability of protein interactions [Den03a]. As in other existing methods, a basic assumption is that proteins in the same signal pathway tend to interact with a high probability and be involved in the same process, which results in high expression correlation. In a weighted network, a linear path with specific length m from the starting node to another node is assigned a score that equals the sum of the weights for the edges in the path, where the length of the path is the number of proteins involved in the path. Similarly, the score of a subnetwork is the sum of the weights for the edges of the network, and the network size is the number of proteins in the subnetwork. Given an undirected weighted network $G(V, E, W)$ and the possible starting and ending points of signaling pathways (membrane proteins and TFs in this case), detecting signaling networks is formulated as an optimization problem, specifically to find a maximum-weight subnetwork from the network G, which is viewed as the putative STN [ZhX08c].

Let x_i be a binary variable for protein i to denote whether protein i is selected as a component of the STN; also let y_{ij} be a binary variable to denote whether the biochemical reaction represented by $E(i, j)$ is a part of the STN. Then, an ILP model formulated as follows can accomplish the mission:

$$\min_{\{x_i, y_{ij}\}} S = -\sum_{i=1}^{|V|} \sum_{j=1}^{|V|} w_{ij} y_{ij} + \lambda \sum_{i=1}^{|V|} \sum_{j=1}^{|V|} y_{ij} \tag{10.10}$$

$$\text{s.t. } y_{ij} \leq x_i \tag{10.11}$$

$$y_{ij} \leq x_j \tag{10.12}$$

$$\sum_{j=1}^{|V|} y_{ij} \geq 1 \quad \text{if } i \text{ is either a starting or ending protein} \tag{10.13}$$

$$\sum_{j=1}^{|V|} y_{ij} \geq 2x_i \quad \text{if } i \text{ is not a starting or ending protein} \tag{10.14}$$

$$x_i = 1 \quad \text{if } i \text{ is a protein known in STN} \tag{10.15}$$

$$x_i \in \{0, 1\}, \quad i = 1, 2, \ldots, |V| \tag{10.16}$$

$$y_{ij} \in \{0, 1\}, \quad i, j = 1, 2, \ldots, |V| \tag{10.17}$$

Here, $|V|$ is the total number of proteins in G. Constraint (10.13) means that each start protein has at least one link with other proteins, whereas constraint (10.14) ensures that x_i has at least two linking edges once it is selected as a component of the STN. These two constraints ensure that the components in the detected subnetwork are as connected as possible. On the other hand, constraints (10.11) and (10.12) reflect the relationships between component variables x_i and reaction variables y_{ij}, which means that if and only if proteins i and j are selected as components of the signaling network, the biochemical reaction denoted by the edge $E(i, j)$ can be considered. Constraint (10.15) incorporates prior knowledge from the experimental results or literature.

The first term of the abovementioned cost function S implies that a STN with maximum weights should be extracted, while the second term is used to control the STN size, that is, the number of biochemical reactions in the STN since each interaction represented by $E(i, j)$ actually corresponds to a biochemical reaction. The idea behind the model is that we want to find a minimum-weight subnetwork of specific size that accomplishes the signal transduction process with as few biochemical reactions as possible. The assumption is consistent with the parsimony principle widely adopted in other areas of biology [ZhaX06]. λ is used to control the tradeoff between the first term and the second term. When λ is small, many possible links are selected. The derived subnetwork is large and dense; otherwise, it is a small and sparse subnetwork. Since ILP is NP-hard, to make the model suitable for large-scale interaction networks, the integer constraints $x_i \in \{0, 1\}$, $y_{ij} \in \{0, 1\}$ can be relaxed into a real number $x_i \in [0, 1]$, $y_{ij} \in [0, 1]$. With such relaxations, the model becomes a LP model that can be exactly solved in polynomial time. Although without theoretical guarantee, experiment results show that the solutions by LP are always integers for test examples [ZhX08c].

The scalar parameter λ has clear geometric meaning and thereby can be tuned in a relatively easy manner. Furthermore, the parameter λ enables the biologists to view the STN in a hierarchical and nesting framework. Therefore, biologists are allowed some flexibility in choosing interesting STNs of different sizes in this way by adjusting λ. Because of the complexity of signaling networks, there is no absolutely optimal λ. Zhao et al. formulated a rule of thumb for selecting the parameter λ by defining the density of the extracted signaling network as [ZhaX08c]

$$D = \frac{\sum_{ij} w_{ij}}{n} \tag{10.18}$$

where w_{ij} is the weight of edge (i, j) and n is the total number of nodes in the signaling network. λ, which corresponds to the largest value of D, is determined as the optimal parameter setting, and the corresponding signaling network is regarded as the detected signaling network accordingly.

10.4.2 Significance Measures

To evaluate the significance of the STN found by the ILP method, two quality measures—p-value and functional enrichment—are used in the paper by Zhao et al. [ZhaX08c]. Assume that a STN starting from a membrane protein M and ending at a TF T is found by ILP with the cost of S from a real protein interaction network. To see the significance of the STN, that is, to prove that it is not detected by chance, a number of random networks are generated by shuffling the edges of the real network, while preserving the degree of each vertex. Totally, 100 random networks are generated. For each random network, the ILP model is employed to find a subnetwork starting from M and ending at T, where λ is chosen by the way described above. The p value of the STN detected in the real network is defined as the percentage of subnetworks found from the random networks that have a cost of S or below.

In addition, the functional enrichment of the components in a detected signaling network is calculated to evaluate it from a biological viewpoint [ZhX08c]. Specifically, the biological process annotations in Gene Ontology [GO08] are assigned to the proteins in STN. The probability that the components of the signaling network have the same function can be calculated through a hypergeometric distribution (8.1). Furthermore, the p value is corrected for multiple testing by Bonferroni correction.

10.4.3 Numerical Validation

Figure 10.4 shows the four yeast MAPK signaling pathways deposited in KEGG. These signaling pathways are used as a gold standard to test the effectiveness of the ILP approach in extracting signaling networks from protein interaction data and gene expression data [ZhX08c].

10.4.3.1 High-Throughput Data Three protein interaction datasets are employed in the study, including DIP, DIP Core, and SPA data [Arg07]. The DIP dataset and DIP Core dataset (2007-01-07 version) are obtained from the DIP database [Xen02]. The confidence scores of the DIP data were calculated as described by Sharan et al. [Sha05b]. The DIP Core dataset contains interactions determined by at least one small-scale experiment or at least two independent experiments. The SPA dataset consists of proteins that are possibly involved in cellular communication and signal transduction, and has been successfully applied to recover signaling pathways [Arg07].

Five gene expression datasets are used, including carbon sources, stress response, rosetta compendium, diauxic shift, and phosphate metabolism [OgN00]. All the gene expression data except diauxic shift (from GEO, accession number GSE28) are obtained from the authors' Websites. In particular, the expression data measured under shock conditions (at temperatures decreasing from 37°C to 25°C) recorded in the stress response dataset are used. For the combination of carbon sources and diauxic

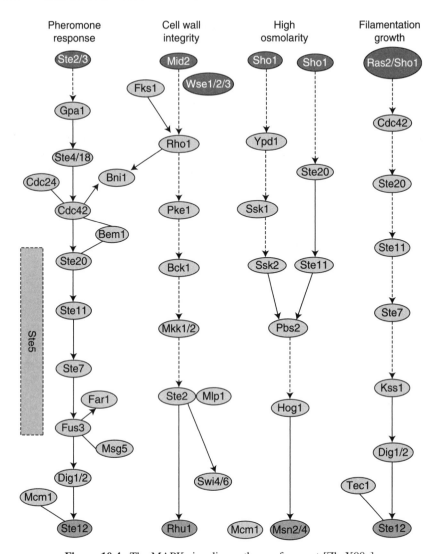

Figure 10.4. The MAPK signaling pathways for yeast [ZhaX08c].

shift, only genes with twofold expression change are selected. On the basis of gene expression levels, irrelevant protein interactions corresponding to low expression changes of genes are eliminated to reduce false positives and improve the accuracy.

10.4.3.2   Using Only Interaction Data   If only protein interaction data are used to extract signaling pathways, the weights in the objective function (10.10) of ILP are defined as the confidence scores of protein interactions. The ILP model is applied to find pheromone response and filamentous growth signaling pathways in yeast. In a large protein interaction network, many components are far from the starting or ending nodes that do not likely belong to the signaling network. Therefore, the depth-first search algorithm is employed to preprocess the interaction data to reduce computation cost [ZhX08c]. In other words, a small protein interaction network is generated by the depth-first search algorithm, which constructs all possible paths of length 6–9 starting from membrane proteins and ending at TFs. In this way, two smaller interaction networks are generated by depth-first search for the two MAPK signaling pathways, respectively. ILP is applied to these two reduced networks. Such preprocessing has been widely used in the literature [Arg07, Liu04, Sco06, Ste02]. Precision measure and recall measure are employed for the performance of different methods by adopting KEGG pathways as a gold standard. Precision measure is defined as the percentage of components found in STN that are also in the KEGG pathway, and recall measure is the percentage of components in the KEGG pathway found in STN [ZhX08c].

By varying λ from 0 to 1 in the ILP model, signaling networks with different sizes (from a complicated network to a linear pathway) can be obtained. Numerical results confirm that a detected larger network always covers a smaller one [ZhX08c]. Therefore, a smaller one is viewed to be more likely involved in the STN because it is covered by all larger networks, but a larger one includes more predictions. For the pheromone response pathway, the ILP model is applied to find a signaling network starting from membrane protein STE3 and ending at transcription factor STE12. The results are summarized in Figure 10.5, where the upper circles are starting points and the lowest ones are ending points. The size of each circle is proportional to the sum of the scores of the paths that it is involved in Figure 10.5a shows the pheromone response pathways detected by color coding and by ILP model with $\lambda = 0.85$. Comparing the results of ILP and color coding on the same dataset [Sco06], we can see that the signaling pathway detected by the ILP model covers the one by color coding. Furthermore, other proteins (i.e., STE18, AKR1, FAR1, STE20, CDC42, STE50 and STE11), are also detected by the ILP model. Figure 10.5b shows the signaling network recovered by ILP with $\lambda = 0.8$. Clearly, it covers the one with $\lambda = 0.85$. By comparing the detected signaling network with those found by NetSearch and color coding, we can see that most components of the three signaling networks are common. In addition, the ILP model successfully detected STE20 in the main chain (see Fig. 10.4). Furthermore, ILP identified two new components, CLN2 and CDC28, which repress the pheromone signaling.

Table 10.2 compares the ILP model and other methods, including color coding, NetSearch, and Pathfinder with respect to precision measure and recall measure. It can be seen that Pathfinder performs best, and color coding ranks second. Despite its simplicity, the ILP model performs well compared with other methods. The p values of functional enrichment on five GO terms (response to pheromone, pheromone-dependent signal transduction, regulation of conjugation with cell fusion, sexual reproduction, signal transduction) for members in the signaling network found by ILP show that most components involve similar functions. The p value of the detected STN is smaller than 10^{-15}. From these results, ILP can be considered as a good complement to the existing algorithms.

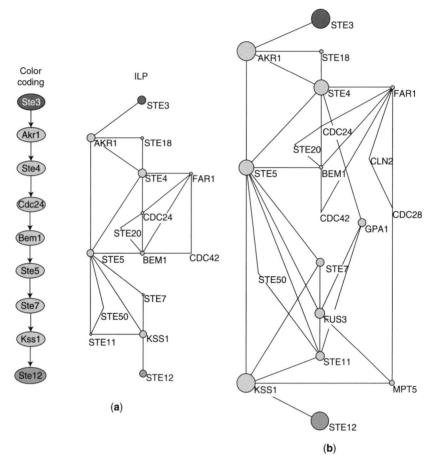

Figure 10.5. (a) Pheromone response signaling pathways—pathways recovered by color coding and ILP model, respectively; (b) pheromone response signaling network discovered by ILP model with a smaller λ [ZhaX08c].

TABLE 10.2. Comparison of Different Methods for Detecting Pheromone Pathway on the Basis of Protein Interaction Data

Methods	Precision (%)	Recall (%)
ILP ($\lambda = 0.85$)	80	60
ILP ($\lambda = 0.80$)	70	70
Color coding (linear path)	78	35
Color coding (signaling network)	83	75
Pathfinder	88	75
NetSearch	74	70

Source: Zhao et al. [ZhaX08c].

For the filamentous growth invasion pathway, the ILP approach was applied to detect a signaling network starting from membrane protein RAS2 and ending at transcription factor STE12 [ZhX08c]. Figure 10.6a shows the signaling pathways detected by the color-coding method and by the ILP model with $\lambda = 0.90$. It can be seen that the signaling pathway recovered by the ILP model matches the known signaling pathway to a large extent. The CDC25 and HSP82, which do not appear in the pathway of KEGG, were detected because of the missing links between RAS2 and CDC42 in the interaction network. Using the same dataset, the ILP model can find the identical

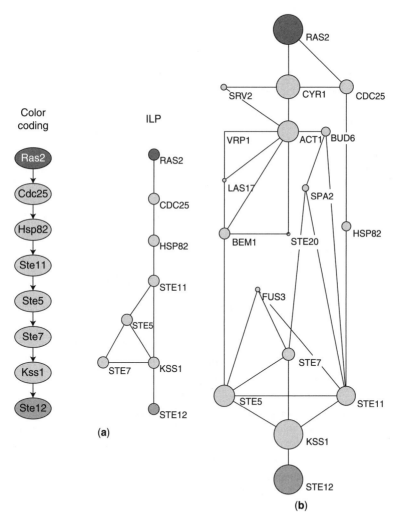

Figure 10.6. Signaling pathways of filamentous growth: (a) filamentation signaling pathways—from left to right, the pathways from KEGG, detected by color coding and by ILP model with $\lambda = 0.90$ respectively; (b) filamentation signaling network by the ILP model with $\lambda = 0.50$ [ZhaX08c].

TABLE 10.3. Comparison of Different Methods in Detecting
Filamentation Pathway on the Basis of Protein Interaction Data

Methods	Precision (%)	Recall (%)
ILP ($\lambda = 0.90$, no prior information)	62.5	45
ILP ($\lambda = 0.95$, with prior information)	33	55
Color coding (linear path)	62.5	45
Pathfinder	28	82
NetSearch	33	64

Source: Zhao et al. [ZhX08c].

signaling pathway of the same size as that detected by color coding. In addition, the ILP model found several additional links compared against the color-coding method. The additional links may imply alternative signaling pathways since such redundant mechanisms can compensate single protein disruptions and maintain unblocked signal transduction. Figure 10.6b shows the filamentation signaling network of a larger size detected by the ILP model with $\lambda = 0.10$. The signaling network consists of 18 proteins, where we assume that the proteins CDC25, SPA2, CYR1, FUS3, HSP82, and BEM1 are known to be involved in the signaling pathway to test the effectiveness of the additional information. It can be seen that the detected signaling network matches the one found by NetSearch to a large extent. The HSC82 detected by NetSearch is not contained in the network because there is a direct interaction between STE11 and HSP82. In particular, the ILP model found STE20 in the main chain of the filamentation pathway (Fig. 10.4), while NetSearch fails to detect it.

Table 10.3 compares five different methods. In this case, the Pathfinder detects a maximum number of components involved in the KEGG filamentation pathway but has the lowest precision. This example demonstrates that no method can always perform the best and different methods can complement each other. The p values of functional enrichment on five GO terms (reproduction, growth, filamentous growth, signal transduction, cell communication) for members in the signaling network show that most components in the signaling network have similar functions. On the other hand, the p value calculated from random networks is smaller than 10^{-15}, which indicates that the detected signaling network by ILP is statistically significant.

10.4.3.3 Using Integrated Data

The ILP approach works well by using only protein interaction data, partly because the confidence scores of yeast protein interaction data are estimated with high accuracy. However, protein interaction data from many databases have no confidence scores or have not been estimated properly. On the other hand, a tremendous amount of gene expression data are currently available, and provide additional information for studying signaling pathways. As in previous work, the integration of gene expression profiles with protein–protein interactions can improve the accuracy of signaling network inference. In addition to the two signaling pathways described above, the ILP method is also applied to detect cell wall integrity pathway and the high osmolarity glycerol (HOG) pathway. Table 10.4 shows the protein interaction and gene expression datasets used in Zhao et al.'s

TABLE 10.4. Protein Interaction Data and Gene Expression Data for Detecting Yeast MAPK Pathways[a]

Pathway	Protein Interaction	Gene Expression
Pheromone response	DIP core	Carbon sources
		Diauxic shift
Filamentous growth	DIP core	Carbon sources
		PHO regulatory pathway
Cell wall integrity	DIP core	Rosetta compendium
High-osmolarity (HOG)	SPA	Stress response

[a]Used by Zhao et al. [ZhaX08c].

study [ZhX08c]. For three pathways including pheromone response, filamentation, and cell wall integrity, the DIP core dataset is employed. For the high-osmolarity pathway, the SPA interaction data constructed by Arga et al. is used because there are many missing interactions in DIP core data for the HOG pathway [Arg07]. Since different signaling pathways are activated under different conditions, different gene expression data and their combination are used to discover signaling pathways. In the integrated data, the weight w_{ij} in the objective function of the ILP model is the absolute value of expression correlation coefficients.

The signaling networks discovered by the ILP model are illustrated in Figure 10.7. Figure 10.7a shows the pheromone response signaling networks detected by the ILP approach with $\lambda = 0.50$. It can be seen that all the components in the main chain have been successfully discovered, especially CDC42 and STE20, which are not found by NetSearch. STE20 is not found by the color-coding method. Compared to the signaling networks detected by NetSearch and color coding, the ILP model can uncover almost all the components found by the two existing methods except for GPA1, SST2, and SPH1, which are not in the main chain and have low expression correlations with other members in the signaling network. However, the ILP model successfully identified STE20 and BNI1, where the former is in the main chain and the latter has been confirmed in KEGG. Furthermore, the detected signaling network contains several additional proteins. Among these proteins, it has been confirmed that they are relevant to the pheromone response. Table 10.5 shows the functional enrichment of the pheromone signaling network, where we can see that most components have similar functions. On the other hand, the p value of the detected signaling network is smaller than 10^{-15}.

Figure 10.7b shows the filamentation signaling network detected by the ILP model with $\lambda = 0.50$. It can be seen that the ILP model can detect all the components in the main chain except CDC42, due to the incompleteness of the interaction data. Compared to NetSearch, the ILP model successfully found STE20, but missed ABP1, HSC82, FUS1, and HSP82, which are not in the main chain. Instead of ABP1, the ILP model identified three other members, including actin assembly factor LAS17, actin-associated protein RVS167, and profilin-, actin-, and phosphatidylinositol-4,5-bisphosphate-binding protein PFY1. These three proteins are in the same complex with SRV2, BUD6, and ABP1, which implies that they have similar

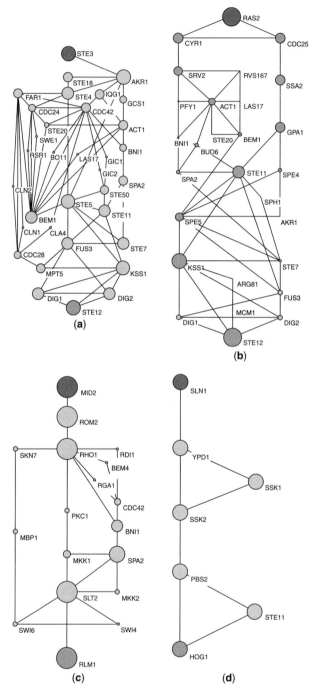

Figure 10.7. Yeast MAPK signaling networks detected by ILP model from integrated data: (a) pheromone response; (b) filamentous growth; (c) cell wall integrity; (d) HOG [ZhaX08c].

TABLE 10.5. p Values of Functional Enrichment for Pheromone Response Signaling Network Found by ILP

GO Term	p Value	Annotated Proteins in Signaling Network	Total Annotated Proteins
Response to pheromone	4.71×10^{-30}	21	94
Signal transduction during conjugation	3.08×10^{-27}	15	28
Pheromone-dependent signal transduction	3.08×10^{-27}	15	28
Signal transduction	6.40×10^{-26}	23	209
Cell communication	3.36×10^{-25}	23	224

Source: Zhao et al. [ZhaX08c].

functions. SPH1 is included because of its strong correlation with STE7 and STE11, where SPH1 activates STE7. The rest of the proteins are included because these proteins are shared among different pathways and have strong correlations. The functional enrichments of the filamentation signaling network in terms of five GO terms (filamentous growth, signal transduction, reproduction, cell surface receptor, growth) are significant, which indicate that most of the components in the signaling network have similar functions. On the other hand, the p value of the detected signaling network is smaller than 10^{-15}, which also demonstrates the effectiveness of the ILP method and the significance of the identified network.

Figure 10.7c shows the cell wall integrity signaling network recovered by the ILP model with $\lambda = 0.15$. All the members in the main chain were successfully detected except BCK1. Compared to the one found by NetSearch, the ILP model did not find FKS1, GIC2, ACT1, BUD6, BCK1, SPH1, and SMD3 because of the missing interactions in the network, but successfully detected two transcription factors: SWI4 and SWI6. In addition, the ILP model found several other members, including MBP1, which forms a complex with SWI6p, RHO1 effectors SKN7, and BEM4p involved in the RHO1-mediated signaling pathway. The functional enrichments of the uncovered cell wall signaling network in terms of five GO terms (signal transduction, cell communication, intracellular signaling cascade, small GTPase-mediated signal transduction, cell structure morphogenesis) are significant. The p value of the detected signaling network is 0.002, which implies the significance of the recovered signaling network.

Figure 10.7d shows the HOG signaling pathway found by the ILP model with $\lambda = 0.90$. The main chain was successfully recovered. Furthermore, the member STE11 involved in the signaling network was also detected. Aside from this, several new links among the members were also discovered, which may correspond to alternative signaling pathways. The other methods utilizing the pairwise correlation between proteins failed to detect the HOG pathway in this case because the HOG pathway is nonlinear and there are additional links among members in the main chain of the pathway. On the other hand, the ILP model handles the HOG pathway as a global entity and therefore performs better.

TABLE 10.6. Performance of ILP Model in Detecting MAPK Signaling Networks

Signaling Network	Precision (%)	Recall (%)
Pheromone (ILP, $\lambda = 0.50$)	47	80
Filamentation (ILP, $\lambda = 0.90$)	29	73
Cell wall (ILP, $\lambda = 0.15$)	56	63
Cell wall (NetSearch)	50	56
HOG (ILP, $\lambda = 0.89$)	100	58
HOG (pairwise correlation based on SPA)	47	75

Source: Zhao et al. [ZhX08c].

Table 10.6 shows the performance of ILP model in detecting MAPK signaling networks on the basis of the protein interaction data and gene expression data, along with NetSearch in detecting cell wall signaling pathway and the results described by Arga et al. [Arg07] in the HOG pathway. It can be seen from the results that the performance of the ILP model is improved by using the integrated data in comparison with using only interaction data in unraveling signaling networks. Although comparison of different methods may be biased by lack of knowledge of true signaling networks, the results demonstrate that the ILP model performs comparably to or better than other methods in inferring signaling networks.

10.4.4 Inferring Signaling Networks by Network Flow Models

As mentioned previously, the ILP approach can identify signaling networks as a whole without the need to rank and assemble individual pathways. However, the ILP approach cannot guarantee the connectedness of signaling networks. Although the parameter λ can be tuned small enough in order to ensure connectivity of the detected signaling networks, it is only a heuristic manipulation. In other words, there is no theoretical guarantee for the connectivity of a signaling network. To overcome this problem, we can modify the constraints of the ILP and make the connectivity constraint enforceable by adopting a network flow model. Lee and Dooly discussed a constrained maximum-weight connected graph problem [Lee98]. Specifically, given a positive integer R, a weight for each vertex in a graph, and a predetermined vertex v_0, find a connected subgraph with R vertices containing v_0 such that the sum of the weights is maximized. They presented three optimization algorithms for this problem, including mixed-integer linear programming (MILP). In this section, this MILP is extended to a maximum edge-weighted graph problem with two predetermined vertices (membrane protein and transcription factor) for detecting signaling networks, which guarantee connectivity of the detected network.

For detecting linear signal transduction pathways, we aim to find a maximum edge-weighted path with R vertices starting from a membrane protein S and ending at a TF T in a weighted protein interaction network $G(V, E, W)$. Let x_i be a binary variable for protein i to denote whether protein $i \in V$ is selected as a component of the signaling pathway. y_{ij} is also a binary variable to denote whether the biochemical reaction represented by $E(i, j) \in E$ is a part of the signaling pathway. The network flow model, formulated as the following MILP, can accomplish the mission described above

$$\max_{x_i, y_{ij}, z_{ij}} S = \sum_{i \in V} \sum_{j \in V} w_{ij} y_{ij} \tag{10.19}$$

$$\text{s.t.} \quad y_{ij} \leq x_i \tag{10.20}$$

$$y_{ij} \leq x_j \tag{10.21}$$

$$\sum_{j \in V} y_{ij} = 1 \qquad \text{if } i = s \text{ or } t \tag{10.22}$$

$$\sum_{j \in V} y_{ij} = 2x_i, \qquad \text{if } i \neq s \text{ and } t \tag{10.23}$$

$$y_{ij} + y_{ji} = 1 \tag{10.24}$$

$$\sum_{j \in V'} z_{sj} = R - 1 \tag{10.25}$$

$$\sum_{j \in V} z_{ij} \leq (R - 1)x_j \tag{10.26}$$

$$\sum_{j \in V} z_{ij} - \sum_{k \in V'} z_{jk} = x_j \tag{10.27}$$

$$\sum_{i \in V} z_{it} = 1 \tag{10.28}$$

$$z_{ij} \leq y_{ij} \tag{10.29}$$

$$x_i, y_{ij} \in \{0, 1\}, z_{ij} \in \{0, 1, \ldots, R - 1\} \tag{10.30}$$

where $i, j = 1, 2, \ldots, |V|$, $V' = V - \{s\}$, $w_{ij} \in W$ is the weight of edge $E(i, j)$ in G. Constraint (10.22) ensures that each membrane protein or TF has exactly one link to other proteins. Constraint (10.23) ensures that x_i has exactly two linking edges once it is selected as a middle component of the linear signaling pathway. Constraint (10.24) indicates that each edge can be selected at most once. z_{ij} represents a flow from node i to node j. Constraint (10.25) means that there are $R - 1$ units of flow entering the network from the source node s. In other words, R components will be chosen by the network flow model to form a maximum edge-weighted path. Constraint (10.26) denotes that if a node (component) is selected (i.e., $x_j = 1$), the maximum flow entering this node is no more than $R - 1$ since the total flow is $R - 1$. Constraint (10.27) denotes that if a node i is selected, the number of the possible components is reduced by 1, and thus the flow is reduced by 1. Constraint (10.28) indicates that the remaining flow with one unit enters the sink node t. Constraint (10.29) denotes that only an edge selected as a part of the path can have a flow on it. Equations (10.25)–(10.29) are network flow constraints to ensure that the path from s to t is connected. Since the flow is from a starting node to an ending node, in order to satisfy constraint (10.28), there must be a path from the starting node to the ending node so that the detected linear signal pathway is connected. The defect lying in this model is that z_{ij} is not a binary variable but an integer variable, thereby increasing the computational complexity.

This network flow model can detect linear signaling transduction pathways. In order to detect signaling pathways with general network structures, the objective function and some constraints must be modified further. Hence, we adopt a more sophisticated MILP as follows:

$$\max_{x_i, y_{ij}, z_{ij}} S = \sum_{i \in V} \sum_{j \in V} w_{ij} y_{ij} - \lambda \sum_{i \in V} \sum_{j \in V} y_{ij} \tag{10.31}$$

$$\text{s.t. } y_{ij} \leq x_i \tag{10.32}$$

$$y_{ij} \leq x_j \tag{10.33}$$

$$\sum_{j \in V} y_{ij} \geq 1 \quad \text{if } i = s \text{ or } t \tag{10.34}$$

$$\sum_{j \in V} y_{ij} \geq 2x_i \quad \text{if } i \neq s \text{ and } t \tag{10.35}$$

$$y_{ij} + y_{ji} = 1 \tag{10.36}$$

$$\sum_{j \in V'} z_{sj} = R - 1 \tag{10.37}$$

$$\sum_{j \in V} z_{ij} \leq (R - 1)x_j \tag{10.38}$$

$$\sum_{j \in V} z_{ij} - \sum_{k \in V'} z_{jk} = x_j \tag{10.39}$$

$$\sum_{i \in V} z_{it} = 1 \tag{10.40}$$

$$z_{ij} \leq y_{ij} \tag{10.41}$$

$$x_i, y_{ij} \in \{0, 1\}, z_{ij} \in \{0, 1, \ldots, R - 1\} \tag{10.42}$$

Here, the first term of the cost function implies that we intend to find a maximum edge-weighted subnetwork, while the second term is used to control the number of biochemical reactions involved in the subnetwork. The idea behind the model is that we aim to find a maximum edge-weighted subnetwork with a specific size R that accomplishes the signal transduction process with as few biochemical reactions as possible. Note that without the second term of the cost function, the model tends to find a dense subgraph with R nodes since more edges will definitely correspond to the larger weight of the subgraph. Constraints (10.34) and (10.35) are respectively the relaxed counterparts of constraints (10.22) and (10.23), which ensure that we can find a general signaling network instead of a linear pathway. All other constraints have the same meanings as in the previous model.

In most cases, R, the number of components in a signaling network, is unknown. Hence, it is more appropriate to set R as an upper abound. For such a general case, we reformulate (10.31)–(10.42) by holding all constraints except changing the constraint (10.40), into

$$\sum_{i \in V} z_{it} = R - \sum_{i \in V'} x_i$$

which denotes that all the remaining flow (not exactly 1) enters the ending node t. Totally, before the flow just arrives at the ending node, $\sum_{i \in V} x_i - 1$ components are selected. Hence, the remaining flow is $R - \sum_{i \in V} x_i$, which enters into the ending node t. This constraint, along with the second term of the cost function, controls the numbers of components and biochemical reactions in the signaling network. The models described above are all ILP models for which it is difficult to find optimal solutions within an acceptable timeframe if the network is large. To make them tractable and suitable for large-scale interaction networks, we can relax the constraints $x_i \in \{0, 1\}$, $y_{ij} \in \{0, 1\}$ to $0 \leq x_i \leq 1$, $0 \leq y_{ij} \leq 1$, and $z_{ij} \in \{0, 1, \ldots, R - 1\}$ to $0 \leq z_{ij} \leq R - 1$, which can be handled through linear programming algorithms. A variant of the network flow models mentioned above has been used to detect connected signaling networks [ZhaX09].

10.5 INFERRING SIGNALING NETWORKS FROM EXPERIMENTAL EVIDENCE

In contrast to extracting signaling pathways from high-throughput data, much fragmentary knowledge of components and reactions involved in a biological process can be collected from experimental observations and existing literature, which provides valuable information for determining signal transduction networks. For example, Yuryev et al. presented a methodology for automatic compilation of biological association networks from the literature. These data are used for automatic signaling pathway reconstruction [Yur06]. Albert et al. presented a network synthesis framework that determines a sparsest graph consistent with available experimental observations [Alb07, Alb08]. Network synthesis is quite reasonable and very useful in assembling such fragmentary knowledge into a relatively complete signal transduction pathway.

As stated by Albert et al. [Alb07, Alb08], experimental information about the involvement of a component in a signaling pathway can be classified into three categories. Enzymatic activity and protein–protein interactions provide biochemical evidence indicating direct relationships between two components. Chemical or exogenous treatments of a component provide pharmacological evidence of indirect relationships between components. Biochemical evidence and pharmacological evidence can be represented as component-to-component relationships such as "A promotes B" (denoted by A → B) and "A inhibits B" (denoted by A ⊣ B), which correspond to directed edges from A to B in a graph representing a signaling network. Different responses to a stimulus in wild-type organisms versus mutant organism provide genetic evidences for the involvement of the product of the mutated gene in the signal transduction process. Genetic evidence leads to double causal inferences like "C promotes the process through which A promotes B." If C is an enzyme-catalyzing a reaction in which A is transformed into B, then such genetic evidence is represented by A $\rightarrow$ B and C $\rightarrow$ B [Alb07]. If the interaction between A and B is direct and C is not a catalyst of the A–B interaction, C is assumed to activate A. In all other cases, an unknown intermediary vertex (pseudovertex) is introduced into path AB and C is assumed to activate this pseudovertex, which corresponds to the intersection of two paths A $\Rightarrow$ B and C $\Rightarrow$ B. The main idea of the network synthesis method is to find a minimal graph in terms of pseudovertex number and edge number such that it is consistent with all reachability relationships between real vertices [Alb07, Alb08]. This is a combinatorial optimization problem. The algorithm for solving it consists of two parts:

1. Transitive reduction of the resulting graph subject to the constraints that no edges denoting direct relationships are eliminated. This process is formulated as the binary transitive reduction (BTR) problem defined below.
2. Pseudovertex collapse subject to the constraints that real vertices are not eliminated. This process is formulated as the pseudovertex collapse (PVC) problem.

Given a directed graph $G = (V, E)$, an edge labeling function $w : E \mapsto \{0, 1\}$ is defined on E, where $u \xrightarrow{0} v$ and $u \xrightarrow{1} v$ correspond to the biological relationships "u promotes v" and "u inhibits v," respectively. The parity of a path P from u to v is $\sum_{e \in P} w(e)$ (mod)2. A path of parity of 0 (respectively 1) is called a path of even (respectively odd) parity. $u \xRightarrow{x} v$ denotes a path from u to v with parity $x \in \{0, 1\}$. Reachable(E) is the set of all order triples (u, v, x); for instance, $u \xRightarrow{x} v$ is a path of $G = (V, E)$. With these notations, the BTR problem [Alb07] is defined as

- Given a directed graph $G = (V, E)$ with an edge labeling function $w : E \mapsto \{0, 1\}$ and a set of critical edges $E_c \subseteq E$, find a minimal subgraph $G' = (V, E')$ such that $E_c \subseteq E' \subseteq E$ and reachable(E') = reachable(E).

The BTR problem is NP-hard and thus cannot be solved within polynomial time unless P $=$ NP. A $2 + o(1)$-approximation algorithm is given by Albert et al. [Alb08]. The BTR problem can be solved in polynomial time if G is a directed acyclic graph. On the other hand, the PVC problem [Alb07] is defined as

- Given a directed graph $G = (V, E)$ with an edge labeling function $w : E \mapsto \{0, 1\}$ and a pseudovertex set $v' \subseteq V$, find a subgraph $G'' = (V'', E'')$ with minimum V'' such that G'' is obtained from G by a sequence of permissible collapse operations,

where collapsing two pseudovertices u and v is permissible if and only if in(u) $=$ in(v) and out(u) $=$ out(v), where in(v) $= [(u, x)|u \xRightarrow{x} v, x \in \{0, 1\}] - \{v\}$ and

$\text{out}(v) = [(u, x)| \ v \overset{x}{\Rightarrow} u, x \in \{0, 1\}] - \{v\}$. The PVC problem can be solved in polynomial time [Alb07].

The BTR problem describes how to reduce the graph by eliminating spurious inferred edges, and the PVC problem is to reduce the unnecessary redundancy of the resulting graph. With these two main operations, the formal framework of the network synthesis procedure is given as follows [Alb07]:

Step 1: Encoding Single Causal Inferences. Build a network from all causal inferences of type $A \overset{0}{\to} B$ or $A \overset{1}{\to} B$ which correspond to critical edges. Solve the BTR problem for this network.

Step 2: Encoding Double Causal Inferences. Consider each indirect causal relationship $A \overset{x}{\to} (B \overset{y}{\to} C)$ where $x, y \in \{0, 1\}$. New nodes or edges are added on the basis of the following cases:

If $B \overset{y}{\to} C$ is a critical edge, add $A \overset{x}{\to} B$.

If there is no subgraph of the form

$$A$$
$$\Downarrow x$$
$$B \overset{a}{\Rightarrow} D \overset{b}{\Rightarrow} c$$

for some node D where $b = a + b = y \pmod 2$, then add the subgraph

$$A$$
$$\downarrow x$$
$$B \overset{a}{\longrightarrow} P \overset{b}{\longrightarrow} c$$

to the network and P is the added pseudonode. Solve the PVC problem for the resulting graph.

Step 3: Final Reduction. Solve the BTR problem for the network.

The network synthesis procedure was applied to synthesize a signaling network for abscisic acid (ABA)-induced stomatal closure. The result was also compared with the manually curated network [LiS06], which shows that network synthesis approach performs well.

10.6 SUMMARY

In this chapter, we introduced some methods for modeling and inferring signal transduction pathways. Particularly, we described integer linear programming approaches which are able to uncover signaling networks as a whole integrity instead of using a scoring-assembling strategy like most of other methods. For inferring signaling networks from high-throughput data, although the computational methods demonstrated the ability to recover known signaling pathways, such methods heavily depend on the quality of data. On the other hand, for inferring signaling networks from partial experimental observations, a reliable pathway can be obtained only if prior experimental observations are sufficient. Although much progress has been made in this important area, an iterative refining process between theoretical prediction and experimental confirmation is still necessary to identify accurate biological signaling networks.

CHAPTER 11

OTHER TOPICS AND NEW TRENDS

11.1 NETWORK-BASED PROTEIN STRUCTURAL ANALYSIS

In this book, we described mainly the topics related to macromolecule interaction networks in living organisms. However, besides those biomolecular networks, many sequence and structure problems have also been studied by network-based methods, and such network-based analysis is an emerging topic in the area of bioinformatics and systems biology. Proteins are the machinery of a cellular system, and are responsible for almost all the functions. It is generally believed that protein functions are determined by or closely related to their 3D structures. Therefore, there has been much research work analyzing protein structures, including protein structure prediction, protein structure alignment, protein structure classification [WaY09b], and function prediction from protein structure [Liu08]. In this section, we do not intend to cover all of these contents, but focus on function-related analysis based on network representation of proteins.

Networks have been employed to represent proteins and solve many problems related to protein structure analysis. Much work has been conducted on the study of the topology and biological significance of networks formed by residues in contact [Gre03]. For instance, a protein structure can be converted into a network where the nodes represent the C_α atoms of the residues and the links denote the interactions (contacts or distances) between these residues. In such a network representation, a protein with N residues can be represented as an $N \times N$ matrix. If two residues in a protein are in contact (i.e., the distance between C_α atoms is smaller than a threshold),

Biomolecular Networks. By Luonan Chen, Rui-Sheng Wang, and Xiang-Sun Zhang
Copyright © 2009 John Wiley & Sons, Inc.

the corresponding entry is set as 1, otherwise 0. This matrix is actually the adjacency matrix of the network representation of a protein. Vendruscolo et al. have reported that networks formed by protein interresidue contacts [Ven02], where a contact is defined as a C_α separation ≤ 8.5 Å, have small-world properties and that residues with high network betweenness make important contacts in the model of folding intermediates. Taylor and Vaisman introduced residue contact networks defined in a more robust way with Delaunay tessellation [Tay06]. Using this kind of representation, they analyzed the protein contact graph in terms of complex networks. They found that protein contact networks have small-world characteristics but technically are not small-world networks. It has been also found that networks formed by native structures and by most misfolded decoys can be differentiated by their respective graph properties. Currently, contact maps and Delaunay tessellated graphs are the two most commonly used representations of protein 3D structures.

Jiao et al. proposed a method to construct a weighted amino acid network [Jia07]. The weight of a link is based on the contact energy between residues. They studied the statistical properties of such networks and the influence of the edge weights on network properties. Besides the position of residues, the interactions between different residues are also critically important for a protein's function and stability. Brinda and Vishveshwara represented a protein structure as a network of noncovalent connections between amino acids [Bri05], in which each amino acid is a node, and the strength of the noncovalent interactions between two amino acids is used for edge determination. They found that the aromatic residues along with arginine, histidine, and methionine act as strong hubs at high interaction cutoffs, whereas the hydrophobic leucine and isoleucine residues are usually added to these hubs at low interaction cutoffs and form weak hubs. Atilgan et al. represented proteins as networks of interacting amino acid pairs [Ati04] and analyzed the local and global properties of these networks with their spatial locations in the three-dimensional structure of the protein. By conducting statistics on a set of nonhomologous proteins, their study indicates that regular packing is preserved in short-range interactions and the shortest path lengths in the networks, and residue fluctuations are highly correlated. In the network representation of a protein, since residues act as nodes, such networks are usually called residue networks, to distinguish them from protein networks whose vertices are proteins.

In addition to studies on statistical properties, residue networks have wide real-world applications. As an application of network representation of a protein structure in classification, Muppirala and Li used the network pattern of conserved hydrophobic residues for discriminating nonnative structures from native ones [Mup06]. Kucukural et al. treated protein fold as a classification problem and used network topological properties to discriminate protein folds [Kuc08]. Using the characteristic path length of contact networks, Dokholyan et al. reported being able to classify hypothetical pretransition and posttransition structures that could not be distinguished via RMSE deviation, solvent accessible area, or radius of gyration [Dok02].

Identifying active-site residues from a protein three-dimensional structure is an important and difficult task. A number of more recent studies use the network representation of protein structures to identify critical functional residues. A relatively early attempt was conducted by Amitai et al. [Ami04], with amino acid residues as the graph nodes and their interactions with each other as the graph edges. They found that active-site, ligand-binding, and evolutionary conserved residues typically have high closeness values. Closeness and surface accessibility are combined as features that can identify active-site residues with reasonably high accuracy. Sol and O'Meara represented protein complexes as small-world networks in which highly central amino acid residues occurring frequently at protein–protein interfaces are found to correspond to or be in direct contact with an experimentally annotated hotspot [Sol05]. Instead of using betweenness, Cusack et al. defined the dynamic connectivity of a residue, that is, the number of times that the residue is traversed in connecting every pair of residues using shortest paths in the network; the residues with the largest dynamic connectivity are predicted as critical residues for protein function [Cus07]. More recently, pocket, as an extension to functional residues has been used as a bridge between protein structure and protein function. In particular, the pocket similarity network is adopted to annotate protein functions [Liu07], which demonstrates remarkable effectiveness of such a technique. For comprehensive comparison of phylogenetic approaches and network-based methods for predicting critical residues, the reader is referred to the paper by Thibert et al. [Thi05], which shows that a combination of phylogenetic and network-based methods has a superior performance.

11.2 INTEGRATION OF BIOMOLECULAR NETWORKS

In this book, we discuss mainly five types of biomolecular networks: transcriptional regulatory networks, gene regulatory networks, protein interaction networks, signaling networks, and metabolic networks. Along with coexpression networks, those biomolecular networks represent biochemical networks at different cellular levels such as transcription, translation, and posttranslation, and account for specific biological functions. Each type of network lends insight into a different slice of biological organization and system. For example, signaling networks are responsible for reflecting external stimuli through interacting proteins. Transcriptional regulatory networks cause some genes to be expressed so as to perform certain functions. Integrating different types of networks may paint a more comprehensive picture of the overall biological system under study [Sha06], and is able to describe cellular systems more accurately and systematically, and as a result helps us better understand biological mechanisms. With rapid accumulation of biomolecules data, new analysis methods are being developed to integrate data from transcriptome, proteome, interactome, and metabolome. One type of integration is defined over the same set of components and achieved by merging different networks into a single network with multiple types of interactions. The other type of integration is defined over different sets of components with overlapping, and the integrated heterogeneous network for those components reveals biological information at different levels.

There are many examples for the first type of integration. Commonly, a fundamental problem in this kind of integration is to identify functional modules, predict protein functions, or study network motifs that are supported by interactions of multiple types. Kelly and Ideker studied the combination of protein–protein and genetic interactions in yeast [Kel05], and found that a large proportion of genetic interactions are significantly associated with between-pathways in the physical interactions network, which suggests that genetic interactions tend to bridge genes operating in two pathways with complementary functions. Gunsalus et al. integrated protein interaction networks, coexpression networks, and phenotypic similarity networks to provide a system-level model for studying the development processes of *Caenorhabditis elegans* [Gun05]. Yeger-Lotem et al. investigated the overrepresentation of network motifs in a combined network of protein–protein interactions and protein–DNA interactions, and found several types of motifs exhibiting coregulation and complex formation [Yeg04]. Zhang et al. integrated protein–protein interactions, genetic interactions, coexpression correlation, and transcriptional interactions in yeast, and studied motifs in the combined network [Zha05]. They combined enriched network motifs with network themes, thereby providing a useful simplification of complex biological relationships.

The second type of integration has been studied in several ways. Integrating protein complexes and transcriptional interactions reveals that members of protein complexes tend to be coregulated on the transcriptional level, which can be used to predict previously uncharacterized transcription interactions by cross-species analysis [Sim04, Tan07]. Yeang and Vingron proposed a joint model of gene regulation and metabolic reactions [Yea06]. The links bridging regulatory networks and metabolic networks specify the feedback control from the substrates of metabolic reactions to enzyme gene expressions. Their study provides insight into the mechanisms of the coupling between the two systems and enzyme gene regulation. Pir et al. investigated the relationship between transcriptomic and metabolic data [Pir06]. Specifically, according to the variation in transcriptome data in response to three genetic perturbations, genes whose expression levels change significantly are identified. Then, the metabolic variables are modeled by the expression levels of significant genes through partial least squares (PLS). The study helps discriminate the effects among the growth medium, dilution rate, and the deletion of specific genes on the transcriptome and metabolite profiles. In addition, some preliminary dynamic analyses of integrated regulation and metabolic systems have been completed, and revealed novel mechanisms in *S. cerevisiae* and *E. coli* [Her06b]. A kinetic model integrating signal transduction, metabolism, and regulation has been constructed to describe the response of *S. cerevisiae* to osmotic shock [Kli05]. A major drawback of the kinetic modeling is that it requires an exhaustive list of kinetic parameters for the reactions, which is difficult to obtain. To overcome this limitation, flux balance analysis–based strategies are proposed to simulate the dynamic behavior of integrated metabolic, regulatory, and signaling networks [LeJ08, Cov08]. As is well known to us, intracellular biomolecular networks are highly integrated and interlaced, which means that developing sophisticated modeling methods for different types of biological processes is urgently demanded so as to eventually elucidate complicated biological phenomena at a whole-cell level.

11.3 POSTTRANSCRIPTIONAL REGULATION OF NONCODING RNAs

Noncoding RNA (ncRNA) is a kind of RNA that is transcribed from DNA but not translated into proteins. MicroRNA (miRNA), a single-stranded RNA molecule with about 21–23 nucleotides in length, is a family of small noncoding RNAs and has been found to play unique roles in posttranscriptional regulation in both prokaryotes and eukaryotes. More recently, miRNAs have attracted much attention from researchers in molecular biology. Until now, hundreds of miRNAs have been found in worms, flies, plants, and mammals. Initially, the miRNA family was discovered as small temporal RNAs that regulate developmental transitions in *C. elegans*, and are now found to have diverse expression patterns and probably regulate many aspects of development and physiology. Although the detailed regulation mechanisms of miRNAs are largely unknown, some of them have already been found to possess the characteristic targets and are also recognized to negatively regulate the expression of target genes at the posttranscriptional level by base-pairing with mRNAs.

An important potential of the roles of miRNAs is that they can inhibit the expression of target genes through RNA interference pathways and are commonly downregulated in human cancers. For example, one study shows that miRNA acts as a new component of the p53 signaling pathway and has an intrinsic function in tumor suppression [HeL07]. In the study, three miRNAs have been validated as direct transcriptional targets of the p53 tumor suppressor protein, which provide a novel mechanism of p53-mediated growth arrest in mammalian cells. In addition, miRNAs are also found to have tissue-specific expression patterns, and mRNA targets of several highly tissue-specific miRNAs are expressed in the same tissue as the miRNAs but at significantly lower levels than in tissues where the miRNAs are not present [Soo06]. Therefore, measuring the expression of miRNAs in tissues of different conditions is important for investigating the functions of miRNAs. Liang et al. provided expression data of 345 miRNAs in 40 normal human tissues and presented a global view of tissue distribution of miRNAs in relation to their chromosomal locations and genomic structures [Lia07]. Lu et al. used the miRNA expression profiling method to analyze mammalian miRNAs [LuJ05] and found that the miRNA profiles are surprisingly informative in reflecting the developmental lineage and differentiation state of the tumors. These findings make it possible to classify different types of human tumors according to miRNA profiling and provide the potential of miRNA profiling in cancer diagnosis.

With an increasing number of ncRNAs shown to mediate posttranscriptional processes and regulate critical pathways in prokaryotes and eukaryotes, quantitatively characterizing their regulation roles in gene expression is a new and challenging task [Shi07, Lev07]. Levine et al. adopted a quantitative approach to study bacterial small RNAs (sRNAs) in *E. coli* and found that the mode of gene regulation of sRNAs has characteristics distinct from those of TF regulation [Lev07]. These include a threshold-linear response with a tunable threshold, a robust noise resistance characteristic, and a built-in capability for hierarchical crosstalk. Shimoni et al. used dynamical simulations to characterize the regulation modes of sRNAs and compared them with the transcriptional regulation mediated by TFs and posttranslational regulation achieved by protein interactions [Shi07]. They showed quantitatively that the regulation by sRNA is advantageous when fast responses to external signals are needed, which is consistent with experimental data on its involvement in stress responses. In a more recent study, Mehta et al., used a quantitative approach to compare the regulation of sRNAs with conventional transcription factors (TFs) in terms of steady-state behavior, noise properties, frequency-dependent amplification, and dynamical response to large input signals and gain important insight into the advantages of sRNA regulation [Meh08]. In addition, there are a large number of methods for predicting mRNA targets of noncoding RNAs. With the availability of more expression data on ncRNAs, a promising goal is to discover regulatory networks with transcription and posttranscription events, that is, reconstruct TF–ncRNAs–gene regulatory networks of two levels through expression profiles [WaR09].

11.4 BIOMOLECULAR INTERACTIONS AND HUMAN DISEASES

As described in this book, biomolecular networks have been systematically investigated from various perspectives. In particular, in recent years (as of 2009), integration of heterogeneous biomolecular networks at different levels is being touched on and provides comprehensive insights into our understanding of the fundamental mechanisms of cellular systems. All of these studies are enhanced by the roles of systems biology approaches played in uncovering the etiology of important human diseases. Actually, some researchers already turn their attention to study the relations between biomolecular interactions and human diseases, which provide the clues for diagnosis, drug treatment, and medical therapy before costly experiments are conducted.

At the transcriptome level, in much earlier years, gene expression data were utilized to identify specific disease-related genes by differential expression analysis with respect to a certain disease. More recently, with network-based tools available, gene regulatory networks and transcription regulatory networks provide a platform for conducting systemwide analysis on human disease. Tuck et al. constructed sample-specific regulatory networks to identify links between transcription factors (TFs) and regulated genes that differentiate between healthy and diseased states [Tuc06]. Compared with those approaches merely using gene expression profiles, their approach can identify specific TF–gene pairs with differential activity between healthy and diseased states, and thus can reveal biological processes in addition to individual genes. Ergün et al. used reverse-engineered gene networks combined with expression profiles to identify genes and associated pathways that mediate a disease [Erg07]. By applying their method to nonrecurrent primary and metastatic prostate cancer data, they found the androgen receptor gene and the androgen receptor pathway, which is a highly enriched pathway for metastatic prostate cancer. Döhr et al. developed a method to associate disease genes with gene regulatory networks by promoter analysis [Doh07]. This approach was applied to "mature-onset diabetes of the young" (MODY)-associated genes, which helps find MODY-related insulin/glucose signaling pathways.

At the interactome level, a large number of studies have been conducted to unravel the molecular basis of human disease by analyzing human molecular interaction networks. Some of them focus on identifying new disease genes [WuX08] and disease-related subnetworks [ChJ06], whereas some others focus on network-based disease classification [Chu07]. Disease genes and nondisease genes may have different local topological features in protein interaction networks, which can be used to predict disease genes. Wachi et al. studied the degree distribution and centrality of the genes that are differentially expressed with respect to lung squamous cell cancer in a human protein interaction network [Wac05]. They found that upregulated genes in the cancerous tissues tend to be highly connected and central, which suggests that upregulated genes are essential for proliferation of the cancerous tissue. Jonsson and Bates performed a systematic computation study of a subset of proteins related to cancer, and derived some common topological features of cancer proteins in the human protein interaction network [Jon06]. In particular, they showed that these proteins tend to have, on average, twice as many interaction partners as noncancer proteins. By defining several topological features of nodes, Xu and Li used a k-nearest-neighbor classifier to predict genes related to disease on the basis of protein interaction networks [XuJ06]. In addition to the discovery of some novel diseases, another interesting finding in their work is that disease genes tend to be clustered in literature compiled protein interaction networks (which is believed to be more reliable), which implies that proteins related to a disease tend to interact with other proteins involved in the same disease. A similar observation was made by Lim et al. [Lim06], who developed an interaction network of proteins related to ataxias and disorders of Purkinje cell degeneration. Chen et al. presented a computational method based on a heuristic score to mine the Alzheimer's disease subnetwork of interacting proteins from protein interaction data [ChJ06]. In contrast to the study of a single disease in protein interaction networks, Goh et al. explored the properties of the human disease network (the associations between human genetic diseases) and disease gene network (the associations between disease genes) [Goh07]. Their study indicates that genes associated with similar disorders/diseases show both higher likelihood of physical interactions between their products and higher expression profiling similarity for their transcripts, which again supports the finding that proteins related to a disease are more likely to interact with proteins already known to cause similar diseases and confirms the existence of distinct disease-specific functional modules. Comprehensive reviews on computational approaches for analyzing human diseases through protein interactions are given in the literature [Kan07, Ide08].

Finally, at metabolic and signaling network level, there is also much work on disease-related studies [LeD08, Fin03]. Using network systems biology approaches to uncover the molecular mechanisms of human disease represents an important step forward in biomedical science. With the great advances in cell biology, the pathogeny of many complicated diseases will be much clearer to us, and their therapies and treatments are expected to be largely improved.

11.5 SUMMARY

In this chapter, we briefly described several new network-based topics, including network analysis of protein structures, integration of molecular networks, and the post-transcriptional regulation of ncRNAs, which are becoming important research cores. It should be noted that unlike basic disciplines, the research topics of bioinformatics and systems biology are constantly changing, with new technologies always appearing. As time goes by, only those models that are able to reveal biological mechanisms will be deposited, and those methods that really provide practical utility will become permanently useful tools.

REFERENCES

[Abu06]   Aburatani, S., Saito, S., Toh, H., Horimoto, K., A graphical chain model for inferring regulatory system networks from gene expression profiles, *Stat. Methodol.* **3**:17–28 (2006).

[Ada06]   Adamcsek, B., Palla, G., Farkas, I. J., Derenyi, I., Vicsek, T., CFinder: Locating cliques and overlapping modules in biological networks, *Bioinformatics* **22**:1021–1023 (2006).

[Ait06]   Aittokallio, T., Schwikowski, B., Graph-based methods for analyzing networks in cell biology, *Brief. Bioinform.* **7**:243–255 (2006).

[Aku99]   Akutsu, T., Miyano, S., Kuhara, S., Identification of genetic networks from a small number of gene expression patterns under the Boolean network model, *Pac. Symp. Biocomput.* 17–28 (1999).

[Aku00]   Akutsu, T., Miyano, S., Kuhara, S., Inferring qualitative relations in genetic networks and metabolic pathways, *Bioinformatics* **16**:727–734 (2000).

[Alb00]   Albert, R., Jeong, H., Barabasi, A. L., Error and attack tolerance of complex networks, *Nature* **406**(6794):378–382 (2000).

[Alb02]   Albert, R., Barabási, A. L., Statistical mechanics of complex networks, *Rev. Modern Phys.* **74**:47–97 (2002).

[Alb05]   Albert, R., Scale-free networks in cell biology, *J. Cell Sci.* **118**:4947–4957 (2005).

[Alb07]   Albert, R., DasGupta, B., Dondi, R., et al., A novel method for signal transduction network inference from indirect experimental evidence, *J. Comput. Biol.* **14**:927–949 (2007).

[Alb08]   Albert, R., DasGupta, B., Dondi, R., Sontag, E., Inferring (biological) signal transduction networks via transitive reductions of directed graphs, *Algorithmica* **51**:129–159 (2008).

[Alo07]   Alon, U., Network motifs: Theory and experimental approaches, *Nature Rev. Genet.* **8**:450–461 (2007).

[Alt00]   Alter, O., Brown, P. O., Botstein, D., Singular value decomposition for genome-wide expression data processing and modeling, *Proc. Natl. Acad. Sci. USA* **97**:10101–10106 (2000).

[Alt03]   Alter, O., Brown, P. O., Botstein, D., Generalized singular value decomposition for comparative analysis of genome-scale expression data sets of two different organisms, *Proc. Natl. Acad. Sci. USA* **100**:3351–3356 (2003).

[Ami04]   Amitai, G., Shemesh, A., Sitbon, E., Shklar, M., Netanely, D., et al., Network analysis of protein structures identifies functional residues, *J. Mol. Biol.* **344**:1135–1146 (2004).

[Api01]   Apic, G., Gough, J., Teichmann, S. A., Domain combinations in archaeal, eubacterial and eukaryotic proteomes, *J. Mol. Biol.* **310**(2):311–325 (2001).

[Ara07]   Aragues, R., Sali, A., Bonet, J., Marti-Renom, M. A., Oliva, B., Characterization of protein hubs by inferring interacting motifs from protein interactions, *PLoS Comput. Biol.* **3**(9):e178 (2007).

[Arg07]   Arga, K. Y., Önsan, Z., Kiidar, B., Ölgen, K., Nielsen, J., Understanding signaling in yeast: Insights from network analysis, *Biotechnol. Bioeng.* **97**:1246–1258 (2007).

[Ari04]   Arita, M., The metabolic world of *Escherichia coli* is not small, *Proc. Natl. Acad. Sci. USA* **101**(6):1543–1547 (2004).

[Arn05]   Arnau, V., Mars, S., Marin, I., Iterative cluster analysis of protein interaction data, *Bioinformatics* **21**:364–378 (2005).

[Ast01]   Asthagiri, A. R., Lauffenburger, D. A., A computational study of feedback effects on signal dynamics in a mitogen-activated protein kinase (MAPK) pathway model, *Biotechnol. Prog.* **17**:227–239 (2001).

[Ati04]   Atilgan, A. R., Akan, P., Baysal, C., Small-world communication of residues and significance for protein dynamics, *Biophys. J.* **86**(1):85–91 (2004).

[Bab04]   Babu, M. M., Luscombe, N. M., Aravind, L., Gerstein, M., Teichmann, S. A., Structure and evolution of transcriptional regulatory networks, *Curr. Opin. Struct. Biol.* **14**:283–291 (2004).

[Bad03]   Bader, G. D., Hogue, C. W., An automated method for finding molecular complexes in large protein interaction networks, *BMC Bioinform.* **4**:2 (2003).

[Bad04]   Bader, J. S., Chaudhuri, A., Rothberg, J. M., Chant, J., Gaining confidence in high-throughput protein interaction networks, *Nature Biotechnol.* **22**:78–85 (2004).

[Baj03]   Bajic, V. B., Seah, S. H., Dragon Gene Start Finder identifies approximate locations of the 5′ ends of genes, *Nucleic Acids Res.* **31**(13):3560–3563 (2003).

[Bal03]   Balaji, S., Babu, M. M., Iyer, L. M., Luscombe, N. M., Aravind, L., Comprehensive analysis of combinatorial regulation using the transcription regulatory network of yeast, *J. Mol. Biol.* **360**:213–227 (2003).

[Ban03]   Banerjee, N., Zhang, M. Q., Identifying cooperativity among transcription factors controlling the cell cycle in yeast, *Nucleic Acids Res.* **31**:7024–7031 (2003).

[Ban06]   Bandyopadhyay, S., Sharan, R., Ideker, T., Systematic identification of functional orthologs based on protein network comparison, *Genome Res.* **16**(3):428–435 (2006).

[BaM06]   Bansal, M., Gatta, G. D., Bernardo, D. D., Inference of gene regulatory networks and compound mode of action from time course gene expression profiles, *Bioinformatics* **22**(7):815–822 (2006).

[Bar99]   Barabasi, A. L., Albert, R., Emergence of scaling in random networks, *Science* **286**:509–512 (1999).

[Bar04]   Barabasi, A. L., Oltvai, Z. N., Network biology: Understanding the cell's functional organization, *Nature Rev. Genet.* **5**:101–113 (2004).

[Bar06]   Barenco, M., Tomescu, D., Brewer, D., Callard, R., Stark, J., et al., Ranked prediction of p53 targets using hidden variable dynamic modeling, *Genome Biol.* **7**:R25 (2006).

[Bas05]   Basso, K., Margolin, A. A., Stolovitzky, G., Klein, U., Dalla-Favera, R., Califano, A., Reverse engineering of regulatory networks in human B cells, *Nature Genet.* **37**(4):382–390 (2005).

[Bat06a]   Batada, N. N., Hurst, L. D., Tyers, M., Evolutionary and physiological importance of hub proteins, *PLoS Comput. Biol.* **2**(7):e88 (2006a).

[Bat06b]   Batada, N. N., Reguly, T., Breitkreutz, A., Boucher, L., Breitkreutz, B. J., et al., Stratus not altocumulus: A new view of the yeast protein interaction network, *PLoS Biol.* **4**(10):e317 (2006b).

[Bat04]   Bateman, A., Coin, L., Durbin, R., Finn, R., Hollich, V., Griffiths-Jones, S., Khanna, A., Marshall, M., Moxon, S., Sonnhammer, E. L. L., Studholme, D., Yeats, C., Eddy, S., The Pfam protein families database, *Nucl. Acids. Res.* **32**:D138–D14 (2004).

[BaC06]   Barrett, C. L., Palsson, B. O., Iterative reconstruction of transcriptional regulatory networks: An algorithmic approach, *PLoS Comput. Biol.* **2**(5):e52 (2006).

[BaZ06]   Barutcuoglu, Z., Schapire, R. E., Troyanskaya, O. G., Hierarchical multi-label prediction of gene function, *Bioinformatics* **22**(7):830–836 (2006).

[Bea01]   Beasley, J. E., Planes, F. J., Recovering metabolic pathways via optimization, *Bioinformatics* **23**(1):92–98 (2001).

[Bea05]   Beal, M. J., Falciani, F., Ghahramani, Z., Rangel, C., Wild, D. L., A Bayesian approach to reconstructing genetic regulatory networks with hidden factors, *Bioinformatics* **21**:349–356 (2005).

[Beb07]   Bebek, G., Yang, J., PathFinder: Mining signal transduction pathway segments from protein–protein interaction networks, *BMC Bioinform.* **8**:335 (2007).

[Ben05]   Ben-Hur, A., Noble, W. S., Kernel methods for predicting protein–protein interactions, *Bioinformatics* **21**:i38–i46 (2005).

[Ber04a]   Berg, J., Lässig, M., Local graph alignment and motif search in biological networks, *Proc. Natl. Acad. Sci. USA* **101**:14689–14694 (2004a).

[Ber04b]   Berg, J., Lässig, M., Wagner, A., Structure and evolution of protein interaction networks: A statistical model for link dynamics and gene duplications, *BMC Evol. Biol.* **4**:51 (2004b).

[Ber05] Bernardo, D. D., Thompson, M. J., Gardner, T. S., et al., Chemogenomic profiling on a genome-wide scale using reverse-engineered gene networks, *Nature Biotechnol.* **23**:377–383 (2005).

[Ber06] Berg, J., Lässig, M., Cross-species analysis of biological networks by Bayesian alignment, *Proc. Natl. Acad. Sci. USA* **103**:10967–10972 (2006).

[BeS04] Bergmann, S., Ihmels, J., Barkai, N., Similarities and differences in genome-wide expression data of six organisms, *PLoS Biol.* **2**(1):e9 (2004).

[Bha99] Bhalla, U. S., Iyengar, R., Emergent properties of networks of biological signaling pathways, *Science* **283**:381–387 (1999).

[Bor98] Bork, P., Dandekar, T., Diaz-Lazcoz, Y., Eisenhaber, F., Huynen, M., Yuan, Y., Predicting function: From genes to genomes and back, *J. Mol. Biol.* **283**(4):707–725 (1998).

[Bou05] Boulesteix, A. L., Strimmer, K., Predicting transcription factor activities from combined analysis of microarray and ChIP data: A partial least squares approach, *Theor. Biol. Med. Model* **2**:23 (2005).

[Bow04] Bowers, P. M., Cokus, S. J., Eisenberg, D., Yeates, T. O., Use of logic relationships to decipher protein network organization, *Science* **306**:2246–2249 (2004).

[Boy03] Boyer, F., Viari, A., Ab initio reconstruction of metabolic pathways, *Bioinformatics* **19**:ii26–ii34 (2003).

[Bra02] Brazhnik, P., Fuente, A., Mendes, P., Gene networks: How to put the function in genomics, *Trends Biotechnol.* **20**(11):467–472 (2002).

[Bri05] Brinda, K. V., Vishveshwara, S., A network representation of protein structures: Implications for protein stability, *Biophys. J.* **89**:4159–4170 (2005).

[Bro02] Brown, T. A., *Genomes*, 2nd ed., BIOS Scientific Publishers, 2002.

[Bro06] Brohée, S., van Helden, J., Evaluation of clustering algorithms for protein–protein interaction networks, *BMC Bioinform.* **7**:488 (2006).

[Bru04] Brun, C., Herrmann, C., Guénoche, A., Clustering proteins from interaction networks for the prediction of cellular functions, *BMC Bioinform.* **5**:95 (2004).

[Bu03] Bu, D., Zhao, Y., Cai, L., Xue, H., Zhu, X., Lu, H., Zhang, J., Sun, S., Ling, L., Zhang, N., Li, G., Chen, R., Topological structure analysis of the protein–protein interaction network in budding yeast, *Nucleic Acids Res.* **31**(9):2443–2450 (2003).

[Buc04] Buck, M. J., Lieb, J. D., ChIP-chip: Considerations for the design, analysis, and application of genome-wide chromatin immunoprecipitation experiments, *Genomics* **83**:349–360 (2004).

[Bur03a] Burgard, A. P., Maranas, C. D., Optimization-based framework for inferring and testing hypothesized metabolic objective functions, *Biotechnol Bioeng.* **82**(6):670–677 (2003a).

[Bur03b] Burgard, A. P., Pharkya, P., Maranas, C. D., Optknock: A bilevel programming framework for identifying gene knockout strategies for microbial strain optimization, *Biotechnol Bioeng.* **84**(6):647–657 (2003b).

[Bur08] Burger, L., Nimwegen, E., Accurate prediction of protein–protein interactions from sequence alignments using a Bayesian method, *Mol. Syst. Biol.* **4**:165 (2008).

[Car06] Carninci, P., Sandelin, A., Lenhard, B., Katayama, S., Shimokawa, K., Ponjavic, J., Semple, C. A., Taylor, M. S., Engstrom, P. G., Frith, M. C., et al.,

Genome-wide analysis of mammalian promoter architecture and evolution, *Nature Genet.* **38**:626–635 (2006).

[Cas02]   Cascante, M. et al., Metabolic control analysis in drug discovery and disease, *Nature Biotechnol.* **20**(3):243–249 (2002).

[Cha06]   Chang, Y. H., Wang, Y. C., Chen, B. S., Identification of transcription factor co-operativity via stochastic system model, *Bioinformatics* **22**:2276–2282 (2006).

[Cha07]   Chaouiya, C., Petri net modelling of biological networks, *Brief. Bioinform.* **8**:210–219 (2007).

[Che08]   Chen, C. C., Zhu, X., Zhong, S., Selection of thermodynamic models for combinatorial control of multiple transcription factors in early differentiation of embryonic stem cells, *BMC Genomics* **9**(Suppl. 1):S18 (2008).

[ChC08]   Cheng, C., Li, L. M., Inferring microRNA activities by combining gene expression with microRNA target prediction, *PLoS ONE* **3**(4):e1989 (2008).

[ChG08]   Chen, G., Larsen, P., Almasri, E., Dai, Y., Rank-based edge reconstruction for scale-free genetic regulatory networks, *BMC Bioinform.* **9**(1):75 (2008).

[ChH04]   Chen, H. C., Lee, H. C., Lin, T. Y., Li, W. H., Chen, B. S., Quantitative characterization of the transcriptional regulatory network in the yeast cell cycle, *Bioinformatics* **20**, 1914–1927 (2004).

[ChH07]   Choi, H., Shen, R., Chinnaiyan, A. M., Ghosh, D., A latent variable approach for meta-analysis of gene expression data from multiple microarray experiments, *BMC Bioinform.* **8**(1):364 (2007).

[ChJ06]   Chen, J. Y., Shen, C., Sivachenko, A. Y., Mining Alzheimer disease relevant proteins from integrated protein interactome data, *Pac. Symp. Biocomput.* **11**:367–378 (2006).

[ChK05]   Chen, K. C., Wang, T. Y., Tseng, H. H., Huang, C. Y., Kao, C. Y., A stochastic differential equation model for quantifying transcription regulatory network in *Saccharomyces cerevisiae*, *Bioinformatics* **21**:2883–2890 (2005).

[ChL02]   Chen, L., Aihara, K., Stability of genetic regulatory networks with time delay, *IEEE Trans. Circuits Syst. I* **49**(5):602–608 (2002).

[ChL04]   Chen, L., Wang, R., Kobayashi, T., Aihara, K., Dynamics of gene regulatory networks with cell division cycle, *Phys. Rev. E* **70**:011909 (2004).

[ChL05]   Chen, L., Wang, R., Zhou, T., Aihara, K., Noise-induced cooperative behavior in a multi-cell system, *Bioinformatics* **21**:2722–2729 (2005).

[ChL06]   Chen, L., Wu, L., Wang, Y., Zhang, X. S., Inferring protein interactions from experimental data by association probabilistic method, *Proteins* **62**:833–837 (2006).

[Cho03]   Cho, K.-H., Wolkenhauer, O., Analysis and modelling of signal transduction pathways in systems biology, *Biochem. Soc. Trans.* **31**:1503–1509 (2003).

[Cho07]   Cho, Y. R., Hwang, W., Ramanathan, M., Zhang, A., Semantic integration to identify overlapping functional modules in protein interaction networks, *BMC Bioinform.* **8**:265 (2007).

[ChR08]   Cheong, R., Hoffmann, A., Levchenko, A., Understanding NF-κB signaling via mathematical modeling, *Mol. Syst. Biol.* **4**:192 (2008).

[ChT99]   Chen, T., He, H. L., Church, G. M., Modeling gene expression with differential equations, *Pac. Symp. Biocomput.* **4**:29–40 (1999).

[Chu06]   Chua, H. N., Sung, W. K., Wong, L., Exploiting indirect neighbours and topological weight to predict protein function from protein–protein interactions, *Bioinformatics* **22**(13):ô1623–1630 (2006).

[Chu07]   Chuang, H. Y., Lee, E., Liu, Y. T., Lee, D., Ideker, T., Network-based classification of breast cancer metastasis, *Mol. Syst. Biol.* **3**:140 (2007).

[ChX05]   Chen, X. W., Liu, M., Prediction of protein–protein interactions using random decision forest framework, *Bioinformatics* **21**:4394–4400 (2005).

[ChY04]   Chen, Y., Xu, D., Global protein function annotation through mining genome-scale data in yeast *Saccharomyces cerevisiae*, *Nucl. Acids. Res.* **32**:6414–6424 (2004).

[Cli03]   Cliften, P., Sudarsanam, P., Desikan, A., Fulton, L., Fulton, B., Majors, J., Waterston, R., Cohen, B. A., Johnston, M., Finding functional features in Saccharomyces genomes by phylogenetic footprinting, *Science* **301**:71–76 (2003).

[Cli07]   Climescu-Haulica, A., Quirk, M. D., A stochastic differential equation model for transcription regulatory networks, *BMC Bioinform.* **8**:S4 (2007).

[Coo06]   Cooper, S. J., Trinklein, N. D., Anton, E. D., Nguyen, L., Myers, R. M., Comprehensive analysis of transcriptional promoter structure and function in 1% of the human genome, *Genome Res.* **16**:1–10 (2006).

[Cov08]   Covert, M. W., Xiao, N., Chen, T. J., Karr, J. R., Integrating metabolic, transcription regulatory and signal transduction models in *Escherichia coli*, *Bioinformatics* **24**(18):2044–2050 (2008).

[Cra04]   Crampina, E. J. et al., Mathematical and computational techniques to deduce complex biochemical reaction mechanisms, *Prog. Biophys. Mol. Biol.* **86**:77–112 (2004).

[Cro06]   Croes, D. et al., Inferring meaningful pathways in weighted biochemical networks, *J. Mol. Biol.* **356**:222–236 (2006).

[Cus07]   Cusack, M. P., Thibert, B., Bredesen, D. E., Del Rio, G., Efficient identification of critical residues based only on protein structure by network analysis, *PLoS ONE* **2**(5):e421 (2007).

[Dai07]   Dai, X., He, J., Zhao, X., A new systematic computational approach to predicting target genes of transcription factors, *Nucleic Acids Res.* **35**(13):4433–4440 (2007).

[Das04]   Das, D., Banerjee, N., Zhang, M. Q., Interacting models of cooperative gene regulation, *Proc. Natl. Acad. Sci. USA* **101**:16234–16239 (2004).

[DaM04]   Dasika, M., Gupta, A., Maranas, C. D., Varner, J. D., A mixed integer linear programming (MILP) framework for inferring time delay in gene regulatory networks, *Pac. Symp. Biocomput.* **9**:474–485 (2004).

[Dat08]   Datta, D., Zhao, H., Statistical methods to infer cooperative binding among transcription factors in *Saccharomyces cerevisiae*, *Bioinformatics* **24**:545–552 (2008).

[Den02]   Deng, M., Mehta, S., Sun, F., Chen, T., Inferring domain–domain interactions from protein–protein interactions, *Genome. Res.* **12**:1540–1548 (2002).

[Den03a]   Deng, M., Sun, F., Chen, T., Assessment of the reliability of protein–protein interactions and protein function prediction, *Pac. Symp. Biocomput.* 140–151 (2003a).

[Den03b] Deng, M., Zhang, K., Mehta, S., Chen, T., Sun, F., Prediction of protein function using protein–protein interaction data, *J. Comput. Biol.* **10**(6):947–960 (2003b).

[Dep06] Deplancke, B., Mukhopadhyay, A., Ao, W., et al., A gene-centered *C. elegans* protein-DNA interaction network, *Cell* **125**(6):1193–1205 (2006).

[Dha99] D'haeseleer, P., Wen, X., Fuhrman, S., Linear modeling of mRNA expression levels during CNS development and injury, *Pac. Symp. Biocomput.* 41–52 (1999).

[Dha00] D'haeseleer, P., Liang, S., Somogyi, R., Genetic network inference: From coexpression clustering to reverse engineering, *Bioinformatics* **16**(8):707–726 (2000).

[Doh05] Döhr, S., Klingenhoff, A., Maier, H., Hrabé de Angelis, M., Werner, T., Schneider, R., Linking disease-associated genes to regulatory networks via promoter organization, *Nucleic Acids Res.* **33**(3):864–872 (2005).

[Doj06] Dojer, N., Gambin, A., Mizera, A., Wilczyński, B., Tiuryn, J., Applying dynamic Bayesian networks to perturbed gene expression data, *BMC Bioinform.* **7**:249 (2006).

[Dok02] Dokholyan, N. V., Li, L., Ding, F., Shakhnovich, E. I., Topological determinants of protein folding, *Proc. Natl. Acad. Sci. USA* **99**:8637–8641 (2002).

[Don00] Dongen, S., *Graph Clustering by Flow Simulation*, PhD thesis, Univ. Utrecht, May 2000.

[Dos07] Dost, B., Shlomi, T., Gupta, N., Ruppin, E., Bafna, V., Sharan, R., QNet: A tool for querying protein interaction networks, *Lect. Notes Bioinform.* **4453**:1–15 (2007).

[Dro05] Droit, A., Poirier, G. G., Hunter, J. M., Experimental and bioinformatic approaches for interrogating protein–protein interactions to determine protein function, *J. Mol. Endocrinol.* **34**:263–280 (2005).

[Dug99] Duggan, D. J., Bittner, M., Chen, Y., et al., Expression profiling using cDNA microarrays, *Nature Genet.* **21**(Suppl. 1):10–14 (1999).

[Dun05] Dunn, R., Dudbridge, F., Sanderson, C. M., The use of edge-betweenness clustering to investigate biological function in protein interaction networks, *BMC Bioinform.* **6**:39 (2005).

[Dut07] Dutkowski, J., Tiuryn, J., Identification of functional modules from conserved ancestral protein–protein interactions, *Bioinformatics* **23**(13):i149–i158 (2007).

[Edw00] Edwards, J. S., Palsson, B. O., Metabolic flux balance analysis and the in silico analysis of *Escherichia coli* K-12 gene deletions, *BMC Bioinform.* **1**:1 (2000).

[Eis03] Eisenberg, E., Levanon, E. Y., Preferential attachment in the protein network evolution, *Phys. Rev. Lett.* **91**:138701 (2003).

[Eka06] Ekman, D., Light, S., Björklund, K., Elofsson, A., What properties characterize the hub proteins of the protein–protein interaction network of *Saccharomyces cerevisiae?Genome Biol.* **7**:R45 (2006).

[Ela07] Elati, M., Neuvial, P., Bolotin-Fukuhara, M., Barillot, E., Radvanyi, F., et al., LICORN: Learning cooperative regulation networks from gene expression data, *Bioinformatics* **23**:2407–2414 (2007).

[Eln06] Elnitski, L., Jin, V. X., Farnham, P. J., Jones, S. J., Locating mammalian transcription factor binding sites: A survey of computational and experimental techniques, *Genome Res.* **16**(12):1455–1464 (2006).

[Enr99]   Enright, A. J., Iliopoulos, I., Kyrpides, N. C., Ouzounis, C. A., Protein interaction maps for complete genomes based on gene fusion events, *Nature* **402**:86–90 (1999).

[Erg07]   Ergün, A., Lawrence, C. A., Kohanski, M. A., Brennan, T. A., Collins, J. J., A network biology approach to prostate cancer, *Mol. Syst. Biol.* **3**:82 (2007).

[Est06]   Estrada, E., Virtual identification of essential proteins within the protein interaction network of yeast, *Proteomics* **6**:35–40 (2006).

[Eun04]   Eungdamrong, N. J., Iyengar, R., Modeling cell signaling networks, *Biol. Cell* **96**:355–362 (2004).

[Evl07]   Evlampiev, K., Isambert, H., Modeling protein network evolution under genome duplication and domain shuffling, *BMC Syst. Biol.* **1**:49 (2007).

[Fam03]   Famili, I., Palsson, B. O., Systemic metabolic reactions are obtained by singular value decomposition of genome-scale stoichiometric matrices, *J. Theor. Biol.* **224**:87–96 (2003).

[Fel00]   Fell, D. A., Wagner, A., The small world of metabolism, *Nature Biotechnol.* **18**:1121–1122 (2000).

[Fer07]   Ferro, A., Giugno, R., Pigolal, G., Pulvirenti, A., Skripin, D., Bader, G. D., Shasha, D., NetMatch: A cytoscape plugin for searching biological networks, *Bioinformatics* **23**:910–912 (2007).

[Fin03]   Finkel, T., Gutkind, J. S. (eds.), *Signal Transduction and Human Disease*, Wiley, Hoboken, NJ, 2003.

[Fla06]   Flannick, J., Novak, A., Srinivasan, B. S., McAdams, H. H., Batzoglou, S., Graemlin: General and robust alignment of multiple large interaction networks, *Genome Res.* **16**:1169–1181 (2006).

[Fle95]   Fleischmann, R. D. et al., Whole-genome random sequencing and assembly of *Haemophilus influenzae*, *Science* **269**:496–512 (1995).

[For03]   Föster, J., Famili, I., Fu, P., Palsson, B., Nielsen, J., Genome-scale reconstruction of the *Saccharomyces cerevisiae* metabolic network, *Genome Res.* **13**:244–253 (2003).

[For07]   Fortunato, S., Barthélemy, M., Resolution limit in community detection, *Proc. Natl. Acad. Sci. USA* **104**(1):36–41 (2007).

[Fri00]   Friedman, N., Linial, M., Nachman, I., Pe'er, D., Using Bayesian networks to analyze expression data, *J. Comput. Biol.* **7**:601–620 (2000).

[Fri04]   Friedman, N., Inferring cellular networks using probabilistic graphical models, *Science* **303**:799–805 (2004).

[Gao04]   Gao, F., Foat, B. C., Bussemaker, H. J., Defining transcriptional networks through integrative modeling of mRNA expression and transcription factor binding data, *BMC Bioinform.* **5**:31 (2004).

[Gar03]   Gardner, T. S., Bernardo, D. D., Lorenz, D., Collins, J. J., Inferring genetic networks and identifying compound mode of action via expression profiling, *Science* **301**:102–105 (2003).

[Gar79]   Garey, M. R., Johson, D. S., *Computers and Intractability: A Guide to the Theory of NP-Completeness*, Freeman, San Francisco, CA, 1979.

[Gav06]   Gavin, A. C., Aloy, P., Grandi, P., et al., Proteome survey reveals modularity of the yeast cell machinery, *Nature* **440**:631–636 (2006).

[GeH03]   Ge, H., Walhout, A. J. M., Vidal, M., Integrating "omic" information: A bridge between genomics and systems biology, *Trends Genet.* **19**:551–560 (2003).

[Gei07]   Geier, F., Timmer, J., Fleck, C., Reconstructing gene-regulatory networks from time series, knock-out data, and prior knowledge, *BMC Syst. Biol.* **1**:11 (2007).

[Gha97]   Ghahramani, Z., Hinton, G., *The EM Algorithm for Mixtures of Factor Analyzers*, Technical Report CRG-TR-96-1, 1997.

[Gib04]   Gibson, M., Mjolsness, E., Modeling the activity of single genes, in *Computational Modeling of Genetic and Biochemical Networks*, Bower, J. M., Bolour, H. (eds.), MIT Press, Cambridge, MA, 2004.

[Gil06a]   Gilbert, D., Heiner, M., From Petri nets to differential equations—an integrative approach for biochemical network analysis, *Lecture Notes in Computer Science* **4024**:181–200 (2006a).

[Gil06b]   Gilbert, D., Fuss, H., Gu, X., Orton, R., Robinson, S., Vyshemirsky, V., Kurth, M. J., Downes, C. S., Dubitzky, W., Computational methodologies for modelling, analysis and simulation of signalling networks, *Brief. Bioinform.* **7**(4):339–353 (2006b).

[Gil77]   Gillespie, D. T., Exact stochastic simulation of coupled chemical reactions, *J. Phys. Chem.* **81**(25):2340–2361 (1977).

[Gio03]   Giot, L., Bader, J. S., Brouwer, C., Chaudhuri, A., Kuang, B., et al., A protein interaction map of *Drosophila melanogaster*, *Science* **302**:1727–1736 (2003).

[Gir02]   Girvan, M., Newman, M. E. J., Community structure in social and biological networks, *Proc. Natl. Acad. Sci. USA* **99**(12):7821–7826 (2002).

[Gla98]   Glass, L., Hill, C., Ordered and disordered dynamics in random networks, *Europhys. Lett.* **41**(6):599–604 (1998).

[Gla05]   Glazov, E. A., Pheasant, M., McGraw, E. A., Bejerano, G., Mattick, J. S., Ultraconserved elements in insect genomes: A highly conserved intronic sequence implicated in the control of homothorax mRNA splicing, *Genome Res.* **15**:800–808 (2005).

[GO08]   Gene Ontology Consortium, The Gene Ontology project in 2008, *Nucleic Acids Res.* **36**(database issue):D440–D444 (2008).

[Goh02]   Goh, C. S., Cohen, F. E., Co-evolutionary analysis reveals insights into protein–protein interactions, *J. Mol. Biol.* **324**:177–192 (2002).

[Goh07]   Goh, K. I., Cusick, M. E., Valle, D., et al., The human disease network, *Proc. Natl. Acad. Sci. USA* **104**:8685–8690 (2007).

[Gom02]   Gomperts, B. D., Kramer, I. M., Tatham, P. E. R., *Signal Transduction*, Academic Press, San Diego, CA, 2002.

[Gre03]   Greene, L. H., Higman, V. A., Uncovering network systems within protein structures, *J. Mol. Biol.* **334**:781–791 (2003).

[Gui06]   Guimaraes, K., Jothi, R., Zotenko, E., Przytycka, T., Predicting domain–domain interactions using a parsimony approach, *Genome Biol.* **7**:R104 (2006).

[Gui08]   Guimaraes, K., Przytycka, T., Interrogating domain–domain interactions with parsimony based approaches, *BMC Bioinform.* **9**:171 (2008).

[Gui05]   Guimerà, R., Amaral, L. A. N., Functional cartography of complex metabolic networks, *Nature* **433**(7028):895–900 (2005).

[Gui07]   Guimerà, R., Sales-Pardo, M., Amaral, L. A. N., A network-based method for target selection in metabolic networks, *Bioinformatics* **23**:1616–1622 (2007).

[Gun05]   Gunsalus, K. C. et al., Predictive models of molecular machines involved in *Caenorhabditis elegans* early embryogenesis, *Nature* **436**:861–865 (2005).

[Hac07]   Hackney, J. A., Ehrenkaufer, G. M., Singh, U., Identification of putative transcription regulatory networks in *Entamoeba histolytica* using Bayesian inference, *Nucleic Acids Res.* **35**:2141–2152 (2007).

[Hah05]   Hahn, M. W., Kern, A. D., Comparative genomics of centrality and essentiality in three eukaryotic protein-interaction networks, *Mol. Biol. Evol.* **22**(4):803–806 (2005).

[Hal06]   Hallén, K., Bjökegren, J., Tegnér, J., Detection of compound mode of action by computational integration of whole-genome measurements and genetic perturbations, *BMC Bioinform.* **7**:51 (2006).

[Han04]   Han, D., Kim, H., Jang, W., Lee, S., Suh, J., PreSPI: A domain combination based prediction system for protein–protein interaction, *Nucl. Acids Res.* **32**:6312–6320 (2004).

[Han05]   Han, J. D. J., Dupuy, D., Bertin, N., Cusick, M. E., Vidal, M., Effect of sampling on topology predictions of protein–protein interaction networks, *Nature Biotechnol.* **23**:839–844 (2005).

[Han07]   Han, S., Yoon, Y., Cho, K. H., Inferring biomolecular interaction networks based on convex optimization, *Comput. Biol. Chem.* **31**(5–6):347–354 (2007).

[HaJ04]   Han, J. D., Bertin, N., Hao, T., Goldberg, D. S., Berriz, G. F., Zhang, L. V., Dupuy, D., Walhout, A. J., Cusick, M. E., Roth, F. P., Vidal, M., Evidence for dynamically organized modularity in the yeast protein–protein interaction network, *Nature* **430**:88–93 (2004).

[Har05]   Harbers, M., Carninci, P., Tag-based approaches for transcriptome research and genome annotation, *Nature Meth.* **2**:495–502 (2005).

[Har04]   Harbison, C. T., Gordon, D. B., Lee, T. I., et al., Transcriptional regulatory code of a eukaryotic genome, *Nature* **431**:99–104 (2004).

[Har99]   Hartwell, L. H., Hopfield, J. J., Leibler, S., Murray, A. W., From molecular to modular cell biology, *Nature* **402**:C47–C52 (1999).

[Hav04]   Haverty, P. M., Hansen, U., Weng, Z., Computational inference of transcription regulatory networks from expression profiling and transcription factor binding site identification, *Nucleic Acids Res.* **32**(1):179–188 (2004).

[Haw06]   Hawkins, R. D., Ren, B., Genome-wide location analysis: Insights on transcriptional regulation, *Human Mol. Genet.* **15**:R1–R7 (2006).

[Hay03]   Hayashida, M., Ueda, N., Akutsu, T., Inferring strengths of protein–protein interactions from experimental data using linear programming, *Bioinformatics* **19**:ii58–ii65 (2003).

[Hay04]   Hayashida, M., Ueda, N., Akutsu, T., A simple method for inferring strengths of protein–protein interactions, *Genome Inform.* **15**(1):56–68 (2004).

[Hei04]   Heiner, M., Koch, I., Will, J., Model validation of biological pathways using Petri nets-demonstrated for apoptosis, *Biosystems* **75**(1–3):15–28 (2004).

[HeL07]   He, L. et al., A microRNA component of the p53 tumour suppressor network, *Nature* **447**(7148):1130–1134 (2007).

[Her07]   Heron, E. A., Finkenstädt, B., Rand, D. A., Bayesian inference for dynamic tran-
            scriptional regulation: The Hes1 system as a case study, *Bioinformatics*
            23:2596–2603 (2007).

[Her06a]   Herrgård, M. J., Lee, B. S., Portnoy, V., Palsson, B. Ø., Integrated analysis of
            regulatory and metabolic networks reveals novel regulatory mechanisms in
            Saccharomyces cerevisiae, *Genome Res.* **16**:627–635 (2006a).

[Her06b]   Herrgård, M. J., Fong, S. S., Palsson, B. Ø., Identification of genome-scale meta-
            bolic network models using experimentally measured flux profiles, *PLoS Comput.
            Biol.* **2**(7):e72 (2006b).

[HeX06]   He, X., Zhang, J., Why do hubs tend to be essential in protein networks?*PLoS
            Genet.* **2**(6):e88 (2006).

[His01]   Hishigaki, H., Nakai, K., Ono, T., Tanigami, A., Takagi, T., Assessment of pre-
            diction accuracy of protein function from protein–protein interaction data, *Yeast*
            18:523–531 (2001).

[Hof94]   Hofestädt, R., A Petri net application to model metabolic processes, *J. Syst. Anal.
            Model. Simul.* **16**:113–122 (1994).

[Hol00]   Holter, N. S., Mitra, M., Maritan, A., Cieplak, M., Banavar, J. R., Fedoroff, N. V.,
            Fundamental patterns underlying gene expression profiles: Simplicity from com-
            plexity, *Proc. Natl. Acad. Sci. USA* **97**:8409–8414 (2000).

[Hol01]   Holter, N. S., Maritan, A., Cieplak, M., Fedoroff, N. V., Banavar, J. R., Dynamic
            modeling of gene expression data, *Proc. Natl. Acad. Sci. USA* **98**(4):1693–1698
            (2001).

[Hop86]   Hopfield, J. J., Tank, D. W., Computing with neural circuits: A model, *Science*
            233(4764):ô625–633 (1986).

[Hua07]   Huang, C., Morcos, F., Kanaan, S. P., Wuchty, S., Chen, D. Z., Izaguirre,
            J. A., Predicting protein–protein interactions from protein domains using
            a set cover approach, *IEEE/ACM Trans. Comput. Biol. Bioinform.* **4**:78–87
            (2007).

[Hua96]   Huang, C.Y., Ferrell, J.E. Jr., Ultrasensitivity in the mitogen-activated protein
            kinase cascade, *Proc. Natl. Acad. Sci. USA* **93**(19):10078–10083.

[Huh03]   Huh, W. K., Falvo, J. V., Gerke, L. C., Carroll, A. S., Howson, R. W., Weissman,
            J. S., O'shea, E. K., Global analysis of protein localization in budding yeast,
            Nature **425**(6959):686–691 (2003).

[Hus03a]   Husmeier, D., Reverse engineering of genetic networks with Bayesian networks,
            Biochem. Soc. Trans. **31**:1516–1518 (2003a).

[Hus03b]   Husmeier, D., Sensitivity and specificity of inferring genetic regulatory inter-
            actions from microarray experiments with dynamic Bayesian networks,
            Bioinformatics **19**(17):2271–2282 (2003b).

[Ide08]   Ideker, T., Sharan, R., Protein networks in disease, *Genome Res.* **18**:644–652
            (2008).

[Iro07]   Irons, D. J., Monk, N. A., Identifying dynamical modules from genetic regulatory
            systems: Applications to the segment polarity network, *BMC Bioinform.* **8**:413
            (2007).

[Ito01]   Ito, T., Chiba, T., Ozawa, R., Yoshida, M., Hattori, M., Sakaki, Y., A comprehen-
            sive two-hybrid analysis to explore the yeast protein interactome, *Proc. Natl.
            Acad. Sci. USA* **98**:4569–4574 (2001).

[Itz06]   Itzhaki, Z., Akiva, E., Altuvia, Y., Margalit, H., Evolutionary conservation of domain–domain interactions, *Genome Biol.* **7**:R125 (2006).

[Jan03]   Jansen, R., Yu, H., Greenbaum, D., Kluger, Y., Krogan, N. J., et al., A Bayesian networks approach for predicting protein–protein interactions from genomic data, *Science* **302**:449–453 (2003).

[Jan04]   Jansen, R., Gerstein, M., Analyzing protein function on a genomic scale: The importance of gold-standard positives and negatives for network prediction, *Curr. Opin. Microbiol.* **7**(5):535–545 (2004).

[Jeo00]   Jeong, H., Tombor, B., Albert, R., Oltvai, Z. N., Barabási, A. L., The large-scale organization of metabolic networks, *Nature* **407**(6804):651–654 (2000).

[Jeo01]   Jeong, H., Mason, S. P., Barabási, A. L., Oltvai, Z. N., Lethality and centrality in protein networks, *Nature* **411**(6833):41–42 (2001).

[Jia07]   Jiao, X., Chang, S., Li, C., Chen, W., Wang, C., Construction and application of the weighted amino acid network based on energy, *Phys. Rev. E* **75**:051903 (2007).

[Jin07]   Jin, G., Zhang, S., Zhang, X. S., Chen, L., Hubs with network motifs organize modularity dynamically in the protein–protein interaction network of yeast, *PLoS ONE* **2**(11):e1207 (2007).

[Jin09]   Jin, G., Sun, Y., Zhang, X., Zhang, S., Zhang, X. S., Chen, L., Uncovering functional roles of network motif clusters in cancers and type II diabetes mellitus, in submission (2009).

[Jon02]   Jong, H. D., Modeling and simulation of genetic regulatory systems: A literature review, *J. Comput. Biol.* **9**(1):67–103 (2002).

[Jon06]   Jonsson, P. F., Bates, P. A., Global topological features of cancer proteins in the human interactome, *Bioinformatics* **22**:2291–2297 (2006).

[Jot06]   Jothi, R., Cherukuri, P. F., Tasneem, A., Przytycka, T. M., Co-evolutionary analysis of domains in interacting proteins reveals insights into domain–domain interactions mediating protein–protein interactions, *J. Mol. Biol.* **362**:861–875 (2006).

[Joy05]   Joy, M. P., Brock, A., Ingber, D. E., Huang, S., High-betweenness proteins in the yeast protein interaction network, *J. Biomed. Biotechnol.* **2005**(2):96–103 (2005).

[Joy06]   Joyce, A. R., Palsson, B. O., The model organism as a system: Integrating "omics" data sets, *Nature Rev. Mol. Cell Biol.* **7**:198–210 (2006).

[Jun06]   Junker, B. H., Koschützki, D., Schreiber, F., Exploration of biological network centralities with CentiBiN, *BMC Bioinform.* **7**:219 (2006).

[Kal08]   Kalaev, M., Bafna, V., Sharan, R., Fast and accurate alignment of multiple protein networks, *Lect. Notes Bioinform.* **4955**:246–256 (2008).

[Kan00]   Kanehisa, M., Goto, S.KEGG: Kyoto encyclopedia of genes and genomes, *Nucleic Acids Res.* **28**:27–30 (2000).

[Kan07]   Kann, M. G., Protein interactions and disease: Computational approaches to uncover the etiology of diseases, *Brief. Bioinform.* **8**(5):333–346 (2007).

[Kao04]   Kao, K., Yang, Y., Boscolo, R., Sabatti, C., Roychowdhury, V., et al., Transcriptome-based determination of multiple transcription regulator activities in *Escherichia coli* by using network component analysis, *Proc. Natl. Acad. Sci. USA* **101**:641–646 (2004).

[Kar02] Karp, G., *Cell and Molecular Biology: Concepts and Experiments*, Wiley, Hoboken, NJ, 2002.

[Kar04] Karaoz, U., Murali, T. M., Letovsky, S., Zheng, Y., Ding, C., Cantor, C. R., Kasif, S., Whole-genome annotation by using evidence integration in functional-linkage networks, *Proc. Natl. Acad. Sci. USA* **9**:2888–2893 (2004).

[Kas04] Kashtan, N., Itzkovitz, S., Milo, R., Efficient sampling algorithm for estimating subgraph concentrations and detecting network motifs, *Bioinformatics* **20**:1746–1758 (2004).

[Kat04] Kato, M., Hata, N., Banerjee, N., Futcher, B., Zhang, M. Q., Identifying combinatorial regulation of transcription factors and binding motifs, *Genome Biol.* **5**:R56 (2004).

[Kau69] Kauffman, S. A., Homeostasis and differentiation in random genetic control networks, *Nature* **224**:177–178 (1969).

[Kau03] Kauffman, K. J., Prakash, P., Edwards, J. S., Advances in flux balance analysis, *Curr. Opin. Biotechnol.* **14**:491–496 (2003).

[Kel03] Kelley, B. P., Sharan, R., Karp, R., Sittler, E. T., Root, D. E., Stockwell, B. R., Ideker, T., Conserved pathways within bacteria and yeast as revealed by global protein network alignment, *Proc. Natl. Acad. Sci. USA* **100**:11394–11399 (2003).

[Kel04] Kelley, P. B., Yuan, B., Lewitter, F., Sharan, R., Stockwell, B. R., Ideker, T., PathBLAST: A tool for alignment of protein interaction networks, *Nucl. Acids Res.* **32**:83–88 (2004).

[Kel05] Kelley, R., Ideker, T., Systematic interpretation of genetic interactions using protein networks, *Nature Biotechnol.* **23**:561–566 (2005).

[Kha06] Khanin, R., Vinciotti, V., Wit, E., Reconstructing repressor protein levels from expression of gene targets in *E. coli*, *Proc. Natl. Acad. Sci. USA* **103**:18592–18596 (2006).

[Kha07] Khanin, R., Vinciotti, V., Mersinias, V., Smith, P., Wit, E., Statistical reconstruction of transcription factor activity using Michaelis-Menten kinetics, *Biometrics* **63**:816–823 (2007).

[KiC07] Kim, C. S., Bayesian orthogonal least squares (BOLS) algorithm for reverse engineering of gene regulatory networks, *BMC Bioinform.* **8**:251 (2007).

[KiJ07] Kim, J., Bates, D. G., Postlethwaite, I., Heslop-Harrison, P., Cho, K. H., Least-squares methods for identifying biochemical regulatory networks from noisy measurements, *BMC Bioinform.* **8**:8 (2007).

[Kim03] Kim, S. Y., Imoto, S., Miyano, S., Inferring gene networks from time series microarray data using dynamic Bayesian networks, *Brief. Bioinform.* **4**:228–235 (2003).

[Kim06] Kim, P. M., Lu, L. J., Xia, Y., Gerstein, M. B., Relating three-dimensional structures to protein networks provides evolutionary insights, *Science* **314**:1938–1941 (2006).

[Kim07] Kim, H., Lee, J. K., Park, T., Boolean networks using the chi-square test for inferring large-scale gene regulatory networks, *BMC Bioinform.* **8**:37 (2007).

[Kin04] King, A. D., Przulj, N., Jurisica, I., Protein complex prediction via cost-based clustering, *Bioinformatics* **20**:3013–3020 (2004).

[Kin05]   King, R. D. et al., On the use of qualitative reasoning to simulate and identify metabolic pathways, *Bioinformatics* **21**:2017–2026 (2005).

[Kle96]   Klemm, J., Pabo, C., Oct-1 POU domain-DNA interactions: Cooperative binding of isolated subdomains and effects of covalent linkage, *Genes Devel.* **10**:27–36 (1996).

[Kli05]   Klipp, E., Nordlander, B., Kruger, R., Gennemark, P., Hohmann, S., Integrative model of the response of yeast to osmotic shock, *Nature Biotechnol.* **23**:975–982 (2005).

[Kli06]   Klipp, E., Liebermeister, W., Mathematical modeling of intracellular signaling pathways, *BMC Neurosci.* **7**(Suppl. 1):S10 (2006).

[Koc05]   Koch, I., Junker, B. H., Heiner, M., Application of Petri net theory for modelling and validation of the sucrose breakdown pathway in the potato tuber, *Bioinformatics* **23**(7):1219–1226 (2005).

[Koy06]   Koyutürk, M., Grama, A., Szpankowski, W., Pairwise alignment of protein interaction networks, *J. Comput. Biol.* **13**(2):182–199 (2006).

[Kra99]   Krauss, G., *Biochemistry of Signal Transduction and Regulation*, Wiley-VCH, 1999.

[Kro06]   Krogan, N. J., Cagney, G., Yu, H., Zhong, G., Guo, X., Ignatchenko, A., Global landscape of protein complexes in the yeast *Saccharomyces cerevisiae*, *Nature* **440**:637–643 (2006).

[Kuc08]   Kucukural, A., Sezerman, O. U., Ercil, A., Discrimination of native folds using network properties of protein structures, *Adv. Bioinform. Comput. Biol.* 59–68 (2008).

[Lah03]   Lähdesmäki, H., Shmulevich, I., Yli-Harja, O., On learning gene regulatory networks under the Boolean network model, *Machine Learn.* **52**:147–167 (2003).

[Lan04]   Lanckriet, G. R., Deng, M., Cristianini, N., Jordan, M. I., Noble, W. S., Kernel-based data fusion and its application to protein function prediction in yeast, *Pac. Symp. Biocomput.* 300–311 (2004).

[LeD08]   Lee, D. S., Park, J., Kay, K. A., Christakis, N. A., Oltvai, Z. N., Barabsi, A. L., The implications of human metabolic network topology for disease comorbidity, *Proc. Natl. Acad. Sci. USA* **105**(29):9880–9985 (2008).

[Lee98]   Lee, H. F., Dooly, D. R., Algorithms for the constrained maximum-weight connected graph problem, *Naval Res. Logist.* **43**(7):985–1008 (1998).

[Lee04]   Lee, D.-Y., Zimmer, R., Lee, S.-Y., et al., Knowledge representation model for systems-level analysis of signal transduction networks, *Genome Inform.* **15**(2):234–243 (2004).

[Lee06a]   Lee, H., Deng, M., Sun, F., Chen, T., An integrated approach to the prediction of domain–domain interactions, *BMC Bioinform.* **7**:269 (2006a).

[Lee06b]   Lee, H., Tu, Z., Deng, M., Sun, F., Chen, T., Diffusion kernel based logistic regression models for protein function prediction, *OMICS: J. Integr. Biol.* **10**(1):40–55 (2006b).

[LeJ08]   Lee, J. M., Gianchandani, E. P., Eddy, J. A., Papin, J. A., Dynamic analysis of integrated signaling, metabolic, and regulatory networks, *PLoS Comput. Biol.* **4**(5):e1000086 (2008).

[LeM06]   Lee, J. M., Gianchandani, E. P., Papin, J. A., Flux balance analysis in the era of metabolomics, *Brief. Bioinform.* **7**(2):140–150 (2006).

[LeT02]   Lee, T. I., Rinaldi, N. J., Robert, F., et al., Transcriptional regulatory networks in *Saccharomyces cerevisiae, Science* **298**:799–804 (2002).

[Let03]   Letovsky, S., Kasif, S., Predicting protein function from protein–protein interaction data: A probabilistic approach, *Bioinformatics* **19**:i197–i204 (2003).

[Lev07]   Levine, E., Zhang, Z., Kuhlman, T., Hwa, T., Quantitative characteristics of gene regulation by small RNA, *PLoS Biol.* **5**:e229 (2007).

[LeW06]   Lee, W. P., Jeng, B. C., Pai, T. W., Tsai, C. P., Yu, C. Y., Tzou, W. S., Differential evolutionary conservation of motif modes in the yeast protein interaction network, *BMC Genomics* **7**:89 (2006).

[Lia98]   Liang, S., Fuhrman, S., Somogyi, R., Reveal, a general reverse engineering algorithm for inference of genetic network architectures, *Pac. Symp. Biocomput.* 18–29 (1998).

[Lia03]   Liao, J. C., Boscolo, R., Yang, Y. L., et al., Network component analysis: Reconstruction of regulatory signals in biological systems, *Proc. Natl. Acad. Sci. USA* **100**(26): 15522–15527 (2003).

[Lia07]   Liang, Y. et al., Characterization of microRNA expression profiles in normal human tissues, *BMC Genomics* **8**:166 (2007).

[LiC06a] Li, C., Chen, L., Aihara, K., Transient resetting: A novel mechanism for biological synchrony, *PLoS Comput. Biol.* **2**(8):e103 (2006a).

[LiC06b] Li, C., Chen, L., Aihara, K.Stability of genetic networks with SUM regulatory logic: Lur'e system and LMI approach, *IEEE Trans. Circuits Syst. I* **53**:2451–2458 (2006b).

[LiC07a] Li, C., Chen, L., Aihara, K., A systems biology perspective on signal processing in genetic network motifs, *IEEE Signal Process. Mag.* **24**:136–147 (2007a).

[LiC07b] Li, C., Chen, L., Aihara, K., Stochastic stability of genetic networks with disturbance attenuation, *IEEE Trans. Circuits Syst. II* **54**:892–896 (2007b).

[LiD06]   Li, D., Li, J., Ouyang, S., Wang, J., et al., Protein interaction networks of *Saccharomyces cerevisiae, Caenorhabditis elegans* and *Drosophila melanogaster*: Large-scale organization and robustness, *Proteomics* **6**:456–461 (2006).

[LiG07]   Li, C., Ge, Q.-W., Nakata, M., Matsuno, H., Miyano, S., Modelling and simulation of signal transductions in an apoptosis pathway by using timed Petri nets, *J. Biosci.* **32**(1):113–127 (2007).

[Lim06]   Lim, J., Hao, T., Shaw, C., et al., A protein–protein interaction network for human inherited ataxias and disorders of Purkinje cell degeneration, *Cell* **125**:801–814 (2006).

[LiS04]   Li, S., Armstrong, C. M., Bertin, N., Ge, H., Milstein, S., et al., A map of the interactome network of the metazoan *C. elegans, Science* **303**:540–543 (2004).

[LiS06]   Li, S., Assmann, S., Albert, R., Predicting essential components of signal transduction networks: Dynamic model of guard cell abscisic acid signaling, *PLoS Biol.* **4**(10):e312 (2006).

[LiP08]   Liu, P. K., Wang, F. S., Inference of biochemical network models in *S*-system using multi-objective optimization approach, *Bioinformatics* **24**:1085–1092 (2008).

[Liu04]   Liu, Y., Zhao, H., A computational approach for ordering signal transduction pathway components from genomics and proteomics data, *BMC Bioinform.* **5**:158 (2004).

[Liu05]   Liu, Y., Liu, N., Zhao, H., Inferring protein–protein interactions through high-throughput interaction data from diverse organisms, *Bioinformatics* **21**:3279–3285 (2005).

[Liu07]   Liu, Z., Wu, L. Y., Wang, Y., Chen, L., Zhang, X. S., Predicting gene ontology functions from protein's regional surface structures, *BMC Bioinform.* **8**:475 (2007).

[Liu08]   Liu, Z., Wu, L. Y., Wang, Y., Zhang, X. S., Chen, L., Bridging protein local structures and protein functions, *Amino Acids* **35**(3):627–650 (2008).

[LiZ06]   Li, Z., Shaw, S. M., Yedwabnick, M. J., Chan, C., Using a state-space model with hidden variables to infer transcription factor activities, *Bioinformatics* **22**(6):747–754 (2006).

[LiZ07]   Li, Z., Zhang, S., Wang, Y., Zhang, X. S., Chen, L., Alignment of molecular networks by integer quadratic programming, *Bioinformatics* **23**(13):1631–1639 (2007).

[LiZ08]   Li, Z., Zhang, S., Wang, R. S., Zhang, X. S., Chen, L., Quantitative function for community detection, *Phys. Rev. E* **77**:036109 (2008).

[LiZ09]   Li, Z., Wang, R. S., Zhang, X. S., Chen, L., Detecting drug targets in metabolic networks by integer linear programming, *IET Syst. Biol.* minor revision (2009).

[Lju99]   Ljung, L, *System Identification: Theory for the User*, Prentice-Hall, Upper Saddle River, NJ, 1999.

[LuH04]   Lu, H., Zhu, X., Liu, H., Skogerbo, G., et al., The interactome as a tree—an attempt to visualize the protein–protein interaction network in yeast, *Nucleic Acids Res.* **32**:4804–4811 (2004).

[LuJ05]   Lu, J. et al., MicroRNA expression profiles classify human cancers, *Nature* **435**(7043):834–838 (2005).

[Lus04]   Luscombe, N. M., Babu, M. M., Yu, H., Snyder, M., Teichmann, S. A., Gerstein, M., Genomic analysis of regulatory network dynamics reveals large topological changes, *Nature* **431**(7006):308–312 (2004).

[LuX04]   Lu, X., Zhai, C., Gopalakrishnan, V., Buchanan, B. G., Automatic annotation of protein motif function with gene ontology terms, *BMC Bioinform.* **5**:122 (2004).

[Ma07]   Ma, S., Gong, Q., Bohnert, H. J., An *Arabidopsis* gene network based on the graphical Gaussian model, *Genome Res.* **17**:1614–1625 (2007).

[Mah05]   Mahadevan, R., Palsson, B. O., Properties of metabolic networks: Structure versus function, *Biophys. J.* **88**(1):L07–L09 (2005).

[Mar99]   Marcotte, E., Pellegrini, M., Ng, H., Rice, D., Yeates, T., Eisenberg, D., Detecting protein function and protein–protein interactions from genome sequences, *Science* **285**:751–753 (1999).

[Mas02]   Maslov, S., Sneppen, K., Specificity and stability in topology of protein networks, *Science* **296**:910–913 (2002).

[Mat03]   Matsuno, H., Tanaka, Y., Aoshima, H., Doi, A., Matsui, M., Miyano, S., Biopathways representation and simulation on hybrid functional Petri net, *In Silico Biol* .**3**(3):389–404 (2003).

[McA97]   McAdams, H. M., Arkin, A., Stochastic mechanisms in gene expression, *Proc. Natl. Acad. Sci. USA* **94**:814–819 (1997).

[McD05]   McDermott, J., Bumgarner, R., Samudrala, R., Functional annotation from predicted protein interaction networks, *Bioinformatics* **21**(15):3217–3226 (2005).

[McS03]   McShan, D. C., et al., PathMiner: Predicting metabolic pathways by heuristic search, *Bioinformatics* **19**:1692–1698 (2003).

[Meh08]   Mehta, P., Goyal, S., Wingreen, N. S., A quantitative comparison of sRNA-based and protein-based gene regulation, *Mol. Syst. Biol.* **4**:221 (2008).

[Mew06]   Mewes, H., Frishman, D., Mayer, K., Munsterkotter, M., Noubibou, O., Pagel, P., Rattei, T., Oesterheld, M., Ruepp, A., Stumpflen, V., MIPS: Analysis and annotation of proteins from whole genomes in 2005, *Nucl. Acids Res.* **34**:D169–D172 (2006).

[Mil02]   Milo, R., Shen-Orr, S., Itzkovitz, S., et al., Network motifs: Simple building blocks of complex networks, *Science* **298**:824–827 (2002).

[Moz06]   Moza, B., Buonpane, R., Zhu, P., Herfst, C., Rahman, A., McCormick, J., Kranz, D., Sundberg, E., Long-range cooperative binding effects in a T cell receptor variable domain, *Proc. Natl. Acad. Sci. USA* **103**:9867–9872 (2006).

[Muk01]   Mukherjee, S., Bal, S., Saha, P., Protein interaction maps using yeast two-hybrid assay, *Curr. Sci.* **81**:458–464 (2001).

[Mup06]   Muppiralal, U. K., Li, Z., A simple approach for protein structure discrimination based on the network pattern of conserved hydrophobic residues, *Protein Eng. Design Select.* **19**:265–275 (2006).

[Nab05]   Nabieva, E., Jim, K., Agarwal, A., Chazelle, B., Singh, M., Whole proteome prediction of protein function via graph-theoretic analysis of interaction maps, *Bioinformatics* **21**:i302–i310 (2005).

[Nac04]   Nachman, I., Regev, A., Friedman, N., Inferring quantitative models of regulatory networks from expression data, *Bioinformatics* **20**:i248–i256 (2004).

[Nag05]   Nagamine, N., Kawada, Y., Sakakibara, Y., Identifying cooperative transcriptional regulations using protein–protein interactions, *Nucleic Acids Res.* **33**:4828–4837 (2005).

[Naj08]   Najafabadi, H. S., Salavati, R., Sequence-based prediction of protein–protein interactions by means of codon usage, *Genome Biol.* **9**:R87 (2008).

[Nar07]   Narayanan, M., Karp, R. M., Comparing protein interaction networks via a graph match-and-split algorithm, *J. Comput. Biol.* **14**:892–907 (2007).

[Nar05]   Nariai, N., Tamada, Y., Imoto, S., Miyano, S., Estimating gene regulatory networks and protein–protein interactions of Saccharomyces cerevisiae from multiple genome–wide data, *Bioinformatics* **21**:ii206–ii212 (2005).

[Nem07]   Nemenman, I., Escola, G. S., Hlavacek, W. S., Unkefer, P. J., Unkefer, C. J., Wall, M. E., Reconstruction of metabolic networks from high-throughput metabolite profiling data: In silico analysis of red blood cell metabolism, *Ann. NY Acad. Sci.* **1115**:102–115 (2007).

[New04a] Newman, M. E. J., Detecting community structure in networks, *Eur. Phys. J. B* **38**:321–330 (2004a).

[New04b] Newman, M. E. J., Girvan, M., Finding and evaluating community structure in networks, *Phys. Rev. E* **69**:026113 (2004b).

[New06]   Newman, M. E. J., Modularity and community structure in networks, *Proc. Natl. Acad. Sci. USA* **103**:8577–8582 (2006).

[Ng03]   Ng, S. K., Zhang, Z., Tan, S. H., Integrative approach for computationally inferring protein domain interactions, *Bioinformatics* **19**:923–929 (2003).

[Ngu06]   Nguyen, D. H., D'haeseleer, P., Deciphering principles of transcription regulation in eukaryotic genomes, *Mol. Syst. Biol.* **2**:2006–2012 (2006).

[Nye05]   Nye, T. M., Berzuini, C., Gilks, W. R., Babu, M. M., Teichmann, S. A., Statistical analysis of domains in interacting protein pairs, *Bioinformatics* **21**:993–1001 (2005).

[Oga00]   Ogata, H., Fujibuchi, W., Goto, S., Kanehisa, M., A heuristic graph comparison algorithm and its application to detect functionally related enzyme clusters, *Nucleic Acids Res.* **28**:4021–4028 (2000).

[OgN00]   Ogawa, N. et al., New components of a system for phosphate accumulation and polyphosphate metabolism in Saccharomyces cerevisiae revealed by genomic expression analysis, *Mol. Biol. Cell.* **11**:4309–4321 (2000).

[Old06]   Oldham, M., Horvath, S., Geschwind, D., Conservation and evolution of gene co-expression networks in human and chimpanzee brain, *Proc. Natl. Acad. Sci. USA* **103**(47): 17973–17978 (2006).

[Ort05]   Orton, R. J., Sturm, O. E., Vyshemirsky, V., Calder, M., Gilbert, D. R., Kolch, W., Computational modelling of the receptor-tyrosine-kinase-activated MAPK pathway, *Biochem. J.* **392**:249–261 (2005).

[Pag04]   Pagel, P., Wong, P., Frishman, D., A domain interaction map based on phylogenetic profiling, *J. Mol. Biol.* **344**:1331–1346 (2004).

[Pal05]   Palla, G., Derenyi, I., Farkas, I., Vicsek, T., Uncovering the overlapping community structure of complex networks in nature and society, *Nature* **435**:814–818 (2005).

[Pal06]   Palsson, B. O., *Systems Biology: Properties of Reconstructed Networks*, Cambridge Univ. Press, 2006.

[PaM05]   Palumbo, M. C. et al., Functional essentiality from topology features in metabolic networks: A case study in yeast, *FEBS Lett.* **579**:4642–4646 (2005).

[Pap02]   Papin, J. A., Price, N. D., Palsson, B. O., Extreme pathway lengths and reaction participation in genome-scale metabolic networks, *Genome Res.* **12**:1889–1900 (2002).

[Pap03]   Papin, J. A., Price, N. D., Wiback, S. J., Fell, D. A., Palsson, B. O., Metabolic pathways in the post-genome era, *Trends Biochem. Sci.* **28**(5):250–258 (2003).

[Pap04]   Papin, J. A., Stelling, J., Price, N. D., Klamt, S., Schuster, S., Palsson, B. O., Comparison of network-based pathway analysis methods, *Trends Biotechnol.* **22**(8):400–405 (2004).

[Par03]   Patterson, S. D., Aebersold, R. H., Proteomics: The first decade and beyond, *Nature Genet.* **33**(Suppl.):311–323 (2003).

[Pee01]   Pe'er, D., Regev, A., Elidan, G., Friedman, N., Inferring subnetworks from perturbed expression profiles, *Bioinformatics* **17**:S215–S224 (2001).

[Pel99]   Pellegrini, M., Marcotte, E. M., Thompson, M. J., Eisenberg, D., Yeates, T. O., Assigning protein functions by comparative genome analysis: Protein phylogenetic profiles, *Proc. Natl. Acad. Sci. USA* **96**:4285–4288 (1999).

[Per04]   Pereira-Leal, J. B., Enright, A. J., Ouzounis, C. A., Detection of functional modules from protein interaction networks, *Proteins* **54**:49–57 (2004).

[Pil01]   Pilpel, Y., Sudarsanam, P., Church, G., Identifying regulatory networks by combinatorial analysis of promoter elements, *Nature Genet.* **29**:153–159 (2001).

[Pin03]   Pinney, J. W., Westhead, D. R., McConkey, G. A., Petri net representations in systems biology, *Biochem. Soc. Trans.* **31**:1513–1515 (2003).

[Pin05]   Pinter, R. Y., Rokhlenko, O., Yeger-Lotem, E., Ziv-Ukelson, M., Alignment of metabolic pathways, *Bioinformatics* **21**:3401–3408 (2005).

[Pir06]   Pir, P., Kıdar, B., Hayes, A., Ösan, Z., Ügen, K. Ö., Oliver, S. G., Integrative investigation of metabolic and transcriptomic data, *BMC Bioinform.* **7**:203 (2006).

[Pou07]   Pournara, I., Wernisch, L., Factor analysis for gene regulatory networks and transcription factor activity profiles, *BMC Bioinform.* **8**:61 (2007).

[Pou08]   Pournara, I., Wernisch, L., Using temporal correlation in factor analysis for reconstructing transcription factor activities, *EURASIP J. Bioinform. Syst. Biol.* 172840 (2008).

[Pri03a]   Price, N. D., Reed, J. L., Papin, J. A., Famili, I., Palsson, B. O., Analysis of metabolic capabilities using singular value decomposition of extreme pathway matrices, *Biophys. J.* **84**:794–804 (2003a).

[Pri03b]   Price, N. D., Reed, J. L., Papin, J. A., Wiback, S. J., Palsson, B. O., Network-based analysis of regulation in the human red blood cell, *J. Theor. Biol.* **225**(2):185–194 (2003b).

[PrT06]   Przytycka, T., Davis, G., Song, N., Durand, D., Graph theoretical insights into evolution of multidomain proteins, *J. Comput. Biol.* **13**(2):351–363 (2006).

[Prz04a]   Przulj, N., Wigle, D. A., Jurisica, I., Functional topology in a network of protein interactions, *Bioinformatics* **20**:340–348 (2004a).

[Prz04b]   Przulj, N., Corneil, D. G., Jurisica, I., Modeling interactome: Scale-free or geometric?*Bioinformatics* **20**:3508–3515 (2004b).

[Prz06]   Przulj, N., Corneil, D. G., Jurisica, I., Efficient estimation of graphlet frequency distributions in protein–protein interaction networks, *Bioinformatics* **22**:974–980 (2006).

[Pta02]   Ptashne, M., Gann, A, *Genes and Signals*, Cold Spring Harbor Press, New York, 2002.

[Qia03]   Qian, J., Lin, J., Luscombe, N. M., Yu, H., Gerstein, M., Prediction of regulatory networks: Genome-wide identification of transcription factor targets from gene expression data, *Bioinformatics* **19**:1917–1926 (2003).

[Qin03]   Qin, H., Lu, H. H. S., Wu, W. B., Li, W. H., Evolution of the yeast protein interaction network, *Proc. Natl. Acad. Sci. USA* **100**:12820–12824 (2003).

[Rav02]   Ravasz, E., Somera, A. L., Mongru, D. A., Oltvai, Z. N., Barabási, A. L., Hierarchical organization of modularity in metabolic networks, *Science* **297**:1551–1555 (2002).

[Red93]   Reddy, V. N., Mavrovouniotis, M. L., Liebman, M. N., Petri net representation in metabolic pathways, *Proc. Int. Conf. Intell. Syst. Mol. Biol.* 328–336 (1993).

[Red07]   Redestig, H., Weicht, D., Selbig, J., Hannah, M. A., Transcription factor target prediction using multiple short expression time series from *Arabidopsis thaliana*, *BMC Bioinform.* **8**:454 (2007).

[Ree03]   Reed, J. L., et al., An expanded genome-scale model of *Escherichia coli* K-12 (iJR904 GSM/GPR), *Genome Biol.* **4**:R54 (2003).

[Rem04]   Reményi, A., Schöer, H. R., Wilmanns, M., Combinatorial control of gene expression, *Nature Struc. Mol. Biol.* **11**:812–815 (2004).

[Rem01]   Remm, M., Storm, C. E. V., Sonnhammer, E. L., Automatic clustering of orthologs and in-paralogs from pairs species comparisons, *J. Mol. Biol.* **314**:1041–1052 (2001).

[Ril05]   Riley, R., Lee, C., Sabatti, C., Eisenberg, D., Inferring protein domain interactions from databases of interacting proteins, *Genome Biol.* **6**:R89 (2005).

[Riv03]   Rives, A. W., Galitski, T., Modular organization of cellular networks, *Proc. Natl. Acad. Sci. USA* **100**:1128–1133 (2003).

[Rob00]   Roberts, C. J., Nelson, B., Marton, M. J., Stoughton, R., Meyer, M. R., Bennett, H. A., He, Y. D., Dai, H., Walker, W. L., Hughes, T. R., et al., Signaling and circuitry of multiple MAPK pathways revealed by a matrix of global gene expression profiles, *Science* **287**:873–880 (2000).

[Rog05]   Rogers, S., Girolami, M., A Bayesian regression approach to the inference of regulatory networks from gene expression data, *Bioinformatics* **21**(14):3131–3137 (2005).

[Rog07]   Rogers, S., Khanin, R., Girolami, M., Bayesian model-based inference of transcription factor activity, *BMC Bioinform.* **8**:S2 (2007).

[Ros07]   Rosvall, M., Bergstrom, C. T., An information-theoretic framework for resolving community structure in complex networks, *Proc. Natl. Acad. Sci. USA* **104**:7327–7331 (2007).

[Roy08]   Roy, S., Werner-Washburne, M., Lane, T., A system for generating transcription regulatory networks with combinatorial control of transcription, *Bioinformatics* **24**(10):1318–1320 (2008).

[Rue04]   Ruepp, A., Zollner, A., Maier, D., Albermann, K., et al., FunCat, a functional annotation scheme for systematic classification of proteins from whole genomes, *Nucleic Acids Res.* **32**:5539–5545 (2004).

[Rus06]   Russell, P. J., *iGenetics: A Molecular Approach*, 2nd ed., Benjamin-Cummings Pub Co, San Francisco, CA, United States, 2006.

[Sab06]   Sabatti, C., James, G. M., Bayesian sparse hidden components analysis for transcription regulation networks, *Bioinformatics* **15**:739–746 (2006).

[Sac06]   Sackmann, A., Heiner, M., Koch, I., Application of Petri net based analysis techniques to signal transduction pathways, *BMC Bioinform.* **7**:482 (2006).

[Sad06]   Sadava, D., Heller, H. C., Orians, G. H., Purves, W. K., Hillis, D., *Life: The Science of Biology*, 8th ed., Sinauer Associates Inc., W. H. Freeman & Co., San Francisco, CA, 2006.

[Sal06]   Salgado, H., Gama-Castro, S., Peralta-Gil, M., Diaz-Peredo, E., RegulonDB (version 5.0): *Escherichia coli* K-12 transcriptional regulatory network, operon organization, and growth conditions, *Nucleic Acids Res.* **34**:D394–D397 (2006).

[Sam03]   Samanta, M. P., Liang, S., Predicting protein functions from redundancies in large-scale protein interaction networks, *Proc. Natl. Acad. Sci. USA* **100**:12579–12583 (2003).

[Sam06]   Samal, A., Singh, S., Giri, V., et al., Low degree metabolites explain essential reactions and enhance modularity in biological networks, *BMC Bioinform.* **7**:118 (2006).

[San06a]   Sanguinetti, G., Lawrence, N. D., Rattray, M., A probabilistic dynamical model for quantitative inference of the regulatory mechanism of transcription, *Bioinformatics* **22**:1753–1759 (2006a).

[San06b]   Sanguinetti, G., Lawrence, N. D., Rattray, M., Probabilistic inference of transcription factor concentrations and gene-specific regulatory activities, *Bioinformatics* **22**:2775–2781 (2006b).

[Sat05]   Sato, T., Yamanishi, Y., Kanehisa, M., Toh, H., The inference of protein–protein interactions by co-evolutionary analysis is improved by excluding the information about the phylogenetic relationships, *Bioinformatics* **21**:3482–3489 (2005).

[Say07]   Sayyed-Ahmad, A., Tuncay, K., Ortoleva, P. J., Transcriptional regulatory network refinement and quantification through kinetic modeling, gene expression microarray data and information theory, *BMC Bioinform.* **8**:20 (2007).

[Sch95]   Schena, M., Shalon, D., Davis, R. W., Brown, P. O., Quantitative monitoring of gene expression patterns with a complementary DNA microarray, *Science* **270**(5235):467–470 (1995).

[Sch02]   Schoeberl, B., Eichler-Jonsson, C., Gilles, E. D., Muller, G., Computational modeling of the dynamics of the MAP kinase cascade activated by surface and internalized EGF receptors, *Nature Biotechnol.* **20**(4):370–375 (2002).

[Sch05]   Schreiber, F., Schwobbermeyer, H., MAVisto: A tool for the exploration of network motifs, *Bioinformatics* **21**:3572–3574 (2005).

[ScB00]   Schwikowski, B., Uetz, P., Fields, S., A network of protein–protein interactions in yeast, *Nature Biotechnol.* **18**:1257–1261 (2000).

[ScB07]   Schuster-Bökler, B., Bateman, A., Reuse of structural domain–domain interactions in protein networks, *BMC Bioinform.* **8**:259 (2007).

[ScJ02]   Schug, J., Diskin, S., Mazzarelli, J., Brunk, B. P., Stoeckert, C. J., Jr., Predicting gene ontology functions from ProDom and CDD protein domains, *Genome Res.* **12**(4):648–655 (2002).

[ScJ06]   Schwartz, J. M., Kanehisa, M., Quantitative elementary mode analysis of metabolic pathways: The example of yeast glycolysis, *BMC Bioinform.* **7**:186 (2006).

[ScS00]   Schuster, S., Fell, D. A., Dandekar, T., A general definition of metabolic pathways useful for systematic organization and analysis of complex metabolic networks, *Nature Biotechnol.* **18**:326–332 (2000).

[Sco06]   Scott, J., Ideker, T., Karp, R. M., Sharan, R., Efficient algorithms for detecting signaling pathways in protein interaction networks, *J. Comput. Biol.* **13**(2):133–144 (2006).

[Sed02]   Sedaghat, A. R., Sherman, A., Quon, M. J., A mathematical model of metabolic insulin signaling pathways, *Am. J. Physiol. Endocrinol. Metab.* **283**(5): E1084–E1101 (2002).

[Seq02]   Segré, D., Vitkup, D., Church, G. M., Analysis of optimality in natural and perturbed metabolic networks, *Proc. Natl. Acad. Sci. USA* **99**(23):15112–15117 (2002).

[Sha05a] Sharan, R., Ideker, T., Kelley, B., Shamir, R., Karp, R. M., Identification of protein complexes by comparative analysis of yeast and bacterial protein interaction data, *J. Comput. Biol.* **12**:835–846 (2005a).

[Sha05b] Sharan, R., Suthram, S., Kelley, R. M., Kuhn, T., McCuine, S., Uetz, P., Sittler, T., Karp, R. M., Ideker, T., Conserved patterns of protein interaction in multiple species, *Proc. Natl. Acad. Sci. USA* **102**:1974–1979 (2005b).

[Sha06] Sharan, R., Ideker, T., Modeling cellular machinery through biological network comparison, *Nature Biotechnol.* **24**:427–433 (2006).

[Sha07] Sharan, R., Ulitsky, I., Shamir, R., Network-based prediction of protein function, *Mol. Syst. Biol.* **3**:88 (2007).

[She07] Shen, J., Zhang, J., Luo, X., Zhu, W., Yu, K., Chen, K., Li, Y., Jiang, H., Predicting protein–protein interactions based only on sequences information, *Proc. Natl. Acad. Sci. USA* **104**(11):4337–4341 (2007).

[Shi07] Shimoni, Y., Friedlander, G., Hetzroni, G., Niv, G., Altuvia, S., et al., Regulation of gene expression by small non-coding RNAs: A quantitative view, *Mol. Syst. Biol.* **3**:138 (2007).

[ShiY07] Shi, Y., Mitchell, T., Bar-Joseph, Z., Inferring pairwise regulatory relationships from multiple time series datasets, *Bioinformatics* **23**(6):755–763 (2007).

[Shl06] Shlomi, T., Segal, D., Ruppin, E., Sharan, R., QPath: A method for querying pathways in a protein–protein interaction network, *BMC Bioinform.* **7**:199 (2006).

[Shm02] Shmulevich, I., Dougherty, E. R., Zhang, W., From boolean to probabilistic boolean networks as models of genetic regulatory networks, *Proc. IEEE* **90**:1778–1792 (2002).

[Sho07a] Shoemaker, B. A., Panchenko, A. R., Deciphering protein–protein interactions. Part I. Experimental techniques and databases, *PLoS Comput. Biol.* **3**(3):e42 (2007a).

[Sho07b] Shoemaker, B. A., Panchenko, A. R., Deciphering protein–protein interactions. Part II. Computational methods to predict protein and domain interaction partners, *PLoS Comput. Biol.* **3**(4):e43 (2007b).

[Sim04] Simonis, N., Helden, J., Cohen, G. N., Wodak, S. J., Transcriptional regulation of protein complexes in yeast, *Genome Biol.* **5**:R33 (2004).

[Sin08] Singh, R., Xu, J., Berger, B., Global alignment of multiple protein interaction networks with application to functional orthology detection, *Proc. Natl. Acad. Sci. USA* **105**:12763–12768 (2008).

[Smi05] Smith, A. D., Sumazin, P., Das, D., Zhang, M. Q., Mining ChIP-chip data for transcription factor and cofactor binding sites, *Bioinformatics* **21**:i403–i412 (2005).

[Sol05] Sol, A., O'Meara, P., Small-world network approach to identify key residues in protein–protein interaction, *Proteins* **58**(3):672–682 (2005).

[Soo06] Sood, P. et al., Cell-type-specific signatures of microRNAs on target mRNA expres-sion, *Proc. Natl. Acad. Sci. USA* **103**(8):2746–2751 (2006).

[Spe98] Spellman, P. T., Sherlock, G., Zhang, M. Q., Iyer, V. R., Anders, K., et al., Comprehensive identification of cell cycle-regulated genes of the yeast *Saccharomyces cererisiae* by microarray hybridization, *Mol. Biol. Cell* **9**:3273–3297 (1998).

[Spi03]   Spirin, V., Mirny, L. A., Protein complexes and functional modules in molecular networks, *Proc. Natl. Acad. Sci. USA* **100**:12123–12128 (2003).

[Spr01]   Sprinzak, E., Margalit, H., Correlated sequence-signatures as markers of protein–protein interaction, *J. Mol. Biol.* **311**:681–692 (2001).

[Sri07]   Sridhar, P., Kahveci, T., Ranka, S., An iterative algorithm for metabolic network-based drug target identification, *Pac. Symp. Biocomput.* **12**:88–99 (2007).

[Sri08]   Sridhar, P., Song, B., Kahveciy, T., Ranka, S., Mining metabolic network for optimal drug targets, *Pac. Symp. Biocomput.* **13**:291–302 (2008).

[SrJ07]   Srividhya, J., Crampin, E. J., McSharry, P. E., Schnell, S., Reconstructing biochemical pathways from time course data, *Proteomics* **7**:828–838 (2007).

[Sta02]   Standafer, E., Wahlgren, W., *Modern Biology*, Holt, Rinehart and Winston, 2002.

[Ste02]   Steffen, M., Petti, A., Aach, J., D'haeseleer, P., Church, G., Automated modelling of signal transduction networks, *BMC Bioinform.* **3**:34 (2002).

[Ste06]   Steuer, R., Gross, T., Selbig, J., Blasius, B., Structural kinetic modeling of metabolic networks, *Proc. Natl. Acad. Sci. USA* **103**(32):11868–11873 (2006).

[Stu03]   Stuart, J. M., Segal, E., Koller, D., Kim, S. K., A gene-coexpression network for global discovery of conserved genetic modules, *Science* **302**:249–255 (2003).

[Stu05]   Stumpf, M. P., Wiuf, C., May, R. M., Subnets of scale-free networks are not scale-free: Sampling properties of networks, *Proc. Natl. Acad. Sci. USA* **102**(12):4221–4224 (2005).

[Sug05]   Sugimotoa, M., Kikuchia, S., Tomitaa, M., Reverse engineering of biochemical equations from time-course data by means of genetic programming, *BioSystems* **80**:155–164 (2005).

[Sun06]   Sun, N., Carroll, R. J., Zhao, H., Bayesian error analysis model for reconstructing transcription regulatory networks, *Proc. Natl. Acad. Sci. USA* **103**:7988–7993 (2006).

[SuS06]   Sun, S., Zhao, Y., Jiao, Y., Yin, Y., et al., Fast and more accurate global protein function assignment from protein interaction networks using MFGO algorithm, *FEBS Lett.* **580**:1891–1896 (2006).

[Sut06]   Suthram, S., Shlomi, T., Ruppin, E., Sharan, R., Ideker, T., A direct comparison of protein interaction confidence assignment schemes, *BMC Bioinform.* **7**(1):360 (2006).

[Tan07]   Tan, K., Shlomi, T., Feizi, H., Ideker, T., Sharan, R., Transcriptional regulation of protein complexes within and across species, *Proc. Natl. Acad. Sci. USA* **104**(4):1283–1288 (2007).

[Tan05]   Tanaka, R., Yi, T.-M., Doyle, J., Some protein interaction data do not exhibit power law statistics, *FEBS Lett.* **579**:5140–5144 (2005).

[Tay06]   Taylor, T. J., Vaisman, I. I., Graph theoretic properties of networks formed by the Delaunay tessellation of protein structures, *Phys. Rev. E* **73**:041925 (2006).

[Tei06]   Teixeira, M. C., Monteiro, P., Jain, P., The YEASTRACT database: A tool for the analysis of transcription regulatory associations in *S. cerevisiae*, *Nucleic Acids Res.* **34**:D446–D451 (2006).

[Thi05]   Thibert, B., Bredesen, D. E., del Rio, G., Improved prediction of critical residues for protein function based on network and phylogenetic analyses, *BMC Bioinform.* **6**:213 (2005).

[Tho04]   Thomas, R., Mehrotra, S., Papoutsakis, E. T., Hatzimanikatis, V., A model-based optimization framework for the inference on gene regulatory networks from DNA array data, *Bioinformatics* **20**(17):3221–3235 (2004).

[Tho07]   Thomas, R., Paredes, C. J., Mehrotra, S., Hatzimanikatis, V., Papoutsakis, E. T., A model-based optimization framework for the inference of regulatory interactions using time-course DNA microarray expression data, *BMC Bioinform.* **8**:228 (2007).

[Tia07]   Tian, Y., McEachin, R. C., Santos, C., States, D. J., Patel, J. M., SAGA: A subgraph matching tool for biological graphs, *Bioinformatics* **23**:232–239 (2007).

[Toh00]   Tohsato, Y., Matsuda, H., Hashimoto, A., A multiple alignment algorithm for metabolic pathway analysis using enzyme hierarchy, *Proc. 8th Int. Conf. Intell. Syst. Mol. Biol. (ISMB)* 376–383 (2000).

[Toh02]   Toh, H., Horimoto, K., Inference of a genetic network by a combined approach of cluster analysis and graphical Gaussian modeling, *Bioinformatics* **18**:287–297 (2002).

[Tom05]   Tompa, M., Li, N., Bailey, T. L., Assessing computational tools for the discovery of transcription factor binding sites, *Nature Biotechnol.* **23**(1):137–144 (2005).

[Too05]   Tootle, T. L., Rebay, I., Post-translational modifications influence transcription factor activity: A view from the ETS superfamily, *BioEssays* **27**:285–298 (2005).

[Tsa05]   Tsai, H. K., Lu, H. H. S., Li, W. H., Statistical methods for identifying yeast cell cycle transcription factors, *Proc. Natl. Acad. Sci. USA* **102**(38):13532–13537 (2005).

[Tuc06]   Tuck, D. P., Kluger, H. M., Kluger, Y., Characterizing disease states from topological properties of transcriptional regulatory networks, *BMC Bioinform.* **7**:236 (2006).

[Uet00]   Uetz, P. et al., A comprehensive analysis of protein–protein interactions in *Saccharomyces cerevisiae*, *Nature* **403**:623–627 (2000).

[Val06]   Valente, A. X., Cusick, M. E., Yeast protein interactome topology provides framework for coordinated-functionality, *Nucleic Acids Res.* **34**:2812–2819 (2006).

[Vas06]   Vasilescu, J., Figeys, D., Mapping protein–protein interactions by mass spectrometry, *Curr. Opin. Biotechnol.* **17**:394–399 (2006).

[Vaz03]   Vazquez, A., Flammini, A., Maritan, A., Vespignani, A., Global protein function prediction in protein–protein interaction networks, *Nature Biotechnol.* **21**:697 (2003).

[Vaz04]   Vazquez, A., Dobrin, R., Sergi, D., Eckmann, J. P., Oltvai, A. N., Barabási, A.-L., The topological relationship between the large-scale attributes and local interaction patterns of complex networks, *Proc. Natl. Acad. Sci. USA* **101**:17940–17945 (2004).

[Vei03]   Veitia, R. A., A sigmoidal transcriptional response: Cooperativity, synergy and dosage effects, *Biol. Rev.* **78**:149–170 (2003).

[Ven01]   Venter, J. C., Adams, M. D., Myers, E. W., et al., The sequence of the human genome, *Science* **291**:1304–1351 (2001).

[Ven02]   Vendruscolo, M., Dokholyan, N. V., Paci, E., Karplus, M., Small-world view of the amino acids that play a key role in protein folding, *Phys. Rev. E* **65**:061910 (2002).

[Ver07]   Vera-González, J., Curto, R., Cascante, R., Torres, N. V., Detection of potential enzyme targets by metabolic modelling and optimization: Application to a simple enzymopathy, *Bioinformatics* **23**:2281–2289 (2007).

[VeV07]   Vermeirssen, V., Deplancke, B., Barrasa, M. I., Matrix and Steiner-triple-system smart pooling assays for high-performance transcription regulatory network mapping, *Nature Meth.* **4**:659–664 (2007).

[Vos03]   Voss, K., Heiner, M., Koch, I., Steady state analysis of metabolic pathways using Petri nets, *In Silico Biol.* **3**(3):367–387 (2003).

[VuT07]   Vu, T. T., Vohradsky, J., Nonlinear differential equation model for quantification of transcriptional regulation applied to microarray data of *Saccharomyces cerevisiae*, *Nucleic Acids Res.* **35**:279–287 (2007).

[Wac05]   Wachi, S., Yoneda, K., Wu, R., Interactome-transcriptome analysis reveals the high centrality of genes differentially expressed in lung cancer tissues, *Bioinformatics* **21**:4205–4208 (2005).

[WaC06]   Wang, C., Ding, C., Meraz, R. F., Holbrook, S. R., PSoL: A positive sample only learning algorithm for finding non-coding RNA genes, *Bioinformatics* **22**(21):2590–2596 (2006).

[WaM06]   Wang, M., Caetano-Anolles, G., Global phylogeny determined by the combination of protein domains in proteomes, *Mol Biol Evol* **23**:2444–2454 (2006).

[WaR07a]   Wang, R. S., Wang, Y., Zhang, X. S., Chen, L., Inferring transcription regulatory networks from high-throughput data, *Bioinformatics* **23**:3056–3064 (2007a).

[WaR07b]   Wang, R. S., Zhang, X. S., Chen, L., Inferring transcriptional interactions and regulator activities from experimental data, *Mol. Cells* **24**(3):307–315 (2007b).

[WaR07c]   Wang, R. S., Wang, Y., Wu, L. Y., Zhang, X. S., Chen, L., Analysis of multi-domain cooperation for predicting protein–protein interactions, *BMC Bioinform.* **8**:391 (2007c).

[WaR09]   Wang, R. S., Jin, G., Zhang, X. S., Chen, L., Modeling post-transcriptional regulation activity of small non-coding RNAs in *Escherichia coli*, *BMC Bioinformatics* **10**(Suppl4):S6 (2009).

[WaR08]   Wang, R., Li, C., Chen, L., Aihara, K., Modeling and analyzing biological oscillations in molecular networks, *Proc. IEEE* **96**:1361–1385 (2008).

[WaY06]   Wang, Y., Joshi, T., Zhang, X. S., Xu, X., Chen, L., Inferring gene regulatory networks from multiple microarray datasets, *Bioinformatics* **22**:2413–2420 (2006).

[WaY07]   Wang, Y., Wang, R. S., Zhang, X. S., Chen, L., Establishing protein functional linkage in a systematic way, *Lect. Notes Oper. Res.* **7**:75–88 (2007).

[WaY09a]   Wang, Y., Wang, R. S., Joshi, T., Xu, D., Zhang, X. S., Chen, L., Xia, Y., A linear programming framework for inferring gene regulatory networks by integrating heterogeneous data, in *Computational Methodologies in Gene Regulatory Networks*, Das, S., Caragea, D., Hsu, W. H., Welch, S. M. (eds.), IGI Global, in press. (2009a).

[WaY09b]   Wang, Y., Wu, L. Y., Zhang, J., Zhan, Z., Zhang, X. S., Chen, L., Evaluating protein similarity from coarse structures, *IEEE/ACM Trans. Comput. Biol. Bioinform.* (2009b) 10.1109/TCBB.2007.70250.

[Web92]   Webb, E. C., (ed.), *Enzyme Nomenclature*, Academic Press, 1992.

[Wer06]   Werhli, A. V., Grzegorczyk, M., Husmeier, D., Comparative evaluation of reverse engineering gene regulatory networks with relevance networks, graphical gaussian models and bayesian networks, *Bioinformatics* **22**(20):2523–2531 (2006).

[WeS06]   Wernicke, S., Rasche, F., FANMOD: A tool for fast network motif detection, *Bioinformatics* **22**:1152–1153 (2006).

[Wes03]   West, M., Bayesian factor regression models in the "Large *p*, Small *n*" paradigm, *Bayesian Stat.* **7**:733–742 (2003).

[Wib03]   Wiback, S. J., Mahadevan, R., Palsson, B. O., Reconstructing metabolic flux vectors from extreme pathways: Defining the α-spectrum, *J. Theor. Biol.* **224**(3):313–324 (2003).

[Wic04]   Wichert, S., Fokianos, K., Strimmer, K., Indentifying periodically expressed transcripts in microarray time series data, *Bioinformatics* **20**:5–20 (2004).

[Wil04]   Wille, A., Zimmermann, P., Vranov, E., Sparse graphical Gaussian modeling of the isoprenoid gene network in *Arabidopsis thaliana*, *Genome Biol.* **5**:R92 (2004).

[Wu05]   Wu, H., Su, Z., Mao, F., Olman, V., Xu, Y., Prediction of functional modules based on comparative genome analysis and Gene Ontology application, *Nucl. Acids Res.* **33**:2822–2837 (2005).

[Wuc01]   Wuchty, S., Scale-free behavior in protein domain networks, *Mol. Biol. Evol.* **18**(9):1694–1702 (2001).

[Wuc04]   Wuchty, S., Evolution and topology in the yeast protein interaction network, *Genome Res.* **14**:1310–1314 (2004).

[WuX08]   Wu, X., Jiang, R., Zhang, M. Q., Li, S., Network-based global inference of human disease genes, *Mol. Syst. Biol.* **4**:189 (2008).

[Xen02]   Xenarios, I., Salwnski, L., Duan, X. J., Higney, P., Kim, S. M., Eisenberg, D., DIP the Database of Interacting Proteins: A research tool for studying cellular networks of protein interactions, *Nucleic Acids Res.* **30**:303–305 (2002).

[Xie05]   Xie, X., Lu, J., Kulkobas, E. J., Golub, T. R., Mootha, V., Lindblad-Toh, K., Lander, E. S., Kellis, M., Systematic discovery of regulatory motifs in human promoters and 3'UTRs by comparison of several mammals, *Nature* **434**:338–345 (2005).

[Xin06]   Xing, H., Garder, T. S., The mode-of-action by network identification (MNI) algorithm: A network biology approach for molecular target identification, *Nature Protocols* **1**:2551–2554 (2006).

[XuJ06]   Xu, J., Li, Y., Discovering disease-genes by topological features in human protein–protein interaction network, *Bioinformatics* **22**:2800–2805 (2006).

[Yam04]   Yamanishi, Y., Vert, J. P., Kanehisa, M., Protein network inference from multiple genomic data: A supervised approach, *Bioinformatics* **20**:I363–I370 (2004).

[Yan07]   Yang, Q., Sze, S. H., Path matching and graph matching in biological networks, *J. Comput. Biol.* **14**(1):56–67 (2007).

[Yea06]   Yeang, C. H., Vingron, M., A joint model of regulatory and metabolic networks, *BMC Bioinform.* **7**:332 (2006).

[Yeg04]   Yeger-Lotem, E., Sattath, S., Kashtan, N., Itzkovitz, S., Milo, R., Pinter, R. Y., Alon, U., Margalit, H., Network motifs in integrated cellular networks of transcription-regulation and protein–protein interaction, *Proc. Natl. Acad. Sci. USA* **101**:5934–5939 (2004).

[Yeu02]   Yeung, M. K. S., Tegner, J., Collins, J., Reverse engineering gene networks using singular value decomposition and robust regression, *Proc. Natl. Acad. Sci. USA* **99**:6163–6168 (2002).

[Yil07]   Yildirim, M. A., Goh, K. I., Cusick, M. E., Barabsi, A. L., Vidal, M., Drug-target network, *Nature Biotechnol.* **25**(10):1119–1126 (2007).

[Yoo04]   Yook, S. H., Oltvai, Z. N., Barabási, A. L., Functional and topological characterization of protein interaction networks, *Proteomics* **4**:928–942 (2004).

[YuH04]   Yu, H., Zhu, X., Greenbaum, D., Karro, J., Gerstein, M., TopNet: A tool for comparing biological subnetworks, correlating protein properties with topological statistics, *Nucleic Acids Res.* **32**(1):328–337 (2004).

[YuH07]   Yu, H., Kim, P. M., Sprecher, E., Trifonov, V., Gerstein, M., The importance of bottlenecks in protein networks: Correlation with gene essentiality and expression dynamics, *PLoS Comput. Biol.* **3**(4):e59 (2007).

[Yur06]   Yuryev, A., Mulyukov, Z., Kotelnikova, E., Maslov, S., Egorov, S. Nikitin, A.,Daraselia, N., Mazo, I., Automatic pathway building in biological association networks, *BMC Bioinform.* **7**:171 (2006).

[YuT05]   Yu, T., Li, K. C., Inference of transcription regulatory network by two-stage constrained space factor analysis, *Bioinformatics* **21**:4033–4038 (2005).

[Zak03]   Zak, D. E., Gonye, G. E., Schwaber, J. S., Francis, J., Doyle, I., Importance of input perturbations and stochastic gene expression in the reverse engineering of genetic regulatory networks: Insights from an identifiability analysis of an *in silico* network, *Genome Res.* **13**:2396–2405 (2003).

[Zha05]   Zhang, L. V., King, O. D., Wong, S. L., Goldberg, D. S., Tong, A. H., Lesage, G., Andrews, B., Bussey, H., Boone, C., Roth, F. P., Motifs, themes and thematic maps of an integrated *Saccharomyces cerevisiae* interaction network, *J. Biol.* **4**(2):6 (2005).

[Zha06]   Zhang, A. D., *Advanced Analysis of Gene Expression Data*, World Scientific, Singapore, 2006.

[Zha07]   Zhang, S., Jin, G., Zhang, X. S., Chen, L., Discovering functions and revealing mechanisms at molecular level from biological networks, *Proteomics* **7**:2856–2869 (2007).

[Zha08]   Zhang, S., Zhang, X. S., Chen, L., Biomolecular network querying: A promising approach in systems biology, *BMC Syst. Biol.* **2**:5 (2008).

[ZhaX06]   Zhang, X. S., Wang, R. S., Wu, L. Y., Zhang, S., Chen, L., Inferring protein–protein interactions by combinatorial models, *IFMBE Proc.* **14**:181–184 (2006).

[ZhaX07]   Zhao, X., Xuan, Z., Zhang, M. Q., Boosting with stumps for predicting transcription start sites, *Genome Biol.* **8**:R17 (2007).

[ZhaX08a]   Zhao, X. M., Wang, Y., Chen, L., Aihara, K., Gene function prediction using labeled and unlabeled data, *BMC Bioinform.* **9**:57 (2008a).

[ZhaX08b]   Zhao, X. M., Wang, Y., Chen, L., Aihara, K., Protein domain annotation with integration of heterogeneous information sources, *Proteins* **72**:461–473 (2008b).

[ZhaX08c]   Zhao, X. M., Wang, R. S., Chen, L., Aihara, K., Uncovering signal transduction networks from high-throughput data by integer linear programming, *Nucleic Acids Res.* **369**(9):e48 (2008c).

[ZhaX08d]   Zhao, X. M., Aihara, K., Chen, L., Protein function prediction with high-throughput data, *Amino Acids* **35**(3):517–530 (2008d).

[ZhaX09]   Zhao, X. M., Wang, R. S., Chen, L., Aihara, K., Automatic modeling of signaling pathways based on network flow model, *J. Bioinform. Comput. Biol.* **7**(2):309–322 (2009).

[ZhaZ06]   Zhang, Z., Liu, C., Skogerbo, G., Zhu, X., Lu, H., Chen, L., Shi, B., Zhang, Y., Wu, T., Wang, J., Chen, R., Dynamic changes in subgraph preference profiles of crucial transcription factors, *PLoS Comput. Biol.* **2**(5):e47 (2006).

[Zhe07]   Zheng, M., Barrera, L. O., Ren, B., Wu, Y. N., ChIP-chip: Data, model, and analysis, *Biometrics* **63**:787–796 (2007).

[Zho05]   Zhou, T., Chen, L., Aihara, K., Molecular communication through stochastic synchronization induced by extracellular fluctuations, *Phys. Rev. Lett.* **95**:178103 (2005).

[Zho08]   Zhou, T., Zhang, J., Yuan, Z., Chen, L., Synchronization of genetic oscillators, *Chaos* **18**:037126 (2008).

[Zho04]   Zhou, X. J., Gibson, G., Cross-species comparison of genome-wide expression patterns, *Genome Biol.* **5**(7):232 (2004).

[Zho02]   Zhou, X., Kao, M. C. J., Wong, W. H., Transitive functional annotation by shortest-path analysis of gene expression data, *Proc. Natl. Acad. Sci. USA* **99**(20):12783–12788 (2002).

[Zhu05]   Zhu, D., Qin, Z. S., Structure comparison of metabolic networks in selected single cell organisms, *BMC Bioinform.* **6**:8 (2005).

[ZhuH02]   Zhu, H., Snyder, M.,"Omic" approaches for unraveling signaling networks, *Curr. Opin. Cell Biol.* **14**:173–179 (2002).

[ZhZ05]   Zhu, Z., Shendure, J., Church, G. M., Discovering functional transcription-factor combinations in the human cell cycle, *Genome Res.* **15**:848–855 (2005).

[Zou05]   Zou, M., Conzen, S. D., A new dynamic Bayesian network (DBN) approach for identifying gene regulatory networks from time course microarray data, *Bioinformatics* **21**:71–79 (2005).

INDEX

Biomolecular Networks. By Luonan Chen, Rui-Sheng Wang, and Xiang-Sun Zhang
Copyright © 2009 John Wiley & Sons, Inc.

quadratic programming, 208
quasi steady-state, 97, 287
quasibipartite, 237
quasiclique, 237
quasiequilibrium, 96

Radial Basis Function, 262
random network, 165, 170, 242
random sampling, 325
ratio association, 199
ratio cut, 199
reaction, 281
reaction-rate equation, 54
recall measure, 261, 331
regulation matrix, 56, 78, 96, 108
regulatory motif abundance, 179
regulatory region, 25
relevance network, 53, 87
replication, 3, 5
repression, 56, 68, 94, 110
repressor, 35, 103
residue network, 346
ribosome, 4, 7
RNA, 2
    miRNA, 349
    mRNA, 3, 5, 6
    ncRNA, 99, 349
    tRNA, 9
RNA polymerase, 26
RNA synthesis, 6, 27
ROC curve, 262
ROC score, 262
root mean square error, 131

SAGA, 227
sample imbalance, 256
scale-free property, 172
second messenger, 313
Selective Permissibility Algorithm, 326
sensitivity, 133
sequence alignment, 211, 213
sequence logo, 90
sequence signature, 127
set-cover problem, 148
short cycle, 178
shortest path, 170, 174, 235, 243
shortest path distribution, 169
shortest-path distance, 235
shortest-path profile, 243

sigmoidal function, 94, 105
signal transduction, 313
signal transduction pathway, 313
signaling molecule, 314, 315
signaling network, 9, 12, 315, 321, 326, 341
signaling network detection, 326
similar length-p path, 213
simulated annealing, 239, 252
single-input motif, 117, 178
single organism data, 139
Singular Value Decomposition, 56, 256, 259, 290
sink compound, 295
small G protein, 314
small GTPase, 315
small RNA, 349
small-world property, 169, 172
socioaffinity score, 245
SOS network, 84
source compound, 295
spatial distribution, 180, 181
specificity, 133
splicing, 5, 8, 28
    alternative splicing, 5
steady state, 48, 55, 56, 73, 96, 287
stochastic differential equation, 55, 92, 95, 317
stoichiometric matrix, 286
stoichiometric reaction equation, 286
stoichiometry, 96, 286
strongly cooperative domain, 151
structure alignment, 227
subgraph distribution, 187
subgraph-isomorphism problem, 207
subtree comparison, 213
superdomain, 151, 152
superparamagnetic clustering, 236
Support Vector Machine, 98, 256, 267
    one-class SVM, 259
    two-class SVM, 260
system identification, 73, 102

tandem affinity purification, 12, 123, 161
TF binding site, 89, 90
thermodynamic equilibrium, 42
thermodynamic model, 102
three-domain pair, 151, 152
three-node motif, 178
time delay, 51, 54, 58